Violence Against Women

Violence Against Women: Vulnerable Populations investigates under-researched and underserved groups of women who are particularly vulnerable to violent victimization from an intimate male partner. In the past, there has been an understandable reluctance to address this issue to avoid stereotyping vulnerable groups of women. However, developments in the field, particularly intersectionality theory, which recognizes women's diversity in experiences of violence, suggest that the time has come to make the study of violence in vulnerable populations a new sub-field in the area. As the first book of its kind, *Violence Against Women: Vulnerable Populations* identifies where violence on vulnerable populations fits within the field, develops a method for studying vulnerable populations, and brings vital new knowledge to the field through the analysis of original data (from three large-scale representative surveys) on eight populations of women who are particularly vulnerable to violence.

Douglas A. Brownridge, Ph.D., is an Associate Professor with the Department of Family Social Sciences at the University of Manitoba. Dr. Brownridge is an expert on family violence with numerous publications and recognitions, including the 2006 Rh Award for Outstanding Contributions to Scholarship and Research in the Social Sciences.

Contemporary Sociological Perspectives
Edited by **Valerie Jenness**,
University of California, Irvine
and
Jodi O'Brien
Seattle University

This innovative series is for all readers interested in books that provide frameworks for making sense of the complexities of contemporary social life. Each of the books in this series uses a sociological lens to provide current critical and analytical perspectives on significant social issues, patterns, and trends. The series consists of books that integrate the best ideas in sociological thought with an aim towards public education and engagement. These books are designed for use in the classroom as well as for scholars and socially curious general readers.

Published:

Political Justice and Religious Values
Charles F. Andrain

GIS and Spatial Analysis for the Social Sciences
Robert Nash Parker and Emily K. Asencio

Hoop Dreams on Wheels
Disability and the competitive wheelchair
Ronald J. Berger

Forthcoming:

The Internet and Inequality
James C. Witte

Media and Middle Class Moms
Lara Descartes and Conrad Kottak

Sociology of Music
Michael B. MacDonald

Race, Justice and the New Genetics
Sandra Soo-Jin Lee

Watching T.V. Is Not Required
Bernard McGrane and John Gunderson

Intimate Impostors
The social psychology of romantic deception
Sally Caldwell

Regression Unplugged
Sally Caldwell and Robert Abbey

Gender Circuits
Eve Shapiro

Violence Against Women

Vulnerable Populations

Douglas A. Brownridge

Routledge
Taylor & Francis Group

NEW YORK AND LONDON

First published 2009
by Routledge
270 Madison Ave, New York, NY 10016

Simultaneously published in the UK
by Routledge
2 Park Square, Milton Park, Abingdon, Oxon OX14 4RN

Routledge is an imprint of the Taylor & Francis Group, an informa business

Typeset in Minion by Wearset Ltd, Boldon, Tyne and Wear
Printed and bound in the United States of America on acid-free paper by
Sheridan Books, Inc

Library of Congress Cataloging in Publication Data
Brownridge, Douglas A., 1969–
Violence against women: vulnerable populations/Douglas A. Brownridge.
p. cm. – (Contemporary sociological perspectives)
Includes bibliographical references and index.
1. Women–Violence against. 2. Abused wives. 3. Abused women. 4. Marital violence.
5. Family violence. I. Title.
HV6250.4.W65B76 2008
362.82'92–dc22
2008031539

ISBN10: 0-415-99607-4 (hbk)
ISBN10: 0-415-99608-2 (pbk)
ISBN10: 0-203-87743-8 (ebk)

ISBN13: 978-0-415-99607-5 (hbk)
ISBN13: 978-0-415-99608-2 (pbk)
ISBN13: 978-0-203-87743-2 (ebk)

Contents

Contents

Figures

Tables

Series Editors' Foreword

Violence Against Women: Vulnerable Populations skilfully utilizes three compelling Canadian data sets—the 1993 Violence Against Women Survey and the 1999 and 2004 General Social Survey—to present a comprehensive statistical analysis of the contours of violent victimization against women by an intimate male partner. Drawing on a decade-long award-winning programme of research and adopting an intersectionality approach, this book directs sustained empirical attention to special populations of women—those who are cohabitating, separated/divorced, in stepfamilies, living in rental housing, and living in rural settings as well as Aboriginal women, immigrant women, and women with disabilities—who are uniquely vulnerable with respect to risk. By focusing analytic attention on these groups of women on their own terms and by making comparisons across these groups, this book provides much-needed "fundamental statistics" on violence against women and it puts these empirical facts in service to theorizing. Throughout, Brownridge is attentive to patterns and trends as well as nuances and particularities, all the while making a compelling case that the study of vulnerable populations deserves a place in the extant violence against women literature. He does so without falling prey to invoking and reifying stereotypes that surround women in these populations or simplifying the complicated nature of violence against women. Instead, *Violence Against Women* sheds insight into the processes and structures that surround this type of human suffering. And it does so in a way that ensures we better understand violence against women as a social problem, including implications for prevention and intervention.

Preface

Why are some groups of women particularly vulnerable with respect to violent victimization? Not long ago such a question was politically incorrect. An episode of the Oprah Winfrey Show (which aired December 5, 2002), the topic of which was domestic violence in the military, is illustrative. A representative of the United States military, seeming quite defensive, repeatedly made the point that domestic violence occurs in all segments of society, not just the military. Understandably, this attitude of not wanting to be "singled out" is common. Oprah's conclusion was that we should not be pointing the proverbial finger at the military, but see violence in the military as a wake-up call to everyone about domestic violence. Indeed, examining populations of women that are uniquely vulnerable to violence not only will help to address effectively this social problem, but the lessons learned will also contribute to the prevention of violence against women in general.

Although, in the past, there was reluctance to study vulnerable groups, we have reached a crucial point in the field where stakeholders are recognizing the need to understand the unique experiences of violence in vulnerable groups. Intersectionality theorists are currently on the cutting edge of this movement, raising awareness that violence against women is a complex intersectional puzzle. However, an intersectionality approach is limited by its focus on oppression. I argue that, in addition to focusing on oppression, we also need to include a focus on violence against women in vulnerable populations.

This book investigates populations of women that are particularly vulnerable with respect to violent victimization from an intimate male partner. It represents the culmination of an award-winning program of research that has spanned the last decade. I have published several preliminary studies on specific vulnerable populations, which are cited accordingly. On this basis, in this book I am able, for the first time, to define vulnerable populations, identify these groups as such, argue for the importance of studying them, and show how the study of them fits within the field of family violence. I am also able to articulate my method for studying vulnerable populations in general, apply this method as well as unique theoretical treatments to each vulnerable population using multiple data sets, and draw specific as well as more general conclusions based on an examination of the data.

I would like to thank Statistics Canada for its continuing commitment to collecting data on family violence and the Manitoba Regional Data Centre of Statistics Canada for providing access to the data from the 2004 General Social Survey. Special thanks are owed to all respondents of the three surveys analysed in this book. I began this project in the winter of 2006 while on research leave from the University of Manitoba. I wish to thank the University and the Department of Family Social Sciences for this opportunity. I am also grateful to several agencies that funded the preliminary studies in my pro- gramme of work. These include the Social Sciences and Humanities Research Council of Canada (SSHRC), the University of Manitoba, the Prairie*action* Foundation, and the Prairie Centre of Excellence for Research on Immigra- tion and Integration (PCERII).

I would also like to thank all of the individuals at Routledge for their encouragement and support during the production of this book. I am espe- cially thankful to my publisher, Stephen D. Rutter, for all of his efforts in the process of seeing this book to fruition. Thanks also to Professor Valerie Jenness (University of California, Irvine and Co-Editor, Contemporary Soci- ology Series) and the anonymous reviewers for their helpful comments. I also owe a debt of gratitude to Leah Babb-Rosenfeld for her editorial assistance and to both Beth Renner and my graduate student, Ms. Tamara Taillieu, for their editorial comments.

1
Introduction

Nearly four decades have passed since the first studies of family violence were published in a 1971 issue of the *Journal of Marriage and the Family*. During that time research on and interventions for violence against women, and family violence in general, have burgeoned. There are now several academic journals devoted to family violence, including the increasingly influential international periodical *Violence Against Women*. In Canada alone, violence prevention programmes are available across the nation and there are more than 550 shelters for victimized women and their children (Taylor-Butts, 2007). Innovative court responses exist in several locations and domestic violence legislation is present almost everywhere in the country (Johnson, 2006). Although such efforts have been crucial, family violence continues to be a major national and global social problem and there is much to learn to improve the efficacy of prevention efforts. For example, while batterer intervention programmes are useful and undoubtedly save lives, research on their efficacy for preventing recidivism has shown that their effect is minimal beyond the effect of being arrested (Babcock, Green, & Robie, 2004).

A more complete understanding of this phenomenon is required for adequately addressing family violence. There remains much to learn about family violence before we can eradicate, or substantially reduce, this social ill. Among the gaps in knowledge that need filling is an examination of violence against women in vulnerable populations. *Vulnerable populations* are defined here as groups of individuals who share some common characteristic not held by the rest of the population and who are uniquely vulnerable with respect to risk and/or experiences surrounding violence. This is not to say that all persons falling outside of a given vulnerable population are not themselves vulnerable to violence. When examining a given vulnerable population there will be members from other vulnerable populations in the comparison group. But the factors leading to each group's vulnerability may be unique. It is possible that the common characteristic shared by a given vulnerable population is also connected to circumstances that require the application and testing of unique explanatory frameworks. By studying these vulnerable populations in this way one can better understand their unique vulnerability to violence and be in an improved position to address the risk for, and experiences of, violence faced by each vulnerable population.

While epidemiological data on violence against women have intimated the existence of these vulnerable populations, there has been a reluctance to tackle the unpleasant realities of violence within these vulnerable groups. Understandably, in the past there were concerns about "singling out" vulnerable groups. Correlations can, unfortunately, lead to stereotypes. For instance, a stereotype based on a correlation between low socioeconomic status (SES) and violence against women has led to a fashion trend in recent years of referring to tank tops as "wife-beaters," presumably based on the stereotypical image of a violent male partner as an unemployed/low-income, poorly educated, beer-bellied man lying about in his undershirt. When I confront this stereotypical image in my lower-level undergraduate class on family violence, I project a bar graph from a national survey of Canada that shows that men who had an annual income of less than $15,000 had twice the likelihood of violence compared to men who earned more than this amount, men with less than high school education had twice the likelihood of violence compared to men with a university degree, and unemployed men had twice the likelihood of violence compared to employed men. While this graph clearly illustrates an association between low SES and male-to-female violence in Canada, it also shows that men in the highest SES echelons are violent. Taking the example of employment, the bar graph shows that 3% of employed men and 6% of unemployed men were violent against their partner in the previous year. I then ask students what else they observe in the graph. After several thoughtful, but usually unsuccessful, attempts, I point out to the class that the graph also indirectly shows (because it is not a bar in the graph) that the overwhelming majority of unemployed men in Canada, 94%, were not violent against their partner in the previous year. The message: we should not stereotype based on vulnerabilities to violence.

Social science researchers should not shy away from studying vulnerable populations out of fear of stereotypes. To do so is a disservice to members of these groups who have experienced, continue to suffer from, or will experience, violence from their male partners. In fact, conducting research on violence in vulnerable populations will contribute to an understanding of these populations' unique vulnerabilities, and so is a way to avoid such stereotypes. As the literature reviews in the chapters of this book show, some scholars have studied individual vulnerable populations to varying degrees. However, as the first book devoted to the study of violence in vulnerable populations, this book develops the study of vulnerable populations as a new focal area within the field of family violence. In addition to defining vulnerable populations, it identifies how to approach theorizing about, and develops a method for approaching the study of, violence in vulnerable populations. For each vulnerable population, explanatory frameworks are articulated for understanding their vulnerability to violence. As well, original and novel analyses are conducted using large-scale samples that are representative of Canada to gain a better sense of trends in risk for violence, patterns in post-violence experiences, the importance of risk factors for violence, and the adequacy of explanatory frameworks. From this, implications are derived for understanding and preventing violence against women in vulnerable populations, as well as violence against women in general.

Before beginning the investigation of individual vulnerable populations, it is necessary to show where research on vulnerable populations fits within the field of family violence. This is accomplished in Chapter 2, showing how the study of vulnerable populations can complement other approaches to family violence research through providing pieces of the intersectional puzzle of violence against women. The next chapter discusses methodological matters including the data sets employed in the analyses, how variables are measured, and the innovations in the methodological approach used for studying violence in vulnerable populations. On this theoretical and methodological basis, Chapters 4 through 11 investigate violence against women who are cohabiting, separated/divorced, in stepfamilies, living in rental housing, living in rural settings, Aboriginal, immigrants, and who have disabilities, respectively. This is not an exhaustive list of vulnerable populations. These vulnerable populations were selected for inclusion because they were identifiable in at least two of the three data sets that were used. Other vulnerable populations, such as lesbian relationships, were excluded because there were insufficient data for analyses.

How one reads Chapters 4 through 11 will depend on what they wish to glean from these chapters. Each of these chapters is generally organized with an introduction, review of the literature, articulation of an explanatory framework, analysis of results, discussion, and conclusion. Since these chapters are research based, the evidence for the conclusions in each chapter is presented in detail beforehand in the results. Readers interested in examining the basis for the conclusions may therefore want to digest these chapters in their entirety. Readers interested in the main findings of one or more of these chapters may wish to refer only to the discussion and conclusion parts of the relevant chapters. Those who desire more background may want to read the introduction, literature review, and explanatory framework in addition to the results and conclusions of each chapter.

Finally, the concluding chapter integrates the new knowledge provided in the book to help assemble pieces of the intersectional puzzle of violence against women. This includes a discussion of the utility of studying vulnerable populations and implications for prevention.

2
Situating Research on Vulnerable Populations Within the Family Violence Field

It is important to begin by discussing some issues that must be understood in order to situate where research on vulnerable populations fits within the family violence field. The type(s) of violence being studied, the context within which questions about violence are asked, and the type of sample employed, each has implications for understanding research on intimate partner violence (IPV). Having touched on these issues, this chapter briefly discusses general theoretical approaches relevant to the study of vulnerable populations. More attention is given to an intersectionality approach because of its focus on oppressed groups that are vulnerable to violence. This culminates in a discussion of how the study of violence against women in vulnerable populations in this book differs from typical applications of intersectionality.

Defining Violence

Definitions of violence vary widely. In the context of intimate partner relationships, violence is most commonly defined as an act carried out with the intention, or perceived intention, of causing physical pain or injury to another person (Lupri, Grandin, & Brinkerhoff, 1994; Straus, Gelles, & Steinmetz, 1980). Definitions of violence typically include physical violence, sexual violence, and threats of physical and/or sexual violence (Barnett, Miller-Perrin, & Perrin, 2005). Violent behaviours also vary in their severity. "Minor," or less severe forms of violence, are considered to be less dangerous and, therefore, less likely to be physically injurious, whereas severe forms of violence are more likely to cause a physical injury to the victim (Straus & Gelles, 1990). This distinction between less severe and severe violence also alludes to a distinction between IPV and battering. Battering is a form of IPV. IPV encompasses violence in relationships that involve, or have involved, intimacy. Therefore, IPV includes minor and severe violence. There are various definitions of battering, but its most basic definition involves "repeated forceful blows" (Dutton, 2006, p. 4). Thus, battering in intimate relationships encompasses a subset of IPV in which there is repeated severe violence.

Crime Victim versus Conflict Tactics Scale Surveys

An important distinction in survey research on IPV is whether the data are based on a crime victim survey or a Conflict Tactics Scale (CTS) survey. *CTS surveys* employ some version of Straus' CTS (Straus, 1979). With respect to IPV, the CTS consists of a list of actions that one partner may employ during a conflict with another partner, beginning with less coercive tactics and moving towards more coercive and aggressive tactics. Hence, the CTS presents questions measuring violence in the context of conflict. *Crime victim surveys*, on the other hand, are concerned with determining whether respondents have been victims of crimes by asking what crimes they have experienced. Since not all victims and perpetrators consider acts of violence to be criminal, the result is that crime victim surveys tend to underestimate the prevalence of violence (DeKeseredy & Schwartz, 2003a). In other words, asking questions about violence in the context of crime yields lower rates of reporting as compared to asking questions about violence in the context of conflict. Indeed, a comparison of reported rates of violence showed those from CTS surveys to be six times greater than those from crime victim surveys (Dutton, 2006).

Representative versus Clinical Samples and their Connections to Theories

The most contentious issue in the field of family violence concerns gender differences in rates of IPV; some researchers find that males and females experience violence at similar rates while others report that women are more likely to be victimized. In that regard, Kurz (1989) identified two major social science perspectives on IPV. Although both perspectives emphasize the importance of patriarchy in contributing to violence against women, the *family violence* perspective views patriarchy as one of several contributing factors while the *feminist* approach views patriarchy as the key factor in violence against women. Family violence researchers usually employ CTS surveys, which tend to examine representative samples of the general population and generally find similar rates of IPV for males and females. Feminist theorists, who tend to use clinical samples of identified victims (e.g., samples drawn from shelter residents), cite data showing that women have higher rates of victimization in support of their approach.

In an attempt to clarify this disjuncture between feminist and family violence approaches, Straus (1990) suggested that the findings of researchers from both camps were correct, but differed as a result of disparate approaches to sampling (i.e., representative vs. clinical samples). Straus cautioned that survey researchers should not assume that their findings apply to cases known to the police and to shelters (what he called the representative sample fallacy) just as feminist researchers, and others using clinical samples, should not conclude that the higher proportion of male perpetrators applies to the general population (the clinical sample fallacy).

This distinction points to the close connection between the phenomena captured in different samples and, consequently, the theories that are relevant for understanding those phenomena. Clinical samples are more likely to include cases of battering. Violence that is severe and repeated has been estimated to have ever occurred in about 5.4% of unions in Canada (Dutton, 2006). On the other hand, when asked about any occurrence of violence in the 1993 Violence Against Women Survey, a large-scale representative sample survey, 29% of Canadian women reported having ever experienced violence by an intimate partner (Johnson, 1996). Hence, battering is far less common than other forms of IPV. The greater the proportion of cases of battering in a data set, the more relevant will be theories designed to understand the perpetration of severe repeated violence. For example, the more severe the violence, the more likely it is that a personality style, trait, or disorder underlies the violence (O'Leary, 1993). Indeed, research has identified different types of batterers (Hamberger & Hastings, 1986; Holtzworth-Munroe & Stuart, 1994; Jacobson & Gottman, 1998; Saunders, 1992) and connected battering behaviour to insecure attachment as well as both antisocial and borderline personality disorders (Mauricio, Tein, & Lopez, 2007).

Representative samples, on the other hand, contain relatively few cases of severe repeated violence such that there are insufficient cases to analyse separately (Straus, 1993). In fact, it has been estimated that about only 10% of violent incidents are caused by mental illness while the remaining 90% require explanations that move beyond the purely psychological (Gelles, 1993; Straus et al., 1980). There are a number of theories that are useful for studying violence in representative samples (e.g., cf. Bersani & Chen, 1988). Those that are particularly useful for investigating violence against women include feminist, evolutionary psychology, and ecological approaches.

Feminist Approach

There are several different types of feminism. Although it is beyond the scope of this chapter to review all of these variants, it is generally agreed that feminist theorists share the common view that violence against women is generated from patriarchy (Kurz, 1989). *Patriarchy* refers to "the supremacy of the father over his family members and the domination of men over women and children in every aspect of life and culture" (O'Neil & Nadeau, 1999). Patriarchy, present in both the social structure and ideology (Dobash & Dobash, 1979), and taking on social and familial forms (Ursel, 1986), creates a condition under which men feel entitled to use violence to dominate women.

Evolutionary Psychology

From an evolutionary psychology perspective, men are evolutionarily hardwired to ensure their contribution to the gene pool. Since men have no guarantee of paternity, they are prone to sexually proprietary behaviour. Male proprietariness essentially refers to a set of beliefs and values that view a female romantic partner as a type of property (Hannawa, Spitzberg, Wiering, & Teranishi, 2006). This sexually proprietary behaviour is conceptually similar to sexual jealousy but is broader in the sense that it includes attitudes towards social relationships that lead men to attempt to sequester women from other men (i.e., possessiveness; Wilson & Daly, 1992). Sexual proprietariness is, in turn, associated with violence against women.

Ecological Framework

No single theory, including feminist and evolutionary psychology approaches, has been able fully to explain IPV. The literature on IPV suggests that each theoretical perspective (variously stemming from biology, psychiatry, psychology, sociology, and criminological and feminist approaches) has strengths and weaknesses. When one examines these theories it becomes evident that their contributions tend to be complementary. Thus, the strengths of these approaches can be built upon in multilevel models, such as the ecological framework.

This framework began with the seminal contribution of Bronfenbrenner (1977) and has subsequently been applied to understand both child abuse (Belsky, 1980, 1993) and partner violence (e.g., Brownridge, 2006b, 2006c; Brownridge & Halli, 2002a; Carlson, 1984; Dutton, 1995, 2006; Heise, 1998; Sobsey, 1994). In each of these applications the framework has been modified to suit the subject under study and the author's personal style. For example, both the nomenclature and the indicators of the systems in the framework vary across these applications. In addition, as Heise (1998) has noted, "considerable room exists for interpretation as to exactly where a particular factor most appropriately fits into the framework" (p. 266).

As it is typically applied to IPV, there are four levels of the ecological framework in which micro-level variables are nested within macro-level variables (Dutton, 2006). At the broadest level, the *macrosystem* refers to cultural attitudes, values, and beliefs that foster violence. The *exosystem* refers to the formal and informal social networks in which the family is involved. The *microsystem* consists of the family or immediate setting in which violence occurs. Finally, the *ontogenic* level concerns the individual's development, and what a given individual's unique developmental history brings to the other levels. By drawing our attention to factors linked to violence from various theories at all levels of the environment, the ecological framework naturally lends itself to theoretical integration. Applying such multilevel models where relevant helps contribute to a more comprehensive examination and understanding of IPV.

Universal Risk versus Differing Vulnerabilities

There has been a reluctance in the family violence field to address the fact that some groups are more vulnerable to violence than others. Even feminist theory has traditionally emphasized women's universal risk for violence (Sokoloff & Dupont, 2005) and, as discussed above, identified patriarchy as "the" source of women's experiences of violence (Kurz, 1989). These theorists typically focused their attention on women's common experiences of violence.

Since the last decade of the twentieth century, there has been increasing recognition that it is an insufficient reflection of reality to restrict analyses of violence against women to views based on women's universal risk and the primacy of gender inequality. For example, in terms of universal risk, Fine (1985) noted that

> feminists have dealt inadequately with the question of whether some women are *more* vulnerable than others. Eager to repudiate class- and race-biased analyses of abuse, we have promoted universal risk arguments, critiquing methodologies that define some women as more vulnerable than others. But this refutation of classism and racism obscures our ability to wrestle with the question of vulnerability.
>
> (p. 397)

As well, commenting on the feminist focus on patriarchy, Heise (1998) wrote that

> The feminist community has been especially reluctant to acknowledge factors other than patriarchy in the etiology of abuse. This reluctance, however, must be seen in the context of a discourse on violence that has traditionally been very slow to acknowledge the significance of gender inequalities and power differentials in the etiology of violence directed toward women. For years, academic social science failed to acknowledge even the presence of the problem, much less to incorporate issues of power, gender and rights into its reigning analysis. As a result, feminist researchers and activists have been understandably reluctant to endorse any theory that isn't grounded in a thorough understanding of the way that male privilege operates to perpetuate gender-based abuse.
>
> (p. 263)

It is understandable, then, why feminist theorists were reluctant to focus on issues of vulnerability and to recognize factors in addition to patriarchy. To be sure, overcoming a history of ignoring gender and the desire to avoid racist and classist analyses of violence were essential tasks. However, in more recent years there has been increasing recognition among some feminist theorists that not all women have an equal risk for violence as well as of the potential importance of factors other than patriarchy. These are key insights of an intersectional approach to understanding domestic violence.

An Intersectional Approach to Recognizing Differing Vulnerabilities

It has been said that "intersectionality is the most important theoretical contribution that women's studies, in conjunction with related fields, has made so far" (McCall, 2005, p. 1771). Intersectionality was born to grapple with essentialism, which sees all women as sharing the same essence: born female, biological mothers, and the primary sexual choice of men (Zack, 2005). Traditional feminism was critiqued by those who recognized that white middle-class feminists did not speak for all women, especially women of colour and working-class women. Given the important role that intersectionality has played in drawing attention to differing vulnerabilities among women, it is necessary to discuss this approach in some detail.

Early writings on intersectionality were by Black feminists, most notably Crenshaw (1989) who coined the term "intersectionality." Black feminists argued that the feminist thinking of the day did not address problems that were unique to Black women. For example, unlike White women, women of colour did not necessarily view patriarchy as primordial. For Black women, the main concern was White racism (Zack, 2005).

Intersectionality focuses on how forms of oppression and inequality intersect. Depending on an individual's circumstances, gender is modified by other forms of oppression and markers of difference. To illustrate her view of intersectionality, in a conference presentation Crenshaw used the image of a woman standing at an intersection with vehicles coming at her from an indeterminate number of cross-cutting roads (Yuval-Davis, 2006). Forms of oppression and markers of difference interrelate based on which of these oppressions and markers apply to each individual. Oppression based in gender inequality, prejudice, class stratification, and heterosexist bias are typically the foci of intersectional analyses. In addition, other inequalities/axes/markers of difference that have been identified include nation/state, culture, ability, age, sedentariness/origin, wealth, north–south, religion, and stage of social development (Yuval-Davis, 2006).

Diversity Among Intersectional Approaches

There is no single intersectional approach. For instance, Yuval-Davis (2006) has observed that

> one of the differences among the different approaches to intersectionality ... is that while some ... focus on the particular positions of women of colour, others ... have been constructed in more general terms,

applicable to any grouping of people, advantaged as well as disadvantaged.

(p. 201)

In addition, two major approaches to intersectionality have been identified (Prins, 2006). The *systemic* approach, from North America, focuses on "the impact of system or structure upon the formation of identities" (p. 279). Generally, this means that outside influences impact individuals to create identities. The other is the *constructionist* approach, from Britain, which focuses on "the dynamic and relational aspects of social identity" (p. 279). In short, this approach considers identity to be constructed in an environment where power relations are dynamic.

Although intersectionality approaches have been criticized for not having any accompanying methods (Phoenix & Pattynama, 2006), McCall (2005) has identified three approaches to studying intersectionality (anticategorical, intracategorical, and intercategorical) that differ in terms of "how they understand and use analytical categories to explore the complexity of intersectionality in social life" (p. 1773). While McCall (2005) requests researchers to "embrace multiple approaches to the study of intersectionality" (p. 1795), intersectionality research is not positivistic. Rather than being quantitative, research in this area tends to be qualitative and consistent with the argument of Kanuha (1996) that "the methods of research must be participatory, empowering, and based in a community action model" (p. 45).

Main Criticism of Intersectionality

While a number of criticisms have been levelled at intersectionality, the main weakness identified in the literature is the difficulty in applying it to empirical analyses. The seemingly endless list of markers of difference has been referred to as the "Achilles heel" of intersectionality because it is not possible to specify precisely how the axes of difference operate in producing a phenomenon (Ludvig, 2006). In response to the critique that the social divisions are limitless, Yuval-Davis (2006) notes that

in specific historical situations and in relation to specific people there are some social divisions that are more important than others in constructing specific positionings. At the same time, there are some social divisions, such as gender, stage in the life cycle, ethnicity and class, that tend to shape most people's lives in most social locations, while other social divisions such as those relating to membership in particular castes or status as indigenous or refugee people tend to affect fewer people globally.

(p. 203)

This suggests that axes of difference are not limitless for a given individual. Rather, in addition to core oppressions that are nearly universally relevant, there are also other axes of difference that can be applied as relevant depending upon an individual's social location.

Intersectionality and Violence Against Women

The central statement in the application of intersectionality to violence against women is that "intersectionalities color the meaning and nature of domestic violence, how it is experienced by self and responded to by others, how personal and social consequences are represented, and how and whether escape and safety can be obtained" (Bograd, 1999, p. 276). Intersectionality can be applied to understanding definitions, risk, causes, experiences, consequences of, and responses to violence. For example, Renzetti (1998) wrote that "attention to intersectionality requires us to include in our work a careful analysis of how racism, social class inequality, sexism and heterosexism affect both the causes and the consequences of intimate violence" (p. 123).

In terms of the traditional feminist notion of the primacy of gender, from an intersectionality view the existence of violence in lesbian relationships illustrates that gender is not always the primary locus of oppression in understanding violence. For example, Renzetti (1998) noted that homophobia is an important factor in violence in lesbian relationships with unique tactics, such as "outing" (i.e., disclosure of the victim's sexual preference), often used by lesbian batterers to control their partners.

Also, although traditional feminists were weary of acknowledging differing vulnerabilities to violence, Sokoloff and Dupont (2005) have identified how such concerns can be contextualized as being largely due to economic or structural factors. The example given is that Black women are overrepresented in their rates of severe violence and femicide (i.e., the killing of a female by her intimate partner). Without a context this finding serves to reinforce negative stereotypes. Sokoloff and DuPont provide a context to this finding by noting that African Americans are overrepresented on a number of factors that are associated with violence and by citing research that shows that socioeconomic variables largely account for this overrepresentation. In other words, an appropriate and unbiased focus on vulnerable groups is, in fact, a way to avoid negative stereotypes.

An intersectionality approach to violence against women has also highlighted the need for services to be tailored to specific groups. According to Crenshaw (1993), "structures of subordination which intersect ... limit the utility of interventions that are not constructed with them in mind" (p. 232). Women of differing class, race, and religious backgrounds as well as lesbian, bisexual, transgendered, and intersexed battered women have all been identified as facing unique obstacles to effective intervention (Sokoloff & Dupont, 2005). For example, it has been suggested that Latina women in the United

States may not report violence to authorities from fear of deportation and language barriers (Swan & Snow, 2006).

How the Study of Vulnerable Populations Differs from Typical Applications of Intersectionality

What is clear is that we need to recognize differing vulnerabilities and understand why some groups are more vulnerable to violence than others, so that we will have a more complete understanding of IPV, which can then inform efforts to prevent this social problem. I argue that, to complement extant work on IPV, we need to examine violence in vulnerable populations. However, my view on the major issues of risk and explanation differs somewhat from applications of intersectionality to IPV.

First, we need to identify all groups that are uniquely vulnerable with respect to violence. As defined in the Introduction of this book, *vulnerable populations* are groups of individuals who share some common characteristic not held by the rest of the population and who are uniquely vulnerable with respect to risk and/or experiences surrounding violence. The greatest difference between the approach offered here and that of intersectionality concerns the issues of focusing only on oppression/inequality and of providing contextualization with economic/structural factors.

Although not characteristic of all applications of intersectionality, the focus in much of the research relies only on intersections of oppressions. Vulnerable populations are broader than forms of oppression, though they may include many of the same markers of difference. That is, vulnerable populations are not necessarily oppressed groups, but such groups can be, and often are, vulnerable populations. The distinction between intersectionality and my approach to investigating vulnerable populations is that vulnerable populations vis-à-vis violence are based on some unique vulnerability with respect to violence, not necessarily with respect to oppression. It is insufficient only to focus on intersections of oppression, or even markers of difference; we must also combine this with other variables and/or circumstances drawn from research on and explanations for IPV. Analyses based on classic theories of IPV can provide an overall picture but, as an intersectionality approach suggests, the picture may be very different for vulnerable populations. An analysis of IPV in vulnerable populations also needs to engage in more than just contextualization à la the suggestion of intersectionality theorists Sokoloff and DuPont (2005). It is not enough for each vulnerable population to be contextualized. We need to bring in other theories and explanations as appropriate to a particular vulnerable population. A given theory or explanation may not be equally relevant, or relevant at all, across specific vulnerable populations. Hence, we need to apply and assess all relevant explanations for violence in each vulnerable population.

Second, it is important to examine various aspects of violence for each vulnerable population. As Bograd (1999) has noted, "care must be taken not to generalize from one population to others, since the chronicity, level, frequency, and types of violence may be important distinguishing factors among couples and their dynamics" (p. 279). Indeed, we need to examine prevalence, forms of violence, and so on for each vulnerable population. The use of statistics in applications of intersectionality to violence against women is generally not in keeping with proponents of an intersectional approach, which tend not to be quantitative. But gathering such statistics on vulnerable populations serves to fill an important gap in the literature. Bograd, who appears to be in the minority of intersectionality theorists in this regard, suggested that

> the invisibility of certain populations reflects more their social importance in the eyes of the dominant culture than the absence of domestic violence in their midst. The lack of statistics is also not of minor consequence. These statistics are fundamental to the distribution of funds and the creation of social policy, which in turn shape the development of mental health initiatives, the availability of services, and the possibility of safety for disenfranchised populations.
>
> (p. 279)

Hence, we need to examine all vulnerable populations and all methods in this larger project are valuable and should be pursued. This must include quantitative data that provide these "fundamental" statistics.

Of course, the importance of an understanding of violence in vulnerable populations rests on more than an issue of differential risk and cause. Intersectional approaches have identified how examining the complexity of experiences of violence suggests important policy implications. For example, the fact that some shelters do not allow adolescent boys has been identified as placing these women in the position of having to make the difficult decision between finding safety for themselves or leaving sons behind (Bograd, 1999). While this book will examine some post-violence experiences in terms of consequences and help-seeking, it is beyond the scope of the book to examine services. Nevertheless, this is an important enterprise for future research.

Finally, it is important to add that the focus on vulnerable populations in this book is intended to be a complement to, rather than a replacement for, other approaches to understanding IPV. In many ways, the approach herein comes closest to intersectionality. As identified above, there are multiple approaches and methods within the burgeoning area of intersectionality. Although this approach to studying vulnerable populations is too different from most articulations of intersectionality to be considered as such, the research contained in this book can certainly contribute to intersectional analyses since it provides pieces of the complex puzzle that intersectionality attempts to capture.

Conclusion

It is clear that the time has come to address the gap in the literature on violence against women in vulnerable populations. In so doing, one needs to be mindful of the meaning of violence, the type of data being used, the type of sample on which the data are based, and how that impacts relevant theories. Although intersectionality has been the key theoretical approach for recognizing women's differing vulnerabilities to violence, it is not without its weaknesses. This book differs from the typical intersectionality approach to violence against women and in so doing suggests that an examination of violence against women in vulnerable populations, through the application of unique explanatory frameworks to each vulnerable population as well as the analysis of quantitative data based on representative sample surveys, will contribute new knowledge to help assemble pieces of the intersectional puzzle of violence against women. This approach to vulnerable populations is intended to complement extant research in the field of family violence, through filling a niche that is requisite for a more complete understanding of violence against women. Before delving into the examination of vulnerable populations, it is necessary in the next chapter to discuss some specifics about the materials and methods used in this book.

3
Materials and Methods

The investigation of vulnerable populations rests on a number of important methodological matters. This chapter identifies and discusses the following: the data that are employed; the use of relative rates; how risk factors, violence, and post-violence variables are measured; the methods of analysis; and how the data are weighted.

The Data Sets

Three data sets produced by Statistics Canada are used in the analyses contained in this book: the 1993 Violence Against Women Survey (VAWS), and the 1999 and 2004 iterations of the General Social Survey (GSS).[1] In the 1993 VAWS, Statistics Canada randomly sampled 12,300 women 18 years of age or older and conducted in-depth interviews by telephone concerning their experiences of physical and sexual violence since reaching the age of 16. The GSS was designed to monitor changes in Canadian society over time and provide information on policy issues of current or emerging interest. Since 1985, 19 cycles of the GSS have been collected. In cycle 13 of the GSS conducted in 1999, a random sample of 25,876 men and women 15 years of age or older completed in-depth telephone interviews concerning the nature and extent of their criminal victimization, including experiences of partner violence. Cycle 18 of the GSS was very similar to cycle 13 and was administered in 2004, resulting in a random sample of 23,766 men and women 15 years of age or older.[2]

The data analysed in this book for the 1993 VAWS and 1999 GSS are from the public use microdata files released by Statistics Canada. Statistics Canada did not release several variables in the 2004 GSS for public use, including the measures of violence. Consequently, it was necessary to obtain access to the masterfile (i.e., the file that has not been prepared for public use and, therefore, contains all of the variables in the data in their original format) at the Manitoba Regional Data Centre (RDC) of Statistics Canada. Since the results from the masterfile needed to be vetted to protect respondent confidentiality, as noted where applicable in the tables throughout the book, not all estimates from the bivariate analyses of the 2004 data were released.

While cycles 13 and 18 of the GSS are largely comparable, there are a couple of general differences in the methodology used for the VAWS that limit its comparability with the GSS.[3] One difference concerns the manner in which the questions in the section on physical and sexual violence were asked. Although, as will be discussed later in this chapter, the questions were the same across all three data sets, in cycles 13 and 18 of the GSS the respondents were asked all questions in the section on physical and sexual violence. In the VAWS, to prevent respondent fatigue, after every three questions on violence respondents who did not report any occurrences of violence were screened out with a question that asked if their partner had been violent towards them in any other way. The authors of the VAWS reasoned that, because the ten items increased in severity, respondents who said no to all three items in a set were unlikely to endorse any of the subsequent items. The method used in the GSS was preferable because specific behavioural items may have triggered recall of a violent event(s) that was not captured by asking the screening question.

A second difference between the VAWS and GSS concerned the context of the surveys. As discussed in the previous chapter, crime surveys contribute to underreporting of violence as a result of some respondents not considering acts of violence to be criminal. Cycles 13 and 18 of the GSS were crime surveys. In both iterations of the GSS, the survey questionnaire was introduced to respondents as follows: "We are calling you for a study on Canadians' safety. The purpose of the study is to better understand people's perceptions of crime and the justice system, and the extent of victimization in Canada" (Statistics Canada, 2000, 2005b). Although this introduction may be understood to differentiate perceptions of crime from victimization, it is reasonable to assume that some respondents would hear the word "crime" and think about victimization in the context of a crime. The introduction to the VAWS questionnaire, on the other hand, read as follows: "I'm calling you for a survey about the safety of Canadians" (Statistics Canada, 1994b). Thus, in the introduction to the VAWS there was no mention of safety in the context of crimes. It must also be added, however, that the VAWS has been criticized for its narrow, legal definitions of violence such that it could also be deemed to be a variation of a crime survey (DeKeseredy, 2000). Nevertheless, the mention of "crime" at the outset of the GSS would suggest that respondents in the GSS might have been more likely to underreport violence they felt not to be criminal. While there was no difference in 1-year rates of violence across the three surveys, the 5-year prevalence rates of violence against women were larger in the VAWS than in the GSS (Johnson, 2005), and so this difference in context may have been one contributing factor to the differential rates.

Use of Relative Rates

The study of populations that are uniquely vulnerable as a result of their risk for violence inherently implies the need for a comparison group. That is to say, identifying a population as being vulnerable implies an inherent comparison to a population that is less vulnerable. Vulnerability with respect to risk is determined based on comparing the risk for violence in a given vulnerable population relative to the risk for individuals who are not members of that population. In this way, one can determine whether a given vulnerable population has an elevated risk for violence relative to its comparison group. For example, Chapter 4 of this book shows that cohabiting women have a higher risk for violence relative to married women.

The use of such relative rates is also a key strategy in attenuating methodological differences across the surveys in this book. Any methodological differences across the surveys that may have affected prevalence rates likely had the same impact on the rates both for women in a vulnerable population and women in the comparison group within a given survey. That is to say, methodological differences across surveys were likely to impact the prevalence rate of violence for each vulnerable population and its comparison group in the same manner within a given survey. Consequently, the primary focus in comparisons across the surveys is on the relative rates rather than the actual prevalence rates of violence.

Measurement

Risk Factors

A total of 26 independent variables, discussed below, are examined across various chapters in this book. Those that are applicable to a given chapter are listed in that chapter. What follows describes how each variable was measured. Unless otherwise indicated, the independent variables in each applicable survey were measured on the basis of the same items.

DURATION OF RELATIONSHIP

Union duration was measured with a variable derived from the respondent's report of the year in which she became married or began living with her common-law partner. For the descriptive analyses, this variable was grouped into the following categories: less than 4 years; 4 to 9 years; and 10 or more years.

EDUCATION COMPATIBILITY

Education compatibility was measured by calculating the ratio of the respondent's years of education to the couple's total years of education. For the analyses, education compatibility was grouped into the following categories: the woman had much less education (ratio < 0.46); the woman had less education (ratio $= 0.46$ to 0.49); the woman had the same years of education as her partner (ratio $= 0.50$); the woman had more education (ratio $= 0.51$ to 0.54); and the woman had much more education (ratio > 0.54).

WOMAN'S AND PARTNER'S EDUCATION

Woman's and partner's education referred to the highest level of education obtained by the respondent and her partner, respectively. In the descriptive analysis, these variables are grouped into the following categories: less than high school; high school; some post-secondary; community college; and university degree. For the multivariate analysis, the categories are converted into the number of years of education by estimating the average number of years of education in each category.

WOMAN'S AND PARTNER'S EMPLOYMENT

In the VAWS, woman's and partner's employment was measured with a question that simply asked whether she/her partner had worked at a business or paid job in the past 12 months. In both iterations of the GSS, woman's and partner's employment was measured with a more sophisticated question that referred to whether the main activity in the 12 months prior to the interview was working at a paid job or business (i.e., employed) or looking for work, caring for children, or housework (i.e., unemployed). The major difference concerned the coding of retired respondents. Since the question did not allow such a distinction in the VAWS, a portion of those responding "no" to the question were probably referring to a situation of retirement. However, in both iterations of the GSS, the coding of this variable allowed the exclusion of retired persons.

AGE

Age referred to the woman's age at the time of the interview. The age range was not identical in the VAWS and the GSS. The VAWS sampled women 18 years of age and over while both iterations of the GSS interviewed women 15 years of age and over. Since most women in a marital or common-law union are at least age 18, and the vulnerable populations involved women who were currently or had been in a marital or common-law union, this subtle difference between the youngest age groups to which each survey was administered did not affect the results of the analyses.

ABORIGINAL STATUS

Aboriginal status was not available in the public use microdata file for the 1993 survey. In the 1999 and 2004 iterations of the GSS, Aboriginal status was measured in terms of whether the respondent identified her cultural or racial background as being Aboriginal (i.e., North American Indian, Métis, or Inuit) or some other racial background (i.e., non-Aboriginal).

PATRIARCHAL DOMINANCE

Patriarchal dominance was measured with an item that asked the respondent if her partner prevented her from knowing about or having access to the family income, even if she asked.[4] Control of family finances is one indicator of patriarchal domination (Biesenthal et al., 2000; Hamby, 2000; Hamby & Skupien, 1998).

SEXUAL JEALOUSY

The measure of sexual jealousy was based on an item that asked the respondent if her partner was jealous and did not want her to talk to other men.

POSSESSIVE BEHAVIOUR

Possessiveness was measured with a question that asked the respondent if her partner demanded to know who she was with and where she was at all times.

HEAVY ALCOHOL CONSUMPTION

Heavy alcohol consumption was measured with a question that asked the respondent how many times in the month prior to the interview that her partner had five or more drinks on one occasion. For descriptive analyses the variable was coded as: none; once; two to four times; or five or more times.

PRESENCE OF CHILDREN

The presence of children referred to whether or not there were children reported by the respondent to be residing in the household. The VAWS included children aged 0 to 24 years. The GSS, in both the 1999 and 2004 iterations, included children aged 0 to 14 years.

NUMBER OF CHILDREN

The number of children referred to how many children aged 0 to 14 were reported by the participant to be residing in the household.[5]

SOCIAL ISOLATION

Social isolation was measured with a variable asking the respondent to indicate whether her partner tried to limit her contact with family and friends.

RELIGIOSITY

Religiosity was measured as the grouped number of times the respondent attended religious services, aside from special occasions, in the 12 months prior to the interview. For the descriptive analysis, the frequency of church attendance was divided into the following categories: never; once per year; a few times per year; between one and three times per month; and once per week or more. For the multivariate analysis, midpoints were taken to represent each categorical grouping of the frequency of church attendance.

IMMIGRANT STATUS

Immigrant status referred to whether the respondent was born in Canada or elsewhere.

PLACE OF ORIGIN

Place of origin categorized immigrants as having immigrated from either a developed or developing nation. Immigrants from developed countries referred to those who had migrated from countries in North America or Europe. Immigrants from developing countries were those who migrated from non-North American/non-European countries.[6]

PERIOD OF IMMIGRATION

Period of immigration referred to the range of years in which the respondent came to live permanently in Canada. This variable was categorized as follows: before 1965; 1965 to 1974; 1975 to 1989; and 1990 to 1999/2004.

AGE AT IMMIGRATION

Age at immigration referred to the age group of the respondent when she came to live permanently in Canada. Respondents were categorized into one of three groups: less than age 20; 20 to 29; and 30 and over.

PREVIOUS MARRIAGE/COMMON-LAW UNION

Previous marriage/common-law union was measured by whether the woman had ever been in any other marriage or common-law relationship with a person other than her current partner.

PREVIOUS PARTNER VIOLENCE

Previous partner violence referred to whether the respondent had experienced physical or sexual violence by a previous partner. The time frames for violence by previous partners were not identical in the VAWS and GSS. In the VAWS, respondents were asked about previous partner violence that had ever occurred. In both iterations of the GSS, respondents who reported having had contact with their previous partner in the 5 years prior to the survey were asked about previous partner violence that had occurred within those 5 years.

CULTURE

Culture was determined by whether the respondent lived within or outside of Québec.[7]

DEPRESSION

Depression referred to whether or not the respondent reported having used medication or drugs to help her get out of depression in the month prior to the interview.[8]

RURAL/URBAN RESIDENCE

In all three surveys, rural/urban residence was derived from the postal code of the participant's residence. However, while the coding of which areas were rural or urban was the same in the 1993 and 1999 surveys, a different coding was used by Statistics Canada in the 2004 survey. In the 1993 and 1999 surveys, urban areas had a minimum population concentration of 1,000 and a population density of at least 400 per square kilometre based on the previous census counts.[9] All territories outside urban areas were considered rural (Statistics Canada, 1999). The 2004 survey distinguished between larger urban centres and rural/small towns. Larger urban centres encompassed large urban areas or cores as well as adjacent urban and rural areas that possessed a high degree of social and economic integration with the urban cores. Rural and small town areas were outside the commuting zone of larger urban centres. Rural areas had populations of less than 1,000 and small towns had a population of 1,000 to 9,999 and a population density of 400 inhabitants per square kilometre according to the previous census (Statistics Canada, 2006).

TYPE OF DWELLING

The type of dwelling was derived from a question that asked the respondent in what type of dwelling she was living at the time of the survey. The types of dwellings are: single-detached house; low-rise apartment (less than five storeys); high-rise apartment (five or more storeys); and other (semi-detached or double/side by side, garden-/town-/row-house, duplex—one above the other, mobile home, or trailer).

Violence

The VAWS and both versions of the GSS measured violence by husbands and common-law partners with ten behavioural items from a modified version of the CTS (Straus, 1979). Male partner violence against women was defined as acts of physical assault, physical threat, and/or sexual assault perpetrated by a woman's current marital or common-law partner within a specified time frame preceding the interview. Hence, if respondents reported having experienced any of the aforementioned forms of violence within the specified time frame preceding the interview they were coded as having experienced violence.

It is important to add that the items not only measure violence in the sense that they have the potential for harm, but they also can be classified as assault. Assault includes forms of violence that are unlawful (Barnett, Miller-Perrin, & Perrin, 1997). The measures of violence used in the VAWS and GSS are offences under the Canadian Criminal Code (Johnson, 1996, 2006).

The module on IPV in the GSS was modelled after the VAWS, with the intention of allowing monitoring of changes across time (Federal-Provincial-Territorial Ministers Responsible for the Status of Women, 2002; Johnson,

2006). The introduction to the items measuring violence by a current partner in the VAWS and GSS were as follows:

VAWS: We are particularly interested in learning more about women's experiences of violence in their homes. I'd like you to tell me if your husband/partner has ever done any of the following to you. This includes incidents that may have occurred while you were dating.

1999 and 2004 GSS: It is important to hear from people themselves if we are to understand the serious problem of violence in the home. I'm going to ask you ten short questions and I'd like you to tell me whether in the past 5 years, your current spouse/partner has done any of the following to you. Your responses are important whether or not you have had any of these experiences. Remember that all information provided is strictly confidential.

In addition to the specification of different time frames ("ever" for the VAWS and "past 5 years" for the GSS), the main difference between the two introductions is the specification in the VAWS that the incidents may include violence that occurred while dating. This probably did not have a large impact on the rates because the introduction to the GSS, asking about violence in the past 5 years by a current partner, would include dating violence if the couple had been dating in the past 5 years. So, when comparing a 5-year rate in the VAWS to a 5-year rate in the GSS, both rates may or may not include violence that occurred while the couple was dating, depending on whether the couple had been dating in the previous 5 years. Nevertheless, the fact that the VAWS explicitly mentioned violence experienced while dating suggested that respondents in the VAWS may have been more likely to include incidents that occurred while dating, thereby potentially contributing to a lower prevalence rate in the GSS.

Both surveys used virtually identical questions to measure male-to-female violence. The ten questions were:[10]

1. Has your husband/partner threatened to hit you with his fist or anything else that could (have) hurt you?
2. Has he thrown anything at you that could (have) hurt you?
3. Has he pushed, grabbed, or shoved you (in a way that could have hurt you)?
4. Has he slapped you?
5. Has he kicked, bit (you), or hit you with his fist?
6. Has he hit you with something that could (have) hurt you?
7. Has he beaten you up (GSS did not include 'up')?
8. Has he choked you?

9. Has he threatened to or used a gun or knife on you (used or threatened to use a gun or knife on you)?
10. Has he forced you into any (unwanted) sexual activity when you did not want to, by threatening you, holding you down, or hurting you in some way?

The most important difference between the VAWS and GSS questions measuring violence concerns Question 3. This question tends to be the most common form of IPV reported on the CTS. Presumably, Statistics Canada added the "in a way that could have hurt you" to this question in the GSS to ensure that they were measuring assaultive behaviours. This difference could also contribute to a lower prevalence of violence in the GSS. As discussed above, the use of relative rates in this book is key to attenuating such methodological differences when comparing the data for vulnerable populations across the surveys.

A separate section of the surveys asked respondents about their experiences of violence by previous partners.[11] The introductory statements and violence questions essentially paralleled those in the section on violence by current partners.[12]

TIME FRAMES OF THE VIOLENCE VARIABLES

The maximum time frame of violence in the VAWS was a lifetime rate while the maximum time frame in the GSS was 5 years prior to the survey. Where applicable three time frames were employed in examining the prevalence of violence in this book: (a) lifetime of the current relationship; (b) 5 years prior to the survey; and (c) 1 year prior to the survey. For analyses, the 5-year period is used because it provides a more adequate account of the women in the sample who had experienced violence compared to the 1-year rate. An exception is the chapter on post-separation violence, in which a 1-year time frame was used in the analyses to maximize the likelihood that ex-partner violence occurred after the physical separation began.

Post-Violence Variables

Not only is it important to understand factors in the prevalence and prediction of violence against women in vulnerable populations, but also it is useful to examine the post-violence experiences of victims in vulnerable populations relative to victims in their comparison group. For instance, as Shannon, Logan, Cole, and Medley (2006) note,

Women's help seeking should be considered within the broader social context, for this may influence service availability and accessibility.... Contextual factors specific to certain geographic areas and groups, such as cultural values/norms about gender and class, predominant religious institutions, and attitudes toward the acceptability of violence may all affect women's perceptions of whether their partner's behaviours are problematic, as well as acceptability of help seeking.

(p. 168)

Most of the past research on victims has been based on women who have sought help by either leaving the relationship or staying in a shelter, and those who seek help are believed to be different from those who do not leave an abusive relationship (Ting, 2007). The value of the post-violence data in this book is that it is based on representative samples, and so provides access to victims who did not necessarily leave the relationship and/or seek help in a shelter. Examining women's post-violence experiences in the context of vulnerable populations provides more specific data to inform secondary prevention efforts. The post-violence variables, which were variously available in all three surveys, involved the consequences of violence, help-seeking behaviours, and the involvement of the police.

CONSEQUENCES OF THE VIOLENCE

Several indicators of the consequences of violence are included in the analyses in this book. These include physical injury, psychopathology,[13] altered psyche, anger, taking time off from everyday activities, staying in bed for all or most of the day, and whether the victim perceived children to have witnessed the violence.

HELP-SEEKING BEHAVIOURS

Victims were also asked a number of questions about if and how they sought help for the violent incident. This encompassed seeking medical treatment, confiding in others, using services, and whether the respondent was interested in mediation/conciliation.

POLICE INTERVENTION

Victims were asked several questions about police intervention in the violence. This included whether the police found out about the violence and, if so, if they found out from the respondent. Victims who reported to the police were asked their reason for doing so. Victims for whom the police found out about the violence were asked a number of questions about the action(s) the police took and whether police intervention impacted the frequency of the violence. Victims who did not contact the police were asked a number of questions about why they did not contact the police.

Methods of Analysis

To document the prevalence of violence among subpopulations and their comparison groups and to investigate risk factors, descriptive analyses are conducted using bivariate comparisons that examine cross-tabulations with Chi-square tests of significance. Logistic regression was used to calculate zero-order odds ratios,[14] which are odds ratios that have been calculated without adjusting for the effects of other variables, and to conduct multivariate analyses. In the latter regard, logistic regression is an appropriate technique for predicting a dichotomous dependent variable from a set of independent variables. Logistic regression essentially allows one to predict group membership (e.g., victim or non-victim of violence) through evaluating the odds (or probability) of membership in one of the groups (e.g., victim of violence) based on the combined values of predictor variables (i.e., risk and protective factors for violence; Tabachnick & Fidell, 2001). This technique also has a very simple interpretation. For a given variable it provides a ratio of the odds of violence occurring. If the value of the odds is greater than one the variable is positively related to violence, meaning that the variable increases the odds of violence occurring. If the value of the odds is less than one the variable is negatively related to violence, meaning that the variable decreases the odds of violence occurring. For example, Table 9.5 (see Chapter 9) includes the impact of rural/urban residence on the odds of violence for Aboriginal and non-Aboriginal women in the 1999 survey. The odds of violence for rural-dwelling Aboriginal women were 4.717. This means that living in a rural area was associated with increased odds of violence compared to living in an urban area for Aboriginal women in the 1999 survey. Specifically, if one subtracts the odds ratio for rural women from the odds ratio for urban women (which is fixed at 1.000 since it is the comparison group) and then converts the difference to a percentage we find that Aboriginal women living in a rural area had 372% greater odds of violence compared to Aboriginal women living in an urban area in the 1999 survey (4.717 − 1.000 = 3.717 * 100 = 372). Non-Aboriginal women living in a rural area in the 1999 survey had an odds ratio of 0.577. Subtracting 1.000 (i.e., the odds for those in urban areas) from this odds ratio, we learn that non-Aboriginal women living in a rural area had 42.3% lower odds of violence compared to their counterparts living in an urban area (0.577 − 1.000 = −0.423 * 100 = −42.3). Independent variables that are in discrete categories (measured at the nominal or interval level) are interpreted in this way. Those that are continuous (measured at the interval or ratio level) are interpreted based on the scale of the variable as per the following example. In the same table in Chapter 9, the independent variable of age is included. Looking at the results from the analysis of the 2004 survey, one finds that the odds ratio on the age variable for Aboriginal women was 1.017. This means that for each additional year older that an Aboriginal respondent was, her odds of violence increased by 1.7% (1.017 − 1.000 = 0.017 * 100 = 1.7). However, the lack of any stars behind this odds ratio in Table 9.5 indicates that this variable did not have a significant effect on violence for Aboriginal women in the 2004 survey. In other words, a 1.7% increase in odds for each

1-year increase in age was not a significant increase in the probability of violence. Looking at the same variable and survey, but in this case for non-Aboriginal women, the odds ratio was 0.971. This means that each additional year of increase in a non-Aboriginal woman's age in the 2004 survey was associated with 3% decrease in her odds of violence (0.971 − 1.000 = −0.029 * 100 = −2.9). The stars behind the odds ratio indicates that age had a significant effect on non-Aboriginal women's odds of violence in the 2004 survey.

Two different types of logistic regressions are used in the analyses in this book. The first type is direct logistic regression. This means that all of the independent variables are entered into the model simultaneously. These analyses are conducted for women in a given vulnerable population and for women in the comparison group. These direct logistic regressions allow examination of the operation of each risk factor (e.g., whether it is significantly positively or negatively associated with violence) in the prediction of violence for women in a given vulnerable population and the comparison group holding constant the effects of all other variables in the model. The second type is sequential logistic regression. This involves running several logistic regression models in sequence. In the first model, only the variable representing the odds of violence for the vulnerable population relative to its comparison group is entered into the regression model. Therefore, the output from this analysis simply provides the ratio of the odds of violence occurring for women in the vulnerable population relative to women who are not in the vulnerable population.[15] This allows identification of the extent to which the odds of violence against women in a given vulnerable population are elevated. Then, in subsequent regression models this variable is entered along with variables based on the explanatory framework of the chapter. If the ratio of the odds of violence for women in the vulnerable population relative to women not in the vulnerable population is decreased after controlling for the variables in the subsequent models, then one can infer that these variables help to account for the vulnerable population's elevated odds of violence. The final model is run with all of the variables simultaneously to see if a combination of risk factors contributes to the greatest reduction in relative odds or if one or more groups of risk factors alone accounted for more of the vulnerable population's elevated odds of violence. In short, these sequential logistic regression analyses are conducted to determine the extent to which the risk factors, which are theorized to explain why women in a given vulnerable population face an elevated risk for violence, account for the elevated odds of violence against women in a given vulnerable population relative to its comparison group. Also, where appropriate, t-tests are used to compare differences in odds ratios.[16]

For the post-violence comparison, logistic regression was used to calculate zero-order odds ratios for victims in a given vulnerable population relative to victims in the vulnerable population's comparison group on each post-violence variable. Since the victim subsamples were quite small, the focus of these analyses was not on statistical significance tests because there was undoubtedly a lot of random fluctuation. Rather, the focus of these analyses was on patterns in the data to shed light on post-violence experiences for each vulnerable population relative to its comparison group.

Weighting

Statistics Canada used a stratified sampling design with the Elimination of Non-Working Banks (ENWB) sampling technique for the VAWS and GSS (cf. Statistics Canada, 1994b, 2000, 2005b). Since the data sets are not simple random samples, it is necessary to weight the data so that the population is adequately represented (cf. Brownridge & Halli, 2001). This is because, with the stratified sampling design used by Statistics Canada, some areas in the sample are overrepresented while other areas are underrepresented. Thus, Statistics Canada assigns each respondent in the data set a weight. The weight variable provided by Statistics Canada is applied when analysing the data, thereby accounting for this over- or underrepresentation.[17]

Conclusion

In addition to this book being novel in both its focus on vulnerable populations and its approach to theorizing about women's vulnerability, it is also methodologically novel. The analytical focus on violence in vulnerable populations, the strengthening of findings through the comparison of results across large-scale representative samples, using relative odds to attenuate the effects of methodological differences across surveys, and the use of sequential logistic regressions to test the extent to which risk factors account for the elevated risk of violence in vulnerable populations are, in themselves, methodologically novel contributions. Moreover, as a package, these innovations provide a unique methodological approach for studying violence against women in vulnerable populations. Having established the need for research on vulnerable populations and an approach for doing so, the in-depth investigation of violence against women in vulnerable populations can commence.

4
Violence Against Cohabiting Women
Present Perspective and Future
Prospective

The trend towards increasing rates of cohabitation in Western industrialized nations has continued into the beginning of the new millennium (Ambert, 2005). In Canada, where rates of cohabitation have more than doubled since the Census began to collect data on this phenomenon in 1981 (Statistics Canada, 2002a), the majority of young people aged 20 to 29 now choose a common-law relationship as their first union (Statistics Canada, 2002b).[1]

One consequence of the increasing prevalence of cohabitation has been concern over potential increases in a number of social problems that have been associated with this form of coupling. Among these, several studies have shown that violence is more common in cohabiting relationships. Most of these studies have been from either the United States (Anderson, 1997; Boba, 1996; Jackson, 1996; Lane & Gwartney-Gibbs, 1985; Schulman, 1981; Stets, 1991; Stets & Straus, 1989; Yllö & Straus, 1981) or Canada (Brinkerhoff & Lupri, 1988; Brownridge, 2004b; Brownridge & Halli, 2002b; Kennedy & Dutton, 1989; Smith, 1986; Sommer, 1994; Statistics Canada, 1994a). Research from New Zealand (Magdol, Moffitt, Caspi, & Silva, 1998) and Peru (Flake, 2005) has also found higher rates of violence in common-law unions. Moreover, research has shown that common-law unions are more likely to involve severe violence (Jackson, 1996; Stets & Straus, 1989; Yllö & Straus, 1981). Official report data have demonstrated that cohabiting unions are at greater risk of the most severe violence: intimate femicide. From 1991 to 2000, common-law unions in Canada had six times the intimate femicide rate as marital unions (Johnson & Hotton, 2003). National-level American data from 1976 to 1994 showed that cohabiting relationships in the United States had almost nine times the intimate femicide rate as marital unions (Shackelford, 2001). The latter pattern was subsequently replicated in a similar study of intimate femicide from 1989 to 2002 in Australia (Shackelford & Mouzos, 2005).

Given that violence is more prevalent and severe in common-law unions, one would intuitively expect to see increasing rates of non-lethal and lethal IPV in societies where cohabitation is becoming increasingly common. However, a study from Statistics Canada reported that over the ten-year

28

period from 1991 through 2000, one of the biggest declines in the intimate femicide rate was in common-law unions, which decreased significantly from 35.8 to 24.2 women per million cohabiting couples (Trainor, Lambert, & Dauvergne, 2002). In terms of non-lethal violence, Brownridge (2004b) noted that in Canada the annual prevalence of violence in common-law unions relative to marital unions decreased from 1993 to 1999. The subsequent release of comparable national data from 2004 provided an opportunity to expand this analysis to examine trends and patterns in risk for non-lethal violence in common-law relative to marital unions in Canada.

The purpose of this chapter, then, is to compare women's reports of male partner violence in common-law and marital unions across three nationally representative surveys of Canada conducted between 1993 and 2004 to assess changes in these unions in terms of the prevalence of violence, risk markers of violence, and the extent to which risk markers account for the higher rate of violence in common-law relative to marital unions.[2]

Theoretical Background

The Social Construction of Violence in Common-Law Unions

One way to understand the paradox of declining rates of violence in cohabiting relative to marital unions despite an increase in cohabiting unions is through an application of a theoretical framework that analytically distinguishes risk markers for violence in terms of whether they are characteristics that tend to select people into cohabitation (selection factors) or characteristics that tend to occur within the context of the union (relationship factors; Brownridge & Halli, 2000). This theoretical framework is based on insights from Berger and Kellner's (1994) thesis of reality construction in marriage. According to these theorists, marriage is a nomos-building instrumentality in which the couples' lives become more stable through the unwitting construction of a new reality. In other words, in marriage a couple builds a new reality with norms of interaction and this, in turn, creates stability in their lives. As a result, through marriage two individuals unite, redefine themselves and, as Berger and Kellner (1994) wrote, "in the most far reaching sense of the word, the married individual 'settles down'" (p. 29). It is reasonable to argue that when two individuals begin to cohabit they too build a nomos together. However, if there are differences in the characteristics of people who choose to cohabit from those who choose to marry (selection factors), the objective reality that cohabiting couples construct may well be different, with ensuing consequences for their relationship (relationship characteristics).

Based on past Canadian research (Brownridge, 2004b; Brownridge & Halli, 2001, 2002b), factors such as youth, low education levels, unemployment, past unions, violence by previous partners, and residing in Québec may select some individuals into cohabitation rather than marriage. These selection differences between "cohabitors" and "marrieds" may, in turn, impact their respective relationships. For example, Kalmun and Bernasco (2001) found that those who cohabit tend to live more separated lives compared to those who marry. These researchers speculated that "couples who are cohabiting are less secure of their relationship and may therefore be more reluctant to develop a joint lifestyle" (p. 653). Lower security among cohabitors may lead to more compensatory domineering behaviour, more sexually proprietary behaviour, greater social isolation, a higher probability of depression, more heavy alcohol consumption, and a reduced likelihood of having children. These selection and/or relationship factors may then lead to more dis-agreements, conflict, and violence. For example, conflict may occur if one member of the couple desires children and the other does not, and such dis-parate expectations are more likely to occur in cohabiting relationships (Ambert, 2005).

Predicting Trends in Cohabiting Women's Relative Risk for Violence

Past research has, indeed, shown that controlling for selection and relation-ship factors does account for the elevated risk for violence in common-law unions in Canada (Brownridge, 2004b; Brownridge & Halli, 2002b). However, these variables by definition are not static. As cohabitation becomes more common, the characteristics of persons who choose to engage in such unions will tend to change. For example, based on Sweden's experience, which is the nation that is most advanced in terms of the development of cohabitation, Kiernan (2002) has identified four stages through which cohab-itation progresses in a society. In the first stage, cohabitation is practised by a minority of the single population and is seen as a deviant or avant-garde phe-nomenon. The second stage involves cohabitation as a childless phase in which the couple tests their relationship for its marriage worthiness. In the third stage cohabitors can become parents and cohabitation is seen as an acceptable alternative to marriage. Finally, in the last stage cohabitation and marriage are indistinguishable such that children are born and raised in cohabiting unions. Applying this view of cohabitation as a form of family life in transition draws one's attention to the fact that the characteristics of indi-viduals who choose to cohabit will change over time. In the context of the theoretical framework outlined above it is possible to derive the following overall prediction; as cohabitation in a society progresses towards the fourth stage of development, and hence becomes increasingly normative, the selec-tion bias will be reduced. Consequently, the characteristics of cohabitors' rela-tionships will become more like that of marrieds and the relatively higher rates of violence for cohabitors will become increasingly similar to that of marrieds.

Data Sets and Measurement

The Data Sets

The data from all three surveys were employed in analyses contained in this chapter (see Chapter 3 for details of the surveys and methods). Since this chapter concerns violence against women in their current relationship, the subsamples of heterosexual women living married or common-law at the time of the survey consisted of 8,418 women (1,053 cohabiting and 7,365 married) from the 1993 survey, 7,396 women (996 cohabiting and 6,400 married) from the 1999 survey, and 6,769 women (1,134 cohabiting and 5,635 married) from the 2004 survey.

Risk Factors

The selection and relationship variables in this chapter were chosen based on their availability in all three data sets and their salience from past research (Brownridge, 2004b; Brownridge & Halli, 2002b).

SELECTION VARIABLES

Selection variables were defined as those characteristics of the respondent and/or her partner that tended to be brought with the individual to the union. The selection variables were: age, woman's education, woman's employment, partner's employment, previous marriage/common-law union, previous partner violence, and culture.

RELATIONSHIP VARIABLES

Relationship variables were defined as those characteristics of the respondent and/or her partner that tended to occur within the context of their relationship together. The relationship variables were: duration of relationship,[3] jealousy, possessive behaviour, social isolation, patriarchal dominance, depression, heavy drinking, and the presence of children.

Results

Descriptive Analysis

VIOLENCE BY COHABITING/MARRIED STATUS

The first two columns of Table 4.1 provide the 5-year and 1-year prevalence rates of violence in cohabiting and marital unions for each data set used in this chapter. The results showed that cohabiting women had a significantly higher prevalence of violence than their married counterparts in all of the available time frames across all three surveys. Examining the time frames that were comparable across the surveys, the 1-year and 5-year time frames, there appeared to be an overall pattern of decline in risk for violence for cohabiting relative to married women. To express the relative risk of violence for cohabiting and married women, as shown in the third column of Table 4.1,

Table 4.1 Prevalence rates (%) of violence in cohabiting and marital unions in the 1993 VAWS, 1999 GSS, and 2004 GSS, corresponding zero-order odds ratios, and significance of the change across surveys

	Cohabiting	Married	Odds ratio	Difference in odds
1993 VAWS				
1-year prevalence	8.7	2.2***	4.171***	
5-year prevalence	16.1	6.8***	2.625***	
Lifetime prevalence	18.1	15.1**	1.238**	
1999 GSS				*1993 vs. 1999*
1-year prevalence	3.7	1.4***	2.714***	2.51***
5-year prevalence	7.1	3.2***	2.263***	1.20
2004 GSS				*1999 vs. 2004*
1-year prevalence	2.6	1.1***	2.413***	0.54
5-year prevalence	4.5	3.0**	1.529**	2.51***

Notes

**$p < 0.05$; ***$p < 0.01$ (p values for prevalence rates refer to Pearson Chi-square, for odds ratios the Wald Chi-square was used, and for the difference in odds the t-statistic was used).

zero-order odds ratios were calculated for the marital status variable on rates of violence for each data set. The final column reports whether the differences between the odds on the 1-year and 5-year time frames from 1993 to 1999 and from 1999 to 2004 were statistically significant. The odds of violence for cohabiting relative to married women using a 5-year time frame remained fairly stable from 2.6 times in 1993 to 2.3 times in 1999. However, they dropped significantly from 1999 to 2004. Cohabiting women reported 1.5 times the odds of violence in 2004. With respect to the 1-year time frame, the elevated risk of violence for cohabiting women dropped significantly from 4.2 times in 1993 to 2.7 times 1999. It then remained fairly stable with cohabiting women reporting 2.4 times the odds of violence in the year prior to the 2004 survey.

It is also noteworthy in Table 4.1 that in the two most comparable surveys, the iterations of the GSS, both the 5-year and 1-year prevalence rates of violence against married women remained fairly stable from 1999 to 2004. For cohabiting women, there was a drop in the prevalence of violence of 2.6% in the 5-year time frame and 1.1% in the 1-year time frame.

Figures 4.1, 4.2, and 4.3 contain the 5-year prevalence of each component of violence for each data set. Consistent with the overall prevalence rates, there were few noteworthy differences in the 5-year prevalence of individual forms of violence between the 1993 and 1999 surveys. Although the difference in the rate of being hit for cohabiting relative to married women was significant in both surveys, this rate dropped from 4.5 times (2.7% vs. 0.6%) in the 1993 survey to 3.3 times (1.0% vs. 0.3%) in the 1999 survey. While cohabiting women had 2.3 times (0.9% vs. 0.4%) the rate of being threatened with or having a knife or gun used against them in the 1993 survey, cohabiting and married women were equally unlikely to report having experienced this form

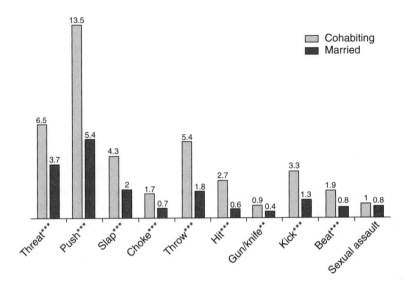

Figure 4.1 Five-year prevalence of each component of violence by cohabiting/married status in the 1993 VAWS (%).

Notes
**$p < 0.05$; ***$p < 0.01$ (p values refer to Chi-square tests of significance).

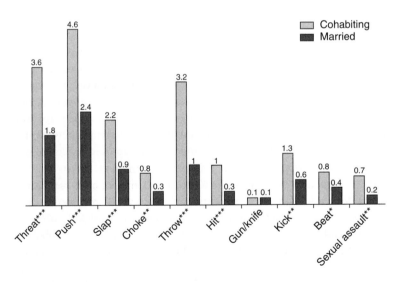

Figure 4.2 Five-year prevalence of each component of violence by cohabiting/married status in the 1999 GSS (%).

Notes
*$p \leq 0.10$; **$p < 0.05$; ***$p < 0.01$ (p values refer to Chi-square tests of significance)

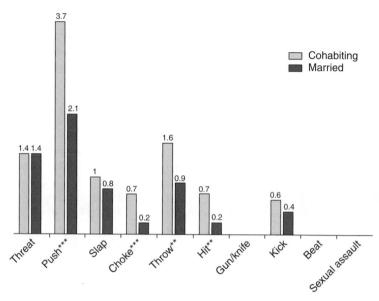

Figure 4.3 Five-year prevalence of each component of violence by cohabiting/married status in the 2004 GSS (%).

Notes

**p < 0.05; ***p < 0.01 (*p* values refer to Chi-square tests of significance).

Blank categories indicate cross-tabulations that were not released by Statistics Canada to ensure respondent confidentiality. Statistical significance test is reported.

of violence in the 1999 survey. Surprisingly, given the overall rates, the prevalence of sexual assault against cohabiting relative to married women more than doubled from 1.3 times (1.0% vs. 0.8%) in the 1993 survey to 3.5 times (0.7% vs. 0.2%) in the 1999 survey. However, in the 2004 data there was not a significant difference in the rate of sexual assault for cohabiting and married women (actual proportions were not released by Statistics Canada due to a small cell size). Indeed, there were several noteworthy differences between the 1999 and 2004 surveys. Although cohabiting women reported twice the rate as married women (3.6% vs. 1.8%) of being physically threatened in the 1999 survey, the two groups were equally likely to report this form of violence in the 2004 survey. Similar reductions were also observed on the measures of being slapped, having something thrown that could hurt, being kicked, bit, or hit with a fist, and being beaten. The relative rate of being pushed, grabbed, or shoved, being hit with something that could hurt, and being choked remained high for cohabiting relative to married women in the 2004 survey.

SELECTION AND RELATIONSHIP VARIABLES BY MARITAL STATUS

Table 4.2 contains the results of the cross-tabulations of the independent variables by whether the respondent was cohabiting or married for each survey. A quick glance at the results for the selection variables in Table 4.2 showed that there were significant differences between cohabitors and marrieds on all of the selection variables in the 1993 and 1999 surveys and on all but one of the variables in the 2004 survey. Compared with married women, cohabiting women were more likely to be young, less likely to be unemployed, more likely to have had a previous marriage or common-law union, more likely to have experienced violence by a previous partner, and more likely to live in Québec. There also was a slight tendency for cohabiting women to be less likely to have low education levels compared to married women, though this difference appeared to have been decreasing over time. The relationship between cohabiting and married men's rates of unemployment varied across the three surveys. In the 1993 survey married men were nearly twice as likely to be unemployed as cohabiting men. However, in 1999 cohabiting men were more than twice as likely to be unemployed. Subsequently, in 2004, 3.6% of cohabiting men were unemployed compared to 2.9% of married men, a difference that was not statistically significant. The difference between the VAWS and both iterations of the GSS was undoubtedly impacted by retired men's inclusion in the VAWS and their exclusion in the iterations of the GSS (see the discussion of how employment was measured in Chapter 3). A comparison of both iterations of the GSS clearly showed increasing similarity in cohabiting and married men's rate of unemployment.

In addition to comparing cohabitors to marrieds on the selection variables, it was also possible to use the data in Table 4.2 to observe whether there were any patterns among those who were cohabiting or married across the three surveys. The results in Table 4.2 showed that the proportion of young cohabiting and married women decreased over time. There also appeared to be a pattern of increasing education for both cohabiting and married women. Although cohabiting women remained unemployed at a similar rate across all three surveys, there was a pattern in which married women were less likely to be unemployed over time. A similar comparison of both iterations of the GSS showed that married men's rate of unemployment remained stable while cohabiting men's unemployment rate dropped slightly. The extent to which cohabitors and marrieds had previous partners remained fairly stable over time. With respect to violence by previous partners, the rates for the 1993 survey cannot be compared to the 1999 and 2004 surveys due to the use of different time frames. For the two iterations of the GSS, there appeared to be little change in the proportion of cohabitors who experienced violence by a previous partner but about half as many married women in 2004 had experienced violence by a previous partner compared to married women in 1999 (8.8% vs. 18.2%). Cohabitation remained very common in Québec relative to the rest of Canada, though the proportion of cohabitors in Québec declined slightly from 51.9% of all cohabitors in the 1999 survey to 46.7% in 2004.

Table 4.2 Independent variables by cohabiting/married status in the 1993 VAWS, 1999 GSS, and 2004 GSS (%)

Independent variables	Cohabiting			Married		
	1993	*1999*	*2004*	*1993*	*1999*	*2004*
Selection variables						
Age						
18/15–34	65.3	55.9	48.2	24.5	19.9	17.4
35–54	30.6	39.6	43.7	47.5	50.3	49.8
55+	4.1	4.5	8.1	28.0***	29.8***	32.8***
Woman's education						
Less than high school	21.3	19.4	16.2	25.2	20.7	16.3
High school	27.7	14.4	16.6	28.9	17.5	18.6
Some post secondary	18.5	16.7	14.7	13.3	13.3	12.6
Community college dip./cert.	16.5	29.7	31.4	16.3	27.5	28.7
University degree	16.0	19.6	21.1	16.2***	21.1**	23.8*
Woman's employment						
Did not work in past year	19.8	20.6	21.0	38.2	31.3	28.3
Worked past year	80.2	79.4	79.0	61.8***	68.7***	71.7***
Partner's employment						
Did not work in past year	12.5	5.4	3.6	23.4	2.6	2.9
Worked past year	87.5	94.6	96.4	76.6***	97.4***	97.1
Previous marriage/common-law						
Yes	52.0	51.5	50.1	15.3	15.3	16.3
No	48.0	48.5	49.9	84.7***	84.7***	83.7***
Previous partner violence (ever/5 yr.)						
Yes	61.5	29.9	28.2	49.2	18.2	8.8
No	38.5	70.1	71.8	50.8***	81.8***	91.2***
Culture						
Québec	43.9	51.9	46.7	23.1	20.6	19.2
Rest of Canada	56.1	48.1	53.3	76.9***	79.4***	80.8***

Relationship variables						
Duration of relationship						
Less than 4 years	57.0	41.9	45.9	8.0	6.9	7.7
4–9 years	29.0	31.6	27.1	15.5	15.0	15.3
10 or more years	13.9	26.5	27.0	76.5***	78.1***	77.0***
Jealousy						
Yes	9.7	6.6	5.0	5.3	4.2	2.4
No	90.3	93.4	95.0	94.7***	95.8***	97.6***
Possessiveness						
Yes	13.2	5.6	3.6	10.0	3.7	2.4
No	86.8	94.4	96.4	90.0***	96.3**	97.6**
Social isolation						
Yes	5.9	2.0	1.5	3.9	2.4	1.4
No	94.1	98.0	98.5	96.1***	97.6	98.6
Patriarchal dominance						
Yes	14.5	1.1	0.6	5.7	1.0	0.9
No	85.5	98.9	99.4	94.3***	99.0	99.1
Depression						
Yes	3.2	3.8	6.1	2.9	4.7	6.9
No	96.8	96.2	93.9	97.1	95.3	93.1
Heavy drinking (past month)						
None	60.5	67.0	60.8	78.5	81.9	78.7
Once	15.8	13.4	18.1	9.2	8.2	8.8
2–4 times	16.7	13.8	14.9	9.3	7.3	9.8
5 or more times	6.9	5.7	6.1	3.0***	2.7***	2.7***
Children <25/15						
Yes	37.4	42.1	41.9	57.1	35.9	35.7
No	62.6	57.9	58.1	42.9***	64.1***	64.3***

Notes

*$p \leq 0.10$; **$p < 0.05$; ***$p < 0.01$ (p values refer to Chi-square tests of significance).

A cursory examination of the relationship variables in Table 4.2 evidenced that in the 1993 survey there were significant differences for all but one relationship characteristic. There were two fewer significant differences in the 1999 survey and this remained the same in the 2004 survey. In all three surveys, cohabitors were significantly more likely to have short-duration unions, to have a partner who was jealous, to have a partner who insisted on knowing who the woman was with and where she was at all times, and to have a partner who consumed alcohol heavily in the month prior to the survey. In none of the surveys was there a significant difference between cohabiting and married women in their rate of depression. Although in the 1993 survey cohabiting women were significantly more likely to have a partner who tried to isolate them from family and friends and who dominated them in a patriarchal manner, these differences disappeared in the 1999 and 2004 surveys. In the 1993 survey cohabiting women were significantly less likely than married women to have children under age 25 living in the household. However, in the 1999 and 2004 surveys cohabiting women were significantly more likely than married women to have children under age 15 living in the household. The extent of the difference between the 1993 survey and the iterations of the GSS was likely impacted by the inclusion of children less than age 25 in the 1993 survey, which would inflate the proportion of married women with children because childbearing in common-law unions is, generally speaking, a more recent event in Canada (Le Bourdais & Lapierre-Adamcyk, 2004).

In terms of patterns in relationship variables among those who were cohabiting or married across the three surveys, the results in Table 4.2 showed that the duration of marital unions was stable while the proportion of cohabiting couples in unions with durations of 10 or more years nearly doubled (13.9% vs. 27.0%) from the 1993 survey to the 2004 survey. There appeared to be a trend for both cohabiting and married women towards decreasing rates of male jealousy, sexually possessive behaviour by monitoring women's whereabouts, and male attempts to isolate women socially. There was a sharp decline in both cohabiting and married women's reports of male patriarchal dominating behaviour between the 1993 and 1999 surveys. By contrast, there appeared to be an increasing trend towards reporting drug/medication use for depression for both cohabiting and married women. Rates of heavy drinking by partners remained fairly stable across all three surveys for both cohabiting and married women. Finally, the proportion of cohabiting and married women with children under age 15 remained stable from 1999 to 2004.

Multivariate Analyses

LOGISTIC REGRESSIONS FOR COHABITORS AND MARRIEDS COMBINED

Table 4.3 provides the results of the sequential logistic regressions on the 5-year prevalence of violence for cohabitors and marrieds in each survey. The

Table 4.3 Results of sequential logistic regressions on the 5-year prevalence of violence in the 1993 VAWS, 1999 GSS, and 2004 GSS

Covariates	Model 1 Cohabiting/married odds ratio	Model 2 Selection variables odds ratio	Model 3 Relationship variables odds ratio	Model 4 Full model odds ratio
1993 VAWS	n = 8,339	n = 8,319	n = 8,023	n = 8,011
Cohabiting/married status				
Cohabiting	2.625***	1.337**	1.239*	1.179
Married	1.000	1.000	1.000	1.000
Selection variables		BLOCK		BLOCK
Relationship variables			BLOCK	BLOCK
Constant	0.073***	0.862	0.098***	0.238***
−2 Log-likelihood	4,542	4,301	3,671	3,633
χ^2	88***	319***	725***	760***
1999 GSS	n = 7,042	n = 6,802	n = 6,448	n = 6,379
Cohabiting/married status				
Cohabiting	2.263***	1.334	1.395*	1.467*
Married	1.000	1.000	1.000	1.000
Selection variables		BLOCK		BLOCK
Relationship variables			BLOCK	BLOCK
Constant	0.033***	0.307*	0.028***	0.033***
−2 Log likelihood	2,213	2,062	1,649	1,610
χ^2	28***	108***	427***	439***
2004 GSS	n = 6,644	n = 6,542	n = 6,329	n = 6,292
Cohabitation/married status				
Cohabiting	1.529**	1.033	0.822	0.873
Married	1.000	1.000	1.000	1.000
Selection variables		BLOCK		BLOCK
Relationship variables			BLOCK	BLOCK
Constant	0.031***	0.108***	0.037***	0.026***
−2 Log likelihood	1,876	1,731	1,553	1,492
χ^2	6**	67***	235***	257***

Notes: $* p \leq 0.10$; $** p < 0.05$; $*** p < 0.01$.

first model in Table 4.3 contains the odds of violence for cohabiting compared to married women without any controls (also found in Table 4.1). In the second model selection variables were controlled; in the third, relationship variables were controlled; and in the fourth, both selection and relationship variables were controlled. With respect to the 1993 data, the results showed that controlling for selection variables substantially reduced the elevated odds of violence for cohabiting women from 163% higher to 34% higher compared to married women. A similarly strong reduction in odds resulted when controlling for relationship variables such that cohabiting women had 24% higher odds of violence after adjusting for these variables. The greatest reduction in odds in the 1993 data occurred when controlling for both the selection and relationship variables, in which case cohabiting women's odds of violence were no longer significantly higher than that of married women.[4]

SEPARATE LOGISTIC REGRESSIONS FOR COHABITORS AND MARRIEDS

To identify the impact of each selection and relationship variable on the odds of violence against cohabiting and married women, separate logistic regressions were run for each group. The results of these analyses are presented in Table 4.4. As shown in Table 4.4, holding all other variables constant, in the 1993 survey the largest differences in the selection variables were on the variables involving a previous partner. In particular, violence by a previous partner was associated with significantly higher odds of violence by a cohabiting partner than a marital partner. In terms of the relationship variables in the 1993 survey, the largest differences in odds were on the union duration and sexual possessiveness variables. Although union duration was not associated with the odds of violence for cohabiting women, for married women each year of increase in union duration was associated with a 3% reduction in their odds of violence. In terms of sexual possessiveness, while having a partner who insisted on knowing who a woman was with and where she was at all times increased a married woman's odds of violence by 101%, having such a partner increased a cohabiting woman's odds by 217%.

The results for the 1999 data in Table 4.3 showed that controlling for selection variables reduced cohabiting women's elevated odds of violence from 126% to 33% higher than married women's odds, the latter representing an insignificant difference. Controlling for relationship variables as well as the full model also substantially reduced the odds, but in both cases the difference remained significant. In other words, in the 1999 data the selection variables accounted for the greatest reduction in cohabiting women's elevated odds of violence. An examination of the separate logistic regressions for cohabiting and married women in Table 4.4 showed that there was a large difference for two of the selection variables. Cohabiting women who had a previous marital or common-law partner did not have significantly different odds of violence compared to cohabiting women who did not have a prior marital or common-law relationship. However, married women with a history of a prior union had 112% greater odds of violence than married women without such a past. While there was no significant difference in odds of violence for cohabiting women in Québec compared to cohabiting women in the rest of Canada, married women in Québec had significantly lower odds of violence compared to married women in the rest of Canada in the 1999 survey.

In terms of the 2004 data, the results of the sequential logistic regressions in Table 4.3 showed once again that controlling for the selection and relationship variables substantially reduced the elevated odds of violence against cohabiting women. In the 2004 data, however, controlling for any combination of either selection and/or relationship variables accounted for the significantly higher odds of violence against cohabiting women. Examining the results in Table 4.4, a comparison of the number of variables for which there were significant differences between the cohabiting and married respondents across the three surveys showed that the 2004 survey had the fewest significant differences on the variables in the study. The only variable that was consistently significantly different across the three surveys was having had a previous marriage or common-law union. In all three surveys, the odds of violence against married women who had a prior marital or common-law union were significantly higher than the odds of violence against a cohabiting woman who had such a history. In the 2004 survey a strong difference emerged with respect to the woman's employment. Unemployed cohabiting women had 159% higher odds of violence than their employed counterparts while there was no difference in odds of violence for married women who were unemployed or employed. With respect to relationship variables in the 2004 survey, the strongest difference was on the patriarchal domination variable. Although cohabiting women with a partner who behaved in a patriarchal domineering manner did not have significantly higher odds of violence than cohabiting women without such a partner, married women who had a partner that prevented them from having access to the family income had 701% greater odds of violence compared to their counterparts without a partner who behaved in such a patriarchal domineering manner. The only other significant differences on relationship variables in the 2004 survey were noteworthy because of their reversal in direction from the 1993 and 1999 surveys. The difference in odds on the union duration variable was significant. For the first time, as union duration increased cohabiting women's odds of violence decreased significantly more than married women's odds of violence. Similarly, for the first time in the 2004 survey cohabiting women with children had significantly higher odds of violence than did married women with children.

Table 4.4 Results of logistic regressions on the 5-year prevalence of violence in the 1993 VAWS, 1999 GSS, and 2004 GSS for cohabitors and marrieds

Covariates	1993			1999			2004		
	Cohabiting n = 965	Married n = 7,046		Cohabiting n = 844	Married n = 5,535		Cohabiting n = 998	Married n = 5,294	
	OR	OR	t	OR	OR	t	OR	OR	t
Selection variables									
Age	0.931***	0.981**	−0.39	0.968	0.960**	0.44	0.975	0.980	−0.25
Woman's education	1.041	1.000	0.96	0.941	1.051	−0.17	1.036	1.121**	−1.19
Woman's employment									
Unemployed	1.163	1.092	0.30	0.753	0.901	−0.54	2.594**	1.059	2.64***
Employed	1.000	1.000		1.000	1.000		1.000	1.000	
Partner's employment									
Unemployed	1.356	0.912	1.51*	0.334	1.091	−1.60*	4.616**	3.488***	0.53
Employed	1.000	1.000		1.000	1.000		1.000	1.000	
Previous marriage/cohab.									
Yes	0.647	1.145	−1.99**	0.818	2.123***	−2.65***	0.729	1.461	−1.71**
No	1.000	1.000		1.000	1.000		1.000	1.000	
Previous partner violence									
Yes	2.648**	1.479*	1.98**	0.283	0.862	1.32*	0.196*	0.000	0.00
No	1.000	1.000		1.000	1.000		1.000	1.000	
Culture									
Québec	0.887	0.881	0.04	1.223	0.627*	2.27**	0.834	0.990	−0.56
Rest of Canada	1.000	1.000		1.000	1.000		1.000	1.000	

Relationship variables

	(1)	(2)	(3)	(4)	(5)	(6)	(7)	(8)	(9)
Duration of relationship	1.011	0.970***	1.83**	1.012	1.002	0.35	0.953	0.991	−1.43*
Jealousy									
Yes	1.793*	2.379***	−1.13	2.172	4.518***	−1.85**	3.353*	4.799***	−0.72
No	1.000	1.000		1.000	1.000		1.000	1.000	
Possessiveness									
Yes	3.173***	2.012***	2.11**	5.728***	2.756***	1.94**	2.775	3.930***	−0.64
No	1.000	1.000		1.000	1.000		1.000	1.000	
Social isolation									
Yes	4.696***	4.782***	−0.06	3.242	3.152***	0.05	1.150	2.130*	−0.92
No	1.000	1.000		1.000	1.000		1.000	1.000	
Patriarchal dominance									
Yes	1.045	1.336	−0.95	24.833***	5.549***	2.20**	1.470	8.014***	−1.77**
No	1.000	1.000		1.000	1.000		1.000	1.000	
Depression									
Yes	2.376*	1.800**	0.74	9.805***	2.276**	3.39***	2.606*	2.302***	0.32
No	1.000	1.000		1.000	1.000		1.000	1.000	
Heavy drinking	1.061**	1.087***	−1.33*	1.131***	1.075***	1.85**	1.099***	1.089***	0.30
Children <25/15									
Yes	0.890	1.140	−1.37*	0.957	1.957***	−2.45***	1.414	0.877	1.59*
No	1.000	1.000		1.000	1.000		1.000	1.000	
Constant	0.514	0.146***		0.198	0.028***		0.059*	0.013***	
−2 Log likelihood	693	2,907		324	1,250		309	1,156	
χ^2	158***	535***		104***	340***		56***	219***	

Notes
*$p \leq 0.10$; **$p < 0.05$; ***$p < 0.01$.

Post-Violence Experiences for Cohabiting Relative to Married Victims

Table 4.5 contains the zero-order odds ratios for the consequences of violence for cohabiting compared to married victims in all three surveys. There were few consistent patterns in the consequence variables across the surveys. Although cohabiting victims did not have higher odds of being injured in the 1993 survey, they did have slightly higher odds of being injured in the 1999 and 2004 surveys. Correspondingly, cohabiting victims also had higher odds of taking time off from everyday activities as a consequence of the violence in the 1999 and 2004 surveys.

The zero-order odds ratios for victims' help-seeking behaviours for all three surveys are presented in Table 4.6. Among victims who were physically injured, cohabiting victims were as likely, or perhaps slightly more likely, to seek medical treatment for their injuries. There was no consistent pattern across the surveys in terms of cohabitors' relative odds of confiding in someone. However, cohabiting victims tended to have lower odds of confiding in a physician or nurse and/or a religious adviser across the surveys. Cohabiting victims also had lower relative odds of contacting a service. The only exception was that cohabiting victims tended to have higher odds of contacting a shelter or transition house compared to married victims.

Table 4.5 Zero-order odds ratios for consequences of violence for cohabiting relative to married victims in the 1993 VAWS, 1999 and 2004 GSS

Dependent variable	Cohabiting/married[a]					
	1993		*1999*		*2004*	
	OR	*n*	OR	*n*	OR	*n*
Physical injury	1.008	619	1.133	265	1.209	218
Psychopathology[b]	0.949	594	1.129	255	0.842	208
Altered psyche[c]	0.639*	594	1.692	255	0.498	208
Anger	1.108	594	0.702	255	0.941	208
Time off everyday activities	0.540*	617	1.412	263	1.766	217
Stay in bed all/ most of day	NA		1.019	265	†	
Children witnessed violence	1.093	521	0.618	213	1.785	156

Notes
*$p \leq 0.10$.
a Married is the reference category with an odds of 1.000.
b Includes depression or anxiety attacks, fear, afraid for children, more cautious or aware, sleep problems, shock or disbelief, hurt or disappointment, and upset, confused, or frustrated.
c Includes ashamed or guilty, lowered self-esteem, problems relating to men, and increased self-reliance.
† Statistics Canada would not release the result to ensure respondent confidentiality. Statistical significance test was not released.
NA Not available in the data.

Table 4.6 Zero-order odds ratios for victims' help-seeking behaviours in cohabiting relative to married victims in the 1993 VAWS, 1999 and 2004 GSS

Dependent variable	Cohabiting/married[a]					
	1993		1999		2004	
	OR	n	OR	n	OR	n
Visit doctor/nurse/ hospital for treatment	1.087	141	1.054	73	†	
Confided in someone:	1.343	615	0.873	261	0.748	217
Family	1.087	615	0.784	261	0.773	216
Friend/neighbour	1.307	615	1.344	260	0.826	217
Co-worker	NA		1.094	259	2.137	217
Doctor/nurse	0.464**	615	0.539*	259	0.560	217
Lawyer	NA		0.534	260	†	
Minister/priest/clergy/ spiritual adviser	0.060	615	0.717	259	†	
Services contacted:	0.780	618	0.568*	261	0.918	217
Crisis centre/line	3.392**	618	0.850	261	†	
Another counsellor/ psychologist	0.951	618	0.753	261	0.713	217
Community/family centre	0.183	618	0.702	261	†	
Shelter/transition house	1.880	618	1.345	261	†	
Women's centre	0.335	618	1.501	261	†	
Police/court-based victim service	NA		1.302	261	†	
Interested in mediation/ conciliation	NA		0.633	253	1.760*	203

Notes
*$p \leq 0.10$; **$p < 0.05$.
a Married is the reference category with an odds of 1.000.
† Statistics Canada would not release the result to ensure respondent confidentiality. Statistical significance test was not released.
NA Not available in the data.

Table 4.7 contains the zero-order odds ratios for police intervention variables for cohabiting relative to married victims in all three surveys. There were few consistent patterns in the police intervention variables across the surveys. The 1999 and 2004 data suggested that cohabiting victims for whom the police found out about the violence might have had lower odds of contacting the police themselves. The data from these surveys also suggested that those cohabiting victims who did contact the police had higher odds of having done so to have their partner arrested or punished and out of a sense of duty.

In terms of action taken by the police, the 1999 data suggested that cohabiting victims had higher odds of reporting that the police visited the scene.

Table 4.7 Zero-order odds ratios for police intervention for cohabiting relative to married victims in the 1993 VAWS, 1999 and 2004 GSS

Dependent variable	Cohabiting/married[a]					
	1993		1999		2004	
	OR	n	OR	n	OR	n
Police found out	1.339	616	0.793	263	1.515	216
Police found out from respondent	NA		0.311*	68	0.857	48
Reason police contacted:						
Stop violence/receive protection	NA		1.174	53	†	
Arrest/punish spouse/partner	NA		2.944	54	6.256**	35
Duty to notify police	NA		1.360	53	1.258	35
Recommendation of someone else	NA		0.730	54	†	
Police action:						
Visited scene	NA		2.154	65	†	
Made report/conducted investigation	NA		1.208	65	†	
Gave warning to spouse/partner	NA		0.927	65	0.840	47
Took spouse/partner away	0.214*	64	1.833	65	1.021	48
Put you in touch with community services	0.252	64	1.953	65	†	
Made arrest/laid charges	NA		NA		1.144	48
None	NA		0.570	65	†	
Respondent satisfied w/police	1.129	63	1.600	66	0.730	48
Post-police violence decreased/stopped	1.154	63	0.542	41	†	
Reasons police not contacted:						
Dealt with in another way[b]	NA		1.365	194	†	
Did not want to get involved with police	0.190	533	2.314**	193	2.818**	168
Fear of spouse/partner	0.147	533	0.955	193	†	
Personal matter that did not concern police	NA		1.458	191	1.063	168

Police couldn't do anything about it	0.891	533	3.119***	193	1.867	168
Police wouldn't help[c]	NA		5.698***	192	†	167
Police wouldn't think it was important enough	NA		1.286	192	2.338*	
Fear of publicity/news coverage	NA		1.548	192	†	166
Did not want spouse/partner arrested or jailed	0.091	533	2.073**	192	1.014	167
Did not want anyone to find out about it (e.g., shame)	0.624	533	1.989**	192	0.503*	
Other reason	3.446	533	0.745	191	†	

Notes

$*p \leq 0.10$; $**p < 0.05$; $***p < 0.01$.

a Married is the reference category with an odds of 1.000.

b Includes left him, reported to another official, private matter that took care of myself, etc.

c Includes police wouldn't think it was important enough, wouldn't believe, wouldn't want to be bothered or get involved, police would be inefficient or ineffective, police would be biased, would harass/insult respondent, offender was police officer.

† Statistics Canada would not release the result to ensure respondent confidentiality. Statistical significance test was not released.

NA Not available in the data.

The 1999 and 2004 data suggested that cohabiting victims were slightly less likely to report that the police gave a warning to their partner. Among victims that did not contact the police, those who were cohabiting had higher odds of having not done so in the 1999 and 2004 surveys because they felt the police would not think it was important enough.

Discussion

The Elevated Risk of Violence Against Cohabiting Women from 1993 to 2004

The elevated risk for partner violence against cohabiting women in Canada has persisted into the millennium. However, the risk for violence against women in common-law unions relative to marital unions has declined over time. The odds of violence in the past 5 years for cohabiting relative to married women declined from being 2.6 times higher in 1993 to 1.5 times higher in 2004. Similarly, the relative odds of violence in the past year declined from being 4.2 times higher for cohabiting women in 1993 to 2.4 times higher in 2004. An examination of the individual forms of violence across the three surveys showed two trends. The first trend documented the magnitude of the differences in rates of violence, which decreased over time. Another trend showed fewer marital status differences on individual forms of violence, such as being slapped or beaten up. The results also suggested that the actual rates of violence declined over time to a larger extent for cohabiting than married women. A comparison of the two most comparable surveys, the 1999 and 2004 GSSs, showed that the prevalence rates remained fairly stable for married women while there was a decline in the prevalence rates for cohabiting women. Thus, consistent with what was predicted based on the theoretical framework of the chapter, which suggested a trend towards convergence in rates of violence for cohabiting and marital relationships, over time Canadian women's risk for violence in cohabiting relationships has become increasingly similar to that of their married counterparts.

Selection Variables Across the Surveys

Extrapolating from the proportion of cohabiting women in the samples, it was evident that cohabitation has continued to increase in Canada. In the 1993 survey 13% of women in a union were in a cohabiting relationship. This figure rose to 14% in 1999 and to 17% in 2004. Despite the increasing prevalence of cohabitation there were surprisingly few changes in selection variables across the surveys. Two such changes were observed. Cohabiting women were increasingly similar to married women in their education levels and cohabiting men were increasingly similar to married men in their rate of unemployment. Perhaps it should not be surprising that there were few changes in selection variables given that the proportion of couples living in common-law unions increased by only 4% from the 1993 to the 2004 survey. That is to say, if cohabitation had become much more common during this time, then one would have expected cohabitors to have become more like marrieds in terms of selection variables such as their average age. Instead, there was a fairly small increase in the prevalence of cohabitation and thus cohabitors as a group remained unique from marrieds (i.e., a bias of selection into cohabitation of individuals who tended, on average, to be different from marrieds had persisted). Based on these results, it is apparent that cohabitation will have to become much more prevalent before the selection bias will be eliminated.

Of course, the associations between marital status and selection variables can also be impacted by societal trends that affect marriage in Canada, as will be seen below. Indeed, marriage is a dynamic institution and this should be considered when using it as a comparison group (Smock & Gupta, 2002). For example, a comparison across each survey within and across both marital status groups showed that both cohabiting and married women appeared to be increasing in age and education. For cohabiting women this may partially reflect the increasing social normativeness of cohabitation. That is, as cohabitation becomes more common, it becomes less and less a relationship choice of those who are young and less educated. So the selection bias for cohabiting women is reduced because the characteristics of cohabitors are increasingly similar to the characteristics of marrieds. An increasing age and education level of married women probably reflects increased rates of delayed marriage resulting from a combination of increasing cohabitation as a first union as well as increasingly prolonged singlehood prior to marriage (Ambert, 2005). This change among married women in their age and education levels in turn offsets the reduced selection bias for cohabiting women in terms of their increased age and education levels. In other words, while the selection bias into cohabitation may have been reduced, there was not a proportionate convergence with marrieds on these variables as a result of concomitant changes in the characteristics of marrieds.

Relationship Variables Across the Surveys

Given that there were few changes in the selection variables across the surveys, based on the theoretical framework of the chapter, it was not surprising that there were also relatively few changes in relationship characteristics across the surveys. Cohabiting women consistently reported shorter duration unions, and higher rates of partner jealousy, sexually possessive behaviour, and partner alcohol abuse. They also consistently reported similar rates of drug/medication use for depression as compared to married women. On the two surveys where the measure of presence of children was comparable, the 1999 and 2004 GSSs, a greater proportion of cohabiting than married women reported having children under the age of 15. Recalling Kiernan's (2002) stages in the development of cohabitation, this finding was indicative that cohabitation in Canada had, in general, achieved a key element of the third stage of cohabitation in which it is acceptable for cohabitors to become parents. However, the large proportion of Canadian cohabitors from Québec would render such a conclusion premature. Indeed, past research has applied Kiernan's (2002) stages of the development of cohabitation to Québec and the rest of Canada (Le Bourdais & Lapierre-Adamcyk, 2004). It was concluded that cohabitation had achieved the stage of being an alternative to marriage in Québec because it was the most common way in which women give birth in that province. On the other hand, cohabitation in the rest of Canada was in the second stage of development because it was accepted as a prelude to marriage but not as a union form in which to become a parent. Given the difference in stages of development of cohabitation between Québec and the rest of Canada, there will be a brief comparison of cohabitors in Québec and the rest of Canada later in the discussion.

In terms of the impact of societal trends on relationship variables, it was evident that across the surveys both cohabiting and married women were less likely to report that their partners were jealous, sexually possessive, socially isolating, and patriarchally dominating. This was a most welcome pattern that at least partly speaks to the success of the feminist movement to change men's behaviour towards women in Canadian society. Although there were not significant marital status differences in rates of drug/medication use for depression, there did appear to be a trend for increasing rates of drug/medication use for depression for both groups of women. To the extent that this variable is a proxy for depression, this could signal a trend towards increasing rates of depression among both cohabiting and married women. It could also be indicative of a trend towards increasing rates of help-seeking to deal with depression.

The Ability of Selection and Relationship Factors to Account for Cohabiting Women's Elevated Odds of Violence

Although cohabitation had become more common in Canada and this appeared to have been reflected in some reduction in differences in selection and relationship variables, as well as in lower rates of violence for cohabiting relative to married women, there remained several differences between cohabitors and marrieds on selection and relationship variables and the elevated risk for violence against women in common-law unions persisted. The multivariate analyses showed that, while different variables seemed to be important across the surveys, these differences, in one combination or another, accounted for cohabiting women's higher odds of violence relative to married women in each survey. Applying the theoretical framework of the chapter, cohabitors remained a select group, which continued to result in relationship differences and these selection and relationship factors accounted for cohabiting women's elevated risk for violence.

Consequences of Violence and Experiences with Services for Cohabiting Relative to Married Victims

There were observations in the post-violence comparison that were consistent with the finding that cohabiting victims tended to be more likely to experience severe violence. This included a tendency for cohabiting victims to have slightly greater odds of physical injury, taking time off from everyday activities, and having contact with a shelter or transition house. The fact that cohabiting victims appeared to be slightly less likely to confide in a religious adviser was consistent with the notion that cohabitors in general are less religious. On the other hand, it is difficult to speculate as to why cohabiting victims would be less likely to confide in a physician or nurse about the violence. With respect to the police intervention data, the finding that cohabitors were less likely to report the violence to the police may have reflected that cohabitors are more likely than marrieds to be living in rental housing, and hence may be more likely to have their violence overheard by neighbours who, in turn, report the violence to the police. The finding that cohabiting victims that did not contact the police tended to have not done so because they felt the police would not think it was important enough suggested that more work needs to be done to ensure that cohabiting victims in particular feel comfortable contacting the police for assistance.

Limitations

The analyses were limited by the use of proxy measures for important selection and relationship variables. These are variables that approximate the concepts of interest, but are not perfect measures. For example, measuring patriarchal domination with a single item that asks about the male partner's control of the family finances taps only one aspect of patriarchy. Consequently, results of analyses using this variable may not adequately represent the true effect of patriarchal domination. Nevertheless, the variables that were included in the analyses in this chapter accounted for cohabiting women's higher odds of violence in all three surveys, hence demonstrating their utility for understanding cohabiting women's elevated risk for violence in Canada.

Future Prospective

With these caveats in mind, the results of the analyses suggest that as cohabitation becomes more normative there will tend to be greater similarity between cohabitors and marrieds on selection and relationship characteristics and, as a consequence, a reduction in cohabiting women's higher odds of violence relative to married women. Referring to Kiernan's (2002) stages of cohabitation, as cohabitation continues to progress towards being indistinguishable from marriage the selection bias into cohabitation should continue to decline. As a result, cohabitors should become more like marrieds in their relationships and, eventually, cohabitors and marrieds should have similar prevalence rates of violence.

It is important to add that differential selection may also occur upon exit from cohabitation. Having compared reports of violence by cohabitors and marrieds at union durations of 1 year and 5 years, Kenney and McLanahan (2006) found that cohabitors did not have significantly higher reports of violence after 1 year together but did have significantly higher reports of violence after 5 years together. The authors argued that cohabiting couples with lower levels of violence select out of cohabitation into marriage, leaving a group of cohabitors that are biased towards violence. Similarly, married couples that experience violence tend to select out of marriage into separation, leaving a group of marrieds that are biased towards non-violence. However, although not discussed, a comparison of violence against cohabiting and married women in the data sets in the current chapter showed that in two of the three data sets cohabiting women reported significantly higher rates of violence than married women even at a union duration of 1 year. Indeed, it is likely that differential selection takes place both upon entry into as well as upon exit from cohabitation. An extrapolation from this chapter suggests that as cohabitation increasingly becomes normative, selection out of cohabitation will also be reduced. That is, as cohabitation becomes an alternative to marriage and then indistinguishable from marriage, non-violent cohabiting couples will increasingly choose to remain cohabiting, hence further contributing to a convergence in the rate of violence for cohabitors relative to marrieds.

Lessons Gleaned from the Special Case of Québec

Given that cohabitation in Québec is at a more advanced stage of development, a comparison of violence among cohabitors in Québec and the rest of Canada can provide further insights into the future of the elevated risk of violence for cohabiting women in the rest of Canada. An application of the results contained in this chapter suggested that a comparison of violence among cohabiting women in Québec and the rest of Canada would show lower rates of violence among cohabitors in Québec. The results in Table 4.8 showed that this was not always the case, but has been, in fact, increasingly the case. The rate of violence against women in cohabiting unions in Québec was generally not significantly lower than the rate in cohabiting unions in the rest of Canada in the 1993 survey. Although the gap widened between the two groups in the 1999 survey, the change in cohabiting women's odds of violence in Québec compared to the rest of Canada was not significant. However, in the 2004 survey the gap widened even more with cohabiting women in Québec having half the rate of violence in the 5-year time frame and about one-third the rate of violence in 1-year time frame compared to cohabiting women in the rest of Canada. This resulted in an odds ratio for the annual rate of violence that was significantly lower in the 2004 survey compared to the 1999 survey. Although the change in odds for the 5-year rate from 1999 to 2004 did not reach statistical significance, the 2004 odds ratio was signifi-

Table 4.8 Prevalence rates (%) of violence in cohabiting unions in Québec and the rest of Canada in the 1993 VAWS, 1999 GSS, and 2004 GSS, corresponding zero-order odds ratios, and significance of the change across surveys

	Québec	Rest of Canada	Odds ratio	Difference in odds
1993 VAWS				
1-year prevalence	7.9	9.4	0.831	
5-year prevalence	14.0	17.7	0.759	
Lifetime prevalence	15.7	19.8*	0.756*	
1999 GSS				*1993 vs. 1999*
1-year prevalence	3.3	4.2	0.776	0.23
5-year prevalence	5.7	8.6*	0.637*	0.79
2004 GSS				*1999 vs. 2004*
1-year prevalence	1.3	3.7**	0.331**	2.10**
5-year prevalence	2.9	6.0**	0.483**	0.95

Notes
*$p \leq 0.10$; **$p < 0.05$ (p values refer to Chi-square tests of significance with the exception of the last column in which the t-statistic was used).

cantly different from the 1993 odds ratio ($t = 1.75$, $p < 0.05$). The fact that a significantly lower rate of violence for cohabiting women in Québec compared to cohabiting women in the rest of Canada was a relatively recent phenomenon, despite cohabitation having been far more prevalent in Québec than in the rest of Canada for some time, suggested that violence rates do not correspond perfectly with the stage of cohabitation in a particular culture. If violence rates did correspond perfectly with stage of cohabitation one would have expected to see a significantly lower rate of violence for cohabiting women in Québec compared to the rest of Canada in the 1993 survey. However, the stage of cohabitation in a culture undoubtedly correlates with selection and relationship variables that impact differences in reported rates of violence. Indeed, as shown in Table 4.4, when controlling for the selection and relationship variables in the study the odds of violence against cohabiting women in Québec were not significantly different from in the rest of Canada in any time period. Thus, it is reasonable to expect that as cohabitation in the rest of Canada moves into the third stage of being an alternative to marriage, all else equal, rates of violence in these unions will eventually move closer to those of cohabitors in Québec in the 2004 survey.

5
Differing Dynamics
Violence Against Women Post-Separation

Most research on domestic violence focuses on violence that takes place prior to separation (Anderson & Saunders, 2003). Relatively few investigations have examined the prevalence and characteristics of violence during separation or divorce (McMurray, Froyland, Bell, & Curnow, 2000). This is despite an increasing pool of potential victims, given reports of a trend over the last century towards increasing divorce rates in all Western nations (Hewitt, Baxter, & Western, 2005) and worldwide (McMurray, 1997), as well as recognition that separation from cohabiting unions is similar to marital separation (Walker, Logan, Jordan, & Campbell, 2004).

Although understudied relative to violence in intact unions, research on violence post-separation has slowly accumulated over the past three decades (Brownridge, 2006c). The purposes of this chapter are: (a) to review relevant research on the prevalence and risk markers of post-separation violence; (b) to integrate the research on risk markers of post-separation violence into an organizational framework that can enhance understanding, and guide analyses to further understanding, of this social problem; and (c) to shed light on the potentially differing dynamics of violence against separated, divorced, and married women. It is necessary to begin, however, with a description of the terminology used in the past and in this chapter.

Naming and Defining Post-Separation Violence

Various terms have been used in the research in this area including separation, estrangement, separation assault, post-separation abuse, post-separation woman abuse, and divorce-related domestic violence. Although most research does not provide specific definitions of these terms, those that do tend to arrive at quite different definitions. The most elaborate of these is Mahoney's (1991/1992) definition of separation assault. Mahoney defines separation assault as

> the attack on the woman's body and volition in which her partner seeks to prevent her from leaving, retaliate for the separation, or force her to return. It aims at overbearing her will as to where and with whom she

will live, and coercing her in order to enforce connection in a relationship. It is an attempt to gain, retain, or regain power in a relationship, or to punish the woman for ending the relationship. It often takes place over time.

(pp. 65–66)

The key element of this definition is the focus on motives, which Mahoney juxtaposes with a focus on the victim's psychology. However, focusing on motives in the definition may also impart too much to the concept. It is not necessarily the case that all occurrences of violence post-separation are based on the motives identified by Mahoney. Rather, it seems more appropriate to define the concept in a manner that identifies the perpetrators and the acts that are potentially included. Then motives and other related factors can be identified to improve our understanding of the phenomenon.

Even the definition of separation is not straightforward. Sev'er (1997) defined separation as "imminent or recent termination of any intimate relationship of some longevity, regardless of divorce outcome" (p. 567). Hardesty (2002) has critiqued this definition, suggesting that its focus on recently ended relationships excludes occurrences of violence that take place sometime after the separation. As well, the definitions of both Mahoney (1991/1992) and Sev'er (1997) allow the inclusion of incidents that occurred before the woman left the relationship. However, the intent of most research in the area is to examine violence after the relationship has ended.

The term estrangement has also been used inconsistently in research. Ellis and DeKeseredy (1997) define estrangement as "the process in which one or both partners become alienated from each other" (p. 592). However, in other research, particularly research on homicide, "estranged" is often used to refer to ex-partners, especially those who are legally separated.

Ellis (1987) has defined post-separation abuse as "the physical harms or threats of physical harm that are intentionally inflicted upon a woman by the man she formerly lived with" (p. 408). This definition is restricted only to physical harm thereby excluding other non-physical forms of violence. It also excludes ex-boyfriends, which is a group that has been included in some of the literature in this body of work. In a subsequent publication, Ellis (1992) defined post-separation woman abuse as "the emotional and/or physical harms that are intentionally inflicted on a woman by the man she lived with formerly in an intimate, heterosexual relationship and from whom she is separated physically" (p. 178). This definition is broader in the sense that it includes acts that can cause emotional harm. However, consistent with the focus of most of the research in the area, it is more restrictive in specifying heterosexual relationships and physical separation.

To be inclusive and at the same time reflect the intent behind the majority of the literature on this topic, this chapter employs the term *post-separation violence.* Post-separation violence is defined here as any type of violence per-petrated by a former married or cohabiting male partner or boyfriend sub-sequent to the moment of physical separation.[1]

The Prevalence of Violence Against Women Post-Separation

Past research on the prevalence of violence against women post-separation has examined both non-lethal and lethal violence.

Non-Lethal Violence Post-Separation

A substantial amount of research has provided indications of the prevalence of non-lethal violence post-separation. This body of research can be divided into studies that showed that a risk of violence exists post-separation and studies that demonstrated the existence of an elevated risk for violence post-separation relative to intact unions.

THE RISK FOR NON-LETHAL VIOLENCE POST-SEPARATION

Several studies, which taken together comprise more than three decades of research, have provided evidence that women are at risk for violence post-separation. Although these investigations used different methodologies and their purposes varied, what follows will briefly describe findings that were applicable to establishing women's risk for post-separation violence.

The earliest study suggesting a risk for violence post-separation appears to be O'Brien's (1971) investigation of 150 individuals in a Midwestern American city who had recently been involved in a divorce action. O'Brien found that overt violent behaviour was reported by 15% of the sample. In a study published a decade later, Schulman (1981) examined a representative sample of 1,793 Kentucky women and reported that 64% of divorced or separated women had experienced violence in the year prior to the study. In a follow-up interview of 24 women 4 to 6 months after their stay in a shelter, Giles-Sims (1983) found that 44% of those women who had not returned to their abuser had experienced violence at least once subsequent to leaving the shelter.

Most of the research establishing the risk for post-separation violence has been published since the early 1990s. Ellis and Stuckless (1992) examined a sample of 73 separated individuals who had at least one dependent child and had participated in marital conflict mediation at one of two participating agencies in Ontario. Over one-quarter of the sample reported threats or actual physical abuse following separation. In Arendell's (1995) sample of 75 divorced fathers in New York State, 40% of the men had threatened or used violence against their ex-wife since their marriage ended. The Canadian VAWS found that, among victims of partner violence during the relationship and who subsequently left, 19% experienced violence during the separation (Johnson & Sacco, 1995). McMurray et al. (2000) reported that 21% of their sample of 146 separated men in Western Australia had been violent during the separation. Based on a sample of 135 women living in an American city who had left their batterer, Fleury, Sullivan, and Bybee (2000) reported that 36% (n = 49) of the women had been assaulted by their ex-partner during a 2-year period. Among these victims of post-separation violence, 20% were raped by their ex-partner. This suggests that sexual assault by ex-partners is an important form of post-separation violence (DeKeseredy, Rogness, & Schwartz, 2004). The 1999 GSS data showed that, among women with a former marital or common-law partner who had been violent during the relationship, 39% reported experiencing violence by their ex-partner post-separation (Hotton, 2001).

In addition to providing a wide array of indications that women are at risk for violence post-separation, it has also been pointed out that the figures resulting from this research tend to be higher than the general average for married couples (Kurz, 1996). That is to say, women are at elevated risk for violence post-separation relative to women who are in intact unions. However, to determine more accurately the extent to which women's risk for non-lethal violence is elevated post-separation, one must examine investigations that allow a comparison of post-separation violence to the rate of violence in intact unions.

THE ELEVATED RISK FOR NON-LETHAL VIOLENCE POST-SEPARATION

Relatively few studies have provided data that allow a comparison of rates of violence post-separation to rates of violence in intact unions. A national survey of 1,834 Canadians reported that 30% of divorced or separated men had perpetrated acts of violence compared to 18% of married or cohabiting men (Lupri, 1990). In a study of 604 women in Toronto, Smith (1990b) found that 31% (n = 52) of those who had divorced, separated, or ended a live-in relationship in the 2 years prior to the study reported having experienced violence, compared to 13% of married or cohabiting women. The disparity was even greater with respect to severe violence; with 19% of divorced, separated, or ex-cohabitors compared to 4% of married or cohabiting women reporting having experienced these acts of violence. These two studies certainly showed that the sampled separated and divorced women in Canada were at elevated risk for violence relative to married women. However, a more precise determination of the elevated risk for post-separation violence requires disentangling the rate of violence for different post-separation marital status groups.

Only five studies were identified that provided prevalence rates of violence separately for divorced, separated, and married women. In an analysis of the National Crime Victimization Survey (NCVS), which was based on a representative sample of approximately 72,000 American households, Gaquin (1977/1978) included a comparison of assault victimization rates by spouses or ex-spouses for women aged 12 or older. From 1973 to 1975, the average spouse/ex-spouse assault victimization rate per 1,000 persons was 2.3 for married women, 21.2 for divorced women, and 62.8 for separated women. In a representative sample of 1,045 residents of Alberta, Kennedy and Dutton (1989) found a 1-year prevalence rate of 8.7% for married women (n = 631), 39.8% for divorced women (n = 4), and 54.8% for separated women (n = 7). Reporting on the results of the 1982 Canadian Urban Victimization Survey, Johnson (1990) showed that two per 1,000 married women, 18 per 1,000 divorced women, and 55 per 1,000 separated women aged 16 or older had been verbally, physically, and/or sexually assaulted by a current or former spouse. Using the redesigned NCVS for 1992 and 1993, Bachman and Saltzman (1995) reported that the average annual rate of violent victimizations per 1,000 females aged 12 or older was 2.7 for married women, 23.1 for divorced women, and 82.2 for separated women. Kershner, Long, and Anderson (2001) studied 1,693 women aged 18 and older who presented to one of eight medical clinics or 17 Women, Infants, and Children (WIC) supplemental food programmes in nine counties of west-central Minnesota. In the year prior to data collection, 16% (n = 172) of married women, 31% (n = 28) of divorced women, and 58% (n = 19) of separated women reported physical, emotional, verbal, and/or sexual abuse. In short, studies that allow a comparison of violence among separated, divorced, and married women show a consistent pattern of separated and divorced women being at elevated risk for violence compared to married women, with separated women having by far the greatest risk for post-separation violence. It appears that separated women have as much as 30 times the likelihood, and divorced women have as much as nine times the likelihood, of reporting non-lethal violence compared to married women.

Lethal Violence Post-Separation

An examination of all femicide cases in Dayton, Ohio, from 1975 through 1979, showed that 89% (n = 65) were killed by men (Campbell, 1992). Among these male-perpetrated femicides, 26.2% were committed by husbands or boyfriends and 16.9% were committed by estranged husbands or estranged boyfriends. Campbell (1992) did not differentiate between common-law and marital couples. Presumably these relationships were subsumed within "husbands." An examination of spousal homicides in Canada from 1994 to 2003 showed that common-law couples accounted for 40% of spousal homicides, followed by married persons (35%), separated persons (23%), and divorced persons (2%; Beattie, 2005). One must bear in mind that the homicide statistics mentioned thus far do not take into consideration the representation of these groups in the population. In recognition of this, in their study of intimate femicide in Ontario from 1974 to 1994, Gartner, Dawson, and Crawford (1998/1999) concluded that both separation and common-law status were risk factors for intimate femicide because they are overrepresented among victims. While less than 1% of the intimate femicides in the study by Gartner et al. (1998/1999) involved divorced women, 16% were legally separated. Since, according to Census data, 3% of women in Ontario were separated, these researchers concluded that "separation appears to be a risk factor for intimate femicide" (p. 158). Similarly, in their study of intimate femicide in Ontario from 1974 to 1990, Crawford and Gartner (1992) found that 59% of intimate femicides involved married or common-law partners and 31% involved men who were estranged from their partners (married and common-law partners who had separated as well as estranged boyfriends). Although the proportion of divorced and married victims was similar to the general population, separated women were overrepresented. Crawford and Gartner concluded that separated women had five times the risk of intimate femicide compared to other women.[2] Johnson and Hotton (2003) examined intimate-partner homicides in Canada from 1991 through 2000. In terms of real numbers, intact marital and common-law unions had the highest percentage of intimate femicides (30% and 27%, respectively). A total of 16% of intimate femicides from 1991 through 2000 were perpetrated by estranged married partners, 9% by estranged lovers, 4% by estranged common-law partners, and 2% by divorced partners. To identify the risk for intimate femicide, Johnson and Hotton calculated rates per million for both separated and intact couples. During the 10-year period of the study, 38.0 per million women were killed by estranged partners, 26.5 per million by current common-law partners, 4.4 per million by current husbands, 2.6 per million by divorced husbands, and 3.5 per million by other intimate partners (includes boyfriends, estranged lovers, and separated common-law partners). Thus, taking into consideration intimate femicides in different relationship groups as a proportion of the population, it is evident that separated women are at the highest risk of intimate femicide.[3]

Integrating Research: An Ecological Framework for Understanding Risk Markers of Post-Separation Violence

Given an elevated risk for violence against women post-separation, attention must be turned towards understanding this relationship. This requires a review of research on risk markers for post-separation violence.

Past research has identified potential risk markers for post-separation violence at all levels of separated women's environments. It is appropriate, then, to organize them within an ecological framework. The application of the ecological framework to post-separation violence divides the environment into four levels; the macrosystem, the exosystem, the microsystem, and the ontogenic level. The literature on risk markers for post-separation violence in the context of each level of the ecological framework is reviewed below.

Macrosystem

The macrosystem includes the cultural values and attitudes that foster violence. Like most research on violence against women, research on post-separation violence has identified patriarchy as playing an important role. A patriarchal culture sets the context for post-separation violence through perpetuation of the notion that men are entitled to an ongoing relationship and the expectations of female obedience, loyalty, and dependence (Hardesty, 2002). This places many separated women at risk given "the most salient gender difference in the divorce literature, that most marriages are ended by women" (Hewitt et al., 2005, p. 180). Indeed, divorced women and men tend to agree that the woman initiated the divorce and wanted the divorce more than the man (Amato & Previti, 2003). When women initiate separation within the context of a patriarchal culture, men may see this as a challenge to their patriarchal authority. In a qualitative study of a convenience sample of 75 divorced fathers in New York State, Arendell (1995) reported that some men used or threatened violence against their former partner because it "served to reassert control in the immediate situation, a function consistent with the position that because their rights had been violated and their power illegitimately diminished by divorce, forceful responses were necessary" (p. 120). Thus, during separation men may use violence to reclaim their rights and their role of dominance over their former partner.

Exosystem

The exosystem refers to the formal and informal social networks/structures in which the family is involved. These networks may impact what takes place in the family setting, and so may influence violence.

DETERRENCE

It can be argued that separation often implies the loss of, or the restriction of access to, some social networks. The loss of at least some of these social networks, such as extended family of the ex-partner and "friends of the couple," may also imply loss of stakes in conformity. According to social control theory, men with the least to lose, that is those with the least stakes in conformity, will be least deterred by the threat of legal or social sanctions. It has been argued both that those who are socially isolated are less likely to view loss of reputation as a sanction and that separated and divorced men have a lower stake in conformity than men who are married (Ellis & DeKeseredy, 1989). It follows that these men may be less deterred from using violence by the threat of legal or social sanctions.

FEMALE SOCIAL ISOLATION

While some social networks may be diminished at separation, for some women separation may provide the opportunity to renew social networks. In

Kurz's (1995) study of 129 divorced mothers with children in Philadelphia, about two-thirds of the women experienced violence during their marriage. These women tended to report that their ex-husbands did not allow them to have friends, to hold a job, or to attend school. In cases where women had an ex-partner who prevented them from having friends or engaging in activities that would allow them to develop social networks, once separated these women may be more able to develop these social networks. However, re-establishing friendships, obtaining employment, or applying for school all take time. Thus, immediately upon separation women in this situation will not necessarily have informal social networks that can help to insulate them from post-separation violence, which may make them more vulnerable to violence during this time.

TYPE OF INTERVENTION AND TIMING OF SUPPORT

There has been some suggestion in the literature that the type of intervention and timing of support can impact a woman's likelihood of post-separation violence. Ellis (1987) has argued that women who have lawyers that adopt an adversarial style are less likely to experience post-separation violence than women whose lawyers have a conciliatory style. Adversarial lawyers are more likely to engage in

> abuse-reducing measures such as advising the woman to leave her home (especially where abuse had occurred), having a friend or relative around when the husband visited the children, and insisting that the woman report direct threats of physical harm and assaults to the police.
>
> (p. 409)

The support provided by adversarial lawyers is also argued to be more effective in its timing. Ellis wrote that "lawyers adopting an adversarial style are more likely to challenge the man at the very time when it is most needed, that is, during the initial months following separation" (p. 409). In later work, Ellis and Wight (1997) noted that the type of conflict resolution process used by the couple was correlated with post-separation violence. The argument was that using marital conflict mediation, as opposed to the legal system, reduced the intensity of conflict, in turn reducing the likelihood of violence. Based on this research, then, it appeared that the choice of mediation over legal intervention, and, for those who choose legal intervention, the choice of a lawyer with an adversarial as opposed to a conciliatory style, may reduce the likelihood of post-separation violence.

MALE PEER SUPPORT

DeKeseredy et al. (2004) have suggested that patriarchal male peer subcultures may play a role in post-separation violence. Referring specifically to sexual violence against former partners, these researchers argued that

sexual assaults committed by men during or after the process of separa-
tion/divorce may have much more to do with their need to sustain their
status among their peers than either a need to satisfy their sexual desires
or a longing to regain a loving relationship.

(p. 687)

In other words, men who are members of patriarchal peer subcultures receive
the message that if they cannot control their partner, including keeping her in
the relationship, their status in the group will be damaged. As a result, those
men receiving patriarchal peer support may engage in post-separation violence to regain status within their peer group.

Microsystem

The microsystem consists of the family or immediate setting in which violence occurs.

MALE DEPENDENCE

It has been suggested that highly dependent men tend to be involved in less
stable marriages, and so separated men tend to be highly dependent (Ellis &
DeKeseredy, 1989). Intense male dependency has been linked to status incompatibility favouring the female (Ellis & DeKeseredy, 1997). Ellis and DeKeseredy
(1997) suggest that for men "who tend to be ranked low in terms of the possession of attributes that indicate superordinate male status (e.g., lower status job
and lower income than his wife/cohabiting partner), separation is likely to be
viewed as abandonment" (p. 595). These researchers add that post-separation
violence rooted in male dependency is typical of cases in which violence rarely
or never occurred prior to separation. Presumably there was no need to be
violent while these men's dependency needs were being fulfilled by their partners. It follows, then, that post-separation violence may be more likely to occur
among ex-partners where the female has a higher status relative to the male.

FEMALE INDEPENDENCE

Female dependence functions to keep women within a marriage. Most
research suggests that the probability that abused women will leave is higher
among those who are economically independent (Dutton & Painter, 1993).
Abusive men have been shown to use violence in an attempt to prevent their
partner from acting independently. For example, in Kurz's (1996) sample of
divorced women, the women reported having experienced violence at times
such as "when they would assert their own point of view, when they decided
to go back to work, or when they wanted to go to school" (p. 77). It is possible, then, that post-separation violence varies by the degree of independence
of the woman. That is, the more independent the woman is from her ex-
partner, for example in terms of education and employment resources, the
more likely she may be to experience post-separation violence.

DURATION SINCE SEPARATION

The risk for post-separation violence has been shown to vary depending upon the time that has passed since the separation. In Arendell's (1995) study of divorced fathers, most of the men who had been violent reported that their violence had decreased over time. Fleury et al. (2000) conducted a longitudinal study of a convenience sample of 135 women who had been with their batterer prior to entering a domestic violence shelter programme and who were no longer with their partner 10 weeks after leaving the shelter. They found that "the majority of the initial assaults by an ex-partner took place soon after the end of the relationship; 51% took place within 10 weeks of shelter exit" (p. 1371). Homicide data also clearly demonstrate that the period shortly after separation is the time of greatest risk for severe post-separation violence. Data from Canada, the United States, New South Wales, and Australia indicate that about half of intimate femicides by ex-partners occur within 2 months following separation (Hotton, 2001). Indeed, Ellis and DeKeseredy (1997) suggested this as an explanation for the low rate of intimate femicide among divorced compared to separated women, given that divorces are usually granted 1 or more years following separation. Of course, it bears noting that some men maintain their levels of violence, others become more violent over time (Arendell, 1995), and that intimate femicide has occurred years after separation (Wilson & Daly, 1993). Nevertheless, it is quite evident from existing research that the risk for post-separation violence generally decreases with the passage of time since separation, peaking within 2 or 3 months following the commencement of the separation.

AVAILABILITY

Separated women may also face increased risk for violence because they are available to be abused at times that are particularly risky (Ellis & DeKeseredy, 1989; Hardesty, 2002). Risky times include court appearances pertaining to property, custody, or support as well as exchanging or visiting any children of the couple (Ellis & DeKeseredy, 1989). In addition, living in the same city as the ex-partner impacts separated women's availability. Fleury et al. (2000) reported that, if the woman's ex-partner no longer resided in the same city as she, and in most cases it was the ex-partner rather than the woman who had moved, her odds of violence by her ex-partner were significantly reduced. Women who lived in the same city as their batterer had 364% greater odds of violence compared to those who did not live in the same city as their batterer.

PRE-SEPARATION VIOLENCE

Researchers have suggested that the population of separated persons is overrepresented by men with a history of violence (Ellis & DeKeseredy, 1989; Gartner et al., 1998/1999). A woman's risk for post-separation violence is increased if her partner used violence pre-separation. For example, by virtue

of having used violence while in an intact union these men have demonstrated a low stake in conformity (Hardesty, 2002), which implies that they may
also be less deterred from using violence during separation compared to men
who did not engage in pre-separation violence. In addition, there are also
indications that the relationship between pre-separation and post-separation
violence is impacted by the duration of the relationship prior to the onset of
pre-separation violence as well as the severity of pre-separation violence.
Fleury et al. (2000) reported that the duration of the relationship prior to the
onset of pre-separation violence was positively related to the odds of post-
separation violence. They conjectured that this may be because men who
waited longer before using violence were more invested in the relationship
and therefore were also more invested in maintaining control over their ex-
partners. In terms of the severity of pre-separation violence, women who
experienced severe violence during their relationship have been found to be
three times as likely to report post-separation violence as those who experienced less severe violence during their relationship (Hardesty, 2002). This fits
with Johnston and Campbell's (1993) categorization of "ongoing or episodic
male battering," suggesting that men who use more severe violence and who
do so on an ongoing basis have a high likelihood of engaging in post-
separation violence. However, with respect to the frequency of pre-separation
violence, a study of battered women who had left their partner following their
stay in a shelter found that the frequency of violence prior to shelter entry did
not significantly impact their odds of post-separation violence (Fleury et al.,
2000). In short, there is evidence for a connection between pre-separation and
post-separation violence, but the relationship may also be impacted by additional variables including union duration prior to pre-separation violence
onset as well as the severity and frequency of pre-separation violence.

PRESENCE OF A NEW PARTNER

"Seeing" other men has been identified as a potential risk marker for post-
separation violence (Ellis & DeKeseredy, 1989). Using a convenience sample
of 146 separated men in Western Australia, McMurray et al. (2000) indicated
that in 10.2% (n = 10) of the cases of post-separation violence a new
lover/partner was present. Similarly, Hotton (2001) reported that in one-
quarter of the cases of violence by ex-partners in Canada, third parties were
threatened or harmed. However, the proportion of third parties who were
new partners was not identified. When examining intimate femicides by ex-
partners where a third party was also killed, Hotton (2001) reported that the
new partner was the most frequent third party victim, representing 38% of all
third party victims. On the other hand, research by Fleury et al. (2000) found
that separated women who were in a new relationship had 58% lower odds of
post-separation violence compared to their counterparts without a new
partner. They speculated that being in a new relationship may be a protective

factor for two reasons. First, the presence of a new partner may make it more difficult for the ex-partner to be alone with the woman. Second, the ex-partner may be avoiding a confrontation with the new partner. Based on available evidence, then, it appears that the presence of a new partner can be either a risk or a protective factor for post-separation violence.

STRESS

Separation has been associated with stress and stress has been associated with an increased likelihood of violence (Ellis, 1992; Ellis & Stuckless, 1992). Noting that separation poses unusually potent stressors, Johnston and Campbell (1993) appear to identify trauma as being solely responsible for violence that occurs only during separation and after divorce, as opposed to violence that begins prior to separation. However, other research contradicts this finding. Among the respondents in a study by McMurray et al. (2000), 130 men identified provocations for violence. Stress was the sixth most common provocation for violence, reported by only seven (5.4%) of the men. Furthermore, even if one were to assume that these seven men all identified stress as the main provocation for their violence, 14 of the men were violent only at separation, indicating that provocations other than stress were primarily involved in at least half of these cases. In short, the extent to which stress is implicated in post-separation violence and the manner in which it acts to increase women's risk of violence remains to be understood.

CHILDREN

The presence of children is an important consideration in understanding the likelihood of post-separation violence for several reasons. Among women who have children, often the reason they provide for staying in, leaving, or returning to an abusive relationship is their children (Mahoney, 1991/1992). In the context of post-separation violence, the presence of children has been identified as potentially being both a protective and a risk factor. In Arendell's (1995) study of divorced fathers, several of the men (the actual number was not provided) reported that they did not become violent out of fear that violence would result in the denial of future access to their children. However, most of the research on post-separation violence points to the children as being a risk factor. McMurray et al. (2000) reported that issues regarding children were the second most identified provocation for violence, reported by 14% (n = 19) of their sample of separated men.

There are a number of different ways in which the presence of children may increase the likelihood of post-separation violence. First, there is the matter of custody. In the literature the most noted way in which custody may impact post-separation violence is where men fight for and win custody simply to prohibit maternal custody (Hardesty, 2002; Kurz, 1998; Pagelow,

1993). In Arendell's (1995) study, 61 of the 75 cases involved maternal custody, and maternal custody outraged most of the men. As Arendell stated,

> In desiring shared custody, what the men wanted was not only greater and more meaningful involvement with their children; they wanted acknowledgment of their parental status and importance. So too, they wanted to "balance out" the power of their former wives by prohibiting maternal custody because it was the prime example of their losses.
>
> (pp. 80–81)

Using custody as a means to balance power may contribute to violence because it allows the man to maintain some power and control over his ex-partner. Elsewhere it has been suggested that conjoint custody may contribute to violence. Noting that with joint custody orders parental authority in specific areas is usually not identified, Walker et al. (2004) wrote that "each circumstance becomes an opportunity for conflict and dispute—and in domestic violence cases, a period for potential harassment and violence" (p. 163). Hence, joint custody may contribute to post-separation violence. This may be an increasingly important factor in post-separation violence given the trend towards joint custody. For example, in Canadian divorce proceedings in 2002, for the first time, custody of less than half of dependants was awarded to the mother (Statistics Canada, 2004). Joint custody was awarded for 41.8% of dependants, which continued a 16-year trend of increases in joint custody arrangements (Statistics Canada, 2004).

A second factor connected to the presence of children and which may impact post-separation violence concerns issues around support. One situation in which this may occur is when men feel that their access visits are obstructed because they are late in their support payments. In McMurray's (1997) study of 43 mothers and 68 fathers without custody, "many of the men reported that one of the most difficult and anger-provoking situations involved ex-spouses who sabotaged the father–child relationship(s) by trading access for maintenance" (p. 549). At least three of these men resorted to post-separation violence as a result of this situation. It has also been pointed out that separation when children are involved may be seen as a costly challenge by those men who fear losing a large portion of their money and possessions (Hardesty, 2002). Presumably, these men may be more likely to respond with post-separation violence.

The presence of children also may increase the likelihood of post-separation violence as a result of access. As already noted with respect to availability, visitation, and the process of exchanging children before and after the visit may result in increased contact with the man and, therefore, increased opportunity for violence to occur (Fleury et al., 2000; Hardesty, 2002; Kurz, 1998). In Arendell's (1995) study, violence and threats happened most often during the "handoff," when children were being exchanged from one parent to the other. As a result, children often witness the violence (Arendell, 1995; Hardesty, 2002; Shalansky, Ericksen, & Henderson, 1999).

Finally, the presence of children can also impact the likelihood of post-separation violence if they are used as tools for violence. Some abusive men, separated or otherwise, threaten to harm or abduct the children or use them to demean and induce guilt in the woman (McCloskey, 2001; Sev'er, 1997).

Ontogenic Level

The ontogenic level comprises the individual's development and, as a result, what they bring to the other levels based on their development.

ANXIOUS ATTACHMENT

Dutton (1995) has identified anxious attachment as playing a role in post-separation violence. According to Dutton, "much of male intimate violence occurs in the process of real or perceived relationship dissolution" (p. 154). When confronted with uncontrollable attachment changes, anxiously attached men feel abandoned (Dutton, 1995). The perception of separation as abandonment leads these men to become angry, which increases aggression and violence.

SEXUAL PROPRIETARINESS

It can be argued that an individual's developmental history is strongly linked to his or her attitudes and behaviour. Men who hold attitudes that lead them to behave in a sexually proprietary way towards their partner have clearly learned at some point that this kind of behaviour is acceptable. Sociobiology also suggests that such behaviours are genetic imperatives (Dutton, 2006). According to Wilson and Daly (1993), "a sexually proprietary masculine psychology ... treats wives as valued sexual and reproductive commodities that might be usurped by rivals" (p. 13). With respect to separation, women may be particularly at risk when it is their "unilateral decision" to leave (p. 11). As noted in the discussion of patriarchy above, most women initiate the ending of their marriage (Hewitt et al., 2005). Upon a woman's physical or psychological exit from a relationship, sexually proprietary men "feel deprived of the power of ownership and thus feel justified in trying to take back their possession(s) by whatever means they can, including physical force" (McMurray, 1997, p. 551).

Research lends support to a connection between sexual proprietariness and post-separation violence. Fleury et al. (2000) found that the odds of post-separation violence against women were positively related to the frequency with which the batterer made accusations about the woman having or wanting other sexual relationships. Analyses of police officers' written descriptions of homicides by ex-partners in Canada have found that the most common motive for femicide was jealousy (Hotton, 2001), with this motive being about twice as common in femicides perpetrated in separated compared to intact relationships (Johnson & Hotton, 2003). In her study of 155 mate homicides in Jacksonville, Florida, Rasche (1993) found possessiveness to be the most common motive for homicide in all cases except "live-in lovers." Rasche's data showed that the relationships with the highest percentage of homicides being attributed to possessiveness were ex-partners. Specifically, this motive was cited in homicides against 62% of ex-spouses, 80% of ex-lovers, and 50% of ex-daters. However, it is important to add that the categorization of possessiveness included subcategories of "jealousy" (n = 12), "infidelity" (n = 17), "rivals" (n = 16), and "termination of the relationship" (n = 23). The fact that "termination of relationship" was a motive included in possessiveness likely confounded the results for ex-partners. Nevertheless, it is clear that empirical support exists for the relationship between sexual proprietariness and post-separation violence.

ALCOHOL AND DRUG ABUSE

Noting that alcohol abuse prevents some men from maintaining a marriage, and that alcohol dependency is associated with violence, Ellis and DeKeseredy (1989) argued that an overrepresentation of men who abuse alcohol among separated men would contribute to a greater likelihood of violence against separated women. This hypothesis was supported in a study of 140 divorcing families, which found that drug and alcohol abuse was "a major precipitant of the violence" perpetrated by those who had engaged in "ongoing or episodic male battering" (Johnston & Campbell, 1993, p. 193). However, not all research finds support for a connection between post-separation violence and drug/alcohol abuse. Among the 130 men who identified provocations for violence in the study by McMurray et al. (2000), drugs/alcohol were identified by only 3.8% (n = 5) of the men. Fleury et al. (2000) reported that batterers' current alcohol or drug problems did not significantly impact the odds of post-separation violence. Thus, existing research on the role of alcohol and drug abuse in post-separation violence is inconsistent.

RACE

Using American data from the National Crime Survey, Schwartz (1988) compared African American to Caucasian women in terms of their prevalence of spousal violence across different marital status groups. African American divorcées had a lower rate compared to Caucasian women (16.5% vs. 33.9%) and African American separated women had a similar rate of partner violence as their Caucasian counterparts (45.6% vs. 47.1%). Among separated women in Canada, Aboriginal women have been shown to have a significantly higher annual prevalence of violence by their ex-partner compared to non-Aboriginal women (45.5% vs. 9.8%; Spiwak & Brownridge, 2005). "Separated" is a particularly pertinent marital status category for Aboriginals. According to Frideres (2001), "because Aboriginal people are frequently poor, they often avoid the court costs and alimony payments that accompany formal divorces by simply separating from or deserting their families" (p. 89). Of course, this does not account for the higher proportion of separated Aboriginal women who experience violence compared to non-Aboriginal separated women. Spiwak and Brownridge (2005) speculated that the colonization of Canada's Aboriginal peoples, to which their higher likelihood of violence is often attributed, also extends to post-separation violence.[4]

AGE

Women who are young are at the greatest risk for violence in general (Johnson, 1996). Youth is also likely to be related to post-separation violence. In Canada the peak union duration for divorce to occur is during the fourth year of the marriage (Statistics Canada, 2004). Hence, divorcées tend to be young. Indeed, the average ages at marriage of women and men who divorced in Canada in 2002 were 26.3 and 28.9, respectively (Statistics Canada, 2004). Research on non-lethal violence has found a woman's age to be negatively related to her odds of post-separation violence (Spiwak & Brownridge, 2005). As well, research on lethal violence has shown that youth has an impact on the rate of intimate femicides of separated and divorced women, but not women in marital or common-law relationships (Hotton, 2001). Thus, it appears evident that age is an important developmental variable for understanding post-separation violence.

Subsamples and Risk Factors

Subsamples

The data from all three surveys were employed in this chapter (see Chapter 3 for details of the surveys and methods). Since this chapter investigates male partner violence against women with current or former partners,[5] the subsamples of heterosexual women who were either married, separated, or divorced included 8,500 women from the 1993 survey (245 separated, 859 divorced, 7,396 married), 7,369 women from the 1999 survey (359 separated, 572 divorced, 6,438 married), and 6,716 women from the 2004 survey (429 separated, 614 divorced, 5,673 married).

Risk Factors

Since not all of the aforementioned risk factors from the ecological framework were available for testing, Table 5.1 contains a summary of those that were available for examination in this chapter. Ex-partner or current partner's patriarchal dominance was measured at the macrosystem level. Respondent's education, employment, and presence of children[6] were available at the microsystem level. Risk factors included at the ontogenic level were age, Aboriginal status, sexual jealousy, and possessive behaviour.

Table 5.1 Application of ecological framework to available risk markers of post-separation violence

System	Definition	Risk markers
Macrosystem	Culture	Patriarchal dominance
Microsystem	Family setting	Education
		Employment
		Children
Ontogenic	Individual development	Age
		Race
		Sexual jealousy
		Possessive behaviour

Results

Descriptive Analysis

In each survey a consistent pattern was evident in which separated women reported, by far, the highest prevalence of violence (13.1% in 1993; 14.0% in 1999; 8.0% in 2004), followed by divorced women (3.3% in 1993; 5.3% in 1999; 2.6% in 2004), and then married women (2.2% in 1993; 1.5% in 1999; 1.1% in 2004). Although the prevalence rates were lower in the 2004 survey, an examination of the relative rates suggested a fairly consistent pattern of elevated risk for separated and divorced women. Across the three surveys separated women had three to four times the prevalence of violence compared to divorced women, and six to nine times the prevalence compared to married women. Divorced women had two to four times the prevalence of violence compared to married women.

INDEPENDENT VARIABLES BY SEPARATED, DIVORCED, AND MARRIED STATUS

Table 5.2 contains the means/frequencies of the independent variables for separated, divorced, and married women. As shown in Table 5.2, across all three surveys separated and divorced women were much more likely to report that their ex-partner dominated them by preventing access to the family income than were married women to have a husband who behaved in such a manner. In each survey all three groups of women had similar education levels with a mean of about 12 to 13 years. Divorced women were most likely to be employed in each survey, followed by separated and then married women. Separated women tended to be the most likely to have children residing in the household. Divorced and married women had about the same mean age, ranging from 46 to 49 years across the surveys. Separated women were consistently younger than divorced or married women, with an average age ranging from 42 to 45 years across the surveys. In both iterations of the GSS, separated women were more likely than divorced or married women to

Table 5.2 Means/frequencies of independent variables for separated, divorced, and married women in the 1993 VAWS, 1999 and 2004 GSS

Independent variables	1993			1999			2004		
	$n = 245$ Separated	$n = 859$ Divorced	$n = 7,396$ Married	$n = 359$ Separated	$n = 572$ Divorced	$n = 6,438$ Married	$n = 429$ Separated	$n = 614$ Divorced	$n = 5,673$ Married
Macrosystem									
Ex-/partner's patriarch.									
Yes	31.7	35.9	5.7	25.2	21.2	1.1	19.3	18.2	0.9
No	68.3	64.1	94.3	74.8	78.8	98.9	80.7	81.8	99.1
Microsystem									
Education	11.9	12.1	12.2	13.2	13.2	12.9	13.1	13.6	13.1
Employment									
Employed	63.6	65.8	61.8	76.0	84.8	68.3	84.2	90.1	71.7
Unemployed	36.4	34.2	38.2	24.0	15.2	31.7	15.8	9.9	28.3
Children <25/15									
Yes	58.5	47.6	57.1	51.5	35.5	37.6	56.7	40.1	35.7
No	41.5	52.4	42.9	48.5	64.5	62.4	43.3	59.9	64.3
Ontogenic									
Age	42.8	46.6	46.0	41.7	46.1	46.6	44.5	49.4	48.8
Aboriginal status									
Aboriginal	NA	NA	NA	3.4	1.4	1.5	5.0	3.6	1.6
Non-Aboriginal	NA	NA	NA	96.6	98.6	98.5	95.0	96.4	98.4
Ex-/partner's jealousy									
Yes	41.8	48.6	5.3	45.7	37.4	4.4	31.2	30.7	2.4
No	58.2	51.4	94.7	54.3	62.6	95.6	68.8	69.3	97.6
Ex-/partner's possessive.									
Yes	40.6	47.8	10.0	36.3	32.1	3.6	26.2	24.9	2.4
No	59.4	52.2	90.0	63.7	67.9	96.4	73.8	75.1	97.6

Note
NA Not available in the data.

be Aboriginal. Separated and divorced women were much more likely to have had a partner who had sexually proprietary behaviour, both in terms of jealousy and possessiveness, compared to married women's reports of their current husband's behaviours.

VIOLENCE BY INDEPENDENT VARIABLES FOR SEPARATED,
DIVORCED, AND MARRIED WOMEN

Table 5.3 provides the results of the cross-tabulations of the independent variables by the 1-year prevalence of violence for separated, divorced, and married women. As shown in Table 5.3, in the VAWS separated women that had an ex-partner who behaved in a patriarchal domineering manner were not significantly more likely to have experienced violence than those whose ex-partner did not behave in this manner. In both iterations of the GSS, separated women whose ex-partners engaged in patriarchal domineering behaviour were about two to three times more likely to report violence by their ex-partner in the previous year. Divorced women with an ex-partner who behaved in a patriarchal domineering manner were about two to five times more likely to report having experienced violence by their ex-partner. While, in the VAWS, married women with a partner who engaged in patriarchal domination reported violence at a rate four times that of their counterparts who did not have a partner that behaved in a patriarchal domineering manner, this difference increased to 13 times in the 1999 GSS and to about 22 times in the 2004 GSS.

Although a few significant differences emerged, overall there did not appear to be a substantive association between education and violence for any of the groups of women. There were also few differences in terms of employment. In the 2004 GSS, unemployed separated women were about twice as likely and unemployed divorced women were 13 times as likely to report having experienced violence by their ex-partner compared to their employed counterparts. The presence of children was consistently associated with violence by ex-partners for separated women, and in two of the three surveys for both divorced and married women. With a couple of exceptions, age was negatively associated with violence for all three groups of women. However, the association between youth and violence was strongest for separated women. Aboriginal status was not associated with violence for divorced women. In the 1999 GSS Aboriginal status was associated with about a fivefold higher rate of violence for separated women and a fourfold higher rate for married women. However, there was no significant difference for these groups in the 2004 GSS. Jealousy and possessiveness were associated with violence for all three groups of women, the only exception being for jealousy of separated women's ex-partners in the 2004 GSS. There was also a tendency for the differences to be larger for married women than for separated and divorced women. Separated women with a jealous/possessive ex-partner were two to four times more likely to experience violence, divorced women with such partners were about four to 16 times more likely to experience violence, and married women with husbands who behaved in a jealous/possessive manner were about five to 17 times more likely to report having experienced violence in the previous year.

MULTIVARIATE ANALYSIS: LOGISTIC REGRESSIONS FOR SEPARATED, DIVORCED, AND MARRIED WOMEN

Table 5.4 provides the results of the logistic regressions on the 1-year prevalence of violence for separated, divorced, and married women. In terms of the macrosystem variable of patriarchal dominance, the results showed that, controlling for all other variables in the models, only married women whose partners behaved in a patriarchal domineering manner consistently reported experiencing significantly elevated odds of violence across all three surveys. Table 5.5 provides the results of the *t*-tests for the difference in odds between the 1993 and 1999 surveys and the 1999 and 2004 surveys for separated, divorced, and married women. As shown in Table 5.4, married women whose husbands prevented them from having access to the family income had similarly elevated odds of violence (about 200% greater) compared to their counterparts whose husbands did not engage in patriarchal domination in the 1993 and 1999 surveys. This difference increased in the 2004 survey, with married women who had partners that behaved in a patriarchal domineering manner having 668% greater odds of violence than married women without such partners. Divorced women whose ex-partner behaved in a patriarchal domineering manner reported significantly higher odds of violence in the 1993 and 2004 surveys, though the results of the *t*-tests in Table 5.5 showed that the odds ratios were not significantly different for divorced women across all three surveys. Separated women with ex-partners who behaved in such a manner had significantly higher odds of violence only in the 2004 survey. The results of the *t*-tests in Table 5.5 suggested a pattern in which the impact of patriarchal domination on the odds of violence for separated women had increased across the three surveys.

At the microsystem level, education did not have a significant impact on the odds of violence for any of the three groups of women in the 1993 and 1999 surveys. However, in the 2004 GSS it was associated with significant effects on the odds of violence for all three groups of women. The results of the *t*-tests in Table 5.5 showed that, for each group of women, the odds ratios in the 1993 and 1999 surveys were not significantly different, while the odds ratios in the 1999 and 2004 surveys were significantly different. Each unit of increase in years of education was associated with a 29% increase in odds of violence for separated women and a 13% increase in odds of violence for married women. For divorced women, on the other hand, each unit of increase in years of education was associated with a 42% decrease in their odds of violence.

Table 5.3 One-year prevalence of violence by independent variables for separated, divorced, and married women in the 1993 VAWS, 1999 and 2004 GSS (%)

Independent variables	Separated			Divorced			Married		
	1993	1999	2004	1993	1999	2004	1993	1999	2004
Macrosystem									
Ex-/partner's patriarch.									
Yes	15.6	18.8	17.1	6.0	8.5	7.2	7.7	16.9	19.6
No	12.0	8.5**	5.9***	1.6***	3.5**	1.6***	1.9***	1.3***	0.9***
Microsystem									
Education									
High school or less	14.1	15.7	6.7	3.0	4.8		2.2	1.4	0.9
Some post secondary	17.1	8.9	7.6	6.8	7.3		1.2	2.0	1.7
Community college dip.	16.7	9.5	7.4	2.6	3.9		2.3	1.2	0.7
University degree	0.0	8.2	12.2	0.9*	2.8	†**	3.2*	1.6	1.4*
Employment									
Employed	13.1	10.6	8.5	3.4	4.5	1.1	2.2	1.6	1.1
Unemployed	13.5	14.3	16.1*	3.1	9.0	14.6***	2.3	1.4	1.0
Children <25/15									
Yes	16.9	14.1	10.9	5.4	5.4		2.8	2.1	1.3
No	8.0**	8.2*	4.3*	1.4***	4.4	†***	1.5***	1.0***	0.9
Ontogenic									
Age									
15/18–34	26.7	19.0		9.0	3.1		3.9	2.5	1.0
35–54	8.3	10.4		2.7	6.0		2.1	1.5	1.3
55+	2.2***	0.0***	†***	1.3***	0.8*	†**	1.0***	0.6***	0.7*
Aboriginal status									
Aboriginal	NA	45.5		NA	0.0		NA	5.3	
Non-Aboriginal	NA	9.8***	†	NA	4.6	†	NA	1.3***	†

Ex-/partner's jealousy									
Yes	17.8	19.1	10.6	6.1	8.5		10.9	12.9	13.7
	7.9**	4.6***	6.9	0.7***	2.4***	†***	1.8***	0.9***	0.8***
No									
Ex-/partner's possessive.									
Yes	21.2	21.7	14.4	6.4	9.4	5.9	8.0	14.7	10.5
	7.7***	5.9***	5.8***	0.4***	2.6***	1.5***	1.6***	0.9***	0.8***
No									

Notes

*$p \leq 0.10$; **$p < 0.05$; ***$p < 0.01$ (p values refer to Pearson Chi-square tests of significance).

† Statistics Canada would not release the cross-tabulation to ensure respondent confidentiality. Statistical significance test is reported.

NA Not available in the data.

Table 5.4 Results of logistic regressions on 1-year prevalence of violence for separated, divorced, and married women in the 1993 VAWS, 1999 and 2004 GSS

Independent variables	Separated			Divorced			Married		
	$n = 240$ 1993	$n = 339$ 1999	$n = 416$ 2004	$n = 850$ 1993	$n = 557$ 1999	$n = 598$ 2004	$n = 7,304$ 1993	$n = 5,910$ 1999	$n = 5,442$ 2004
Macrosystem									
Ex-/partner's patriarch.									
Yes	0.598	1.406	5.139***	2.576**	1.583	3.042*	3.283***	3.095***	7.683***
No	1.000	1.000	1.000	1.000	1.000	1.000	1.000	1.000	1.000
Microsystem									
Education	0.963	1.060	1.289**	0.957	1.061	0.580**	1.063	1.011	1.129*
Employment									
Employed	1.050	0.837	0.782	1.343	0.370*	0.121***	0.604***	0.922	0.925
Unemployed	1.000	1.000	1.000	1.000	1.000	1.000	1.000	1.000	1.000
Children <25/15									
Yes	1.731	0.765	0.944	2.692*	0.591	8.871**	1.089	1.257	1.120
No	1.000	1.000	1.000	1.000	1.000	1.000	1.000	1.000	1.000
Ontogenic									
Age	0.942**	0.924***	0.905***	0.964	0.956*	0.923*	0.961***	0.970**	0.985
Aboriginal status									
Aboriginal	NA	5.509**	1.754	NA	0.011	0.979	NA	2.658*	2.024
Non-Aboriginal	NA	1.000	1.000	NA	1.000	1.000	NA	1.000	1.000
Ex-/partner's jealousy									
Yes	1.183	2.290	0.543	4.864**	1.769	6.672**	3.177***	4.324***	8.540***
No	1.000	1.000	1.000	1.000	1.000	1.000	1.000	1.000	1.000
Ex-/partner's possessive.									
Yes	2.854*	1.969	3.170*	3.937*	2.128	0.508	2.756***	5.859***	3.460***
No	1.000	1.000	1.000	1.000	1.000	1.000	1.000	1.000	1.000
Constant	0.896	0.599	0.119	0.008**	0.219	260.858	0.048***	0.025***	0.002***
−2 Log likelihood	155	192	181	195	190	87	1,395	725	548
X^2	25***	43***	51***	50***	22**	58***	173***	156***	93***
Nagelkerke pseudo r^2	0.185	0.237	0.269	0.228	0.124	0.430	0.121	0.188	0.153

Notes: *$p \leq 0.10$; **$p < 0.05$; ***$p < 0.01$ (p values refer to Wald Chi-square tests of significance). NA Not available in the data.

Table 5.5 T-tests for difference in odds between 1993 and 1999, and 1999 and 2004 for separated, divorced, and married women

Independent variables	Separated		Divorced		Married	
	1993–1999	1999–2004	1993–1999	1999–2004	1993–1999	1999–2004
Macrosystem						
Ex-/partner's patriarch.	-1.861**	-2.915***	1.093	-1.171	0.168	-1.966**
Microsystem						
Education	-0.927	-1.722**	-1.005	3.773***	1.084	-1.821**
Employment	0.485	0.140	-1.407*	5.195***	-1.800***	-0.009
Children <25/15	1.739**	-0.479	2.937***	-3.405***	-0.603	0.375
Ontogenic						
Age	0.791	0.807	0.326	0.915	-0.883	-1.279
Aboriginal status	NA	1.385*	NA	-0.396	NA	0.382
Ex-/partner's jealousy	-1.197	2.571***	1.476*	-1.774**	-1.046	-1.791**
Ex-/partner's possessive.	0.685	-0.891	0.863	2.043**	-2.636***	1.380*

Notes
*p ≤ 0.10; **p < 0.05; ***p < 0.01.
NA Not available in the data.

In terms of employment, there was no significant difference in odds of violence for employed and unemployed separated women in any of the surveys. For divorced women there was no difference in odds of violence for employed and unemployed women in the 1993 survey. However, in the 1999 survey divorced women who were employed had 63% lower odds of violence than their unemployed counterparts. This difference increased to 88% lower odds in the 2004 survey. The results of the *t*-tests in Table 5.5 showed that these differences were significant across the three surveys. Married women who were employed had 40% lower odds of violence in the 1993 survey than unemployed married women. However, in the 1999 and 2004 surveys there were no significant differences in the odds of violence for employed and unemployed married women.

The presence of children did not have a significant impact on the odds of violence for either separated or married women in any of the surveys. For divorced women, on the other hand, the presence of children was associated with significantly increased odds of violence in two of the three surveys. Divorced women with children under age 25 had 169% greater odds of violence in the 1993 survey compared to divorced women without children. Divorced women with children under age 15 had 787% increased odds of violence compared to divorced women without children in the 2004 survey.

With respect to the ontogenic level, age was significantly negatively related to the odds of violence for separated women in all three surveys and for divorced and married women in two of the three surveys. The *t*-tests in Table 5.5 showed that the odds ratios within each group of women were not significantly different across the surveys. For separated women, each year of increase in age reduced their odds of violence by a range of 6% to 9% across the three surveys. For divorced and married women the range of reduction was from 4% to 8% and 1% to 4%, respectively. Table 5.6 contains the results of the *t*-tests for differences in odds between separated, divorced, and married women in the 1993, 1999, and 2004 surveys. The results for the age variable in Table 5.6 showed that the odds ratios for separated and divorced women were statistically similar, with the exception of the 1999 survey in which age had a significantly stronger impact on the odds of violence for separated than divorced women. As also shown in Table 5.6, the differences in odds for the age variable between separated and married women were significant in two of the three surveys.

Aboriginal status had a significant impact on the odds of violence for separated and married women in the 1999 survey. The results of the *t*-tests in Table 5.5 suggested that the 451% greater odds for separated Aboriginal women in the 1999 survey were significantly different from the 75% greater odds of separated Aboriginal women in the 2004 survey. The 166% greater odds of violence for married Aboriginal women in the 1999 survey were not significantly different from the 102% greater odds for married Aboriginal women in the 2004 survey.

Table 5.6 T-tests for difference in odds between separated, divorced, and married women in the 1993 VAWS, 1999 and 2004 GSS

Independent variables	Separated vs. divorced			Separated vs. married			Divorced vs. married		
	1993	1999	2004	1993	1999	2004	1993	1999	2004
Macrosystem									
Ex-/partner's patriarch.	-3.161***	-0.266	0.936	-4.452***	-1.817**	-0.852	-0.716	-1.476*	-1.639*
Microsystem									
Education	0.069	-0.009	4.827***	-1.284*	0.573	1.353*	-1.364*	0.589	-4.445***
Employment	-0.524	-2.375***	3.161***	1.555*	-0.251	-0.376	2.253**	2.561***	-3.775***
Children <25/15	-0.820	0.580	-2.824***	1.192	-1.400*	-0.420	2.148**	-1.979**	2.711***
Ontogenic									
Age	-0.979	-1.360*	-0.514	-1.161	-2.448***	-4.011***	0.168	-0.714	-1.848**
Aboriginal status	NA	0.549	0.476	NA	1.165	-0.160	NA	-0.485	-0.602
Ex-/partner's jealousy	-2.140**	0.445	-3.429***	-2.209**	-1.451*	-5.339***	0.788	-1.737**	-0.372
Ex-/partner's possessive.	-0.463	-0.138	2.705***	0.077	-2.637***	-0.170	0.630	-1.951**	-3.161***

Notes
*$p \leq 0.10$; **$p < 0.05$; ***$p < 0.01$.
NA Not available in the data.

Jealousy had a significant impact on the odds of violence in none of the surveys for separated women, in two of the three surveys for divorced women, and in all three surveys for married women. The results of the *t*-tests in Table 5.6 suggested that the differences in odds between divorced and married women who had jealous ex-partners or current partners were not significant in the 1993 and 2004 surveys, but were significant in the 1999 survey.

Possessiveness had a significant impact on the odds of violence in one survey for divorced women, in two surveys for separated women, and in all three surveys for married women. The results of the *t*-tests in Table 5.6 suggested that the odds ratios on the possessiveness variable for separated and divorced women differed significantly only in the 2004 survey; where separated women with a possessive ex-partner had 217% greater odds of violence while divorced women with such a partner did not have significantly different odds of violence compared to their counterparts whose partners did not behave in such a manner. Married women's odds of violence on the possessiveness variable differed significantly from both separated and divorced women's odds in the 1999 survey and from divorced women's odds in the 2004 survey.

Finally, as shown in Table 5.4, the Nagelkerke pseudo r^2 for each model suggested that the variables analysed in this chapter tended to explain more of the variance for separated and divorced women than for married women. The average explained variance across the three surveys was 23% for separated women (ranging from 19% to 27%), 26% for divorced women (ranging from 12% to 43%), and 15% for married women (ranging from 12% to 18%).

Post-Violence Experiences for Separated Relative to Divorced Victims[7]

There were few consistent differences in separated and divorced victims' post-violence variables across the surveys. Table 5.7 contains the zero-order odds ratios for the consequences of violence for separated compared to divorced victims in all three surveys. The only consistent difference across all three surveys was that separated victims had higher odds of being angry as a result of the violence. The 1999 and 2004 data also showed that separated victims had somewhat higher odds of staying in bed for all or most of the day following the violence.

The zero-order odds ratios for separated relative to divorced victims' help-seeking behaviours for all three surveys are presented in Table 5.8. Among victims who were physically injured, the 1993 and 1999 data suggested that there may have been a tendency for separated victims to have higher odds of visiting a health care professional for treatment. There were no consistent patterns of difference for separated and divorced victims confiding in someone about the violence. In terms of services contacted, the only consistent pattern was separated victims' higher odds of having contacted a police or court-based victim service in the 1999 and 2004 surveys.

Table 5.7 Zero-order odds ratios for consequences of violence for separated relative to divorced victims in the 1993 VAWS, 1999 and 2004 GSS

Dependent variable	Separated/divorced[a]					
	1993		1999		2004	
	OR	n	OR	n	OR	n
Physical injury	0.935	417	1.262	289	1.672*	235
Psychopathology[b]	1.294	408	0.569	280	0.792	228
Altered psyche[c]	0.859	408	0.871	280	1.430	228
Anger	1.312	408	1.324	280	1.514	228
Time off everyday activities	0.737	416	2.390***	286	1.763*	233
Stay in bed all/most of day	NA		1.286	288	1.227	234
Children witnessed violence	0.867	375	1.255	260	0.866	199

Notes
*$p \leq 0.10$; ***$p < 0.01$.
a Divorced is the reference category with an odds of 1.000.
b Includes depression or anxiety attacks, fear, afraid for children, more cautious or aware, sleep problems, shock or disbelief, hurt or disappointment, and upset, confused, or frustrated.
c Includes ashamed or guilty, lowered self-esteem, problems relating to men, and increased self-reliance.
NA Not available in the data.

Table 5.9 contains the zero-order odds ratios for police intervention variables for separated relative to divorced victims in all three surveys. Among victims that contacted the police, the 1999 and 2004 data suggested that separated victims had lower odds of having done so to have their ex-partner arrested or punished. In terms of the police response, separated victims had lower odds of the police giving a warning to their ex-partner in the 1999 and 2004 data, higher odds of being put in touch with community services in the 1993 and 1999 surveys, and they tended to have slightly higher odds reporting that the violence decreased or stopped following police intervention across all three surveys. With respect to victims that did not contact the police, those who were separated had lower odds in the 1999 and 2004 surveys of having not done so because it was a personal matter that did not concern the police. Separated victims also had lower odds across all three surveys of having not contacted the police because the police could not do anything about it. However, separated victims tended to have higher odds across the 1999 and 2004 data of having not contacted the police out of fear of publicity or news coverage.

Discussion

The Elevated Risk of Violence Against Separated and Divorced Women

Consistent with past Canadian (Johnson, 1990; Kennedy & Dutton, 1989) and American (Bachman & Saltzman, 1995; Gaquin, 1977/1978; Kershner et

Table 5.8 Zero-order odds ratios for victims' help-seeking behaviours for separated relative to divorced victims in the 1993 VAWS, 1999 and 2004 GSS

Dependent variable	Separated/divorced[a]					
	1993		1999		2004	
	OR	n	OR	n	OR	n
Visit doctor/nurse/hospital for treatment	1.073	239	1.757	156	†	234
Confided in someone:	1.070	415	1.104	287	0.781	234
Family	1.099	415	0.849	287	1.115	234
Friend/neighbour	1.309	415	1.039	286	0.870	234
Co-worker	NA		0.887	286	0.527**	234
Doctor/nurse	1.051	415	0.818	286	0.910	232
Lawyer	NA		0.993	286	0.562**	234
Minister/priest/clergy/spiritual adviser	1.048	415	1.495	285	0.941	234
Services contacted:	1.032	417	2.061**	286	0.871	233
Crisis centre/line	0.284	417	1.229	286	1.106	233
Another counsellor/psychologist	1.300	417	1.778**	286	0.961	233
Community/family centre	0.701	417	1.480	286	1.159	233
Shelter/transition house	0.488	417	2.143**	286	1.657	233
Women's centre	0.414	417	1.700	286	1.467	233
Police/court-based victim service	NA		1.783	286	1.414	232
Interested in mediation/ conciliation	NA		0.829	281	0.988	228

Notes

** $p < 0.05$.

a Divorced is the reference category with an odds of 1.000.

† Statistics Canada would not release the result to ensure respondent confidentiality. Statistical significance test was not released.

NA Not available in the data.

al., 2001) research, which indicated that the dynamics of risk may be different for separated, divorced, and married women, the results of the analyses in this chapter showed that separated and divorced women consistently reported an elevated risk for violence compared to married women across all three surveys. Separated women had, by far, the greatest risk for violence in the year prior to each survey, followed by divorced women, and then married women.

Examining the Elevated Risk of Violence Post-Separation Using an Ecological Framework

An ecological framework was used to examine the impact of available risk markers on each group of women in an effort to help identify whether there were differing dynamics of risk for the three marital status groups.

MACROSYSTEM

The results showed that a high percentage of separated and divorced women's ex-partners behaved in a patriarchal dominating manner compared to married women's husbands. Although patriarchal dominance tended to be associated with violence for all three groups of women in the descriptive analysis, the multivariate analysis showed that patriarchal dominance was most consistently associated with significantly increased odds of violence for married women. Thus, while ex-partners of separated and divorced women were more likely to engage in patriarchal dominating behaviour, such behaviour tended to be a stronger predictor of marital violence.

MICROSYSTEM

Separated, divorced, and married women possessed similar education levels and education level did not appear to be strongly related to violence. The multivariate analysis showed significant associations with education only in the 2004 survey, where education was positively linked to violence for separated and married women and negatively related to violence for divorced women. While separated and divorced women tended to be more likely to be employed, employment was generally not related to violence and, where it was, it was unemployed women who were more at risk for violence. Although it was not possible to determine with the data, given that unemployed divorced women had significantly greater odds of violence in two of the surveys, it may be that the former husbands of these women were engaging in violence against their ex-wife out of retaliation for having to support them after the divorce. Overall, there was little indication that female independence, in terms of education and employment resources, impacted separated and divorced women's elevated odds of violence.

Separated women tended to be most likely to have children residing in the household and the descriptive analysis showed that the presence of children tended to be positively associated with violence for all three groups of women.

Table 5.9 Zero-order odds ratios for police intervention for separated relative to divorced victims in the 1993 VAWS, 1999 and 2004 GSS

Dependent variable	Separated/divorced[a]					
	1993		1999		2004	
	OR	n	OR	n	OR	n
Police found out	0.361**	416	1.061	286	1.053	234
Police found out from respondent	NA		1.277	156	0.343*	107
Reason police contacted:						
Stop violence/receive protection	NA		0.359	123	†	
Arrest/punish ex-spouse/partner	NA		0.744	121	0.423*	89
Duty to notify police	NA		0.983	123	0.314**	88
Recommendation of someone else	NA		1.596	122	0.649	89
Police action:						
Visited scene	NA		1.399	156	0.891	106
Made report/conducted investigation	NA		0.681	156	1.167	106
Gave warning to ex-spouse/ex-partner	NA		0.611	156	0.680	106
Took ex-spouse/ex-partner away	1.586	163	1.196	156	0.690	107
Put you in touch with community services	5.224**	164	1.694	156	†	
Made arrest/laid charges	NA		NA		0.537	107
None	NA		2.702	156	†	
Respondent satisfied w/police	2.431	162	0.650	156	0.663	105
Post-police violence decreased/stopped	1.903	154	1.064	132	1.095	83

Reasons police not contacted:

Dealt with in another way[b]	NA		0.995	129	0.975	125
Did not want to get involved with police	0.984	237	1.381	129	2.407**	126
Fear of ex-spouse/ex-partner	1.163	237	0.971	129	0.928	126
Personal matter that did not concern police	NA		0.764	129	0.848	125
Police couldn't do anything about it	0.765	237	0.832	129	0.560	126
Police wouldn't help[c]	NA		0.598	129	0.852	126
Police wouldn't think it was important enough	NA		1.356	129	0.922	126
Fear of publicity/news coverage	NA		1.092	129	1.412	126
Did not want ex-spouse/ex-partner arrested or jailed	3.798	237	0.906	129	2.034*	126
Did not want anyone to find out about it (e.g., shame)	0.500	237	1.318	129	1.843*	126
Other reason	1.892	237	0.796	129	1.102	126

Notes

*$p \leq 0.10$; **$p < 0.05$.

a Divorced is the reference category with an odds of 1.000.

b Includes left him, reported to another official, private matter that took care of myself, etc.

c Includes police wouldn't think it was important enough, wouldn't believe, wouldn't want to be bothered or get involved, police would be inefficient or ineffective, police would be biased, would harass/insult respondent, offender was police officer.

† Statistics Canada would not release the result to ensure respondent confidentiality. Statistical significance test was not released.

NA Not available in the data.

However, the multivariate analysis revealed that the presence of children significantly impacted the odds of violence only for divorced women. The impact of this variable was highest in the 2004 survey, in which the measure was restricted to children of the union. Although it is not possible to determine with the data, these results suggest the possibility that issues related to children of the union, such as support, access, and custody arrangements, may play a role in some divorced women's experiences of violence by their ex-partner.

ONTOGENIC LEVEL

Separated women were younger on average than divorced and married women. Youth tended to be associated with violence for all three groups of women. The impact of youth on the odds of violence was strongest for separated and divorced women. Thus, youth was an important risk factor for both separated and divorced women.

The results with respect to the Aboriginal status variable in the 1999 survey suggested that separated and married Aboriginal women were significantly more likely to report violence compared to their non-Aboriginal counterparts. However, there were no significant differences in the 2004 survey, though the multivariate analysis showed insignificant positive associations with the Aboriginal status variable for separated and married women in the 2004 survey and a t-test showed that the odds ratios for married women in the 1999 and 2004 surveys were not significantly different. A consistent finding across both surveys was that Aboriginal women who were divorced did not differ from non-Aboriginal divorced women in their odds of violence. It is possible that divorce may not be a significant risk factor for ex-partner violence against Aboriginal women because so few Aboriginal women are divorced. The GSS was a representative sample of Canada and the small number of divorced Aboriginal women in the sample likely reflects the reality in the population. As noted earlier, Frideres (2001) has pointed out that Aboriginal peoples are less likely to divorce than non-Aboriginal peoples. Nevertheless, the small number of divorced and separated women in the sample who were Aboriginal limited the ability to determine accurately the extent to which these groups experienced violence and readers must extrapolate from these results with caution.

With respect to sexual proprietariness, the results showed that a high percentage of separated and divorced women's ex-partners behaved in a sexually proprietary manner, through jealousy or possessiveness, compared to married women's husbands. Although sexual proprietariness tended to be associated with violence for all three groups of women in the descriptive analysis, the multivariate analysis showed some variability in the impact of jealousy and possessiveness for separated and divorced women. Jealousy did not have a significant impact on the odds of violence for separated women but tended to be related to increased odds of violence for divorced women whereas possessiveness tended not to have a significant impact on the odds of violence for divorced women but did tend to have a significant impact on the odds of violence for separated women. More importantly, both jealousy and possessiveness were consistently related to increased odds of violence for married women across all three surveys. Hence, while ex-partners of separated and divorced women were more likely to engage in sexually proprietary behaviour, such behaviour appeared to be a stronger predictor of marital violence than of post-separation violence.

Limitations

Although this chapter overcame a major limitation of past research through its use of large-scale, nationally representative samples, in addition to the small number of separated and divorced Aboriginal women in the sample, there were some other noteworthy limitations of the analyses contained in this chapter. For example, the study was limited to risk markers that were available in the data. Thus, several risk markers applicable to separated and divorced women's ecology could not be tested, which at least partially accounted for explaining on average at best about one-quarter of the variance in violence. Although the levels of explained variance were within or beyond the 10% to 20% range commonly found in the field of family violence (O'Neil & Harway, 1999), the availability of additional risk markers that had previously been identified as being associated with post-separation violence would likely have increased the explanatory power of the models.

The study was also limited to available measures of risk markers. For example, education and employment status are limited proxies of women's independence (Kaukinen, 2004; MacMillan & Gartner, 1999). More elaborate measures of women's independence, such as those used by Kalmuss and Straus (1990), would have provided a more precise test of the hypotheses. Similarly, for separated and divorced women it was not possible to determine whether measures of some of the risk markers for post-separation violence occurred while the union was intact or post-separation. As well, it has been noted that very little research on post-separation violence has examined sexual assault (DeKeseredy & Joseph, 2006; DeKeseredy et al., 2004). Although this chapter moved ahead of many past studies that focused only on physical violence by including in the measure of post-separation violence an item on sexual assault, it was limited because the data precluded disaggregation of post-separation violence by individual forms of violence.

Finally, like most of the research on non-lethal post-separation violence, the analysis could not distinguish between violence that occurred while the relationship was intact and violence that occurred after the separation began. Some researchers argue that physical separation should not be used as a criterion for establishing separation/divorce because doing so "neglects assaults after women's decisions and/or attempts to leave" (DeKeseredy et al., 2004, p. 680). Indeed, it is likely that some predictors of violence, such as patriarchal domination, jealousy, and possessiveness, would be strongly associated with violence experienced by these women. Although the intent of most of the research in the area is to examine violence that began subsequent to the moment of physical separation, it is also true that most research has been unable to make this distinction. Given that it was also not possible to make this distinction in the present analysis, a 1-year time frame for the violence variable was used to attenuate this problem by maximizing the likelihood that the violence reported was experienced at the respondent's current marital status. The dependent variable nevertheless confounded violence that occurred pre- and post-separation and this limitation should be borne in mind when extrapolating from the results. It must also be noted that some of the divorced women who reported violence may have been reporting violence that occurred while they were separated. Despite this inability to specify exactly when violence occurred, the results for separated and divorced women were sufficiently distinct from married women to suggest some unique dynamics in risk for violence against women who were separated or divorced at the time of the study.

Differing Dynamics in Violence Against Separated, Divorced, and Married Women

Overall the variables included in this chapter consistently explained a sizeable portion of the variance for separated women, a more variable proportion for divorced women, and the least for married women. This lent further credence to the notion that there were some differing dynamics in violence against sep-arated, divorced, and married women. On the whole, it appeared that youth may be a particularly important variable for understanding violence against separated women, and to a slightly less extent for divorced women, in Canada. Unemployment and the presence of children appeared to be particu-larly important predictors for divorced women. For married women patriar-chal domination, jealousy, and possessiveness were particularly strong predictors of violence. This is not to say that these sexual proprietariness vari-ables lacked importance for understanding separated and divorced women's reports of violence by their former partners. Indeed, they were much more likely to report that their former partners engaged in such behaviours com-pared to married women's reports of their husband's behaviour and a significant percentage of these men were violent. However, patriarchal domi-nation, sexual jealousy, and possessiveness were less powerful predictors of violence against separated and divorced women because, as shown in the descriptive analysis (see Table 5.3), there was a tendency for a much larger percentage of these women's ex-partners who did not engage in such behav-iours also to be violent compared to married women's husbands who did not engage in such behaviours. This was consistent with the notion that there were other risk factors and motivations that were unique to ex-partners and that contributed to violence against separated and divorced women. The analysis supports a view of post-separation violence as a complex phenomenon, the dynamics of which can be impacted by much more than domination and ownership. Indeed, a number of potential circumstances and motives have been attributed to post-separation violence such that post-separation violence has "many faces" (Brownridge, 2006c).

Distinguishing Between Risk Markers for and Motives Behind Post-Separation Violence

The above review of risk markers for post-separation violence and their integration within an ecological framework did not focus on motives for post-separation violence. At a conceptual level, our understanding of post-separation violence can be enhanced by first understanding how various risk markers may impact the likelihood of post-separation violence and then considering how a particular risk marker or combination of risk markers in the ecological framework may result in specific motives that incite post-separation violence. As Rasche (1993) notes, "the *causes* of some human social events may not be the same as the *reasons* those humans acted in the first place" (p. 77). Examining reasons for behaviour nevertheless provides some insight into causes. Of course, this distinction between risk markers and motives is for conceptual purposes. In practice it may often be difficult to distinguish the two, which is reflected in the fact that the articulation of some of the risk markers above implied specific motives for post-separation violence. With respect to post-separation violence, motives identified in the literature can be grouped into one of three categories: retaliation, restoration, and reconciliation.

In the literature, the most common motive for post-separation violence involves retaliation. As Hart (1990) has noted, "men who believe they are entitled to their relationship with battered women or that they 'own' their female partners view separation as an ultimate betrayal justifying retaliation" (p. 324). This typically involves men's anger and rage towards their ex-partner resulting from the separation. As already noted in the discussion of anxious attachment, Dutton (1995) implicated anxiously attached men's anger resulting from feelings of abandonment in post-separation violence. More generally, in the study by McMurray et al. (2000), anger was the third most commonly identified provocation for violence (13.1%; n = 17). In an analysis of intimate femicide in Ontario, Canada, Crawford and Gartner (1992) reported that in 45% of the cases where a motive could be established, anger or rage over an actual or impending estrangement was the reason for the murder. Separated non-custodial men in McMurray's (1997) study reported that they had "planned, executed or fantasized about violence against their spouses in retaliation for real or perceived injustices related to child custody, support and/or access" (p. 543).

Hence, it appears that some risk factors that are linked with post-separation violence leave these men feeling betrayed, abandoned, angry, or enraged such that they retaliate with violence.

A second potential motivation for post-separation violence is to restore power and control over the woman. As already discussed with respect to children, Arendell's (1995) research showed that fathers' custody challenges were often an attempt to balance out the power of their former wives. The desire to regain power and control can also be a motivation for post-separation violence (Sev'er, 1997). For example, Johnston and Campbell (1993) found that

> With respect to the power dynamics ... the violence changed the balance dramatically, making the victim very frightened of the other partner, hence giving the offending party more psychological leverage. For this reason, the perpetrator, male or female, might become empowered and gain more control through the use of violence.
>
> (p. 197)

Indeed, in an examination of estranged partner homicides, Campbell (1992) found the underlying issue to be men's efforts to reassert power and control.

A third possible motive for post-separation violence is reconciliation. Some abusive men attempt to sabotage women's ability to work so that the resulting financial need will lead to reconciliation (Hardesty, 2002). Similarly, as McMurray (1997) has noted, "when a wife leaves, either psychologically or physically, many men feel deprived of the power of ownership and thus feel justified in trying to take back their possession(s) by whatever means they can, including physical force" (p. 551). Thus, for these men the use of physical violence is a desperate attempt to force reconciliation.

It is important to add that any combination of these motivations may be behind a particular man's use of post-separation violence. Violence can simultaneously be used for punitive purposes and to ensure subordination (Adelman, 2000). It is also possible that in some cases none of these motives are the primary source of the violence. For example, it is difficult to connect the occurrence of pre-separation violence to one of these motives for post-separation violence. While some men who engaged in pre-separation violence may engage in post-separation violence out of retaliation, restoration, or reconciliation, it is possible that others may be violent post-separation simply because it is part of their normal pattern of interaction with their ex-partner.

The Many Faces of Post-Separation Violence

Given that there are a variety of potential risk markers, which appear to differ somewhat depending on whether a woman is separated or divorced, and motives for post-separation violence, it is not surprising that the relationship between separation and violence is variable. For women who are experiencing violence in their relationship, separation or the threat of separation may be a means to end the violence. Bowker (1983) found that threatening to leave was an effective strategy for ending battering. According to Statistics Canada's 1999 GSS, in 60% of cases of violence against women the violence ceased at separation (Hotton, 2001). However, separation and the threat to separate have also been found to be a source of violence (Johnson & Hotton, 2003). Some women experience violence by their ex-partner for the first time during separation. For many other women post-separation violence is a continuation of violence that began during their relationship with their partner. As already discussed above, pre-separation violence is a risk marker for post-separation violence. In fact, some women experience an escalation in the violence post-separation (Johnson & Sacco, 1995; Sev'er, 1997). Since in many cases violence continues or begins after separation, the common view that separation is a solution to partner violence is a myth in need of debunking (Hardesty, 2002).

We can get an indication of the extent to which post-separation violence either occurs only after separation or is a continuation of violence from studies that report prevalence rates for both phenomena (Hart, 1990; Hotton, 2001; Johnson, 1996; Kurz, 1998; McMurray et al., 2000; Spiwak & Brownridge, 2005). Existing evidence suggests that post-separation violence is often a continuation of violence that occurred during the relationship and also that a sizeable portion of post-separation violence is a new phenomenon. Moreover, some evidence suggests that women in the highest risk group, those who are currently separated and who did not experience violence while the relationship was intact, have a very high risk of violence by their ex-partner.

The finding that some post-separation violence was perpetrated by men who were not reported to be domineering or sexually proprietary was consistent with past research that included a focus on violence that occurred only during separation. In a study of a convenience sample of 140 divorcing parents who had a high degree of conflict over their children, Johnston and Campbell (1993) organized their clinical observations with respect to violence into four profiles. One of these profiles involved violence that occurred only post-separation. In this profile violence was seen as being the result of trauma from unusually potent stressors of the separation/divorce situation. This was distinguished from the profile of "ongoing or episodic male battering," which occurred both pre- and post-separation and was attributed to characteristics of the perpetrator including traditional male chauvinistic attitudes, grandiose notions of their masculinity, and sexual proprietariness. However, Johnston and Campbell's attribution of "separation and postdivorce violence" to trauma does not appear to be fully supported in other research. Among the respondents in a study of post-separation violence by McMurray et al. (2000), 130 men identified provocations for violence. Stress was the sixth most common provocation for violence, reported by only seven (5.4%) of the men.

Even if one were to assume that these seven men all identified stress as the main provocation for their violence, 14 of the men were violent only at separation, indicating that provocations other than stress were primarily involved in at least half of these cases.

More recently, Toews, McKenry, and Catlett (2003) have examined predictors of male-initiated violence during separation among a convenience sample of 80 divorced fathers who were not violent during their marriage. Although a traditional male gender-role identity was a significant predictor of psychological abuse, it was not a significant predictor of physical violence. The odds of these men engaging in physical violence were significantly increased by psychological abuse, anxiety, co-parental conflict, and dependence on the ex-wife. Thus, this research was consistent with the current study in finding that some post-separation violence was perpetrated by men who did not fit the traditional profile of marital violence vis-à-vis possession of a traditional male gender-role identity. An application of the results of these studies to those of the current study suggests the possibility that some of the violence perpetrated by men against separated and divorced women whose partners were not domineering, sexually jealous, or possessive, may have been new violence that occurred as a consequence of the separation. Indeed, among the potential motives that have been identified in the past, post-separation violence perpetrated by this subgroup of men would likely be linked to a desire for retaliation and/or a desire to restore the relationship as opposed to being a means to restore power and control.[8]

Differing Motives for Violence Against Separated, Divorced, and Married Women?

Irrespective of whether violence occurred pre-separation, the results of this chapter suggest the possibility that there may be a tendency for different motives to underlie violence against married, separated, and divorced women. Based on the analyses in this chapter, it appears possible that motives based in control and domination are particularly relevant to violence within intact unions. On the other hand, reconciliation may be a strong motive in violence against separated women. Since the relationship has not yet ended in divorce, the separated man may still cling to hope for reconciliation. As noted above, counterintuitive as it may be, some men attempt to use violence as a means to force reconciliation. In terms of violence against divorced women, the motive of retaliation may be particularly relevant. Since the union has legally terminated, these men's main concern may have shifted to resentment over having to support the woman who betrayed them by leaving. In this way, it is possible to see how the dependence of some divorced women, in terms of lack of gainful employment and the presence of dependent children, may lead to an increased risk of violent victimization.

Consequences of Violence and Experiences with Services for Separated Relative to Divorced Victims

Although the risk factors and dynamics of violence may be somewhat different for separated and divorced women, there were few indications that separated and divorced victims were different in terms of their post-violence experiences. There was no consistent pattern in the data with respect to the relative odds of physical injury for separated and divorced victims (though separated victims did have higher odds in two of the three surveys). But a few patterns in the data did suggest that separated victims may have been more likely to experience more severe violence. Separated victims tended to have higher odds of being angry and staying in bed following the violence, as well as to have higher odds of being treated for their injuries.

There may also have been an element of difference resulting from a relative "newness" of the violence for separated compared to divorced victims. Separated victims' higher odds of being angry (in addition to being a potential indicator of severity), contacting a police or court-based victim service, being put in touch with community services by police, and failure to contact police out of fear of publicity or news coverage may have reflected that violence was a more recent event in separated victims' relationships. Similarly, their slightly higher odds of reporting that the police intervention decreased or stopped the violence may have reflected a higher likelihood that this was these men's first contact with the police. Those men with higher stakes in conformity would be more likely to stop their violence at this point. Perpetrators of violence against divorced victims, on the other hand, may have had their first contact with the police when they were separated. Hence, divorced victims would be more represented with ex-partners who are less deterred by police involvement. As well, separated victims' lower odds of contacting the police to have their ex-partner arrested or punished may have reflected that they still had hope for their relationship. Their lower odds of having not contacted the police because the police could not do anything about it may have reflected that separated victims were less jaded about the efficacy of the police response because of fewer exposures to the police.

Implications for Women

The question then becomes, "What does all of this imply for women?" Women who are in a violent relationship and who want the violence to end are faced with a very difficult and dangerous situation. Despite the risk of post-separation violence, it is typically suggested in the literature that the best solution for these women is to leave their partner. For example, Hart (1990) writes that

> Because leaving may be dangerous does not mean that the battered woman should stay. Cohabiting with the batterer is also dangerous

since violence usually increases in frequency and severity over time and since a batterer may engage in pre-emptive strikes, fearing abandonment or anticipating separation even before the battered woman reaches such a decision.

(p. 324)

Other research, however, suggests that men's violence decreases over time in both frequency and severity. In a longitudinal study spanning 10 years, Timmons Fritz and O'Leary (2004) examined the course of physical and psychological aggression in a sample of 203 wives from Suffolk County, New York, 79 of whom responded to a 120-month follow-up. They found that physical aggression significantly declined, "which suggests that partner aggression is likely to desist across time" (p. 12). Cautioning that their study was not directly comparable to past studies, which had suggested the opposite pattern, because the former was a community sample while the latter were based on clinical samples, Timmons Fritz and O'Leary noted that the pattern of declining violence was evident even when examining severe aggression. Horton and Johnson's (1993) study of 185 former victims of partner violence found that those who stayed in their relationship (n = 27) endured abuse for an average of 10 years before it ended.

Another element to consider regarding separation as a solution for partner violence is the common assumption that separation is a permanent break as opposed to a process involving a series of temporary separations (Mahoney, 1991/1992). Indeed, theories have been developed to account for a pattern of separation and reconciliation among women in the process of leaving a violent partner (Dutton & Painter, 1993; Wuest & Merritt-Gray, 1999). Of course, returning to an abusive partner is not without its risks. Research has suggested that a history of separations and reconciliations may be common in spousal homicide cases (Wilson & Daly, 1993).

Thus, it appears that women in violent relationships are caught between a rock and hard place. For those who stay in the relationship, the violence may decrease or end, but they probably have a long, difficult, and dangerous road ahead. For those who choose to leave their partner to stop the violence, the violence may end but it also may continue and even increase in severity. Fleury et al. (2000) concluded that

Ultimately, the survivors themselves are in the best position to determine whether staying or ending the relationship is the best decision for their lives. We as a community need to ensure that women have the resources and support they need to make that decision.

(p. 1381)

Such support includes strategic planning and legal intervention (Hart, 1990). For example, as discussed above, lawyers whose approaches involve challenging the man may reduce the likelihood of post-separation violence. Ellis (1987) hypothesized that this would be most likely to occur in situations where physical violence occurred during the marriage. In light of the fact that many victims of post-separation violence have not experienced violence by their partner prior to the separation, these women may be even less likely to receive the supports needed to prevent post-separation violence. Thus, all stakeholders need to be aware of the many faces of separation and violence so that all women who decide to separate, regardless of whether violence occurred in their relationship, will have the supports needed to prevent violence post-separation.

Conclusion

This chapter shone light on the differing dynamics of risk for violence against separated, divorced, and married women in Canada. Past research and the results of the analyses in this chapter suggest that post-separation violence is a complex phenomenon with some unique risk factors and motives. Although there were common elements to violence for all three groups, there appeared to be unique aspects to post-separation violence. Moreover, there also appeared to be some unique risk factors and dynamics between respondents who were separated and divorced. Even in separated and divorced victims' post-violence experiences, while being generally similar, there were some indications of difference that may have reflected greater severity and "newness" of violence against separated victims. Only by fully understanding these dynamics and contexts will stakeholders be in the most advantageous position to prevent effectively violence against women post-separation. In the meantime, stakeholders need to ensure that these women have the knowledge and resources necessary to make informed decisions and choices to protect themselves and their children.

6

Violence in "The Future Traditional Family"

Stepfamilies and Violence Against Women

Although stepfamilies have existed for centuries in the Western world, prior to the 1970s stepfamilies were a virtually unstudied phenomenon. In Canada, as elsewhere, changes in divorce legislation that facilitated obtaining a divorce in the latter half of the twentieth century had the side effect of an increase in the number of stepfamilies. This dramatic rise in the number of stepfamilies led some commentators to refer to them as "the future traditional American family" (Berger, 1995). In Canada, while 10% of all couples with children were stepfamilies in 1995, by 2001 this figure had increased to 12% (Statistics Canada, 2002e). However, it appears that the trend towards more stepfamilies in Canada may have levelled off. Extrapolating from the most recent available data, the 2006 GSS, the proportion of families in Canada that were stepfamilies in 2006 remained at 12% (Bechard, 2007). It appears that, for the moment, the "traditional family" in Canada may have a reprieve from the trend towards losing its majority position, at least with respect to the proportion of stepfamilies.

Due to their increasing numbers in the latter half of the twentieth century, scholarly interest in stepfamilies burgeoned in the 1980s (Ganong & Coleman, 1994). Considerable attention was paid to problems associated with stepfamily living, particularly the fact that remarried couples tend to have a slightly higher divorce rate than first marriage couples (Ganong & Coleman, 1994). It is also well established in the literature that child abuse is more common in stepfamilies. Indeed, Daly and Wilson (1996) concluded that "living with a stepparent has turned out to be the most powerful predictor of severe child abuse risk yet discovered" (p. 22). In addition, there has been some indication in the literature that rates of filicide (i.e., the killing of a child by a parent) by stepparents may be increasing. The proportion of stepparents accused of filicide in Canada increased from 4% in the 10-year period from 1984 to 1993 to 12% in the 10-year period from 1994 to 2003 (Dauvergne, 2005). A far less researched phenomenon, however, is the increased risk for partner violence against women in these families.

The purpose of this chapter is to use data from two representative samples of Canadian women to determine: (a) the extent to which those who were in stepfamilies were at an elevated risk for violence; and (b) to obtain an improved understanding of this risk through the examination variables derived from explanations for violence against women in stepfamilies.

Kalmuss and Seltzer (1986) were the first to investigate the effect of remarriage on spousal violence. Using data from the 1976 National Survey on Family Violence in the United States, these researchers found that couples in which at least one spouse was divorced had twice the likelihood of violence compared to those couples in which neither of the spouses had been divorced. The impact of remarriage on violence existed regardless of whether the divorced person had brought children from the previous marriage to the remarriage.

While Kalmuss and Seltzer (1986) found evidence of remarriage as a risk marker for spousal violence, Daly, Singh, and Wilson (1993) were the first to investigate specifically whether stepfatherhood is a risk marker for violence against women. Noting that stepchildren are at particular risk for assault and homicide in Canada and beyond, these researchers set out to determine whether women with children fathered by previous partners were also at elevated risk of violence. Based on a sample of 170 mothers who used a women's shelter in Hamilton, Ontario between 1986 and 1987, Daly et al. (1993) found an overrepresentation of women with children fathered by previous partners. These women used shelters at a per capita rate about five times greater than same-age mothers whose children were fathered by their current partner (Wilson & Daly, 1998).

In a subsequent study, Daly, Wiseman, and Wilson (1997) looked at the effect of stepfatherhood on uxoricide (i.e., wife killing).[1] Based on data from Hamilton, Ontario, these researchers found that among murdered mothers with coresiding children, half had children from previous partners. Data on the population at large showed that only 7% of mothers with coresiding children in the Hamilton-Wentworth region had children from previous partners. In other words, Daly et al. demonstrated that women with children from previous unions were at a disproportionate risk of lethal violence.

Yet another indication of a greater problem with violence among stepfamilies comes from the Canadian National Longitudinal Survey of Children and Youth (NLSCY). Data from the NLSCY showed that children in stepfamilies were twice as likely to witness physical fights between parents compared to biological families (Dauvergne & Johnson, 2001). Not only did these results reflect the fact that children in stepfamilies were more likely to be abused, including abuse in the form of witnessing violence, but they were also consistent with the research discussed above suggesting an increased likelihood for partner violence in stepfamilies.

Taken together the aforementioned research studies provide a strong indication that women in stepfamilies are at an elevated risk for partner violence. However, there are important gaps in our knowledge of violence against women in stepfamilies that remain to be filled. Despite Daly et al.'s (1993) conclusion that "attention to this issue is urgently needed" (p. 210), women's elevated risk of violence in stepfamilies remains a largely ignored phenomenon in research. Moreover, extant research has its limitations. Kalmuss and Seltzer's (1986) data are not directly applicable to the Canadian situation. Although there are other indications that an elevated risk for violence in stepfamilies in Canada exists, the non-representative and small samples used to obtain this information dramatically limit their generalizability. Daly and Wilson (1996) admitted that the presence of stepchildren was not established conclusively as a risk marker for violence against women in their research on women's use of shelters. The demonstration of an elevated risk for uxoricide by Daly et al. (1997) also does not prove the presence of stepchildren as a risk marker for non-lethal violence because, as these researchers noted, "demographic risk patterns for uxoricide differ in some details from those for non-lethal wife assault" (p. 62). A final major gap in our knowledge is that, although there are several potential explanations for an elevated risk of violence against women in stepfamilies, the aforementioned research has not taken a holistic approach and attempted to evaluate the impact of risk makers derived from each potential explanation.

Theoretical Background

A review of the literature on stepfamilies resulted in four explanations that can be applied to understanding an elevated risk for violence against women in stepfamilies. Each will be discussed in turn below.

Institutional Incompleteness

Cherlin (1978) developed the institutional incompleteness explanation for the higher divorce rate in stepfamilies. Cherlin argued that, due to remarriage being an "incomplete institution," stepparents in remarried families lack formalized guidelines and norms to help guide their behaviours in their families. This absence of guidelines and norms, combined with the more complex family dynamics in stepfamilies, leads to greater stress on the remarriage. Greater stress, in turn, leads to more divorces.

Cherlin's (1978) hypothesis has also been applied to inter-partner conflict and violence (Kalmuss & Seltzer, 1986; MacDonald & DeMaris, 1995). Kalmuss and Seltzer (1986) argued that there is empirical evidence for a link between stepfamilies and stress as well as between stress and violence. It is, indeed, well documented that stepfamilies experience stress (Ganong & Coleman, 1994; Giles-Sims & Finkelhor, 1984). Based on Cherlin's (1978) explanation, if the complexity of stepfamilies makes them more likely to experience stress, they will have a higher rate of violence against women.

The institutional incompleteness explanation has not been without its critiques. Cherlin (1978) asserted that other societies exist in which complicated kinship rules are institutionalized and, therefore, have a stable family system. On the other hand, Daly and Wilson (1996) argued that "All available evidence suggests that steprelationships are more conflictual than corresponding genetic relationships in *all* societies, regardless of whether steprelationships are rare or common and regardless of their degree of institutionalization" (p. 21). Although Cherlin (1978) and Daly and Wilson (1996) disagree, the critique of the latter does not rule out the essential insight that can be derived from Cherlin's work; the possibility that higher conflict in stepfamilies could be due to stress that results from the greater complexity of stepfamily relationships.

The presence of dependent children in a family has been linked to increased stress in couples (Salari & Baldwin, 2002). It follows that with more dependent children, stress levels may increase. The number of children in a family has, indeed, been shown to be positively related to violence against women (Brownridge, 2002, 2003). Demographic data suggest that stepfamilies are more likely than biological families to have a large family size. In 2001, half of stepfamilies in Canada contained only the children of the female partner. Only 10% contained just the male partner's children. The remaining 40% were blended, containing either biological children of the new couple or children born in previous unions from both spouses (Statistics Canada, 2002a). The large percentage of stepfamilies that are blended implies that they are more likely to have a larger family size than biological families. Thus, based on the institutional incompleteness explanation, women in stepfamilies should be more likely than women in biological families to report having a large family size, and having a large family size should be linked to an increased likelihood of violence.

Depression has been shown to result from marital stress (Kung, 2000). Research has also demonstrated that women who are depressed are more likely to experience violence (Brownridge & Halli, 2002b). Hence, one would expect that women in stepfamilies would be more likely to report being depressed and that depression would be linked to an increased likelihood of violence against these women.

Alcohol consumption has been identified as a mechanism that men use for coping with stress (Umberson, Anderson, Williams, & Chen, 2003). Research has shown that men's alcohol consumption is positively related to violence against women (Johnson, 2001). Therefore, women in stepfamilies should be more likely to report that their partners consume alcohol heavily and heavy alcohol consumption should be linked to an increased likelihood of violence against women.

A direct challenge to the institutional incompleteness explanation comes from Kalmuss and Seltzer (1986). These researchers compared stepfamilies to remarried families without stepchildren and to families in which both spouses were married for the first time. Cherlin (1978) argued that a lack of institutional support was less serious when no stepchildren were present because most of the norms from the first marriage apply. Thus, remarried families without stepchildren should be similar to families of first marriages. However, Kalmuss and Seltzer's (1986) comparison showed that remarried families with and without stepchildren had similarly higher rates of spousal violence relative to first marriage families. These findings led Kalmuss and Seltzer to conclude that "whether the divorced person has brought children from a previous marriage into the remarriage has less of an effect on the likelihood of marital aggression than the remarriage experience itself" (p. 117). It may, however, have been premature for Kalmuss and Seltzer to have ruled out the special case of stepfamilies based on their analysis. The research discussed above concerning increased shelter use and increased risk for lethal violence against women in stepfamilies suggests that there is something operating specifically with respect to violence against women in stepfamilies. Also, Kalmuss and Seltzer studied spouse abuse either perpetrated or experienced by male and female respondents. Thus, their sample confounded female perpetrated with male perpetrated violence, leaving open the question of whether violence against women is more common in stepfamilies. Kalmuss and Seltzer's analysis may also be overly simplistic. In their analyses they controlled only for income. Most importantly, these researchers did not control for duration of the union; a point that is a potential explanation for an elevated risk of violence against women in stepfamilies in its own right.

Duration of Relationship

Based on Cherlin's (1978) work, MacDonald and DeMaris (1995) set out to test the hypothesis that marital conflict is more frequent in stepfamilies than in biological families. Using a nationally representative sample of the United States conducted in the late 1980s, these researchers found that there is an impact of stepchildren on marital conflict. However, the impact depended on the duration of the marriage. In marriages of longer duration, partners having only stepchildren experienced more conflict than those who had only biological children. Contrary to what one would expect based on Cherlin's work, however, conflict was higher in families with only biological children in shorter duration marriages. MacDonald and DeMaris (1995) reasoned that the lack of norms for couples in stepfamilies and a period of trial parenting during dating may make for an easier initial period in the early years of the marriage. Eventually, however, these initial advantages are overtaken by the complexity of living in a stepfamily. Although this research does not support Cherlin's (1978) explanation, it nevertheless employs the essence of the explanation in terms of complexity leading to stress. Extrapolating from the work of MacDonald and DeMaris (1995), if the duration of the relationship between couples in stepfamilies is long, then the likelihood of violence against women in these families should increase. On the other hand, if the duration of the relationship between couples in biological families is short, then the likelihood of violence against women in these families should increase.

For the purposes of the present chapter, the greatest limitation of the Mac-Donald and Demaris (1995) investigation was that it tested the impact of stepfamilies on perceived conflict rather than violence. Although conflict and violence are undoubtedly strongly related, the group of individuals who take conflict to a violent level may well possess some characteristic(s) that differentiates them from those who restrict themselves to open disagreements, as tapped by MacDonald and DeMaris. Thus, the question of whether duration of relationship would operate in the same manner in understanding violence against women in stepfamilies remained unanswered.

Evolutionary Psychology

An evolutionary perspective argues that there is an "evolutionary tendency of parents to protect their own reproductive efforts and not those of others" (Ganong & Coleman, 1994, p. 88). Stemming from this insight are two main factors that are proposed to explain an elevated risk for violence against women in stepfamilies. First, Daly et al. (1993) suggest that stepfathers "may resent their predecessors' children as living violations of their monopoly over their wives" (p. 209). Indeed, research has suggested that filicide by stepparents is more likely to show signs of bitterness and resentment (Weekes-Shackelford & Shackelford, 2004). From an evolutionary psychology perspective, this resentment of stepchildren stems from the evolutionary need for a man to ensure paternity, which results in sexual possessiveness and jealousy. In other words, stepchildren play on the man's evolutionary need to have sexual control over his wife. This, in turn, may create sexually proprietary insecurity in the male and become a source of conflict and violence against the woman. Sexual jealousy and possessiveness have been shown to be positively related to violence against women (e.g., Brownridge & Halli, 2002b). Thus, if the presence of stepchildren makes men in stepfamilies feel more sexually possessive and jealous, then they will be more inclined to be violent. Second, drawing on literature regarding sources of conflict in remarriages, Daly and Wilson (1996) note that the essence of the two main sources of conflict, children and money, is that "the genetic mother wanted more of the stepfather's resources invested in her children than he was inclined to volunteer" (p. 18). The fewer the resources a woman contributes to the family, the less likely she is to have power to determine the allocation of the family's resources. Since, according to evolutionary psychology theory, stepfathers should tend to be less inclined to put equal resources into their stepchildren, if the woman has fewer resources relative to her partner, then there should be an increased likelihood of conflict between the couple and violence against the woman.

Women who do not work are likely to have less power in the family in terms of resource allocation. According to an evolutionary perspective, this will be particularly problematic in stepfamilies as a result of the man's tendency not to invest resources in the progeny of others. Research has shown that remarried wives are more likely to be employed outside of the home (Ganong & Coleman, 1994) and, hence, women in stepfamilies should be less likely to be unemployed compared to women in biological families. Nevertheless, in keeping with evolutionary psychology, women in stepfamilies who are unemployed should be more likely than unemployed women in biological families to experience violence.

It has been noted that remarried couples tend to be less compatible on demographic characteristics such as education (Ganong & Coleman, 1994). An application of evolutionary psychology suggests that the fewer educational resources women in stepfamilies have relative to their partner, the more likely they should be to report experiencing violence. Hence, couples in stepfamilies should be more educationally incompatible than couples in biological families and education incompatibility favouring the male should be positively associated with violence against women in stepfamilies.

Although evolutionary psychology may well play an important role in understanding the elevated risk of violence against women in stepfamilies, it is essential to assess risk markers derived from this theory in the context of those from other theories to identify the unique contribution of evolutionary psychology to understanding this phenomenon.

Selection Factors

An application of a selection explanation to understanding an elevated risk of violence against women in stepfamilies suggests that stepfamilies contain a select group of people that predisposes them to violence. Selection factors vis-à-vis stepfamilies include the fact simply of having been previously married, violence in a previous relationship, and cohabitation.

Extrapolating from Kalmuss and Seltzer's (1986) study discussed above, it is possible that violence against women in stepfamilies is due to one or both of the partners having been in a previous marriage: "Adults bring attitudes and behaviours from their first marriages into subsequent marriages" (Kalmuss & Seltzer, 1986, p. 114). Those who are previously married have been through a relationship that did not work and may therefore be more prone to relationship problems in general, including violence. Since, as noted above, the vast majority of stepfamilies contain children from the woman's prior relationship, women in stepfamilies should be more likely than women in biological families to have had a previous marriage or common-law union. If those who have been previously married are more prone to relationship problems, then they may also be more prone to relationship violence.

A second selection possibility, as suggested by Kalmuss and Seltzer (1986), is that "marriages ended by divorce are more likely to have involved violence than those not ending in divorce" (p. 114). Thus, the pool of individuals in remarried families might contain a higher percentage of people prone to violence. In this vein, if those who have been previously married are more likely to have experienced violence in that union, then they may also be more likely to experience violence in their current union.

Critics of the notion that problems in remarriage are due to selection characteristics of individuals who have had a previous marriage "would say that the theory ignores the fact that divorce and remarriage often result from a desire for a better family life" (Ganong & Coleman, 1994, p. 90). However, while those who leave a marriage may have a desire for a better family life, this does not necessarily mean that they will realize this desire. This is even less likely to be the case if they possess characteristics that are related to the problems they experienced in their first marriage. As discussed above, Kalmuss and Seltzer's (1986) study suggested that it was the characteristics of divorced adults that led to an elevated risk of spouse abuse rather than the presence of stepchildren. Kalmuss and Seltzer posited previous marriage and previous partner violence as rationales for this explanation. However, their own analysis did not directly address the impact of previous marriage and previous partner violence on violence in stepfamilies. Thus, the specific impact of these variables on violence in stepfamilies remains unknown.

A final potential selection factor is cohabitation. In Canada about half of stepfamilies in 2001 and 2006 were common-law couples (Bechard, 2007). Living common-law is a risk marker for violence against women (cf. Chapter 4). If stepfamilies are more likely to live common-law and cohabitation is linked to an elevated risk for violence against women, then women in stepfamilies who are cohabiting may be more likely to experience violence by their partner.

In a study of lethal violence, Daly et al. (1997) found an almost equal proportion of uxoricide victims with stepchildren in common-law (four out of eight victims) and marital unions (seven out of 15 victims). Thus, these data did not suggest support for cohabitation playing a role in an elevated risk of violence against women in stepfamilies. However, as noted above, findings concerning lethal violence are not directly applicable to non-lethal violence. Moreover, the study by Daly et al. was based on a small sample from Hamilton, Ontario, and thus was not generalizable to all of Canada.

Subsamples and Risk Factors

Subsamples

The subsamples employed in this chapter were from the 1999 and 2004 surveys (see Chapter 3 for details of the surveys and methods). Since this chapter concerns male partner violence against women currently in a stepfamily or biological family, the subsamples consisted of heterosexual women living married or common-law, and with at least one child under age 15 residing in the household at the time of the survey. This selection resulted in a subsample of 2,703 (250 in a stepfamily and 2,453 in a biological family) women from the 1999 survey and 2,383 (284 in a stepfamily and 2,099 in a biological family) women from the 2004 survey.

Risk Factors

Based on the explanations identified above, the indicators of institutional incompleteness were the number of children, depression, and heavy alcohol consumption. Union duration was, of course, measured with the duration of relationship variable. Evolutionary psychology included possessive behaviour, sexual jealousy, and woman's employment and education compatibility. Finally, selection factors were represented by previous marriage/common-law union, previous partner violence, and marital status.

Results

Descriptive Analysis

VIOLENCE BY STEPFAMILY/BIOLOGICAL FAMILY STATUS

The first two columns in Table 6.1 provide the 1-year and 5-year prevalence rates of partner violence against women in stepfamilies and biological families in 1999 and 2004. The results showed that in the 1999 survey women in step-families had a significantly higher prevalence of violence compared to women in biological families in both the 1- and 5-year time frames preceding the interview. There appeared to be an overall pattern of decline in prevalence rates in 2004, particularly for women in stepfamilies with reductions in preva-lence of 2.5% in the 1-year rate and 5.3% in the 5-year rate. An examination of the zero-order odds ratios in the third column of Table 6.1 showed that the risk of violence for women in stepfamilies relative to women in biological families was lower in the 2004 survey. Women in stepfamilies had 138% ($p < 0.05$) greater odds of violence in the year prior to the 1999 survey and 88% greater odds in the year prior to the 2004 survey. Similarly, they had 129% ($p < 0.01$) greater odds of violence in the 5-year period prior to the 1999 survey and 67% ($p \leq 0.10$) greater odds in the 5 years prior to the 2004 survey. While the *t*-tests in the final column of Table 6.1 indicated that the difference in odds ratios across the surveys was not significant, overall it was evident that the odds of violence against women in stepfamilies relative to women in biological families was lower in the 2004 survey.

Since the group of women in stepfamilies was quite small, cross-tabulations of individual forms of violence by step-/biological family status would not have met the release guidelines of Statistics Canada. Consequently, for this chapter the individual forms of violence were combined into minor and severe categories to get a sense of whether or not the severity of violence differed by step-/biological family status in the 5 years prior to the survey.

Table 6.1 Prevalence rates (%) of violence against women in stepfamilies and biological families in the 1999 GSS and 2004 GSS, corresponding zero-order odds ratios, and significance of the change across surveys

	Stepfamily	Biological family	Odds ratio	Difference in odds
1999 GSS				
1-year prevalence	5.1	2.2**	2.384**	
5-year prevalence	11.3	5.2***	2.285***	
2004 GSS				*1999 vs. 2004*
1-year prevalence	2.6	1.5	1.882	0.64
5-year prevalence	6.0	3.7*	1.673*	1.24

Notes
$*p \leq 0.10$; $**p < 0.05$; $***p < 0.01$ (*p* values for prevalence rates refer to Pearson Chi-square, for odds ratios Wald Chi-square was used, and for the difference in odds the *t*-statistic was used).

Forms of violence coded as minor were those that involved being threatened, throwing something, pushing/grabbing/shoving, and slapping. Severe violence was based on items that involved choking, hitting, kicking, the threat or use of a gun or knife, being beaten, and being sexually assaulted.

In the 1999 survey, 10.9% of women in stepfamilies reported minor violence compared to 5.1% of women in biological families ($p < 0.01$). The difference between the two groups was smaller in the 2004 survey, with 5.9% of women in stepfamilies compared to 3.7% of women in biological families reporting minor violence ($p \leq 0.10$). In the 1999 survey, 3.9% of women in stepfamilies reported severe violence compared to 1.7% of women in biological families ($p < 0.05$). The difference in severe violence between the two groups was a bit larger in the 2004 survey, where 3% of women in stepfamilies reported experiencing severe violence compared to 0.8% of women in biological families. Therefore, it appeared that the gap in rates of violence between women in stepfamilies and biological families decreased with respect to minor violence and increased with respect to severe violence from 1999 to 2004.

RISK MARKERS BY STEPFAMILY/BIOLOGICAL FAMILY STATUS

Table 6.2 provides the results of the cross-tabulations of the independent variables by step-/biological family status. The results in Table 6.2 showed that stepfamilies were more likely than biological families to have a large family size in both surveys. Also, women in stepfamilies were more likely to be depressed in both surveys. No difference was found between the two groups in terms of partner's alcohol consumption in the 1999 survey. In the 2004 survey, however, women in stepfamilies were significantly more likely to report that their partners consumed alcohol heavily. Stepfamilies tended to have much shorter duration relationships than biological families in both surveys. Although not the case in the 1999 survey, in the 2004 survey men in stepfamilies were significantly more likely to be possessive in terms of

Table 6.2 Independent variables by stepfamily/biological family status in the 1999 GSS and 2004 GSS (%)

Independent variables	1999		2004	
	Stepfamily	Biological family	Stepfamily	Biological family
Institutional incompleteness				
Children <15				
One	39.4	42.3	43.2	43.1
Two	35.6	42.3	36.5	43.3
Three or more	25.0	15.4***	20.4	13.5***
Depressed				
Yes	9.8	3.6	9.3	5.9
No	90.2	96.4***	90.7	94.1**
Heavy drinking (past month)				
None	73.0	75.2	64.0	72.9
Once	12.4	11.5	15.9	13.3
2–4 times	12.4	10.3	16.3	11.2
5 or more times	2.1	3.0	3.9	2.7**
Duration				
Duration of relationship				
Less than 4 years	40.0	7.1	50.7	9.4
4–9 years	40.4	25.7	33.3	31.4
10 or more years	19.6	67.2***	15.9	59.1***
Evolutionary psychology				
Possessiveness				
Yes	5.8	4.1	6.7	2.1
No	94.2	95.9	93.3	97.9***
Jealousy				
Yes	8.6	4.9	8.2	2.9
No	91.4	95.1**	91.8	97.1***
Woman's employment				
Did not work in past year	27.8	35.2	28.6	36.4
Worked past year	72.2	64.8**	71.4	63.6**
Education compatibility				
Woman has much less education	18.0	13.2	8.2	11.7
Woman has less education	13.9	16.2	10.8	13.7
Woman has same education	24.6	34.5	32.0	35.1
Woman has more education	23.4	20.8	30.9	22.6
Woman has much more education	20.1	15.3**	18.2	17.0**
Selection factors				
Previous marriage/common-law union				
Yes	78.5	15.0	80.9	14.9
No	21.5	85.0***	19.1	85.1***
Previous partner violence				
Yes	34.4	17.2	29.4	18.8
No	65.6	82.8**	70.6	81.2*
Marital status				
Common-law	48.3	12.0	55.3	14.5
Married	51.7	88.0***	44.7	85.5***

Notes
$*p \leq 0.10$; $**p < 0.05$; $***p < 0.01$ (p values refer to Chi-square tests of significance).

insisting on knowing the respondent's whereabouts. In both surveys men in stepfamilies were more likely to be sexually jealous. Women in stepfamilies were less likely to be unemployed in both surveys. In the 1999 survey, women in stepfamilies were more likely to be in an educationally incompatible relationship with a greater proportion of women in stepfamilies compared to biological families in the extreme on the education incompatibility continuum. In the 2004 survey, the category with the largest difference between the groups was for women having more education than their partner. About 31% of women in stepfamilies fell into this category compared to 23% of women in biological families. In both surveys, women in stepfamilies were much more likely than those in biological families to have had a previous marriage or common-law union. Women in stepfamilies were more likely to have experienced violence by a previous partner in both surveys. Finally, women in stepfamilies were much more likely to be living in a common-law union in both surveys. While there was an increase in the proportion of women living common-law in both stepfamilies and biological families, the increase was greater for women living in stepfamilies (7% vs. 2.5%).

Multivariate Analysis

SEPARATE LOGISTIC REGRESSIONS FOR STEPFAMILIES AND
BIOLOGICAL FAMILIES

Table 6.3 provides the results of the logistic regressions on the 5-year prevalence of violence for stepfamilies and biological families in the 1999 and 2004 GSSs. The results showed that, controlling for all other variables in the models, having a large family size was not linked to a significantly increased likelihood of violence for either group in any of the surveys. On the other hand, depression was linked to increased odds of violence against women. Although the impact of depression on violence was strong for both groups in the 1999 survey, as shown by the *t*-test, the impact of depression was greater for women in stepfamilies. The impact of depression on violence appeared to be lower in the 2004 survey. Nevertheless, depression was still positively associated with women's odds of experiencing violence in the 2004 survey.[2] Heavy alcohol consumption by a partner was associated with increased odds of violence for women in biological families, but not for women in stepfamilies, in the 1999 survey. However, in the 2004 survey heavy alcohol consumption did not have a significant impact on the odds of violence for either group of women.

The results regarding the duration of relationship variable showed that the longer the relationship duration the lower were the odds of violence. In the 1999 survey, for each additional year that a couple had been together their odds of violence decreased by 4% for women in biological families and by 6% for women in stepfamilies. While the *t*-test showed that these odds ratios were

Table 6.3 Results of logistic regressions on the 5-year prevalence of violence in the 1999 GSS and 2004 GSS for women in stepfamilies and biological families

Covariates	1999			2004		
	Stepfamily n = 218 OR	Biological family n = 2,176 OR	t	Stepfamily n = 236 OR	Biological family n = 1,989 OR	t
Institutional incompleteness						
Children <15						
One	1.000	1.000		1.000	1.000	
Two	0.440	1.380	−1.99**	0.435	0.661	−0.61
Three or more	0.452	1.572	−1.85**	1.631	1.330	0.23
Depressed						
Yes	45.255***	3.729***	3.29***	2.967	2.191*	0.32
No	1.000	1.000		1.000	1.000	
Heavy drinking	1.034	1.107***	−0.47	0.832	1.055	−1.86**
Duration						
Duration of relationship	0.936	0.964**	−0.55	0.865	0.980	−1.76**
Evolutionary psychology						
Possessiveness						
Yes	2.996	5.790***	−0.82	0.581	5.885***	−2.12**
No	1.000	1.000		1.000	1.000	
Jealousy						
Yes	36.515***	3.968***	2.92***	1,052.672***	3.868***	3.95***
No	1.000	1.000		1.000	1.000	
Woman's employment						
Unemployed	6.077**	0.789	3.51***	0.015*	0.754	−2.60***
Employed	1.000	1.000		1.000	1.000	

Education compatibility						
Woman has much less education	0.168	1.341	−2.42***	72.553**	2.390**	2.69***
Woman has less education	0.483	0.741	−0.55	0.248	1.469	−1.35*
Woman has same education	1.000	1.000		1.000	1.000	
Woman has more education	0.593	1.843**	−1.61*	4.797	1.251	1.35*
Woman has much more education	0.462	0.800	−0.73	3.135	2.368**	0.24
Selection factors						
Previous marriage/common-law						
Yes	9.347*	1.083	2.57***	0.785	1.595	−0.71
No	1.000	1.000		1.000	1.000	
Previous partner violence						
Yes	0.255	0.582	−0.74	0.000	0.000	0.00
No	1.000	1.000		1.000	1.000	
Marital status						
Common-law	0.183**	1.802**	−3.78***	0.125**	1.083	−2.94***
Married	1.000	1.000		1.000	1.000	
Constant	0.019**	0.028***		0.063	0.015***	
−2 Log likelihood	81	729		54	545	
χ^2	73***	159***		56***	62***	
Nagelkerke pseudo r^2	0.561	0.211		0.566	0.117	

Notes

*$p \leq 0.10$; **$p < 0.05$; ***$p < 0.01$.

not significantly different, the corresponding odds ratios in the 2004 survey were shown by the *t*-test to be significantly different. Indeed, in 2004 the duration variable did not significantly impact the odds of violence against women in biological families. However, each additional year the couple was together was associated with a 13% decrease in the odds of violence against women in stepfamilies in 2004.

In terms of the indicators of evolutionary psychology, having a partner that was possessive through insisting on knowing a woman's whereabouts was associated with significantly increased odds of violence against women in biological families in both surveys. For women in stepfamilies, the positive association between having a possessive partner and violence was not statistically significant, though the *t*-test suggested that the odds ratio was not different from the statistically significant impact of this variable for women in biological families. However, in the 2004 survey having a possessive partner was clearly not associated with increased odds of violence. Having a jealous partner was strongly associated with increased odds of violence for both groups in both surveys. However, the results of the *t*-test suggested that having a jealous partner had a larger impact on the odds of violence against women in stepfamilies than for women in biological families in both surveys. Unemployment did not significantly impact the odds of violence against women in biological families in either survey. For women in stepfamilies, in the 1999 survey, those who were unemployed had 508% increased odds of violence whereas, in the 2004 survey, unemployed women had 98% lower odds of violence. In terms of education compatibility, there were no consistent results across the surveys. For women in stepfamilies, in the 1999 survey none of the incompatibility categories significantly differed from couples that had equal levels of education. In the 2004 survey, women in stepfamilies who had much less education than their partner had significantly higher odds of violence compared to those who had the same level of education as their partner. For women in biological families, in the 1999 survey women who had more education than their partner had higher odds of experiencing violence than those who had the same level of education as their partner. On the other hand, in the 2004 survey women in the most educationally incompatible categories at both ends of the continuum had significantly increased odds of violence.

With respect to selection factors, the results showed that having had a previous marriage or common-law union was associated with increased odds of violence only for women in stepfamilies, and this was only the case in the 1999 survey. Having experienced violence by a previous marital or common-law partner did not have a significant impact on the odds of violence against either group of women in any of the surveys. Regarding marital status, in the 1999 survey women in biological families who were living common-law had 80% increased odds of violence compared to their married counterparts.

However, in the 2004 survey these women's odds of violence were similar to their married counterparts. On the other hand, results showed that women in stepfamilies who were living common-law had 82% lower odds of violence compared to their married counterparts in the 1999 survey and 87% lower odds of violence compared to their married counterparts in the 2004 survey.

Finally, the results in Table 6.3 provide the Nagelkerke pseudo r^2 for each model. These results suggested that the variables in the models explained more of the variance in violence for women in stepfamilies than for women in biological families. Specifically, these variables accounted for 56% and 57% of the variance in violence for women in stepfamilies compared to 21% and 12% of the variance in violence for women in biological families in the 1999 and 2004 surveys, respectively.

LOGISTIC REGRESSIONS FOR STEPFAMILIES AND BIOLOGICAL
FAMILIES COMBINED

Table 6.4 provides the results of the sequential logistic regressions on the 5-year prevalence of violence for both surveys. The first model in Table 6.4 contains the odds of violence for women in stepfamilies relative to women in biological families without any controls in the 1999 and 2004 GSS (also found in Table 6.1). The difference in prevalence for the two groups translated to women in stepfamilies having 129% greater odds of violence in the 1999 survey and 67% greater odds of violence in the 2004 survey. The second model in Table 6.4 controlled for the variables derived from the institutional incompleteness explanation. Controlling for these variables reduced the elevated odds of violence against women in stepfamilies by 18% in the 1999 survey and by about 7% in the 2004 survey. The third model in Table 6.4 controlled for the duration variable. With duration of relationship controlled there was a 42% reduction in relative odds of violence in the 1999 survey and a 12% reduction in relative odds of violence in the 2004 survey. The fourth model in Table 6.4 controlled for the evolutionary psychology variables. Although, with these controls, there was no reduction in relative odds in the 1999 survey, in the 2004 survey controls for the evolutionary psychology variables reduced the relative odds by 54%. Controlling for selection factors, in the fifth model of Table 6.4, reduced the relative odds by 27% in the 1999 survey and by 26% in the 2004 survey. The final model in Table 6.4 controlled for all of the independent variables simultaneously. Controlling for all of the variables reduced the elevated odds of violence against women in stepfamilies by 78% in the 1999 survey and by 61% in the 2004 survey. In the 1999 survey, only when the variables derived from all explanations were controlled was the significance of the difference in the relative odds of violence removed. In the 2004 survey, not only was the significance of the difference in odds removed when all of the variables were controlled simultaneously, but individually controlling for duration, evolutionary psychology, and selection factors also

Table 6.4 Results of sequential logistic regressions on the 5-year prevalence of violence in the 1999 GSS and 2004 GSS

Covariates	Model 1 Stepfamily/ biological family Odds ratio	Model 2 Institutional incompleteness Odds ratio	Model 3 Duration Odds ratio	Model 4 Evolutionary psychology Odds ratio	Model 5 Selection factors Odds ratio	Model 6 Full model Odds ratio
1999 GSS	n = 2,603	n = 2,461	n = 2,557	n = 2,507	n = 2,597	n = 2,394
Stepfamily/biological family						
Stepfamily	2.285***	2.105***	1.865**	2.291***	2.011**	1.502
Biological family	1.000	1.000	1.000	1.000	1.000	1.000
Institutional incompleteness		BLOCK1				BLOCK1
Duration			BLOCK2			BLOCK2
Evolutionary psychology				BLOCK3		BLOCK3
Selection factors					BLOCK4	BLOCK4
Constant	0.055***	0.036***	0.075***	0.036***	0.048***	0.027***
−2 Log likelihood	1,138	994	1,127	957	1,135	860
χ^2	12***	89***	14***	5	4	207***
2004 GSS	n = 2,330	n = 2,264	n = 2,313	n = 2,286	n = 2,328	n = 2,225
Stepfamily/biological family						
Stepfamily	1.673*	1.608*	1.556	1.131	1.417	1.064
Biological family	1.000	1.000	1.000	1.000	1.000	1.000
Institutional incompleteness		BLOCK1				BLOCK1
Duration			BLOCK2			BLOCK2
Evolutionary psychology				BLOCK3		BLOCK3
Selection factors					BLOCK4	BLOCK4
Constant	0.039***	0.037***	0.044***	0.019***	0.023***	0.022***
−2 Log likelihood	778	720	775	656	763	621
χ^2	3*	18***	3	81***	17***	102***

Notes
* $p \leq 0.10$; ** $p < 0.05$; *** $p < 0.01$.

removed the significance of the difference in odds. This likely reflects the fact that the difference in odds of violence was much lower to begin with in 2004. Nevertheless, there was a common pattern across both data sets. That is, in both data sets, simultaneously controlling for the variables from all of the explanations had the largest impact on reducing the actual odds of violence against women in stepfamilies compared to women in biological families.

Post-Violence Experiences of Victims in Stepfamilies Relative to Biological Families

Table 6.5 contains the zero-order odds ratios for the consequences of violence for women victimized in stepfamilies relative to women victimized in biological families in both surveys. The results in Table 6.5 showed that there was a pattern for victims in stepfamilies to have greater odds of being physically injured than victims in biological families. The 1999 data also showed a pattern for women in stepfamilies to take time off from everyday activities and to stay in bed for all, or most, of the day as a consequence of the violence. Despite these findings, there was also a pattern across the surveys for women in stepfamilies to have lower odds of psychopathology as a result of the violence.

The results of the victims' reports of help-seeking behaviour in the 1999 and 2004 surveys are presented in Table 6.6. Across the 1999 and 2004

Table 6.5 Zero-order odds ratios for consequences of violence for victims in stepfamilies relative to victims in biological families in the 1999 and 2004 GSS

Dependent variable	Stepfamily/biological family status[a]			
	1999		2004	
	OR	n	OR	n
Physical injury	2.001	162	3.540**	98
Psychopathology[b]	0.843	155	0.769	93
Altered psyche[c]	0.954	155	†	
Anger	0.854	155	1.292	93
Time off everyday activities	3.826***	160	†	
Stay in bed all/most of day	4.309	162	†	
Children witnessed violence	1.052	154	0.846	92

Notes
**$p < 0.05$; ***$p < 0.01$.
a Biological family is the reference category with an odds of 1.000.
b Includes depression or anxiety attacks, fear, afraid for children, more cautious or aware, sleep problems, shock or disbelief, hurt or disappointment, and upset, confused, or frustrated.
c Includes ashamed or guilty, lowered self-esteem, problems relating to men, and increased self-reliance.
† Statistics Canada would not release the result to ensure respondent confidentiality. Statistical significance test was not released.

Table 6.6 Zero-order odds ratios for victims' help-seeking behaviours in stepfamilies relative to biological families in the 1999 and 2004 GSS

Dependent variable	Stepfamily/biological family status[a]			
	1999		2004	
	OR	n	OR	n
Visit doctor/nurse/hospital for treatment	1.235	42	†	
Confided in someone:	0.791	158	†	
Family	1.056	158	1.328	97
Friend/neighbour	1.110	158	0.898	97
Co-worker	1.058	157	†	
Doctor/nurse	1.059	157	†	
Lawyer	0.934	158	†	
Minister/priest/clergy/spiritual adviser	1.001	158	†	
Services contacted:	1.411	159	2.544*	97
Crisis centre/line	0.895	159	†	
Another counsellor/psychologist	1.264	159	4.128**	97
Community/family centre	2.375*	159	†	
Shelter/transition house	0.727	159	†	
Women's centre	0.576	159	†	
Police/court-based victim service	1.021	159	†	
Interested in mediation/conciliation	1.594	155	3.929**	91

Notes

*$p \leq 0.10$; **$p < 0.05$.

a Biological family is the reference category with an odds of 1.000.

† Statistics Canada would not release the result to ensure respondent confidentiality. Statistical significance test was not released.

surveys, there was a pattern for women in stepfamilies to have higher odds of confiding in a family member, to have contacted a service (including a counsellor/psychologist or a community/family centre), and to be interested in mediation or conciliation to deal with the violence. The 1999 survey data also suggested that women in stepfamilies had slightly greater odds of visiting a health care professional for treatment.

Table 6.7 contains the zero-order odds ratios for victims in stepfamilies relative to biological families on the police intervention variables. There was a pattern across the surveys of victims in stepfamilies having higher odds than those in biological families of reporting that the police found out about the violence. The 1999 data suggested that the police were less likely to find out about the violence from the respondent herself when the victim was in a stepfamily. Among those who contacted the police themselves, women in stepfamilies reported greater odds of doing so to stop the violence and receive protection, but lower odds of wanting their partner arrested or punished. There appeared to be greater odds of the police visiting the scene and giving a warning to the partner in cases of violence against women in stepfamilies. However, victims in stepfamilies had lower odds of reporting that the police took their partner away from the scene. These victims also had lower odds of being satisfied with the police response. For those women who did contact the police, the 1999 data suggested that victims in stepfamilies were no less likely to have reported the violence as a result of various concerns about having the police involved. Instead, the results suggested that victims in stepfamilies had higher odds of viewing the violence as a personal matter that did not involve the police.

Discussion

The Elevated Risk of Violence Against Women in Stepfamilies from 1999 to 2004

Data from the 1999 survey suggested that Canadian women in stepfamilies were at double the risk for partner violence than their counterparts in biological families. This rate of relative risk was consistent with that found by Kalmuss and Seltzer (1986) vis-à-vis spousal violence which, as noted earlier, was based on American data from nearly 30 years ago. Taking previous research and the current study into consideration, it appears that violence against women in stepfamilies is an enduring and cross-cultural phenomenon. However, data from the 2004 survey suggested that the overall prevalence of violence against women in stepfamilies relative to women in biological families had declined by 2004. An examination of the prevalence of minor and severe violence suggested that the decline was due to a narrowing of the gap between the two groups in terms of minor violence. Indeed, the gap in favour of women in stepfamilies experiencing severe violence widened in the 2004 survey.

The comparison of women's post-violence experiences across the surveys also produced a number of findings that were consistent with women in stepfamilies having a greater likelihood of experiencing more severe violence than women in biological families. The findings included that women in stepfamilies were more likely to have been physically injured, to take time off from everyday activities, and to stay in bed as a result of the violence. These women also tended to have higher odds of contacting a service and were more likely to report that the police found out about the violence.

The finding that women in stepfamilies had a greater likelihood of experiencing severe violence across both surveys was consistent with the research by Daly et al. (1993) and Daly et al. (1997) showing that women with children fathered by previous partners were disproportionate in terms of shelter use and their risk of lethal violence. Clearly, the results of these studies and the present investigation suggest that Canadian women in stepfamilies are at particular risk for severe violence.

Table 6.7 Zero-order odds ratios for police intervention for victims in stepfamilies relative to victims in biological families in the 1999 and 2004 GSS

Dependent variable	Stepfamily/biological family status[a]			
	1999		2004	
	OR	n	OR	n
Police found out	2.373**	161	1.841	97
Police found out from respondent	0.235*	40	†	
Reason police contacted:				
Stop violence/rec. protection	4,131.977	30	†	
Arrest/punish spouse/partner	0.588	30	†	
Duty to notify police	1.343	30	†	
Recommendation of someone else	0.914	30	†	
Police action:				
Visited scene	1.481	38	†	
Made report/conducted investigation	0.789	38	†	
Gave warning to spouse/partner	2.630	38	†	
Took spouse/partner away	0.215*	38	†	
Put you in touch with community services	1.514	38	†	
Made arrest/laid charges	NA		†	
None	0.000	38	†	
Respondent satisfied w/police	0.337	38	†	
Post-police violence decreased/stopped	0.000	21	†	

Reasons police not contacted:

Dealt with in another way[b]	0.832	120	†	70
Did not want to get involved with police	1.013	120	1.566	
Fear of spouse/partner	1.008	120	†	
Personal matter that did not concern police	1.996	119	†	
Police couldn't do anything about it	0.645	120	†	
Police wouldn't help[c]	0.001	119	†	
Police wouldn't think it was important enough	1.076	119	†	
Fear of publicity/news coverage	1.163	119	†	
Did not want spouse/partner arrested or jailed	0.531	119	†	
Did not want anyone to find out about it (e.g., shame)	0.548	119	†	
Other reason	0.001	118	†	

Notes

$*p \leq 0.10; **p < 0.05$.

a Biological family is the reference category with an odds of 1.000.

b Includes left him, reported to another official, private matter that took care of myself, etc.

c Includes police wouldn't think it was important enough, wouldn't believe, wouldn't want to be bothered or get involved, police would be inefficient or ineffective, police would be biased, would harass/insult respondent, offender was police officer.

† Statistics Canada would not release the result to ensure respondent confidentiality. Statistical significance test was not released.

NA Not available in the data.

Examining Explanations for the Elevated Risk of Violence Against Women in Stepfamilies

What follows will discuss the results as they pertain to each explanation and close with the main conclusions of this chapter.

INSTITUTIONAL INCOMPLETENESS

Among indicators used to study institutional incompleteness in the present chapter, the one that was most directly linked to complexity of family relationships was family size. That is, family interactions should be more complicated with a greater number of people in the family. Interestingly, the results suggested that the number of children did not impact the likelihood of violence against women in a stepfamily. In other words, the impact of being in a stepfamily on violence against women was not a matter of complexity in terms of managing relationships with multiple children. Of course, this result did not rule out the influence of complexity in terms of other family relationships, such as the relationship between the nonresidential biological parent and the stepparent.

The results also showed that, if the complexity of stepfamilies led them to experience stress and violence, heavy alcohol consumption was not responsible for the link between stress and an elevated risk of violence against women in stepfamilies. The one indicator derived from the institutional incompleteness explanation that did operate as expected was depression. Women in stepfamilies were more depressed in both the 1999 and 2004 surveys and those who were depressed did have greater odds of violence in both surveys. Indeed, it appeared that the depression variable was likely largely responsible for the observed reductions in the elevated odds of violence against women in stepfamilies in both surveys when controlling for the institutional incompleteness factors. To the extent that depression experienced by women in stepfamilies is due to stress that results from the complexity of being in a stepfamily, these results provided limited support for the institutional incompleteness explanation. However, based on the fact that only the depression variable operated as expected as well as the finding that the institutional incompleteness variables did not fully account for the significantly elevated odds of violence against women in stepfamilies, it appeared that much more was operating in the relationship between stepfamilies and violence against women than simply differential levels of stress.

DURATION

Contrary to expectations, as with biological families, the likelihood of violence against women in stepfamilies decreased the longer the couple had been together. Thus, MacDonald and DeMaris' (1995) suggestion regarding the operation of duration of relationship and conflict, that the initial period of the relationship may be an easier experience for stepfamilies but that the complexity of stepfamily living catches up with them later in the relationship, did not appear to apply to women's experience of violence in stepfamilies in the current study. Rather, duration of relationship had a similar inverse impact on violence for both groups in the 1999 survey. This finding suggested that working out the complexity of stepfamily relationships in the initial period of the union did not impact violence against the female partner much more than did working out the complexities of the relationship in the early years of biological families. In the 2004 data, having a long duration union had an even larger impact on reducing the odds of violence against women in stepfamilies than it did on reducing the odds of violence against women in biological families.

The importance of the duration variable seemed to lay with the fact that couples in stepfamilies were much more likely to have shorter duration relationships than couples in biological families. In the 1999 data, controlling for duration had the largest impact on reducing the difference in odds of violence between stepfamilies and biological families. However, this was not the case in the 2004 survey; though controlling for duration did remove the elevated odds of violence against women in stepfamilies in that survey.

EVOLUTIONARY PSYCHOLOGY

The results in terms of the evolutionary psychology explanation were inconsistent across the surveys. Although there was not a significant difference in possessiveness between partners of women in stepfamilies and biological families in the 1999 survey, the difference was larger and did reach statistical significance in the 2004 survey. However, while this variable had a similar positive impact on the odds of violence against women in both groups in the 1999 data, in the 2004 data it was significant only for women in biological families. Hence, overall the results did not support the expected relationship between possessiveness and violence against women in stepfamilies. This may have been because the measure of possessiveness was not exclusively sexual in nature. That is, while a man insisting on knowing who his female partner is with and where she is at all times is sexual possessiveness, this measure may be tapping a more general element of controlling behaviour, rather than sexual control, that men in both types of families are relatively equally likely to express.

Being jealous of a female partner talking to other men is clearly a sexually based insecurity that, as evolutionary psychology predicted, was a behaviour in which men in stepfamilies were more likely to engage across both the 1999 and 2004 surveys. Moreover, this variable had a stronger impact on the odds of violence against women in stepfamilies than in biological families in both surveys.

Although couples in stepfamilies were less compatible in terms of relative education resources in both surveys, in the 1999 survey education incompatibility favouring the male did not have a significant impact on violence for either group. In the 2004 survey women who had much less education than their partner had significantly increased odds of violence in both groups. As shown by the *t*-test, this impact was stronger for women in stepfamilies (see Table 6.3). On the other hand, unemployed women in stepfamilies were particularly likely to experience violence in the 1999 survey. This was consistent with the application of evolutionary psychology, which suggested that women in stepfamilies who lacked employment resources would be less able to direct resources towards their own biological children, resulting in greater tension and violence in the relationship. However, in the 2004 data, female unemployment had the opposite effect on the odds of violence against women in stepfamilies. The mixed results on three of the four indicators from the evolutionary psychology explanation across the surveys likely accounted for these variables, on the one hand, having no impact on reducing the elevated odds of violence against women in stepfamilies in the 1999 data and, on the other hand, being responsible for the largest reduction in elevated odds in the 2004 survey compared to any other individual explanation (see Table 6.4). Based on the inconsistent findings in this chapter, it was evident that the indicators of evolutionary psychology did not fully explain women's elevated risk for violence in stepfamilies.

SELECTION FACTORS

Consistent with what was expected, women in stepfamilies were more likely to have had a prior live-in relationship in both surveys. In the 1999 survey, this subgroup of women faced much higher odds of violence than those in stepfamilies without prior union experience. However, the 2004 data showed no difference in odds of violence across these two subgroups. Furthermore, women in biological families who had a live-in relationship with someone other than their husband did not face significantly higher odds of violence than their counterparts who were in their first marriage or common-law union. Overall, these results suggested that an elevated risk for violence against remarried women was not a matter simply of having been in a previous live-in relationship, as Kalmuss and Seltzer's (1986) research implied. Rather, depending on which data set one examines, there may or may not be something specific about the stepfamily experience that makes women who have had a prior live-in relationship particularly prone to violence.

It is possible that an observed differential impact of a prior live-in relationship on violence for women in stepfamilies and biological families could be related to a second selection variable: previous partner violence. Although women in stepfamilies were, indeed, more likely to have experienced violence by a previous partner in both surveys, the results also showed that this variable did not have a significant impact on either group of women's odds of violence in both the 1999 and 2004 surveys. Thus, the data analysed in this chapter suggested that the elevated risk of violence against women in stepfamilies was not a matter of women in stepfamilies being prone to violent unions.

Women in stepfamilies were far more likely to be living common-law than were women in biological families. The proportion of women in stepfamilies living in common-law unions was even larger in the 2004 than in the 1999 survey. Contrary to expectations, women in stepfamilies that lived common-law actually reported significantly lower odds of violence than their married counterparts in both surveys. This was particularly surprising because it is a ubiquitous finding in the research that women in common-law relationships are at increased risk for violence (cf. Chapter 4). The research of Daly et al. (1997) was somewhat unusual in the sense that it showed an almost equal likelihood of violence, albeit lethal violence, between a group of women in common-law and marital unions. The results of the analyses in this chapter dealing with non-lethal violence were even more novel in showing a lower rate of violence for women living in common-law unions in stepfamilies. It may be the case that those women in stepfamilies who chose to live common-law were doing so out of cautiousness because of the failure of their past union. This same cautiousness may lead them to select better partners in general, including partners who are less likely to be violent.

The selection factors were important for understanding the higher odds of violence for women in stepfamilies relative to biological families, having the second largest reduction in the difference in odds between the two groups across both surveys. It is noteworthy that inclusion of the selection factor of a prior live-in relationship did not account for the greatest reduction in the elevated odds of violence against women in stepfamilies. If, based on Kalmuss and Seltzer's (1986) analysis, the key factor is remarriage itself, rather than the presence of stepchildren, one would expect that controlling for a prior live-in relationship as part of the group of selection variables would account for the higher odds of violence for women in stepfamilies in both surveys. The results demonstrated this not to be the case.

Limitations

It is prudent at this point to note that the analyses in this chapter were somewhat limited with respect to indicators of the explanations that were available in the data. Future research needs to be conducted to collect data with more complete indicators of the explanations and that will allow identification of the specific mechanisms through which the key variables are linked to violence against women in stepfamilies. For example, the analyses in this chapter were unable to identify the specific sources of stress that led women in stepfamilies to have higher rates of depression and the precise mechanism through which their depression influenced their experience of violence. More complete information on these mechanisms is needed for identifying specific prevention strategies.

Conclusion

Despite the limitations of the data, this chapter provides clear evidence that women in stepfamilies are at elevated risk for violence. Although an examination of the 1999 and 2004 surveys suggested that the elevated risk of violence against women in stepfamilies has declined with respect to minor violence, it is evident that women in stepfamilies remain particularly at risk of severe violence. Also, while there are several mixed results across the surveys, both data sets point to the same basic conclusion. That is, there appears to be some truth to each explanation for the elevated risk of violence against women in stepfamilies. This is buttressed by the finding that, in both surveys, the actual relative odds are reduced the most when the variables from all of the explanations are controlled simultaneously. Hence, the data suggest that elements from all explanations are required to account most adequately for women's higher odds of violence in stepfamilies. In the final analysis, it appears that the elevated risk of violence against women in stepfamilies is a multifactorial problem, the explanation of which requires insights from institutional incompleteness, duration, evolutionary psychology, and selection factor explanations. It follows that any efforts to address the elevated risk of violence against women in stepfamilies must address elements from each of these explanations for the most efficacious approach to prevention.

7

Exploring the Link Between Homeownership Status and Violence Against Women

For centuries researchers have associated homeownership with social benefits, including psychological and physical health (Green, 2001; Hubbard & Davis, 2002). However, despite increasing recognition of the need for gender-specific research on health (Russo, 1990), the relationship between homeownership and women's health does not appear to be a focus in the housing literature. The objective of this chapter is to examine, in the Canadian context, the relationship between homeownership status and partner violence against women. The extant housing research begs the question of whether living in an occupant-owned dwelling decreases women's risk for violence by an intimate partner. In other words, does living in a renter-occupied dwelling increase a woman's risk of experiencing violence? An application of the research on homeownership and health suggests such a hypothesis. Indeed, the only published article that could be found which tested, albeit tangentially, for a relationship between homeownership and violence against women confirmed this hypothesis. Peterson (1980) reported that women in rental housing had nine times the prevalence of violence compared to those who owned their homes. But the existence of a relationship between homeownership and violence raises a further question. If women living in rental housing face an elevated risk for violence, is this a result of ownership status per se, or some other characteristic(s) associated with lack of ownership? Research on homeownership and its effects on children has shown that children of homeowners have better life outcomes compared to those of renters (Hubbard & Davis, 2002). For example, Green and White (1997) found that children of homeowners are more likely to complete high school and that their teenage daughters are less likely to become pregnant. These researchers controlled for quality of neighbourhood, stability of home environment, and the selection of less effective parents into renting versus owning. Despite these controls, the statistically significant impact of homeowning persisted, leading them to conclude that "the evidence is consistent with homeowning being important in itself, rather then [sic] homeowning being important only because it captures the effect of omitted variables such as parents' personality type" (p. 457). Similarly, after finding that renting was associated with increased wife abuse, Peterson (1980) speculated that this relationship was a result of homeowners' higher social status, which Peterson postulated decreases stress, in turn reducing violence.

The classic policy implication of research showing that homeownership matters is that, if the benefits are due to ownership itself, incentives should be given to people who otherwise would not become owners (Green, 2001). If women in renter-occupied housing face an increased risk for violence as the result of ownership status, then this logic implies that simply encouraging homeownership will help to alleviate the problem of violence against women. Alternatively, if a relationship between ownership status and violence is spurious with some other characteristic(s), then dealing with those circumstances will help to alleviate violence against women in rental housing. The purposes of this chapter are to: (a) investigate whether such a relationship between homeownership and violence against women exists in the contemporary Canadian context; (b) identify potential explanations for such a relationship; (c) determine the operation and impact of variables derived from explanations across the 1999 and 2004 GSSs; (d) examine post-violence experiences of victims in renter- and owner-occupied housing; and (e) identify what the results imply for violence prevention.

Potential Explanations for a Relationship Between Homeownership and Violence Against Women

Control Variables

There are several variables that should be controlled in an analysis of violence against women in rental versus owner-occupied housing. First, Rohe, Zandt, and McCarthy (2001) state, "given that owner-occupied homes, when compared to rental properties, tend to be larger, detached units in better repair, it is not surprising to find positive associations between homeownership and health" (p. 9). Having more space, privacy, and better living conditions is presumably good for one's health. It is also possible that the type of dwelling impacts violence. For example, couples living in an apartment are likely to have less living space than those living in a house. This could impact violence because having less space may make it more difficult to diffuse conflict by retreating into one's "own space," such as a den, sewing room, or games room. Since renters are less likely to be living in single-detached houses, this variable should be taken into account in the analysis. Second, the Aboriginal population in Canada is more likely to rent than the non-Aboriginal Canadian population (Jakubec & Engeland, 2004). It has also been demonstrated that violence against Aboriginal women is a much more common occurrence compared to non-Aboriginal women (cf. Chapter 9). Third, renters are more likely to be found in urban than rural areas (Silver & Diepen, 2004). Some research suggests that women in urban areas have a slightly greater risk of experiencing violence than do women in rural areas (Johnson, 1996; Kennedy

& Dutton, 1989; Lupri, 1990; cf. also Chapter 8). Finally, recent immigrants are more likely than the general population to live in rental housing (Jakubec & Engeland, 2004). More than three-quarters of recent immigrants to Canada are from developing countries (Statistics Canada, 2001). It is thus reasonable to expect immigrants from "developing" nations to be more likely to rent. In addition, research has suggested that immigrant women from "developing" nations may have an elevated risk for violence in Canada (cf. Chapter 10). This combination of risk factors may help to account for an elevated risk of violence against women in rental housing.

Family Life Course

There are a number of ways in which homeowners are different from renters and that could therefore account for any differences found between home-owners' and renters' relative risk for violence against women. Renters and homeowners tend to be in different stages of the family life course. Renters are more likely to be young, unmarried, and childless (Rohe et al., 2001). Given these characteristics, one would also expect couples living in rental housing to have been together for a shorter duration. Youth, cohabitation, and short relationship duration have been associated with an increased risk for violence against women (Brownridge, 2004b; cf. Chapter 4).

Domination and Control

One way in which homeownership is thought to impact psychological health is by increasing both perceived and actual control over one's life. Rohe et al. (2001) define perceived control as "an individual's belief that he or she is largely in command of important life events rather than being subject to fate or to the will of others" (p. 5). These researchers suggested that successfully purchasing a home may increase both perceived and actual control, with both perceived and actual control being interrelated. For example, because home-owners can renovate as desired, they have more actual control over their home, which may increase perceived control over life events.

It is possible that a man's perceived level of control over his life impacts the extent to which he dominates and controls his partner, in turn mediating the relationship between homeownership status and violence against women. According to feminist theory, we live in a patriarchal society characterized by the domination of men over women (O'Neil & Nadeau, 1999; Silverstein, 1999). As well, evolutionary psychology theory suggests that men view women as their sexual property, which they must control to ensure reproductive success (Wilson & Daly, 1998). Research has shown that male patriarchal domination and sexual proprietariness are linked to an elevated risk for violence against women (e.g., Brownridge, 2002; Smith, 1990b; Wilson & Daly, 1998). Of course, not all men exhibit the same levels of patriarchal domination and sexual proprietariness in their behaviour. For example,

Sev'er (2002) writes that "privileged men who occupy much higher rungs in the society may not be as prone [as men in the lower economic rungs] to committing more blatant forms of sexism, because they feel much more secure about their own positions in the system" (p. 55). Similarly, men who feel "in command" of their lives may feel less need to be in command of their partner, and hence may feel less need to behave in a patriarchal dominating and sexually proprietary manner. If men who rent feel less in command, they may be more likely to acquire their sense of command by controlling and dominating their partner, which, in turn, will increase their risk of perpetrating violence.

Socioeconomic Status

Homeowners and renters also tend to be different in terms of SES. Renters are more likely have low SES compared to homeowners (McCracken & Watson, 2004; Rohe et al., 2001). Low SES is generally found to increase the risk for violence against women (Barnett et al., 2005; Johnson, 1996). Thus, a positive relationship between renting and violence against women could simply be the result of differences in the socioeconomic characteristics of those who rent.

Subsamples and Risk Factors

Subsamples

Subsamples needed to examine male partner violence against women in rental and owner-occupied housing were available in the 1999 and 2004 surveys (see Chapter 3 for details of the surveys and methods). The subsample from the 1999 survey consisted of 7,141 heterosexual women living married or common-law at the time of the survey (1,434 in rental housing and 5,707 in a dwelling owned by the occupants) and the subsample from the 2004 survey included 6,665 heterosexual women living married or common-law at the time of the survey (1,168 in rental housing and 5,497 in owner-occupied housing).

Risk Factors

There were risk factors in the data relevant to each of the explanations identified above. The control variables were place of origin, Aboriginal status, rural/urban residence, and type of dwelling. Family life course variables were age, marital status, and duration of relationship. Indicators of male control and domination were possessive behaviour, sexual jealousy, and patriarchal dominance. Socioeconomic indicators were woman's and partner's employment, and woman's and partner's education.

Results

Descriptive Analysis

VIOLENCE BY HOMEOWNERSHIP STATUS

The results in the first two columns of Table 7.1 showed that women living in rental housing had a significantly higher prevalence of violence in both the 1-year and 5-year periods preceding the interview compared to women in owner-occupied housing. Those in rental housing tended to have about twice the likelihood as those in owner-occupied housing of reporting having experienced violence. An examination of relative risk through the calculation and comparison of zero-order odds ratios in the last two columns of Table 7.1 showed that the risk of violence for women in rental housing relative to women in owner-occupied housing remained essentially the same across the surveys in both the 1-year and 5-year time frames.

Figures 7.1 and 7.2 contain the 5-year prevalence of each component of violence for the 1999 and 2004 data sets, respectively. In the 1999 survey, women in rental housing were significantly more likely to report having experienced eight of the ten items measuring violence. Such differences were found on seven of the same forms of violence in the 2004 survey. The only difference was on the reports of being hit with something that could hurt, on which there were no significant differences between women in rental and owner-occupied housing in the 2004 survey.

RISK FACTORS BY HOMEOWNERSHIP STATUS

Table 7.2 provides the results of the cross-tabulations of the independent variables by homeownership status. The results in Table 7.2 showed that, with few exceptions, significant differences in risk markers in the expected direction were found between those in renter- and owner-occupied housing in both surveys. As shown in Table 7.2, immigrants from developing nations,

Table 7.1 Prevalence rates (%) of violence against women in rental and owner-occupied housing in the 1999 GSS and 2004 GSS, corresponding zero-order odds ratios, and significance of the change across surveys

	Rented	Owned	Odds ratio	Difference in odds
1999 GSS				
1-year prevalence	3.3	1.4***	2.471***	
5-year prevalence	6.1	3.1***	1.990***	
2004 GSS				*1999 vs. 2004*
1-year prevalence	2.7	1.0***	2.823***	−0.634
5-year prevalence	5.3	2.7***	2.045***	−0.327

Note
***$p < 0.01$ (p values refer to Chi-square tests of significance with the exception of the last column in which the t-statistic was used).

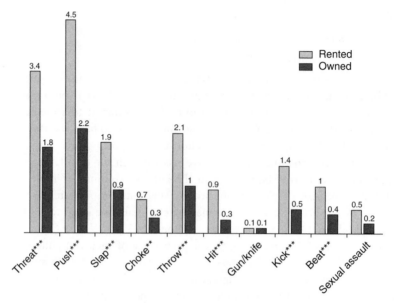

Figure 7.1 Five-year prevalence of each component of violence by homeownership status in the 1999 GSS (%).

Notes
**$p < 0.05$; ***$p < 0.01$ (p values refer to Chi-square tests of significance).

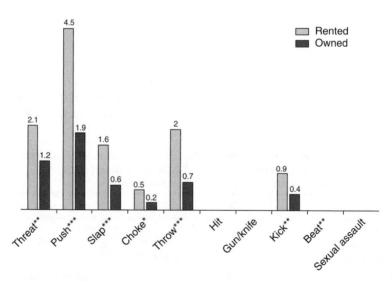

Figure 7.2 Five-year prevalence of each component of violence by homeownership status in the 2004 GSS (%).

Notes
*$p \leq 0.10$; **$p < 0.05$; ***$p < 0.01$ (p values refer to Chi-square tests of significance).
Blank categories indicate cross-tabulations that were not released by Statistics Canada to ensure respondent confidentiality. Statistical significance test is reported.

Table 7.2 Independent variables by homeownership status (%)

Independent variables	1999		2004	
	Rented	Owned	Rented	Owned
Control variables				
Place of origin				
Developed nation	16.0	84.0	14.7	85.3
Developing nation	38.3	61.7	29.9	70.1
Canadian born	18.1	81.9***	16.2	83.8***
Aboriginal status				
Aboriginal	4.6	1.3	4.7	1.8
Non-Aboriginal	95.5	98.7***	95.3	98.2***
Urban/rural residence				
Urban	85.9	73.0	84.6	76.0
Rural	14.1	27.0***	15.4	24.0***
Dwelling type				
Single-detached house	28.1	86.8	23.3	84.9
Low-rise apartment	29.2	1.5	33.1	2.2
High-rise apartment	16.3	1.4	16.5	1.2
Other	26.4	10.2***	27.1	11.8***
Family life course				
Age				
15–34	48.5	19.4	45.9	17.5
35–54	35.4	52.2	37.0	51.3
55 and over	16.1	28.4***	17.1	31.2***
Marital status				
Common-law	39.9	16.3	34.7	13.1
Married	60.1	83.7***	65.3	86.9***
Duration of relationship				
Less than 4 years	31.5	6.8	31.7	10.3
4–9 years	23.4	15.9	25.1	15.5
10 or more years	45.1	77.3***	43.2	74.2***
Male control and domination				
Possessiveness				
Yes	6.8	3.3	5.2	2.0
No	93.2	96.7***	94.8	98.0***
Jealousy				
Yes	7.8	3.7	5.4	2.2
No	92.2	96.3***	94.6	97.8***
Patriarchal domination				
Yes	1.9	0.8	1.6	0.7
No	98.1	99.2***	98.4	99.3***
Socioeconomic indicators				
Woman's employment				
Did not work in past year	29.9	29.6	32.5	25.8
Worked past year	70.1	70.4	67.5	74.2***
Partner's employment				
Did not work in past year	6.0	2.3	7.0	2.2
Worked past year	94.0	97.7***	93.0	97.8***

continued

Table 7.2 continued

Independent variables	1999		2004	
	Rented	Owned	Rented	Owned
Woman's education				
Less than high school	25.0	19.4	19.5	15.6
High school	14.6	17.6	18.7	18.0
Some post secondary	14.4	13.6	14.2	12.7
Community college	26.1	28.2	25.5	30.0
University degree	19.9	21.1***	22.1	23.7***
Partner's education				
Less than high school	27.8	22.8	24.4	21.2
High school	25.4	24.5	23.2	24.6
Some post secondary	8.6	8.1	9.2	8.6
Community college	18.5	20.9	19.0	21.2
University degree	19.7	23.8***	24.1	24.3

Note
***$p < 0.01$ (p values refer to Chi-square tests of significance).

Aboriginals, and urban dwellers were particularly likely to be renting in both surveys. It is noteworthy, however, that the proportion of immigrants from developing countries who were renting declined from 38.3% in 1999 to 29.9% in 2004. In both surveys the overwhelming majority of homeowners lived in single-detached homes, while renters were more evenly distributed among different types of dwellings. Renters were also more likely to be young, to be living common-law, and to have been in their relationship for a shorter duration in both the 1999 and 2004 surveys. Renters were about twice as likely to report that their partners engaged in controlling and dominating behaviours in both surveys. In the 2004 survey, women in rental housing were significantly more likely to be unemployed than women who lived in owner-occupied housing. Partners of women in rental housing were more likely to be unemployed in both surveys. Women in rental housing tended to have lower levels of education than their homeowning counterparts. This was also the case for their partners in the 1999 survey, but not in the 2004 survey.

Multivariate Analysis

SEQUENTIAL LOGISTIC REGRESSIONS FOR RENTAL AND OWNER-OCCUPIED HOUSEHOLDS COMBINED

Table 7.3 provides the results of the sequential logistic regressions. The first model in Table 7.3 contains the odds ratios for the homeownership status variable without any controls (also shown in Table 7.1). Recall that the results of the *t*-tests in Table 7.1 showed that these odds ratios were not significantly different from one another. The second model in Table 7.3 includes the variables labelled as controls. When these variables were entered into the model,

Table 7.3 Results of sequential logistic regressions for rental and owner-occupied households combined in 1999 and 2004

Covariates	Model 1 Ownership status Odds ratio	Model 2 Control variables Odds ratio	Model 3 Family life course Odds ratio	Model 4 Male control and domination Odds ratio	Model 5 Socioeconomic indicators Odds ratio	Model 6 Full model Odds ratio
1999 GSS	n = 7,006	n = 6,960	n = 6,865	n = 6,992	n = 6,678	n = 6,592
Homeownership status						
Rented	1.990***	1.726***	1.383**	1.580***	2.018***	1.121
Owned	1.000	1.000	1.000	1.000	1.000	1.000
Control variables		Block				Block
Family life course			Block			Block
Male control and domination				Block		Block
Socioeconomic indicators					Block	Block
Constant	0.032***	0.028***	0.131***	0.022***	0.039***	0.067***
−2 Log likelihood	2,186	2,138	2,090	1,888	2,097	1,734
χ^2	23***	59***	93***	319***	43***	383***
2004 GSS	n = 6,578	n = 6,498	n = 6,530	n = 6,563	n = 6,422	n = 6,309
Homeownership status						
Rented	2.045***	2.033***	1.643***	1.668***	1.935***	1.418
Owned	1.000	1.000	1.000	1.000	1.000	1.000
Control variables		Block				Block
Family life course			Block			Block
Male control and domination				Block		Block
Socioeconomic indicators					Block	Block
Constant	0.028***	0.026***	0.061***	0.022***	0.014***	0.014
−2 Log likelihood	1,823	1,767	1,785	1,668	1,710	1,490
χ^2	19***	50***	48***	173***	32***	226***

Note
**$p < 0.05$; ***$p < 0.01$.

the odds of violence for women in rental housing relative to those in owner-occupied housing were reduced by 26% in the 1999 survey and by 1% in the 2004 survey. However, the difference in odds remained statistically significant. The third model controlled for the family life course variables. When these variables were controlled the relative difference in odds of violence between the two homeownership status groups were reduced by 61% in the 1999 survey and by 40% in the 2004 survey. As will be shown, in both surveys this was the largest reduction in odds for any of the models based on a single explanation. However, although the statistical significance of the relationship was reduced, women living in rental housing still had significantly elevated odds of violence independent of family life course. The fourth model controlled for the indicators of male control and domination. Although not as great a reduction in odds as the family life course variables, when these variables were controlled there was a 41% reduction in odds in the 1999 survey and a 38% reduction in odds in the 2004 survey. When the socioeconomic indicators were entered in the fifth model, these variables did not reduce the odds of violence in the 1999 survey and they contributed to only an 11% reduction in odds in the 2004 survey. The final model in Table 7.3 simultaneously controlled for all of the variables. When all of the variables were entered simultaneously the odds were reduced by 87% in the 1999 survey and by 63% in the 2004 survey. In both surveys, simultaneously controlling for all of the risk markers in the study removed the significance of the difference in odds of violence between women in rental and owner-occupied housing.

SEPARATE LOGISTIC REGRESSIONS FOR RENTAL AND OWNER-OCCUPIED HOUSEHOLDS

Given that variables derived from a combination of explanations were required to account for the higher odds of violence against women living in rental housing, the final phase of the analysis was to run separate logistic regressions for women in rental and owner-occupied housing in each survey to see how the variables operate within each group. Table 7.4 provides the results of these logistic regressions. The results in Table 7.4 show that, controlling for all other variables in the models, none of the control variables significantly increase the odds of violence against women living in rental housing. In fact, in the 2004 survey immigrant women from developing nations who were living in rental housing had significantly lower odds of violence than Canadian-born women living in rental housing (as did their counterparts in owner-occupied housing). Although in the sequential regression analysis these variables accounted for a 26% reduction in odds of violence in the 1999 survey, when all other variables were controlled it was apparent that these variables lost their importance for understanding the higher odds of violence against women living in rental housing. Of course, this result was not surprising in the 2004 survey since the control variables were responsible for virtually no reduction in the elevated odds of violence against women in rental housing in that survey.

With respect to indicators from the family life course explanation, neither age nor marital status were significant predictors of violence against women living in rental housing in either of the surveys. Duration of relationship, on the other hand, had a significant impact on the odds of violence for women in rental housing in the 1999 survey. For each additional year a woman in rental housing had been living with her partner, her odds of violence were reduced by 4% in the 1999 survey. Union duration did not have a significant impact on the odds of violence for women living in owner-occupied housing in either the 1999 or the 2004 survey. Although the impact of union duration on the odds of violence in rental housing did not reach significance in the 2004 survey and the *t*-test showed that this odds ratio was not statistically different from the corresponding odds ratio for women in rental housing, from a substantive perspective, each additional year a couple living in rental housing had been together was associated with a 3% reduction in their odds of violence. Hence, it seems likely that the union duration variable was responsible for the 61% and 40% reductions in rental women's odds of violence that were observed in the sequential logistic regressions. Also, these findings likely accounted for the fact that the reduction in odds in the sequential logistic regressions was 21% less in the 2004 compared to the 1999 survey.

In terms of the indicators of male control and domination, there was a generally strong positive impact of these variables on the odds of violence against both groups of women. The only exception was for women in rental housing who had a partner that insisted on knowing her whereabouts in the 2004 survey, which was not associated with an increased risk of violence for these women. As shown in the sequential logistic regressions, these variables accounted for about a 40% reduction in the elevated odds of violence against women in rental housing. Given the generally similar impact of these variables for both groups of women, the 40% reduction in odds likely stems from the fact that, as shown in the descriptive analysis (see Table 7.2), women in rental housing were about twice as likely as those in owner-occupied housing to have partners that exhibited these indicators of control and domination.

Not surprisingly, based on the sequential logistic regression analysis in which there was no reduction in odds in the 1999 survey and only an 11% reduction in odds in the 2004 survey, the socioeconomic indicators did not have a significant impact on the odds of violence against women living in rental housing.

Post-Violence Experiences for Victims in Rental Relative to Owner-Occupied Housing

Table 7.5 contains the zero-order odds ratios for the consequences of violence among victims in rental and owner-occupied housing in both surveys. The

Table 7.4 Results of logistic regressions on the 5-year prevalence of violence in the 1999 and 2004 GSS for rental and owner-occupied households

Covariates	1999			2004		
	Rented n = 1,278	Owned n = 5,287		Rented n = 1,035	Owned n = 5,274	
	OR	OR	t	OR	OR	t
Control variables						
Place of origin						
Developed nation	0.416	1.017	−1.84**	0.874	1.318	−0.89
Developing nation	0.524	1.997**	−3.58***	0.333*	0.245**	0.55
Canadian born	1.000	1.000		1.000	1.000	
Aboriginal status						
Aboriginal	0.961	4.031***	−2.93***	1.398	3.659***	−1.88**
Non-Aboriginal	1.000	1.000		1.000	1.000	
Urban/rural residence						
Urban	0.691	1.492*	−2.70***	1.779	0.942	1.75**
Rural	1.000	1.000		1.000	1.000	
Dwelling type						
Low-rise apartment	1.080	0.510	1.16	0.842	2.699**	−2.67***
High-rise apartment	0.855	0.000	0.01	0.393	1.718	−2.13**
Other	0.631	1.586**	−3.08***	1.156	0.640	1.57*
Single-detached house	1.000	1.000		1.000	1.000	
Family life course						
Age	0.995	0.967**	1.86**	1.011	0.974*	2.16**
Marital status						
Common-law	0.924	1.575*	−1.96**	1.049	0.452**	2.54***
Married	1.000	1.000		1.000	1.000	
Duration of relationship	0.956**	0.990	−2.00**	0.967	0.987	−1.11

Male control and domination						
Possessiveness						
Yes	3.859***	4.516***	−0.49	0.892	7.293***	−4.60***
No	1.000	1.000		1.000	1.000	
Jealousy						
Yes	3.523***	5.707***	−1.56*	9.677***	4.848***	1.72**
No	1.000	1.000		1.000	1.000	
Patriarchal domination						
Yes	8.172***	7.387***	0.21	11.658***	6.694***	0.87
No	1.000	1.000		1.000	1.000	
Socioeconomic indicators						
Woman's employment						
Did not work in past year	1.358	0.885	1.63*	1.153	1.179	−0.07
Worked past year	1.000	1.000		1.000	1.000	
Partner's employment						
Did not work in past year	1.470	0.121**	3.10***	1.030	4.596***	−2.21**
Worked past year	1.000	1.000		1.000	1.000	
Woman's education	1.014	1.068	−0.86	1.104	1.142**	−0.48
Partner's education	0.932	0.959	−0.57	0.973	0.975	−0.06
Constant	0.254	0.048***		0.009***	0.019***	
−2 Log likelihood	495	1,193		354	1,092	
χ^2	114***	299***		68***	176***	

Note
*$p \leq 0.10$; **$p < 0.05$; ***$p < 0.01$.

Table 7.5 Zero-order odds ratios for consequences of violence reported by victims living in rental and owner-occupied housing in the 1999 and 2004 GSS

Dependent variable	Rented/owned[a]			
	1999		2004	
	OR	n	OR	n
Physical injury	1.382	263	0.840	211
Psychopathology[b]	2.422**	255	1.519	203
Altered psyche[c]	1.370	255	0.580	203
Anger	0.784	255	1.141	203
Time off everyday activities	2.486***	262	1.959	211
Stay in bed all/most of day	3.414***	263	†	
Children witnessed violence	0.875	212	2.682**	149

Notes
**$p < 0.05$; ***$p < 0.01$.
a Owned is the reference category with an odds of 1.000.
b Includes depression or anxiety attacks, fear, afraid for children, more cautious or aware, sleep problems, shock or disbelief, hurt or disappointment, and upset, confused, or frustrated.
c Includes ashamed or guilty, lowered self-esteem, problems relating to men, and increased self-reliance.
† Statistics Canada would not release the result to ensure respondent confidentiality. Statistical significance test was not released.

results in Table 7.5 showed that victims living in rental housing tended to have higher odds of reporting psychopathology and to have to take time off from everyday activities as a result of the violence.

The results of the victims' reports of help-seeking behaviour in the 1999 and 2004 surveys are presented in Table 7.6. The only pattern that emerged across the surveys with respect to help-seeking was an overall tendency for victims in rental housing to have lower odds of contacting a service compared to women living in owner-occupied housing.

Table 7.7 contains the zero-order odds ratios for women in rental and owner-occupied housing on the police intervention variables. In terms of police response, there was a slight tendency for victims living in rental housing to have higher odds of reporting that the police took their spouse or partner away from the scene. Among those who did not contact the police, victims living in rental housing tended to be less likely than those in owner-occupied housing to report having not contacted the police because it was a personal matter or because of a feeling that the police could not do anything about the violence. However, victims living in rental housing had a pattern of having greater odds of not contacting the police because they did not want anyone to find out about the violence and for some other unspecified reason(s).

Table 7.6 Zero-order odds ratios for victims' help-seeking behaviours in rental and owner-occupied housing in the 1999 and 2004 GSS

Dependent variable	Rented/owned[a]			
	1999		2004	
	OR	n	OR	n
Visit doctor/nurse/hospital for				
Treatment	0.639	73	†	
Confided in someone:	1.093	260	0.961	210
Family	1.095	260	1.127	209
Friend/neighbour	1.328	259	0.775	210
Co-worker	0.781	258	2.523**	210
Doctor/nurse	0.829	258	0.720	210
Lawyer	0.557	259	†	
Minister/priest/clergy/spiritual adviser	0.392	258	0.688	209
Services contacted:	0.615*	261	0.763	210
Crisis centre/line	0.500	261	1.366	209
Another counsellor/psychologist	0.555*	261	0.879	210
Community/family centre	0.985	261	2.795*	210
Shelter/transition house	0.698	261	†	
Women's centre	1.017	261	†	
Police/court-based victim service	0.606	261	†	
Interested in mediation/conciliation	1.031	253	2.468**	197

Notes
*$p \leq 0.10$; **$p < 0.05$.
a Owned is the reference category with an odds of 1.000.
† Statistics Canada would not release the result to ensure respondent confidentiality. Statistical significance test was not released.

Discussion

The Elevated Risk of Violence Against Women in Rental Housing from 1999 to 2004

Similar to the American research of 25 years ago (Peterson, 1980), Canadian women living in rental housing were more likely to be victims of violence at the hands of their male partners compared to their counterparts living in owner-occupied housing. An elevated risk for violence against women in rental housing appears to be an enduring and cross-cultural phenomenon. However, the research in this chapter demonstrates that the magnitude of the difference in risk is much smaller in the Canadian milieu. Peterson (1980) found women in rental housing to have nine times the risk for violence while Canadian women in rental housing had double the risk of violence compared to those who lived in an owner-occupied dwelling. Why is there such a large disparity in relative risk between the American and Canadian research? Although Canadian and American cultures are unique, including as they relate to violence (Dutton, 2006; Grandin & Lupri, 1997), there is no reason

Table 7.7 Zero-order odds ratios for police intervention reported by victims in rental and owner-occupied housing in the 1999 and 2004 GSS

Dependent variable	Rented/owned[a]			
	1999		2004	
	OR	n	OR	n
Police found out	1.082	261	2.849***	209
Police found out from respondent	0.540	68	†	
Reason police contacted:				
Stop violence/receive protection	2.806	53	†	
Arrest/punish spouse/partner	2.622	54	1.100	32
Duty to notify police	4.408**	53	0.302	32
Recommendation of someone else	1.062	54	†	
Police action:				
Visited scene	1.702	65	†	
Made report/conducted investigation	0.797	65	†	
Gave warning to spouse/partner	0.464	65	1.493	41
Took spouse/partner away	1.345	65	1.121	42
Put you in touch with community services	1.090	65	†	
Made arrest/laid charges	NA		1.034	42
None	0.334	65	†	
Respondent satisfied w/police	1.944	66	0.315	42
Post-police violence decreased/stopped	0.489	41	†	
Reasons police not contacted:				
Dealt with in another way[b]	0.563*	192	1.516	167
Did not want to get involved with police	1.183	192	0.863	167
Fear of spouse/partner	1.576	192	†	
Personal matter that did not concern police	0.719	191	0.493	167
Police couldn't do anything about it	0.797	192	0.796	167
Police wouldn't help[c]	1.260	191	†	
Police wouldn't think it was important enough	0.623	192	1.191	166
Fear of publicity/news coverage	1.519	192	1.061	165
Did not want spouse/partner arrested or jailed	0.911	192	1.351	165
Did not want anyone to find out about it (e.g., shame)	1.802*	192	1.176	166
Other reason	1.485	191	1.562	166

Notes

$*p \leq 0.10$; $**p < 0.05$; $***p < 0.01$

a Owned is the reference category with an odds of 1.000.

b Includes left him, reported to another official, private matter that took care of myself, etc.

c Includes police wouldn't think it was important enough, wouldn't believe, wouldn't want to be bothered or get involved, police would be inefficient or ineffective, police would be biased, would harass/insult respondent, offender was police officer.

† Statistics Canada would not release the result to ensure respondent confidentiality. Statistical significance test was not released.

NA Not available in the data.

to believe that renters in Canada are different from renters in the United States. Similarly, despite the fact that Peterson's data were collected more than a quarter of a century ago (the data were collected in 1977/1978), all else equal, it is difficult to speculate why renters would be so much more likely to be violent then compared to now. The most likely source of the disparity in relative risk involves methodological differences between Peterson's and the current study. Peterson's sample included 602 women who were either currently, *or formerly had been,* living with a married or common-law partner. Unlike the current study, Peterson's sample included women who were separated and divorced. Although Peterson did not report statistics by marital status, given that separated and divorced women were from divided households it is probable that these women were more likely to be renters than owners. While not discussed in this chapter, such a comparison within the 1999 GSS data revealed that separated and divorced women were more than twice as likely to rent rather than own their dwelling. Moreover, the chapter on post-separation violence in this book (cf. Chapter 5) demonstrated that the dynamics of violence by ex-partners are different, and it is well known that violence by ex-partners is particularly common and severe. Peterson's comparisons referred to "Abuse," which he operationalized with more severe forms of violence (beating, burning, choking, stabbing, or cutting). Hence, the inclusion of separated and divorced women and the focus on more severe violence could have accounted for much of the disparity in relative rates of violence across Peterson's and the current study. In any case, the fact that Canadian women living in rental housing faced double the risk for violence across both the 1999 and 2004 surveys was both a statistically and substantively significant finding that required deeper investigation.

Examining the Elevated Risk of Violence Against Women in Rental Housing

SOCIOECONOMIC INDICATORS

Peterson (1980) speculated that the association between renting and violence could be due to renters having a lower social status, which in turn could result in more stress that culminates in violence. However, Peterson's study reported only descriptive statistics and so did not delve further into understanding this association. If this relationship was due to renters having lower social status, then one would expect the socioeconomic indicators to have accounted for the relationship. The results of the analyses in this chapter showed this not to be the case, with the socioeconomic indicators accounting for no reduction in odds of violence in the 1999 data and for only an 11% reduction in the 2004 data, and these variables were insignificant for renters when controlling all other variables in the model. It must be mentioned that this chapter was limited with respect to available indicators of SES. But the lack of importance of those indicators that were available suggests that a full measure would not substantively have changed the results. Based on the findings in this chapter, there appeared to be much more going on in the relationship between homeownership and violence than socioeconomic differences. However, it must be noted that these results did not render socioeconomic variables unimportant. Violence in rental housing is associated with a number of additional problems for victims. Menard (2001) writes "battered women ... [who are renting] ... may face eviction as a result of a partner or ex-partner's property damage, his threats against a landlord or other tenants, his theft of rent money, or other abusive behaviour" (pp. 707–708). This can place victims in a disadvantaged position with respect to housing, especially if they are of low SES. Moreover, those on the lower end of the socioeconomic continuum, living in public housing, have been shown to face a number of unique difficulties in relation to partner violence (DeKeseredy & Schwartz, 2003b; Raphael, 2001).

MALE DOMINATION AND CONTROL

The results of the analyses in this chapter showed that male domination and control were important predictors of violence against women in general. However, the descriptive analyses demonstrated that partners of women in rental housing were about twice as likely to exhibit these behaviours and controlling for these variables accounted for a fairly sizeable reduction in the elevated odds of violence for women in rental housing. The review of the literature suggested that this would be the case because renting reduces men's sense of control over life events, thereby possibly increasing their need to control their partner. To disentangle this relationship further would require longitudinal data to determine if there were changes in men's sense of control associated with renting versus owning. However, even if these behaviours were impacted by renting, the results in this chapter showed that they did not account for the higher odds of violence against women in rental housing, nor did they have the largest impact on reducing the elevated odds of violence against women in rental housing.

FAMILY LIFE COURSE

The family life course variables tended to have the largest impact on reducing the difference in odds of violence against women between the groups of renters and owners. In particular, the tendency for renters to have relationships of relatively short duration appeared to impact the odds of violence against women in rental housing.

Conclusion

Given the importance of the family life course and male control and domination variables in this chapter, it is evident that simply encouraging homeownership is not a panacea for dealing with violence against women in rental housing. Rather, the significance of short relationship duration along with male control and domination suggests the policy importance of foci on equality for women and policies directed towards new unions. Eliminating patriarchal domination and male sexual proprietariness will require strengthening existing efforts towards women's equality such as educational efforts to change men's attitudes towards women in general, and violence against women in particular. Stronger supports to help couples that are establishing new relationships might include programmes that promote awareness that violence is particularly likely to occur early in relationships so that women in this situation will know that they are not alone and that there are sources of help. Indeed, the results of the analyses of victims showed that, although women in rental housing had greater odds of reporting having experienced violence, victims living in rental housing had a pattern of lower odds of contacting a service and also a pattern of not contacting the police because they did not want anyone to find out about the violence.

8

Violence Against Women in Rural and Urban Settings
Equal Risk Does Not Imply Equal Prevention

There has been a much needed increase in research on violence against women in rural areas over the past decade. Although there are some indications that rural women in Canada may be at slightly less risk for partner violence (Johnson, 1996; Kennedy & Dutton, 1989; Lupri, 1990), the general consensus in the literature is that rural- and urban-dwelling women experience violence at similar rates (Ulbrich & Stockdale, 2002; Van Hightower & Gorton, 2002; Websdale, 1998). Given approximately equal victimization rates, the focus of this burgeoning body of research has primarily been on providing a better understanding of the unique factors impacting rural women's lived experiences of violence and its aftermath. These research endeavours have provided a rich understanding of the vulnerable position in which many women living in rural areas find themselves (Biesenthal et al., 2000; DeKeseredy & Joseph, 2006; Hornosty & Doherty, 2001; Jiwani, Moore, & Kachuk, 1998; Kershner & Anderson, 2002; Logan, Stevenson, Evans, & Leukefeld, 2004; Logan, Walker, Cole, Ratliff, & Leukefeld, 2003; Martz & Saraurer, 2002; Shannon et al., 2006; Van Hightower & Gorton, 2002; Websdale, 1995, 1998). Nevertheless, these studies have been limited in their ability to generalize findings to the entire population. This chapter is intended to complement existing knowledge with analyses of data from three large-scale representative samples of Canada. Specifically, the purposes of this chapter are: (a) to identify the prevalence of violence against women in rural and urban areas of Canada in the 1993, 1999, and 2004 surveys; (b) to compare the operation of risk factors for violence against women in rural and urban settings across the three surveys; and (c) to compare rural and urban victims of partner violence in terms of the consequences of the violence they experience and their help-seeking behaviours across the three surveys.

Risk Factors for Violence Against Women in Rural Versus Urban Settings

The existing body of research has identified several risk factors for violence against women that may vary across rural and urban settings. What follows is an overview of these risk factors and how they may be related to violence against women living in rural areas.

Socioeconomic Indicators

Persons in rural areas are more likely to be unemployed and to have lower education and income levels (Hornosty & Doherty, 2001; Logan et al., 2004; Logan, Walker, & Leukefeld, 2001; Websdale, 1995). Low SES is generally associated with violence against women (Johnson, 1996). However, although it is widely acknowledged that women's economic dependence in rural areas is a deterrent to leaving an abusive partner (Jiwani et al., 1998), it is largely unknown whether these socioeconomic differences impact rural women's likelihood of violence in general. For example, it has been noted that women in rural areas are more likely to be economically dependent, which in turn may increase their likelihood of experiencing violence (Navin, Stockum, & Campbell-Ruggaard, 1993). On the other hand, Murty et al. (2003) studied 1,310 rural women in an American county and found that education was unrelated to their likelihood of experiencing violence.

Substance Abuse

Using a convenience sample of 1,001 adult female patients of 11 migrant farm worker health care clinics in nine American states, Van Hightower, Gorton, and DeMoss (2000) examined the impact of drug/alcohol abuse, age, race/ethnicity, marital status, children, pregnancy, and migrant status on violence. These researchers reported that only the partner's drug/alcohol use and migrant status significantly increased the sampled women's probability of experiencing violence. Drug/alcohol use by the partner was by far the strongest predictor, rendering women with these partners six times more likely to experience violence. While this research demonstrated that violence experienced by rural women may be strongly impacted by male substance use, it did not compare rural women with urban women to see whether there were any differences in the impact of substance use across these two groups. There are, in fact, indications that substance use may be greater in rural areas. For instance, while Logan et al. (2001) found that men arrested for domestic violence had similar alcohol consumption rates regardless of location, they reported that rural males were more likely to combine nerve pills with alcohol. Elsewhere it has been noted that substance use is, in fact, more prevalent in rural areas and this is compounded by the presence of fewer accessible treatment programmes (Fishwick, 1998).

Isolation

Physical and geographic isolation is typically described as a major characteristic distinguishing rural from urban life. Although levels of isolation in rural areas may differ depending on whether one lives on a farm or in a small town

(Hornosty & Doherty, 2001; Murty et al., 2003), women in rural areas tend to be isolated from metropolitan areas and their accompanying services (Ulbrich & Stockdale, 2002). Rural women's geographic isolation can be compounded by the fact that abusive men tend to socially isolate women from family, friends, and other networks of support (Jiwani et al., 1998; Ulbrich & Stockdale, 2002). Indeed, it has been suggested that some abusive men choose to live in a rural location to facilitate isolation that is conducive to their abusive behaviour (Murty et al., 2003; Websdale, 1998).

Patriarchy

Noting that the domination of women by men is a cross-cultural phenomenon, Websdale (1995, 1998) argued that rural areas possess a distinct articulation of patriarchy, which he called *rural patriarchy*. Rural patriarchy focuses more on the private sphere of life where women's domestic labour and reproductive capacity is exploited. Given that men's individual levels of patriarchal ideology have been connected with violent behaviour, Websdale (1995) suggested that "the possibility that patriarchal ideology may be stronger in rural areas is particularly significant" (p. 335). The Ontario Rural Woman Abuse Study conducted 60 in-depth interviews with rural women who were survivors of domestic violence (Biesenthal et al., 2000). Women typically described their abusive partners as patriarchal, traditional, or conservative. Indeed, one of the ways in which women were patriarchally dominated by their abusive partners was through the control of family finances; "not allowing the woman access to bank accounts or credit cards, often allocating her an 'allowance' to run the household" (p. 19).

Religion

Rural dwellers tend to be more religious (Fishwick, 1998), and more fundamentalist (Grama, 2000; Websdale, 1995), than urban dwellers. It has been argued that this, in turn, bolsters rural patriarchy (Websdale, 1995, 1998). When victimized women seek help, the traditional response of the clergy has included forgiving endlessly and renewing their dedication to the role of wife and mother (Fishwick, 1998). Essentially, women were told to "stay at all costs" (Websdale, 1998). In their study of 50 abused farm and rural women in New Brunswick, Hornosty and Doherty (2001) found that women's religious beliefs impeded leaving their abuser. However, it has also been noted that the religious community has become more aware of the need to be educated about family violence and the need to play a more constructive role in assisting victims (Fishwick, 1998). Given that rural women may be more likely to turn to clergy for assistance, to the extent that they are appropriately counselling women who are victims of violence, the clergy can be a very positive source of help.

Immigrant Status

As will be discussed in Chapter 10, immigrant women have been variously shown to be at an elevated risk for violence in Canada. In addition to the disadvantages faced by some immigrant women, those living in rural areas are typically faced with services that are not culturally sensitive, thereby hampering the likelihood of victimized immigrant women obtaining the assistance they need (Biesenthal et al., 2000; Grama, 2000).

Aboriginal Status

The chapter in this book on violence against Aboriginal women in Canada (Chapter 9) shows that these women have an elevated risk of violence relative to non-Aboriginal women. Moreover, depending on the coding of rural areas, Aboriginal women living in rural areas have an equal or greater risk of violence compared to their urban counterparts. Compounding their likelihood of violence, Aboriginal women in rural areas have reported concerns over access to services, not only because of distance and travel issues, but also because of mistrust of the mainstream Canadian system of services (Biesenthal et al., 2000; Jiwani et al., 1998).

Duration of Union

Rural and urban dwelling women tend to differ in the duration of their unions, with rural women remaining married longer (Fishwick, 1998). Hence, union duration should be controlled in a comparative analysis of partner violence against rural and urban women.

Summary

Based on a review of the literature, then, socioeconomic indicators, isolation, patriarchy, religion, immigrant status, Aboriginal status, and duration of union are all risk factors of violence that may be particularly relevant to understanding violence against women in rural areas. In addition to identifying the prevalence of violence against women in rural and urban areas, and examining consequences and help-seeking behaviours across three large-scale data sets, we need to examine empirically how these risk factors are linked to violence for rural compared to urban women for an improved understanding of the factors contributing to violence against women in rural areas.

Subsamples and Risk Factors

Subsamples

As identified above, the data from all three surveys were employed in this chapter (see Chapter 3 for details of the surveys and methods). Since this chapter concerns violence against women in their current relationship, the subsamples of heterosexual women living married or common-law at the time of the survey consisted of 8,418 women from the 1993 survey (2,303 rural and 6,115 urban), 7,396 women from the 1999 survey (1,948 rural and 5,448 urban), and 6,769 women from the 2004 survey (1,524 rural and 5,245 urban).

Risk Factors

Risk factors included in this chapter were: respondent's and partner's education; respondent's and partner's employment; heavy alcohol consumption; social isolation; patriarchal dominance; religiosity; immigrant status; Aboriginal status; and duration of relationship.

Results

Violence by Rural/Urban Status

Figure 8.1 contains the 1-year, 5-year and lifetime prevalence rates of violence for women living in rural and urban locations in the 1993 survey and Figures 8.2 and 8.3 contain the 1-year and 5-year prevalence rates of violence for women living in rural and urban locations in the 1999 and 2004 surveys, respectively. In the 1993 survey, women in rural areas reported slightly lower rates of violence compared to their urban counterparts in both the 1-year (2.5% vs. 3.2%; $p \leq 0.10$) and 5-year (7.1% vs. 8.3%; $p \leq 0.10$) periods preceding the interview. However, the lifetime rates of violence were virtually identical for rural and urban settings, representing about 15% of rural and urban women in the 1993 survey. There were no differences observed in rates of

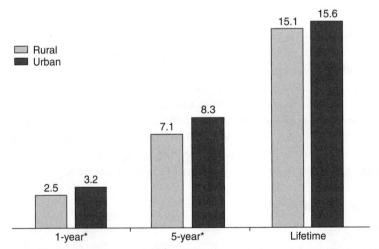

Figure 8.1 One-year, 5-year, and lifetime prevalence of violence by rural/urban location in the 1993 VAWS (%).

Note
*$p \leq 0.10$ (p values refer to Chi-square tests of significance).

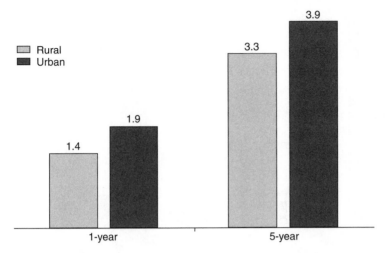

Figure 8.2 One-year and 5-year prevalence of violence by rural/urban location in the 1999 GSS (%).

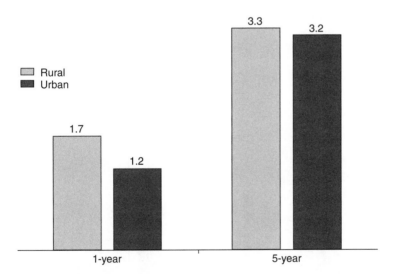

Figure 8.3 One-year and 5-year prevalence of violence by rural/urban location in the 2004 GSS (%).

violence for rural and urban women in the 1-year and 5-year periods prior to the 1999 and 2004 surveys.

Figures 8.4, 8.5, and 8.6 contain the results of each component of the 5-year prevalence of violence cross-tabulated with rural/urban status in all three surveys, respectively. The source of the significance of the difference in the

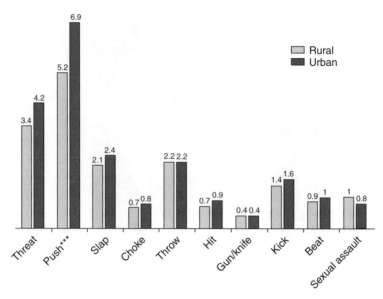

Figure 8.4 Five-year prevalence of each component of violence by rural/urban location in the 1993 VAWS (%).

Note
***$p < 0.01$ (p values refer to Chi-square tests of significance).

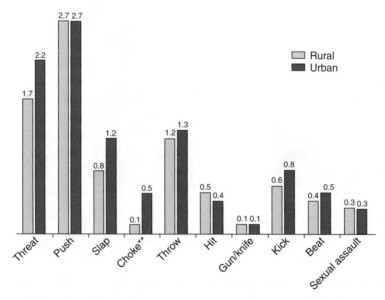

Figure 8.5 Five-year prevalence of each component of violence by rural/urban location in the 1999 GSS (%).

Note
**$p < 0.05$ (p values refer to Chi-square tests of significance).

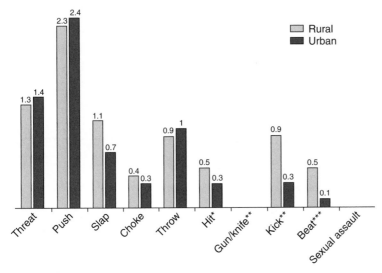

Figure 8.6 Five-year prevalence of each component of violence by rural/urban location in the 2004 GSS (%).

Notes

$*p \leq 0.10$; $**p < 0.05$; $***p < 0.01$ (p values refer to Chi-square tests of significance).

Blank categories indicate cross-tabulations that were not released by Statistics Canada to ensure respondent confidentiality. Statistical significance test is reported.

5-year rate in the 1993 survey appeared to be based on more urban women reporting having been pushed, grabbed, or shoved in a way that could hurt (6.9% vs. 5.2%; $p < 0.01$). Similarly, there was only one significant difference in the 1999 survey, with more urban than rural women reporting having been choked by their partner in the 5 years prior to the survey (0.5% vs. 0.1%; $p < 0.05$). In the 2004 survey, on the other hand, rural women were more likely to report having been hit (0.5% vs. 0.3%; $p \leq 0.10$), threatened with or had a knife or gun used on them, kicked (0.9% vs. 0.3%; $p < 0.05$), and beaten up (0.5% vs. 0.1%; $p < 0.01$).

Risk Factors by Rural/Urban Status

Table 8.1 provides the results of the cross-tabulations of the risk markers by rural/urban status in all three surveys. The results in Table 8.1 showed that rural women and their partners tended to be less educated than their urban counterparts in all three surveys. Rural women were also more likely than urban women to be unemployed in all three surveys. However, no difference in employment levels was found between rural and urban men in any of the surveys. Rural women were significantly more likely than urban women to report that their partners drank heavily one or more times in the month prior to the interview in all three surveys. There was no difference, however, in rural and urban women's reports of their partner's attempts to isolate them socially or to engage in patriarchal dominance across all three surveys. Rural

Table 8.1 Independent variables by rural/urban location in the 1993 VAWS, 1999 and 2004 GSS (%)

Independent variables	1993		1999		2004	
	Rural	Urban	Rural	Urban	Rural	Urban
Respondent's education						
Less than high school	33.6	21.4	26.6	18.5	24.1	14.0
High school	27.9	29.0	18.4	16.6	19.2	18.0
Some post secondary	11.6	14.9	13.6	13.8	12.7	13.0
Community college dip.	15.6	16.6	27.1	28.1	31.2	28.6
University degree	11.2	18.1***	14.3	23.0***	12.8	26.4***
Partner's education						
Less than high school	39.8	25.8	33.9	20.4	35.5	17.8
High school	26.4	25.5	26.3	24.1	26.6	23.8
Some post secondary	7.8	11.5	7.4	8.4	6.6	9.3
Community college dip.	13.4	15.1	18.2	21.1	19.7	21.2
University degree	12.7	22.1***	14.2	25.9***	11.6	27.9***
Respondent's employment						
Unemployed	37.8	35.2	33.5	28.4	30.7	25.9
Employed	62.2	64.8**	66.5	71.6***	69.3	74.1***
Partner's employment						
Unemployed	22.7	21.8	3.3	3.0	3.6	2.9
Employed	77.3	78.2	96.7	97.0	96.4	97.1
Heavy drinking (past month)						
None	75.2	76.7	75.5	81.2	73.1	76.5
Once	10.8	9.8	10.4	8.4	10.9	10.2
2–4 times	11.2	9.8	10.3	7.5	12.4	10.1
5 or more times	2.8	3.7**	3.6	2.9***	3.6	3.2**
Social isolation						
Yes	4.5	4.0	2.4	2.3	1.5	1.4
No	95.5	96.0	97.6	97.7	98.5	98.6

Patriarchal dominance						
Yes	7.0	6.8	1.3	1.0	0.7	0.9
No	93.0	93.2	98.7	99.0	99.3	99.1
Religiosity	NA	NA				
Never			31.5	34.1	18.6	23.3
Once per year			7.8	6.9	9.1	8.9
A few times per year			20.9	20.7	26.0	24.1
Once per month			11.8	12.5	15.9	16.4
Every week			28.0	25.8	30.5	27.3**
Immigrant status	NA	NA				
Immigrant			9.7	24.4	6.8	26.2
Canadian-born			90.3	75.6***	93.2	73.8***
Aboriginal status	NA	NA				
Aboriginal			2.9	1.7	5.4	1.4
Non-Aboriginal			97.1	98.3***	94.6	98.6***
Duration of relationship						
Less than 4 years	11.7	15.0	8.4	12.7	11.7	14.7
4–9 years	15.9	17.7	17.1	17.3	16.0	17.6
10 or more years	72.4	67.3***	74.4	69.9***	72.3	67.7***

Notes

$**p < 0.05$; $***p < 0.01$ (p values refer to Chi-square tests of significance).
NA Not available in the data.

women appeared to be slightly more likely to attend church services, though in the 1999 survey this difference was not statistically significant. Rural women were less likely than urban-dwelling women to be immigrants in both surveys in which the variable was available. On the other hand, they were significantly more likely to be Aboriginal in both surveys containing this variable. Finally, there was a tendency for rural women to have been with their partner for a longer duration relative to their urban counterparts across all three surveys.

A Brief Word on Comparability of the Data

It was noteworthy that, despite the different coding of rural/urban in the 2004 survey, the prevalence rates for rural relative to urban women were, overall, similar across the surveys. As well, there was remarkable similarity in the distribution of the risk factors by rural/urban status across the surveys. These results suggested that the data were largely comparable across the surveys.

Logistic Regression on Risk Markers for Women in Rural and Urban Settings

Table 8.2 provides the results of the logistic regressions on the 5-year prevalence of violence for rural and urban women in each survey. Controlling for all other variables in the models, rural and urban women's education levels did not impact their odds of violence in the 1993 and 1999 surveys. However, in the 2004 survey rural women with higher education levels had increased odds of violence. For each year of increase in a rural woman's education, there was a 34% increase in her odds of violence in the 2004 survey.

The impact of the partner's education was inconsistent across the surveys. In the 1993 survey, each unit of increase in the partner's education was associated with a 7% decrease in the odds of violence against both rural- and urban-dwelling women. A similar impact was observed for urbanites in the 1999 survey, but this variable did not impact rural women's odds of violence in this survey. In the 2004 survey, partner's education did not have a significant impact on the odds of violence against either group of women.

Being unemployed did not impact the odds of violence against women across the surveys, with one exception. Lack of employment decreased rural women's odds of violence by 53% in the 1999 survey. Similarly, men's unemployment did not impact the odds of violence against either group of women in the 1993 and 1999 surveys. In the 2004 survey, male unemployment increased the odds of violence against urban women by 371%.

Heavy alcohol consumption had a strong positive impact on both rural and urban women's odds of violence across all three surveys. Moreover, the t-tests in Table 8.2 showed that the odds ratios for rural compared to urban women were not significantly different in each survey. In general, it appeared that each unit of increase in a man's frequency of heavy alcohol consumption was associated with about a 10% increase in their odds of being violent.

Table 8.2 Results of logistic regressions on the 5-year prevalence of violence in the 1993 VAWS, 1999 and 2004 GSS for women living in rural and urban Canada

Covariates	1993			1999			2004		
	Rural n = 2,643 OR	Urban n = 5,215 OR	t	Rural n = 1,709 OR	Urban n = 4,549 OR	t	Rural n = 1,413 OR	Urban n = 3,770 OR	t
Respondent's education	1.016	1.006	0.24	1.076	1.001	0.99	1.336***	1.045	3.06***
Partner's education	0.932*	0.932**	0.03	1.061	0.920**	2.55***	0.941	0.961	-0.35
Respondent's employment									
Unemployed	1.028	1.109	-0.47	0.470*	1.119	-2.70***	1.384	1.267	0.26
Employed	1.000	1.000		1.000	1.000		1.000	1.000	
Partner's employment									
Unemployed	0.989	0.833	0.77	0.670	0.833	-0.26	1.817	4.708***	1.25
Employed	1.000	1.000		1.000	1.000		1.000	1.000	
Heavy drinking	1.109***	1.098***	0.53	1.092**	1.094***	-0.04	1.137**	1.102***	0.84
Social isolation									
Yes	8.395***	8.354***	0.02	9.168***	9.485***	-0.07	9.926***	3.082**	2.05**
No	1.000	1.000		1.000	1.000		1.000	1.000	
Patriarchal dominance									
Yes	1.563*	1.531**	0.10	15.838***	10.808***	0.78	9.028***	28.356***	-1.64*
No	1.000	1.000		1.000	1.000		1.000	1.000	
Religiosity	NA	NA		1.008	1.000	1.27	1.017**	1.010*	1.15
Immigrant status									
Immigrant	NA	NA		0.161	1.117	-1.86**	2.563*	0.656	3.20***
Canadian-born	NA	NA		1.000	1.000		1.000	1.000	
Aboriginal status									
Aboriginal	NA	NA		6.405***	1.153	3.52***	3.211**	5.174***	-0.95
Non-Aboriginal				1.000	1.000		1.000	1.000	
Duration of relationship	0.946***	0.945***	0.15	0.961**	0.948***	0.98	1.002	0.964***	3.21***
Constant	0.242**	0.330***		0.009***	0.193***		0.001***	0.029***	
−2 Log likelihood	1,175	2,519		365	1,332		318	819	
χ²	194***	401***		87***	224***		57***	127***	
Nagelkerke pseudo r²	0.175	0.173		0.213	0.166		0.169	0.149	

Notes: *$p \leq 0.10$; **$p < 0.05$; ***$p < 0.01$. NA Not available in the data.

Men's socially isolating and patriarchal dominating behaviour was consistently positively associated with their odds of violence for both rural and urban women in each of the surveys. According to the *t*-test, men's attempts to isolate their partners socially were associated with a greater increase in odds of violence against rural (OR = 9.926) compared to urban (OR = 3.082) women in the 2004 survey. However, patriarchal dominance was associated with a greater increase in odds of violence against urban (OR = 28.356) than rural (OR = 9.028) women in the 2004 survey.

Religiosity had no effect on women's odds of violence in the 1999 survey. However, in the 2004 survey, religiosity was positively associated with violence against both rural- and urban-dwelling women. Each unit of increase in the frequency of church attendance was associated with a 2% increase in rural women's odds of violence and a 1% increase in urban women's odds of violence. The *t*-test showed that these effects for rural and urban women in the 2004 survey were not statistically different.

In terms of immigrant status, being an immigrant was not significantly associated with either rural or urban women's odds of violence in the 1999 survey. However, the *t*-test showed that the odds ratios were different. Indeed, the odds ratio for rural women suggested that immigrant women in rural areas had 84% lower odds of violence than their Canadian-born counterparts living in rural areas in the 1999 survey. On the other hand, in the 2004 survey, rural-dwelling immigrant women had 156% greater odds of violence compared to their Canadian-born counterparts.

In the 1999 survey, Aboriginal status was not associated with a significant increase in odds of violence against women in urban areas, but was associated with a significant increase in odds of violence against Aboriginal women living in rural Canada (OR = 6.405). In the 2004 survey, on the other hand, Aboriginal status was associated with significantly increased odds of violence for both rural- (OR = 3.211) and urban- (OR = 5.174) dwelling women.

Duration of relationship was consistently associated with about a 4% to 5% decrease in odds of violence for both rural and urban women across the surveys. There was, however, one exception. In the 2004 survey there was no impact of union duration on the odds of violence against rural-dwelling women.

Finally, an examination of the Nagelkerke pseudo r^2 showed that the variables in the models tended to explain slightly more variance in violence for rural than urban women across the surveys. In the 1993 survey the variables in the models explained 18% of the variance in violence against rural women and 17% of the variance in violence against urban women. In the 1999 survey the corresponding figures were 21% for rural women and 17% for urban women. In the 2004 survey 17% of the variance was explained for rural women and 15% of the variance was explained for urban women.

Victims' Post-Violence Experiences in Rural and Urban Settings

Table 8.3 contains the zero-order odds ratios for the consequences of violence for rural compared to urban women in all three surveys. On balance, rural and urban victims tended to have similar odds of having been physically injured as a result of the violence; although, in the 2004 survey, rural victims had 39% greater odds of reporting having been physically injured compared to urban victims. As well, the 1999 data suggested that rural victims may have greater odds of staying in bed all or most of the day as a result of the violence.

There were no consistent differences across the surveys in rural relative to urban victims' odds of experiencing psychopathology, an altered psyche, anger, or taking time off from everyday activities as a result of the violence. Nor was there any pattern with respect to the odds of children witnessing violence.

The zero-order odds ratios for victims' help-seeking behaviours for each survey are presented in Table 8.4. Among victims who were physically injured, there were contradictory findings for the relative odds of visiting a health care professional for treatment. Although the 1993 data suggested that injured rural victims had 64% lower odds of visiting a health care professional, the 1999 data suggested that victims in rural areas had 183% greater odds of visiting a physician, nurse, or hospital for treatment. Rural victims did, however, tend to have lower odds of confiding in someone about the violence. This was particularly the case in the 1999 and 2004 surveys where

Table 8.3 Zero-order odds ratios for consequences of violence for victims living in rural relative to urban Canada in the 1993 VAWS, 1999 and 2004 GSS

Dependent variable	*Rural/urban status*[a]					
	1993		*1999*		*2004*	
	OR	n	OR	n	OR	n
Physical injury	0.868	619	1.027	265	1.389	218
Psychopathology[b]	0.736*	594	1.014	255	1.144	208
Altered psyche[c]	0.781	594	1.556	255	0.573	208
Anger	0.798	594	1.250	255	1.195	208
Time off everyday activities	0.730	617	1.231	263	1.031	217
Stay in bed all/most of day	NA		1.244	265	†	
Children witnessed violence	0.820	521	1.074	213	0.628	156

Notes
*$p \leq 0.10$.
a Urban is the reference category with an odds of 1.000.
b Includes depression or anxiety attacks, fear, afraid for children, more cautious or aware, sleep problems, shock or disbelief, hurt or disappointment, and upset, confused, or frustrated.
c Includes ashamed or guilty, lowered self-esteem, problems relating to men, and increased self-reliance.
† Statistics Canada would not release the result to ensure respondent confidentiality. Statistical significance test was not released.
NA Not available in the data.

Table 8.4 Zero-order odds ratios for victims' help-seeking behaviours in rural relative to urban Canada in the 1993 VAWS, 1999 and 2004 GSS

Dependent variable	Rural/urban status[a]					
	1993		1999		2004	
	OR	n	OR	n	OR	n
Visit doctor/nurse/hospital for treatment	0.361**	141	2.833*	73	†	217
Confided in someone:	0.825	615	0.651	261	0.486**	216
Family	0.639**	615	0.742	261	0.374***	217
Friend/neighbour	0.958	615	0.934	260	0.804	217
Co-worker	NA		1.018	259	0.389	217
Doctor/nurse	0.466**	615	0.906	259	0.834	217
Lawyer	NA		1.335	260	†	
Minister/priest/clergy/spiritual adviser	1.167	615	1.559	259	1.132	216
Services contacted:	0.921	618	0.786	261	1.078	217
Crisis centre/line	1.023	618	1.167	261	1.218	216
Another counsellor/psychologist	1.055	618	0.976	261	0.904	217
Community/family centre	0.426	618	0.733	261	†	
Shelter/transition house	0.995	618	1.404	261	†	
Women's centre	0.254*	618	1.031	261	†	
Police/court-based victim service	NA		1.795	261	†	
Interested in mediation/conciliation	NA		1.549	253	0.676	203

Notes
*$p \leq 0.10$; **$p < 0.05$; ***$p < 0.01$.
a Urban is the reference category with an odds of 1.000.
† Statistics Canada would not release the result to ensure respondent confidentiality. Statistical significance test was not released.
NA Not available in the data.

rural victims had 35% and 51% lower odds of confiding in someone compared to urban-dwelling victims. Consistent with this finding, rural victims showed a pattern across the surveys of having lower odds of confiding in a family member, a friend or neighbour, and/or a doctor or nurse. The only data in which confiding in a lawyer was available, the 1999 data, suggested that rural victims may be more likely to have confided in a lawyer. There was a consistent pattern for rural victims to have slightly higher odds of confiding in a minister, priest, clergyman, or spiritual adviser (1993 OR = 1.167; 1999 OR = 1.559; 2004 OR = 1.132). The results in Table 8.4 also showed that there was no consistent pattern with respect to rural relative to urban victims' odds of contacting a service or having an interest in mediation/conciliation.

Table 8.5 contains the zero-order odds ratios for the police intervention variables in each survey. The results in Table 8.5 revealed very little in the way of consistent patterns across the surveys. Regarding the police finding out about the violence, the results in Table 8.5 showed that rural victims tended to have lower odds of the police finding out about the violence. The 1999 data suggested the possibility that rural victims had higher odds of contacting the police themselves, of contacting the police to have their partner arrested or punished, and of contacting the police out of a sense of duty. These rural victims also reported 44% lower odds of the police visiting the scene. The results from the 1993 and 1999 data suggested that rural victims have higher odds of being satisfied with the police response. There were no clear patterns across the data sets with respect to reasons why victims did not contact the police.

Discussion

The Prevalence of Violence Against Women in Rural and Urban Canada

Overall, rural- and urban-dwelling Canadian women reported similar prevalence rates of violence across the three surveys, which was consistent with the body of existing literature on rural/urban rates of domestic violence. Women in rural areas were only slightly less likely to report having experienced violence in the 1993 survey. This difference was due to their lower likelihood of being pushed, grabbed, or shoved in a way that could hurt. Moreover, the lifetime prevalence rates were virtually identical for rural and urban women in the 1993 survey. There was no difference in overall prevalence in the 1999 survey, though rural-dwelling women were less likely to have been choked. There was also no overall difference in prevalence rates in the 2004 survey, though there was a pattern for rural-dwelling women to be more likely to experience some of the more severe forms of violence. Thus, violence against women appeared to be as big a problem in rural areas as it was in urban areas.

Table 8.5 Zero-order odds ratios for police intervention for victims in rural relative to urban Canada in the 1993 VAWS, 1999 and 2004 GSS

Dependent variable	Rural/urban status[a]					
	1993		1999		2004	
	OR	n	OR	n	OR	n
Police found out	0.438**	616	0.937	263	0.887	216
Police found out from respondent	NA		2.324	68	†	
Reason police contacted:						
Stop violence/receive protection	NA		0.806	53	†	
Arrest/punish spouse/partner	NA		1.597	54	†	
Duty to notify police	NA		1.983	53	†	
Recommendation of someone else	NA		1.009	54	†	
Police action:						
Visited scene	NA		0.556	65	†	
Made report/conducted investigation	NA		1.486	65	†	
Gave warning to spouse/partner	NA		1.189	65	†	
Took spouse/partner away	0.060*	64	1.305	65	†	
Put you in touch with community services	0.377	64	4.028	65	†	
Made arrest/laid charges	NA		NA		†	
None	NA		0.096	65	†	
Respondent satisfied w/police	10.708**	63	4.576	66	†	
Post-police violence decreased/stopped	1.595	63	1.644	41	†	
Reasons police not contacted:						
Dealt with in another way[b]	NA		1.026	194	0.888	168
Did not want to get involved with police	0.278**	533	1.081	193	1.751	168
Fear of spouse/partner	0.963	533	1.653	193	†	

Reason	Odds	N	Odds	N	Odds	N
Personal matter that did not concern police	NA		1.162	191	2.633	168
Police couldn't do anything about it	0.637	533	3.768***	193	0.559	168
Police wouldn't help[c]	NA		2.641*	192	†	
Police wouldn't think it was important enough	NA		1.628	192	0.702	167
Fear of publicity/news coverage	NA		1.655	192	0.680	166
Did not want spouse/partner arrested or jailed	1.027	533	1.173	192	0.811	166
Did not want anyone to find out about it (e.g., shame)	1.872*	533	1.334	192	0.716	167
Other reason	0.322	533	0.674	191	1.138	167

Notes

$*p \le 0.10$; $**p < 0.05$; $***p < 0.01$.

a Urban is the reference category with an odds of 1.000.

b Includes left him, reported to another official, private matter that took care of myself, etc.

c Includes police wouldn't think it was important enough, wouldn't believe, wouldn't want to be bothered or get involved, police would be inefficient or ineffective, police would be biased, would harass/insult respondent, offender was police officer.

† Statistics Canada would not release the result to ensure respondent confidentiality. Statistical significance test was not released.

NA Not available in the data.

Risk Factors Not Particularly Relevant to the Odds of Violence Against Women in Rural Canada

In terms of risk markers of violence, a somewhat different picture emerged when examining representative samples of Canada from what would be expected based on the extant research. Most of the risk markers examined did not elevate rural women's risk for violence. Moreover, those that did were often similarly related to violence against urban-dwelling women.

As expected, rural respondents tended to score lower on socioeconomic indicators. However, in most cases these disadvantages did not impact rural women's odds of experiencing violence. Although there were indications in the review of the literature that rural women's partners would be more likely to isolate socially and patriarchally dominate them, the results showed no differences in the likelihood of these behaviours and a tendency for these variables to have a very strong positive impact on the odds of violence for both groups of women. Rural women were somewhat more likely to attend church services frequently, but religiosity was only significantly associated with violence in the 2004 survey, and this was in the direction of increasing their odds of experiencing violence. In other words, rural and urban women who were practising their religious faith were faring no better than their non-practising counterparts with respect to their odds of violence. As expected, immigrants were less represented among the rural population. However, the impact of being a rural-dwelling immigrant on women's odds of violence was inconsistent across the surveys. Although the review of the literature identified that rural immigrant women are less likely to have culturally sensitive services, this may be less of a concern for many rural immigrant women in Canada because these women tended to come from developed nations with cultures that are more similar to the mainstream Canadian culture. Nevertheless, in the 2004 survey these women did report significantly greater odds of violence than their urban counterparts. Finally, while there was a tendency for rural women in general to have longer duration unions, longer union duration was generally associated with lower odds of violence for both groups.

Risk Factors Particularly Relevant to the Odds of Violence Against Women in Rural Canada

There were two risk factors, however, that showed differences in their impact on rural and urban women's odds of violence such that rural women were more likely to be represented on them and they were consistently linked to elevated odds of violence across the surveys. It is therefore likely that these two risk markers accounted for the finding that the variables in the logistic regression analyses explained more of the variance in violence for rural compared to urban women in the two models in which both variables were available (i.e., the 1999 and 2004 surveys). Consistent with indications from past research (Fishwick, 1998), rural males had significantly higher rates of frequent alcohol abuse. Heavy alcohol consumption had a strong positive impact on rural and urban women's odds of violence. Thus, the fact that rural men were more likely to engage in alcohol abuse, combined with indications that alcohol treatment programmes are less accessible in rural areas (Fishwick, 1998), suggests that alcohol abuse is a risk factor that warrants special attention in the prevention of violence against women in rural areas.

A second important risk factor was Aboriginal status. Aboriginal women were significantly more likely to live in a rural than urban area, and Aboriginal women living in rural areas consistently had higher odds of reporting having experienced violence than their urban-dwelling counterparts. Statistics Canada (1998, 2003) reported that about 30% of Aboriginals lived on rural reserves and about 20% lived in rural areas off reserves. However, the off-reserve Aboriginals in rural areas were reported by Statistics Canada (1998) mostly to be in isolated northern communities. Since the GSS data did not include the Yukon, North West Territories, and Nunavut, the majority of the rural Aboriginals in the studies were living on reserves. These results suggest that efforts to reduce violence against women in rural areas also require a focus on Aboriginals living on reserves. Given that Aboriginal women on reserves have concerns over distance from and travel to services, as well as mistrust of mainstream Canadian services (Biesenthal et al., 2000; Jiwani et al., 1998), the results of the analyses in this chapter identify the need for appropriate and culturally sensitive services that are readily available to Aboriginal women living on reserves. It is important to add that, while it was beyond the scope of the available data, such services also appear to be needed for Aboriginals in isolated northern communities (Shepherd, 2001).

Consequences of Violence and Experiences with Services for Rural Relative to Urban Victims

In terms of the post-violence comparisons, in the context of a tendency for rural and urban women to have similar prevalence rates of violence at all levels of severity, it was not surprising that rural victims tended not to be more likely to be physically or psychologically injured as a consequence of the violence. Among victims who were physically injured, the contradictory results for seeking medical assistance for treatment were curious. It has been noted that "as a consequence of their isolation, rural women have difficulty accessing health and social services when they experience abuse" (Ulbrich & Stockdale, 2002, p. 85). The 1993 data were consistent with this observation. Yet, in the 1999 data, injured rural women showed a tendency to be more likely to use health services. Further research is needed to bring clarity to the extent to which injured rural- and urban-dwelling victims use health services.

Overall, rural victims had a pattern of being less likely to confide in someone. This included family members, physicians or nurses, and friends or neighbours. This was consistent with past research on a sample of women with protective orders, which showed that rural victims were less likely to discuss the violence with friends (Shannon et al., 2006). The current study was, however, unique in that the victim subsample was from a larger random sample, and so included victims who did not have a protective order and, therefore, who likely experienced less severe forms of violence. Apparently, while physically injured victims in rural areas may (or may not) be more likely to visit a health professional for treatment, rural victims in general are not more likely to confide in these health professionals about the violence. The finding that rural victims consistently had slightly higher odds than their urban counterparts of confiding in a religious adviser suggests that this is an important source of help for rural victims. Although the religious community has become more aware of the need to be educated about family violence and of the need to improve the assistance provided to victims, given that religiosity had either no impact on or increased the odds of violence, efforts to enhance the response of religious institutions to rural victims of violence would appear to be potentially fruitful.

In terms of the involvement of the police, the data indicated that the police were less likely to find out about the violence experienced by women living in rural Canada. The finding that rural victims had higher odds of reporting the violence to the police themselves probably reflected the fact that rural women are more geographically isolated from others who can, for example, overhear or witness the violence taking place. Although participants in one study "suggested that [rural] women may not recognize the violence is wrong given that it is so prevalent throughout their communities" (Logan et al., 2004, p. 57), in this study, rural victims had higher odds of notifying the police out of a sense of duty and to have their partner arrested or punished. This suggests that the sampled rural victims in the 1999 survey clearly recognized the inappropriateness of their partner's violent behaviour.

Overall, the majority of victims, both rural and urban, did not contact the police. This was not surprising. For instance, in a study of 102 clients entering a New Mexico shelter that served surrounding rural communities, it was found that only about half of the victims reported the violence to the police (Krishnan, Hilbert, & VanLeeuwen, 2001). Bearing in mind that the sample was drawn from a shelter, and therefore involved cases severe enough to make the victims feel it necessary to seek shelter, this was a low rate of reporting to the police. Among those victims that did contact the police in the surveys analysed in this chapter, the data indicated that the police may have been less likely to visit the scene in rural areas. This may reflect the challenges presented by travelling to remote rural areas. However, rural victims who had contact with the police had higher odds of reporting being satisfied with the police. Although some research has shown that urban victims find the police more helpful (Shannon et al., 2006), the present study's finding was consistent with other research, which reported that some rural victims have negative experiences and others have positive experiences with the police, perhaps depending on the individual police officer (Martz & Saraurer, 2002). These results implied that rural women should be made aware that a sample of rural victims of violence who contacted the police successfully received help that they found satisfying. The results also suggest that police officers may need to receive more training to become more sensitive to issues of violence against women in rural settings.

Conclusion

Based on three nationally representative samples, we now know that rural women in Canada tend to experience violence at similar rates compared to their urban counterparts. The data suggest that heavy alcohol consumption in rural areas and Aboriginal reserves may be particular foci for the prevention of violence against women in rural areas of Canada. Improvements in and/or the development of new programmes for alcohol abuse and programmes specifically designed for dealing with violence against women on rural reserves appear warranted. Bearing in mind that caution must be exercised when extrapolating from the victim data on post-violence experiences, the data suggest that religious advisers should be aware that rural victims may be particularly likely to turn to them for help and they are, therefore, a good target to improve responses to rural victims. Rural women, as well as urban women, should be made aware that the police can provide effective assistance when a partner becomes violent. Public education campaigns that include a rural focus may be particularly helpful in this regard. Finally, better training of the police in sensitivity to issues of violence against women in rural settings may help to remove variations in the police response and to increase overall rates of victim satisfaction.

9

Violence Against Aboriginal Women
The Role of Colonization

Aboriginal peoples (variously known as Indigenous, Indian, First Nations of Canada, and American Indian/Alaska Native in the United States) comprise 3.8% of the total population of Canada and 1.5% of the total population of the United States (Statistics Canada, 2003, 2008). While representing a small proportion of the total population, Aboriginal peoples are overrepresented as victims of violence, including IPV, in both Canada (Johnson, 2006) and the United States (Rennison, 2001). In a study of Aboriginal women in Manitoba and Saskatchewan, when asked about the health of their communities the vast majority ranked family violence as their most important health concern (Centres of Excellence for Women's Health, 2002). This was despite the existence of other health concerns that are known to be particularly devastating among the Aboriginal population, including diabetes, mental health issues, substance abuse, and Fetal Alcohol Spectrum Disorder (Martens et al., 2002). Indeed, the high rate of violence against Aboriginal women has been linked to several health sequelae including mental health problems, substance abuse, and HIV-risk behaviour (Saylors & Daliparthy, 2006).

Although the problem of violence against Aboriginal women is widely recognized, until recently there was a dearth of research on the topic. It has been argued that this contributed to "epistemic violence" because, as Duran, Duran, Woodis, and Woodis (1998) have commented, "the fact that the problem is almost completely ignored by researchers and funders of research is an indictment of a social science system that chooses to further the violence by ignoring it" (p. 97). While there has been an increase in research attention to the issue in recent years, especially in the United States, there remains a relative paucity of research given the scope and importance of the problem. Moreover, much of the extant research was based on small convenience samples that were not generalizable and did not use comparison groups that would allow an assessment of the extent to which Aboriginal women's risk of violence is elevated. The existing body of research needs to be complemented with studies that use large representative samples and comparison groups to obtain more reliable estimates of the prevalence and relative risk as well as provide a better understanding of factors that place Aboriginal women at elevated risk of partner violence. It is also important to engage in such analyses across different time periods to examine whether the extent of the problem is changing, to gain a better sense of the importance of risk markers, and to derive implications for our understanding of the forces underlying Aboriginal women's elevated risk of violence. The purpose of this chapter is to begin to fill these gaps through the comparison of two large-scale representative surveys of Canada.[1]

Establishing Aboriginal Women's Risk for Partner Violence

Over the past two decades there have been an increasing number of studies providing evidence that Aboriginal women are at risk for partner violence. Although these investigations used different methods and their purposes varied, what follows will briefly describe findings that are applicable to establishing Aboriginal women's risk for partner violence in the United States and Canada.

The Risk for Partner Violence Against Aboriginal Women

Table 9.1 summarizes studies that provide prevalence rates of violence against Aboriginal women. All but the Canadian study by Ridell and Doxtator (1986) were conducted in the United States. The lifetime prevalence rates of violent victimization in Table 9.1 ranged widely, from 12.1% to 91.1%, depending on methodological factors such as the types of violence that were included and whether more than one partner was included (see notes in Table 9.1 for further elaboration). Similarly, Aboriginal women's prevalence of violent victimization in the preceding year was between 3.8% and 47.9%, with most studies reporting rates above 30%. Although methodological differences between the studies largely prohibited a comparison of the various prevalence rates, overall it was evident from past studies that Aboriginal women have typically reported alarmingly high rates of experiencing violence by intimate partners.

A BRIEF SUMMARY OF STUDIES PROVIDING PREVALENCE RATES OF VIOLENCE AGAINST ABORIGINAL WOMEN

Given the methodological differences across the studies providing prevalence rates of violence against Aboriginal women, it is important to provide a brief summary of some key points from each of these studies. Using a convenience sample of 105 Aboriginal women from London, Ontario, and 64 Aboriginal women who lived on the Oneida reserve located just outside London, Riddell and Doxtator (1986) found that 63% identified themselves as having ever been physically or emotionally hurt by a current or past partner. Hamby and Skupien (1998) examined a subsample of 117 women from a larger convenience sample of American Indian women residing on an Apache reservation and who were in a relationship at the time of the study. They reported that

Table 9.1 Rates of partner violence against Aboriginal women

Study	Lifetime (%)	Past year (%)	n	Sample selection	Measurement
Riddell & Doxtator (1986)	63.0[a]		105	convenience	1 item: ever been hurt (physical or emotional) by a current or past partner
Norton & Manson (1995)	46.0[a]		198	convenience	CTS
Hamby & Skupien (1998)	75.2[b]	47.9[b]	117	convenience	CTS2
Fairchild et al. (1998)	41.9[b]	11.4[b]	341	convenience	modified CTS
	12.1[c]	3.8[c]			
Robin et al. (1998)	91.1[d]	31.0[d]	104	convenience	modified CTS
Bohn (2002, 2003)	60.0[e]		30	convenience	punched, slapped, beaten, threatened with weapon, or other acts of physical aggression
	67.0[f]				
Malcoe et al. (2004)	58.7[g]	30.1[g]	312	convenience	modified CTS
Malcoe et al. (2005)		41.1[h]	431	convenience	modified CTS
Manson et al. (2005)	28.9[i]		1,677	random	traumatic events (items not shown)
	31.0[j]				
Yuan et al. (2006)	45.0[k]		793	random	CTS
	14.0[l]				Rape: derived from NVAWS

Notes

a Prevalence of physical or emotional violence by any intimate partner.
b Prevalence of physical violence by any partner.
c Prevalence of sexual violence by any partner.
d Prevalence of any type of intimate violence (includes verbal abuse, threats, indirect violence, physical abuse, medical attention, child involvement, and violence during pregnancy).
e Prevalence of physical violence by a current partner.
f Prevalence of physical violence by a previous partner.
g Prevalence of physical and/or sexual violence by a boyfriend or husband.
h Physical and/or sexual violence by a current partner.
i Prevalence of being physically abused/hurt by a spouse or dating partner in the "Southwest tribe."
j Prevalence of being physically abused/hurt by a spouse or dating partner in the "Northern Plains tribe."
k Prevalence of physical assault since age 18, 80% of which was perpetrated by a romantic partner.
l Prevalence of sexual assault since age 18, 46% of which was perpetrated by a romantic partner.

47.9% of the women had experienced violence in the year prior to the study and 75.2% had ever experienced violence by an intimate partner. Based on a convenience sample of 341 women more than 18 years of age who visited an Indian Health Service comprehensive health care facility, Fairchild, Fairchild, and Stoner (1998) found that 41.9% had experienced physical violence and 12.1% sexual violence by any male partner. In the previous year, 11.4% had experienced physical violence and 3.8% had experienced sexual violence. Robin, Chester, and Rasmussen (1998) studied a convenience sample of 104 men and women from a southwestern American Indian tribal reservation who were in a marital or common-law union for a year or longer. A total of 91% of the women reported being a victim of any type of intimate violence and 31% reported incidents of intimate violence within the previous 12 months.[2] Using a convenience sample of 30 Native American women who were in their third trimester of pregnancy, Bohn (2002, 2003) found that 60% had experienced physical violence by their current partner and 67% had experienced physical violence by a previous partner. Malcoe, Duran, and Montgomery (2004) surveyed 312 Native American women recruited from a tribally operated clinic serving low-income pregnant and childbearing women in southwest Oklahoma. Physical and/or sexual violence by a boyfriend or husband was reported to have been experienced by 58.7% of the women at some time in their life. Of those who had a partner in the previous year (n = 273), 30.1% had experienced physical and/or sexual violence during the year prior to the study. Malcoe, Carson, and Myers (2005) investigated 431 low-income Native American women aged 14 to 45 recruited from tribally operated nutrition clinics, tribal facilities, and a vocational school in western Oklahoma. In the year prior to the study, 41.1% of the women experienced physical and/or sexual violence from their partner. Based on a randomly selected sample of 1,677 women from two large American Indian communities, Manson et al. (2005) reported that 28.9% of the women from the Southwest tribe and 31% of the women from the Northern Plains tribe had ever been physically abused/hurt by a spouse or dating partner. Finally, Yuan, Koss, Polacca, and Goldman (2006) examined a random sample of 793 Native American women from seven tribes. Of the women, 45% reported having been physically assaulted since age 18, of which 80% was perpetrated by a romantic partner. A total of 14% were raped since the age of 18, and 46% of the lifetime sexual assault was by a romantic partner.[3]

The Elevated Risk for Partner Violence Against Aboriginal Women

Table 9.2 summarizes studies that reported prevalence rates of violent victimization for both Aboriginal women as well as for non-Aboriginal comparison groups of women. In addition to including non-Aboriginal comparison groups, these studies were all designed to be representative at either the state or national level. Half of the studies were based on Canadian data

(Brownridge, 2003; Brzozowski, 2004; Trainor & Mihorean, 2001) and half were based on American data (Bachman, 1992; Harwell, Moore, & Spence, 2003; Rennison, 2001). Two studies (Bachman, 1992; Harwell et al., 2003) found that Aboriginal and non-Aboriginal women experienced fairly similar rates of violence, though statistical significance tests were not reported. While Rennison (2001) also did not report tests of statistical significance, her results suggested that Aboriginal women had twice the rate of violent victimization compared to African American women, three times the rate compared to White women, and 12 times the rate compared to Asian women in the United States. Trainor and Mihorean (2001) found that Aboriginal women in Canada had a significantly higher rate of violent victimization compared to non-Aboriginal women, with one-quarter of Aboriginal women and 8% of non-Aboriginal women having experienced physical and/or sexual violence in the previous 5 years by any partner (statistical significance level was not reported). Examining violence by current partners, Brownridge (2003) reported that Aboriginal women had five times the rate of violent victimization in the previous year and four times the rate of violent victimization in the previous 5 years ($p < 0.01$). Similarly, though statistical significance tests were not reported, Brzozowski (2004) found that Aboriginal women in Canada had three times the prevalence rate of violent victimization compared to non-Aboriginal women.[4]

In short, there are several indications that Aboriginal women face a high likelihood of partner violence. Most of these studies, however, are methodologically weak in the sense that they are based on small convenience samples and do not include a comparison group to determine the extent to which their risk is elevated. Nevertheless, four of the six studies that included comparison groups found that Aboriginal women's risk for violence was about three times that of non-Aboriginal women.

The Link Between Violence Against Aboriginal Women and Colonization

In the literature, the high risk of violence against Aboriginal women is often attributed to colonization. Colonization theory essentially argues that the problems faced by many Aboriginal peoples have their roots in Aboriginal peoples' historical experience. For example, Duran et al. (1998) wrote that "the pain and suffering inflicted on Indian people several generations ago can contribute to the suffering that occurs today" (p. 100). This impact of colonization extends to Aboriginal peoples' present-day experiences with violence. Bopp, Bopp, and Lane (2003) stated that "there is a direct relationship between the historical experience of Aboriginal people and current patterns of violence and abuse in Aboriginal communities" (p. 11). The historical trauma exacted on Aboriginal peoples through their colonization experiences is passed from one generation to another and accumulates over time (Duran et

Table 9.2 Rates of partner violence against Aboriginal and non-Aboriginal women

Study	Aboriginal (%)	Non-Aboriginal (%)	n	Sample	Measurement
Bachman (1992)	12.2[a]	11.0[a]	2,211	representative	CTS
Rennison (2001)	2.3[b]	1.1[c] 0.8[d] 0.2[e]	574,000[k]	representative	violent crimes committed by a current or former spouse or boyfriend
Trainor & Mihorean (2001)	25.0[f]	8.0[f]	25,876[k]	representative	modified CTS
Harwell et al. (2003)	3.0[g]	2.0[h]	1,006	representative of Montana reservations	Physical: hit, slapped, kicked, forced to have sex, or otherwise hurt Emotional: frightened for safety of self, family, or friends because of anger or threats; person tried to control most or all of your daily activities
Brownridge (2003)	12.6[i] 8.1[j]	3.5[i] 1.6[j]	7,396	representative	modified CTS
Brzozowski (2004)	24.0[f]	7.0[f]	~24,000[k]	representative	modified CTS

Notes

a Prevalence of physical violence in the previous year.
b Lifetime prevalence of violent crimes by any partner (converted from rates per 1,000).
c Lifetime prevalence of violent crimes against African American women by any partner (converted from rates per 1,000).
d Lifetime prevalence of violent crimes against White women by any partner (converted from rates per 1,000).
e Lifetime prevalence of violent crimes against Asian women by any partner (converted from rates per 1,000).
f Prevalence of physical and/or sexual violence by any partner in the previous 5 years.
g Lifetime prevalence of physical violence by an intimate partner (includes boyfriends or dates).
h Overall rate for women in Montana reported in another study.
i Prevalence of physical and/or sexual violence by a current partner in the previous 5 years.
j Prevalence of physical and/or sexual violence by a current partner in the previous year.
k The size of the subsample from which the estimates were derived was not reported.

al., 1998). This has occurred within a context of continuing colonization (Razack, 1994), which, in the Canadian context, has subjected at least five generations of Aboriginal peoples to an oppressive policy of assimilation (Native Women's Association of Canada, 2003).

Did Violence Against Aboriginal Women Begin with European Contact?

Colonization theory is inherently difficult to prove. Definitive evidence of the impact of colonization on violence against Aboriginal women would be provided by research unequivocally demonstrating that violence against Aboriginal women did not exist prior to colonization. Research, however, suggests that violence against Aboriginal women did occur prior to colonization. The most compelling evidence stems from observations of early Europeans as well as original Indian legends that identified the existence of violence against Aboriginal women (LaRocque, 1994). Other evidence comes from more recent accounts.

Kahn (1980) examined violence among Aboriginals and Islanders in a small urban city in tropical Australia and found that violence against these Aboriginal women stemmed from their traditions. Among these peoples wife beating was almost universal. This was attributed to tribal traditions that viewed women as subservient and the property of their husband and which, in the case of Aboriginals, traditionally allowed them to beat or even spear to death their wives (polygyny was allowed) for being sexually unfaithful. Similarly, in a study of two Arctic communities pre- and post-hydrocarbon development, Durst (1991) concluded that "conjugal violence has been present in native communities for a long time and it was incorrect to suggest that it was a new phenomenon blamed on increased development" (pp. 359–360).

Although definitive evidence for colonization theory is not provided by the generally accepted conclusion that violence against Aboriginal women existed prior to colonization, this does not refute colonization theory. Scholars point out that in pre-colonial times Aboriginal men's and women's roles were delineated in a manner that resulted in violence against women within Aboriginal groups being a rare phenomenon (Duran et al., 1998; McEachern, Winkle, & Steiner, 1998). As givers of life and the key element of family life, women were treated with the utmost respect in North American Indigenous nations (Hukill, 2006). Historical and anthropological research suggests that family violence was not common. As Bopp et al. (2003) wrote,

> in many Aboriginal societies, an abusive man would soon be confronted by his male relatives (or the relatives of the victim) and, if the abuse continued, the abuser could face dire consequences, including banishment, castration and death. On the contrary, the women and children were almost universally honoured, loved, protected and cared for with great respect and, in some Nations, women were accorded high

rank, far-reaching social and political powers, and weighty leadership responsibilities.

(p. 11)

So, while colonization may not be to blame for the existence of violence against women in Aboriginal communities, it nevertheless may be responsible for the increased prevalence of this social problem. In the aforementioned study by Durst (1991), although violence existed prior to hydrocarbon development, it was also found that spousal violence increased in both communities after development. More generally, Hamby (2000) reported a consensus that a dramatic rise in rates of violence among Aboriginal peoples has occurred over the last 150 years.

Mechanisms Through Which Colonization may be Linked to an Increased Prevalence of Partner Violence Against Aboriginal Women

Aboriginal peoples have been affected in a number of ways post-colonization. Those that have been identified as possibly being connected to violence against Aboriginal women include the adoption of a *cosmology of antagonism*, patriarchy, psychopathology, and dependence. Although these are interrelated factors within a larger process of colonization, they are discussed separately here to identify their potential contribution to violence against Aboriginal women.

COSMOLOGY OF ANTAGONISM

Noting that most indigenous peoples have similar cosmologies about the relationship between men and women, Duran et al. (1998) used the Dine' (Navajo) cosmology to illustrate how in pre-colonial times men and women were kept in balance. With colonization, Aboriginal peoples were forced to adopt the cosmology of their colonizers; one which involves a power struggle between men and women. A historical dichotomy was thus created within the psyche of Aboriginal peoples such that

respect between the genders is forgotten and is replaced by Western ideas of power. I am an independent female who is discriminated against therefore I must create a movement against my oppressor, who is the male. On the other hand, the native Indian male simply accepts his stereotypical dominant role but has no power in the dominant or western society.

(Duran et al., 1998, pp. 107–108)

Hence, in the Western cosmology men and women have antagonistic relations with one another. This antagonism is a breeding ground for violence. Duran et al. (1998) conclude that "it is understandable that one of the symptoms suffered by our men and women is that they try to destroy each other" (p. 108).

PATRIARCHY

While related to the cosmology of antagonism, other scholars have emphasized the adoption of patriarchy with colonization. LaRocque (1994) argued that colonization had the largest impact on Aboriginal women. Although many Aboriginal cultures were matriarchal or semi-matriarchal, with colonization European patriarchy was introduced and "the matriarchal character of Aboriginal spiritual, economic, kinship, and political institutions was drastically altered" (LaRocque, 1994, p. 74). Similarly, McEachern et al. (1998) used the example of the Navajos to describe how paternalism and patriarchy were introduced. Prior to 1883, women held power with regard to marriage practices, divorce, and inheritance. Wealth was passed through the mother. In 1883, the government made laws that put the power over these elements of Navajos' culture into the hands of men. The government allotted Indian lands to men and insisted that political leaders be men. According to McEachern et al. (1998), "Navajo men learned several Anglo 'traditions' including robbing women of economic and political power and wife-beating" (pp. 36–37). Support for the role of patriarchy in violence against Aboriginal women comes from past research on Apache women showing that patriarchal domination through partners' control over finances was associated with increased physical violence and injury (Hamby, 2000; Hamby & Skupien, 1998).

There is also reason to believe that patriarchal domination may be compounded by *internalization*. LaRocque (1994) suggested that internalization plays a role in the impact of colonization on Aboriginal peoples' situation, especially that of Aboriginal women. Internalization occurs when Aboriginal people adopt the "White Ideal" and compare themselves according to White standards. This leads Aboriginal peoples, in general, to feel shame and rejection of themselves and other Aboriginal people. According to LaRocque (1994), "Aboriginal men have internalized white male devaluation of women" (p. 75) and "Aboriginal internalization of racist/macho views of Aboriginal men and women has contributed to violence generally and to sexual abuse specifically" (p. 76). Oppression within a dominant patriarchal society can result in Aboriginal men directing their frustrations towards Aboriginal women (McEachern et al., 1998). Hence, violence by Aboriginal men against their female partners may be linked to their own oppression within a European patriarchal system.

PSYCHOPATHOLOGY

According to Kahn (1982) Native Americans (Indians, Eskimos, Aleuts from Alaska, native Hawaiian Polynesians) and Australian Aborigines reacted to similar forms of social and cultural distress with similar forms of psychopathology. Although Kahn did not mention Canadian Aboriginals, it is a well-known fact that their experience has been similar. This psychopathology, according to Kahn, has manifested itself in terms of high rates of alcohol excess, depression, suicide, homicide, crime, delinquency, accidental death, and family disruptions and instability (including domestic violence). From this perspective, high rates of violence against Aboriginal women are simply another symptom of a more general psychopathology that is the result of colonization. Indeed, based on an analysis of 104 members of a Southwest American Indian tribe, Robin et al. (1998) concluded that "intimate violence appears to be another variable in an environmental context of alcoholism, other psychopathology, and overall violent deaths" (p. 342).

Kraus and Buffler (1979) have identified how the Alaskan Native experience of acculturative pressure has been qualitatively different from and of shorter duration than that experienced by other American Indians. These researchers documented the rate of violent death among Alaskan Natives as an indicator of the mental health of the population, the stresses they experienced, and the extent of their social disorganization. They reported a steadily increasing rate of violent death from 1950 to 1974, such that in the 1970 to 1974 period violent death comprised more than 40% of the total Native mortality. Hence, while the experience of acculturation of Alaskan Natives has been different from other Aboriginal peoples, Kraus and Buffler (1979) concluded that "the Alaskan rate seems to be a manifestation of a phenomenon affecting American Indians generally" (p. 139).

Although attempts to assimilate Aboriginal peoples into European culture have been strong, the assimilation of Aboriginals to Western culture has been relatively weak. Kahn (1982) argued that Europeans' view of Aboriginals as inferior resulted in a failure to accept Aboriginal peoples into the new dominant culture. According to Kahn, Aboriginal peoples

> have lived for a considerable period now in a state of social disorganization and stress not fully acceptable to, nor wanting in western society, but with their own culture and ways no longer available or viable. It is this that is the basic social matrix out of which their high rates of severe, emotional disorder has come about and been maintained.
>
> (p. 558)

Hence, from this perspective, the failure to accept fully Aboriginal peoples within the new dominant culture has sustained psychopathology within the Aboriginal community, with all ensuing consequences.

DEPENDENCY

Gagné (1998) suggested a linkage between colonization, dependency, and the social problems faced by Canadian Aboriginals. Across different Aboriginal groups, colonizers followed a similar pattern in which their first priority was to acquire territory, which they did by appropriating traditional lands, forcing Aboriginals to move to what were often the least inhabitable lands and slaughtering those who resisted (Kahn, 1982). Gagné (1998) argued that, due to the loss of families, entire bands, and many Elders who passed on oral traditions, with colonization First Nations peoples were forced to become both economically and politically dependent on external society for their survival. As part of their subordinate position of dependency, Aboriginals were subjected to assimilation attempts, essentially amounting to cultural genocide. Aboriginals were viewed as "pagans who had to be Christianized and civilized" (Kahn, 1982, p. 558), usually via attempts to force conversion to religions, customs, and values of the West. One way in which such attempts were made was through residential schools.

Aboriginal children were placed in residential schools beginning in the early 1800s (Waldram, 1997). The last residential school in Canada closed in 1996 (Blackstock, Trocmé, & Bennett, 2004). Children who attended these schools had little or no contact with their family/community, were not allowed to speak their language, and were Westernized in terms of dress, eating habits, manners, and customs. In addition to being de-culturalized, many children were physically and sexually abused. From this experience they learned an abusive style of parenting, inappropriate attitudes towards sexuality and the opposite sex, and that their language and culture were inferior. Not only did this create self-esteem problems in the children, but they also lost respect for their Elders, which inhibited the transmission of their traditional culture. The term *residential school syndrome* has been coined to refer to the constellation of consequences from the residential school experience, including "the development of self-esteem and identify problems, lack of parenting skills ... alcoholism, and sexual abuse" (Waldram, 1997, p. 182).

The trauma of the residential school experience, attended by at least four generations of Aboriginals, and of this cultural dispossession has been passed to subsequent generations of Aboriginals. The high rates of alcoholism and substance abuse among Aboriginals are at least partially explained as substitutes for grieving their loss of language and culture. This cultural bereavement is also, in turn, linked to the high prevalence of violence among Canadian Aboriginals. Gagné (1998) argued that their dependent state leaves Aboriginal peoples powerless to create change and concludes that "by returning more control to Native communities, they become free to introduce laws that may help them combat particularly harmful behaviour" (p. 368).

The Importance of Examining Risk Markers of Violence Against Aboriginal Women

Colonization theory is at the macro level of explanation. It is difficult to extrapolate from Aboriginal peoples' experience of colonization, with its attendant effects of a cosmology of antagonism, patriarchy, psychopathology, and dependency, why, as evidenced by the prevalence rates discussed above, some Aboriginal women experience violence and others do not. This begs the question of how risk factors are related to violence against Aboriginal women. Brownridge (2003) reasoned that, based on colonization theory, controlling for known risk markers of violence would not fully account for Aboriginal women's elevated odds of violence. For instance, although alcohol abuse is known to be a problem in many Aboriginal communities (Whitbeck, Chen, Hoyt, & Adams, 2004), according to colonization theory, alcohol abuse alone will not fully account for Aboriginal women's elevated risk of violence because this theory points to a complex interplay of a constellation of factors arising out of the experience of colonization. There are several known risk markers of violence against women on which Aboriginal peoples tend to be overrepresented and that therefore may be particularly relevant for understanding violence against Aboriginal women. Since these risk markers do not completely capture all elements of colonization that may be impacting violence against Aboriginal women, colonization theory would suggest that these risk markers will not fully account for the elevated risk of violence against Aboriginal women. The remainder of this part of the chapter will identify those risk markers that were available for examination in the current study of partner violence against Aboriginal women in Canada.[5]

YOUTH

The Aboriginal population is young compared to the general Canadian population (Hull, 2006; Statistics Canada, 2008). It is a well-established fact that youth is a risk marker for partner violence (Johnson, 1996).

EDUCATION

Aboriginal peoples tend to have lower educational attainment than non-Aboriginal Canadians (Brzozowski, Taylor-Butts, & Johnson, 2006). Low educational attainment has been associated with an increased risk of violence (Barnett et al., 1997).

UNEMPLOYMENT

Rates of unemployment are higher among Aboriginal than non-Aboriginal Canadians (Hull, 2006). Unemployment has been associated with an increased risk for violence (Barnett et al., 1997).

COHABITATION/COMMON-LAW UNION

Aboriginal peoples have a higher rate of cohabitation compared to non-Aboriginal Canadians (Frideres, 2001). Cohabitation has been associated with partner violence against women in Canada (Brownridge, 2004b).

PREVIOUS MARRIAGE/COMMON-LAW UNION

Given that Aboriginal peoples have higher rates of cohabitation, as well as the fact that cohabiting unions tend to be of short duration (Burch & Madan, 1986), Aboriginal peoples may be more likely to have a previous marital or common-law partner compared to non-Aboriginal Canadians. Having a previous marital/common-law union has been associated with violence by a current partner (Brownridge, 2002).

RURAL RESIDENCE

Aboriginal peoples are more likely than non-Aboriginal Canadians to live in rural areas (Hull, 2006). About 30% of Aboriginal peoples lived on reserves while about 20% lived in rural non-reserve areas in 2001 (Statistics Canada, 2003). Some factors associated with violence, such as unemployment (Frideres, 1998), are elevated on reserves, which may impact the likelihood of partner violence. Violent crimes are more likely on reserves, with rates of assault that are eight times higher, rates of sexual assault that are seven times higher, and rates of homicide that are six times higher compared to the rest of Canada (Brzozowski et al., 2006).

ALCOHOL ABUSE

With respect to alcohol abuse among Aboriginal peoples, Kahn (1982) commented on the "massive and epidemic nature of this problem for these people" (p. 554). High rates of alcohol abuse have a number of consequences, including death. A study of mortality rates on reserves in Canada between 1979 and 1983 showed that Aboriginal men on reserves were more than twice as likely to die as a result of alcoholism/cirrhosis compared to other male Canadians (Waldram, 1997). A number of sources have linked alcohol abuse with violence among Aboriginal peoples (Durst, 1991; Poelzer & Poelzer, 1986). Bachman (1992) reported that three-quarters of American Indian women from a sample of battered women's shelters were admitted following an assault prior to which the batterer had been drinking. This compared to about one-quarter of the American population.

FAMILY SIZE

The birth rate for Aboriginal women is about 1.5 times that of non-Aboriginal women (Statistics Canada, 2003). The higher fertility rate of Aboriginal peoples translates to a larger average family size compared to non-Aboriginal Canadians. The number of children in a family has been linked to an increased risk of partner violence against women in Canada (Brownridge, 2002).

Subsamples and Risk Factors

Subsamples

The data employed in this study were from the 1999 and 2004 surveys (see Chapter 3 for details of the surveys and methods). Since this chapter concerns violence against women in their current relationship, the subsamples of heterosexual women living married or common-law at the time of the survey consisted of 7,396 women (143 Aboriginal and 6,983 non-Aboriginal) from the 1993 survey and 6,615 women (154 Aboriginal and 6,461 non-Aboriginal) from the 2004 survey.

Risk Factors

Risk factors available in the data were: age, woman's education, woman's employment, partner's employment, marital status, previous marriage/common-law union, rural/urban residence, duration of relationship, patriarchal dominance, heavy alcohol consumption, and number of children.

Results

Descriptive Analysis

VIOLENCE BY ABORIGINAL/NON-ABORIGINAL STATUS

The first two columns in Table 9.3 provide 1-year and 5-year prevalence rates of partner violence for Aboriginals and non-Aboriginals in 1999 and 2004. The results showed that Aboriginal women had a significantly higher prevalence of violence than non-Aboriginal women in both 1- and 5-year time frames across both surveys. There also appeared to be an overall pattern of decline in prevalence rates between 1999 and 2004. This appeared to be more the case for Aboriginal women, with reductions in prevalence of 3.5% in the 1-year rate and 2.1% in the 5-year rate. However, an examination of relative risk through the calculation and comparison of zero-order odds ratios in the

Table 9.3 Prevalence rates (%) of violence against Aboriginal and non-Aboriginal women in the 1999 GSS and 2004 GSS, corresponding zero-order odds ratios, and significance of the change across surveys

	Aboriginal	Non-Aboriginal	Odds ratio	Difference in odds
1999 GSS				
1-year prevalence	8.1	1.6***	5.396***	
5-year prevalence	12.6	3.5***	4.059***	
2004 GSS				*1999 vs. 2004*
1-year prevalence	4.6	1.2***	4.070***	0.77
5-year prevalence	10.5	3.0***	3.860***	0.19

Note

***$p < 0.01$ (p values for prevalence rates refer to Pearson Chi-square, for odds ratios Wald Chi-square was used, and for the difference in odds the t-statistic was used).

last two columns of Table 9.3 showed that the risk of violence for Aboriginal relative to non-Aboriginal women remained essentially the same across the surveys in both the 5-year and 1-year time frames.

Figures 9.1 and 9.2 contain the 5-year prevalence of each component of violence for both data sets, respectively. Consistent with the overall prevalence rate, the prevalence rates for individual indicators of violence tended to be lower in 2004 but the rates for Aboriginals relative to non-Aboriginals were significantly different. In 1999 Aboriginal women had a significantly higher prevalence of each form of violence compared to non-Aboriginal women. The same results occurred in 2004 with the exception of the measure of sexual assault. Aboriginal women's reports of having been pushed, grabbed, or shoved in a way that could hurt were reduced from being five times (12.5% vs. 2.5%) that of non-Aboriginals in 1999 to 2.7 times (5.9% vs. 2.2%) in 2004. On the other hand, from 1999 to 2004 Aboriginal women's reports of being slapped in a way that could hurt increased from 5.2 times (5.2% vs. 1.0%) to 7.4 times (5.2% vs. 0.7%) that of non-Aboriginals. Similarly, Aboriginal women's reports of being choked and being kicked, bit, or hit with a fist increased from 7.3 (2.2% vs. 0.3%) and 6.2 times (3.7% vs. 0.6%) to 19.5 (3.9% vs. 0.2%) and 17.3 times (5.2% vs. 0.3%) that of non-Aboriginals, respectively.

RISK MARKERS BY ABORIGINAL/NON-ABORIGINAL STATUS

Table 9.4 provides the results of the cross-tabulations of independent variables by Aboriginal/non-Aboriginal status in the 1999 and 2004 surveys. With few exceptions, the results in 1999 and 2004 were consistent. Aboriginal women were more likely than non-Aboriginal women to be young, of low education, and both unemployed themselves and to have an unemployed partner. They were also more likely to be living common-law, have been in a previous marriage or common-law union, reside in a rural area, have a partner that consumed alcohol heavily, and have a large family. While there was a tendency for Aboriginal women not to have been with their partner as long as non-Aboriginal women in 1999, in 2004 this difference had strengthened with Aboriginal women having twice the likelihood as non-Aboriginal women of being in their relationship for less than 4 years. On the other hand, although partners of Aboriginal women had five times the rate of behaving in a patriarchal domineering manner through prevention of access to the family income in 1999, in 2004 there was not a significant difference between Aboriginal and non-Aboriginal women's reports of patriarchal dominance by their partners.

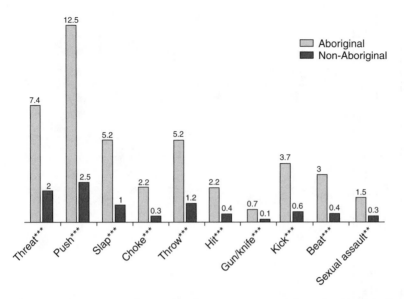

Figure 9.1 Five-year prevalence of each component of violence by Aboriginal/non-Aboriginal status in the 1999 GSS (%).

Note
**$p < 0.05$; ***$p < 0.01$ (p values refer to Chi-square tests of significance).

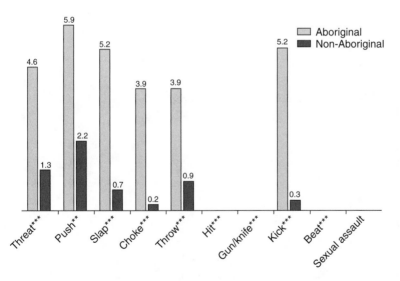

Figure 9.2 Five-year prevalence of each component of violence by Aboriginal/non-Aboriginal status in the 2004 GSS (%).

Notes
**$p < 0.05$; ***$p < 0.01$ (p values refer to Chi-square tests of significance).
Blank categories indicate cross-tabulations that were not released by Statistics Canada to ensure respondent confidentiality. Statistical significance test is reported.

Table 9.4 Independent variables by Aboriginal/non-Aboriginal status in the 1999 GSS and 2004 GSS (%)

Independent variables	1999		2004	
	Aboriginal	Non-Aboriginal	Aboriginal	Non-Aboriginal
Age				
15–24	11.3	4.1	12.3	3.5
25–29	20.6	8.8	13.6	8.1
30–34	11.3	11.9	14.9	10.6
35–39	18.4	13.9	11.7	11.8
40–44	9.9	13.4	15.6	13.5
45–54	17.7	21.6	13.6	23.6
55+	10.6	26.3***	18.2	29.0***
Woman's education				
Less than high school	35.0	20.3	26.0	16.1
High school	7.3	17.3	16.9	18.2
Some post secondary	21.9	13.6	20.8	12.8
Community college diploma/cert.	26.3	27.9	27.9	29.2
University degree	9.5	21.1***	8.4	23.7***
Woman's employment				
Did not work in past year	43.2	29.3	35.2	26.6
Worked past year	56.8	70.7***	64.8	73.4**
Partner's employment				
Did not work in past year	16.4	2.8	8.1	2.9
Worked past year	83.6	97.2***	91.9	97.1***
Marital status				
Common-law	32.9	13.3	43.2	16.3
Married	67.1	86.7***	56.8	83.7***

Previous marriage/common-law union				
Yes	36.8	20.0	41.3	21.6
No	63.2	80.0***	58.7	78.4***
Rural/urban residence				
Rural	36.4	24.2	52.3	21.9
Urban	63.6	75.8***	47.7	78.1***
Duration of relationship				
Less than 4 years	10.5	11.7	27.5	13.6
4–9 years	26.3	18.4	28.1	17.1
10 or more years	63.2	69.9*	44.4	69.3***
Patriarchal dominance				
Yes	5.1	1.0	†	†
No	94.9	99.0***		
Heavy drinking (past month)				
None	68.6	80.0	65.1	75.4
Once	12.4	8.8	13.8	10.5
2–4 times	14.9	8.1	14.5	10.8
5 or more times	4.1	3.1**	6.6	3.3**
Children <15				
None	40.4	63.4	46.8	63.6
One	19.1	15.6	21.4	16.0
Two	20.6	15.2	17.5	15.4
Three or more	19.9	5.8***	14.3	5.0***

Notes

*p ≤ 0.10; **p < 0.05; ***p < 0.01 (p values refer to Chi-square tests of significance).
† Statistics Canada would not release the cross-tabulation to ensure respondent confidentiality. Statistical significance test is reported.

Multivariate Analysis

SEPARATE LOGISTIC REGRESSIONS FOR ABORIGINALS AND NON-ABORIGINALS

Table 9.5 provides the results of the logistic regressions on the 5-year prevalence of violence for Aboriginals and non-Aboriginals in the 1999 GSS and 2004 GSS. Controlling for all other variables in the models, each year of increase in a non-Aboriginal woman's age was associated with a 4% and a 3% reduction in her odds of violence in the 1999 and 2004 surveys, respectively. For Aboriginal women each year of increase in age was associated with a 5% reduction in odds of violence in 1999, though this odds ratio was not statistically significant.[6] In 2004 age was no longer negatively associated with violence for Aboriginal women. The *t*-tests for the age variable suggested that the differences in odds ratios between Aboriginal and non-Aboriginal women were not significant in either 1999 or 2004. Each unit of increase in education was associated with a 22% increase in Aboriginal women's odds of violence and a 4% decrease in non-Aboriginal women's odds of violence in 1999. The *t*-test suggested that this difference was significant. However, in 2004 the opposite pattern was evident, with each unit of increase in education being associated with an 8% reduction in Aboriginal women's odds of violence and a 7% increase in non-Aboriginal women's odds of violence. The *t*-test indicated that this difference was not significant. Being an unemployed woman was not significantly associated with violence for either Aboriginal or non-Aboriginal women in both surveys. Having an unemployed partner was not associated with violence in 1999, but it was significantly associated with violence for both Aboriginal and non-Aboriginal women in 2004. The impact of male unemployment was larger for Aboriginal women and the *t*-test showed that the odds ratios were significantly different in 2004. Although Aboriginal women in common-law unions had significantly greater odds of violence compared to non-Aboriginal women in common-law unions in 1999, this difference was not present in 2004. Both Aboriginal and non-Aboriginal women who had been in a prior marital or common-law union had higher odds of violence than their counterparts without prior unions in 1999. However, in 2004 there did not appear to be a significant impact of this variable for either group. In 1999 Aboriginal women living in a rural area had significantly higher odds of violence than Aboriginal women living in an urban area. On the other hand, non-Aboriginal women living in a rural area had significantly lower odds of violence than non-Aboriginal women who resided in an urban area. This difference was not present in 2004. While the odds of violence on the union duration variable remained the same across the 1999 and 2004 surveys for non-Aboriginal women, for Aboriginal women the impact of union duration changed from being positive in 1999 to negative in 2004. The difference in the impact of union duration on the odds of violence for Aboriginal and non-Aboriginal women was significant in 1999 but was not significant in 2004. In both 1999 and 2004, patriarchal dominance was associated with a strong positive impact on the odds of violence for both Aboriginal and non-Aboriginal women. Similarly, heavy alcohol consumption was linked to significantly increased odds of violence for Aboriginal and non-Aboriginal women in 1999 and 2004. However, while the impact of heavy alcohol consumption remained essentially the same for non-Aboriginal women, for Aboriginal women the impact of this variable increased in 2004 such that the difference between Aboriginal and non-Aboriginal women in 2004 became significant. Although each additional occasion on which an Aboriginal woman's partner consumed alcohol heavily in the month prior to the survey in 1999 was associated with a 17% increased odds of violence, the corresponding change in odds was 28% in 2004. Finally, while family size was positively associated with the odds of violence in 1999, particularly for Aboriginal women, in 2004 this was no longer the case. It is also noteworthy that, according to the Nagelkerke pseudo r^2, in 1999 the variables in the models explained 41% of the variance in violence for Aboriginal women and 13% of the variance in violence for non-Aboriginal women. These figures decreased in 2004 to 31% for Aboriginal women and to 10% for non-Aboriginal women. Hence, in both 1999 and 2004, the variables in the models explained more of the variance for Aboriginal than non-Aboriginal women. As well, these variables explained less of the variance for both groups in 2004 than in 1999.

LOGISTIC REGRESSIONS FOR ABORIGINALS AND NON-ABORIGINALS COMBINED

Table 9.6 provides the results of the sequential logistic regressions on the 5-year prevalence of violence for both surveys. For this analysis the risk markers of violence were divided into three blocks. The first concerned social background variables and included age, education, and previous marriage or common-law union. The second involved situational characteristics of the participants' relationship. The variables in this block were woman's and partner's employment, marital status, rural/urban residence, duration of relationship, frequency of heavy alcohol consumption, and the number of children in the household. The third block consisted of the variable that measured patriarchal dominance.

The first model in Table 9.6 contains the odds of violence for Aboriginal compared to non-Aboriginal women without any controls in the 1999 GSS and 2004 GSS (also found in Table 9.3). Aboriginal women had 306% greater odds of violence compared to non-Aboriginal women in 1999 and 286% greater odds of violence in 2004. Recall that the results in Table 9.3 showed the difference between these odds ratios not to be significant. The second model in Table 9.6 controlled for social background variables. Controlling for

Table 9.5 Results of logistic regressions on the 5-year prevalence of violence in the 1999 GSS and 2004 GSS for Aboriginal and non-Aboriginal women

Covariates	1999			2004		
	Aboriginal n = 119	Non-Aboriginal n = 6,266		Aboriginal n = 164	Non-Aboriginal n = 6,132	
	OR	OR	t	OR	OR	t
Age	0.952	0.958***	−0.16	1.017	0.971**	1.24
Woman's education	1.219	0.962	1.61*	0.918	1.070*	−1.27
Woman's employment						
Unemployed	0.905	0.802	0.20	1.841	1.123	0.84
Employed	1.000	1.000		1.000	1.000	
Partner's employment						
Unemployed	1.289	1.125	0.16	20.338***	2.182**	1.68**
Employed	1.000	1.000		1.000	1.000	
Marital status						
Common-law	3.169	1.128	1.46*	0.595	0.741	−0.39
Married	1.000	1.000		1.000	1.000	
Previous marriage/common-law						
Yes	2.182	1.617**	0.45	1.313	1.324	−0.01
No	1.000	1.000		1.000	1.000	
Rural/urban residence						
Rural	4.717*	0.577***	3.62***	0.558	1.066	−1.24
Urban	1.000	1.000		1.000	1.000	
Duration of relationship	1.104	0.994	2.27**	0.935	0.987	1.19
Patriarchal dominance						
Yes	41.493**	23.850***	0.46	19.150	20.315***	−0.05
No	1.000	1.000		1.000	1.000	

Heavy drinking	1.169**	1.107***	0.10	1.279**	1.101***	2.23**
Children <15						
None	1.000	1.000	0.93	1.000	1.000	-1.82**
One	2.954	1.302	1.63*	0.342	1.184	0.46
Two	6.679*	1.722***	1.95**	0.861	0.631*	-1.21
Three or more	12.457*	1.875**		0.511	1.270	
Constant	0.001**	0.225**		0.225	0.039***	
-2 Log likelihood	61	1,716		85	1,495	
χ^2	29**	229***		28**	139***	
Nagelkerke pseudo r^2	0.408	0.134		0.313	0.096	

Note
*$p \leq 0.10$; **$p < 0.05$; ***$p < 0.01$.

Table 9.6 Results of sequential logistic regressions on the 5-year prevalence of violence in the 1999 GSS and 2004 GSS

Covariates	Model 1 Aboriginal/ Non-Aboriginal	Model 2 Social background	Model 3 Situational	Model 4 Patriarchal dominance	Model 5 Full model
	Odds ratio	Odds ratio	Odds ratio	Odds ratio	Odds ratio
1999 GSS	n = 6,993	n = 6,850	n = 6,443	n = 6,982	n = 6,385
Aboriginal/Non-Aboriginal status					
Aboriginal	4.059***	2.947***	2.733***	3.387***	2.122**
Non-Aboriginal	1.000	1.000	1.000	1.000	1.000
Social background		Block1			Block1
Situational			Block2		Block2
Patriarchal dominance				Block3	Block3
Constant	0.036***	0.290**	0.049***	0.033***	0.183**
−2 Log likelihood	2,179	2,072	1,903	2,090	1,797
χ^2	21***	108***	160***	109***	253***
2004 GSS	n = 6,529	n = 6,492	n = 6,334	n = 6,519	n = 6,296
Aboriginal/Non-Aboriginal status					
Aboriginal	3.860***	3.233***	3.000***	3.703***	3.014***
Non-Aboriginal	1.000	1.000	1.000	1.000	1.000
Social background		Block1			Block1
Situational			Block2		Block2
Patriarchal dominance				Block3	Block3
Constant	0.031***	0.044***	0.046***	0.028***	0.038***
−2 Log likelihood	1,815	1,753	1,684	1,757	1,591
χ^2	18***	57***	98***	76***	167***

Note
**$p < 0.05$; ***$p < 0.01$.

these variables reduced Aboriginal women's elevated odds of violence by 111% in 1999 and 63% in 2004. In the third model, which controlled for situational variables, Aboriginal women's elevated odds of violence were reduced by 133% in 1999 and 86% in 2004. As shown in the fourth model, controlling for patriarchal dominance reduced the elevated odds of violence for Aboriginal women by 67% in 1999 and 16% in 2004. Controlling for all of the risk markers simultaneously, as shown in Model 5, reduced the elevated odds of violence against Aboriginal women by 194% in 1999 and 85% in 2004. In none of the models were the odds of violence against Aboriginal compared to non-Aboriginal women insignificant. In both time periods, then, controlling for the risk markers of violence did not fully account for Aboriginal women's significantly elevated odds of violence compared to non-Aboriginal women.

Post-Violence Experiences of Aboriginal Relative to Non-Aboriginal Victims

Table 9.7 contains the zero-order odds ratios for the consequences of violence for Aboriginal compared to non-Aboriginal victims in the 1999 and 2004 surveys. There was a pattern across both surveys for Aboriginal victims to have slightly greater odds of reporting a physical injury. There was also a pattern across both surveys for Aboriginal victims to report higher odds of having been angry as a consequence of the violence. The data from the 1999 survey suggested that Aboriginal victims may have also had higher odds of an altered psyche, taking time off from everyday activities, and staying in bed for all or most of the day as a consequence of the violence. The data in Table 9.7

Table 9.7 Zero-order odds ratios for consequences of violence against Aboriginal relative to non-Aboriginal victims in the 1999 and 2004 GSS

Dependent variable	Aboriginal/Non-Aboriginal status[a]			
	1999		2004	
	OR	n	OR	n
Physical injury	1.229	261	1.465	210
Psychopathology[b]	0.559	254	1.234	202
Altered psyche[c]	2.270	254	†	
Anger	3.651**	254	1.877	202
Time off everyday activities	2.674*	260	†	
Stay in bed all/most of day	3.401**	261	†	
Children witnessed violence	1.002	210	0.561	149

Notes

$*p \leq 0.10$; $**p < 0.05$.

a Non-Aboriginal is the reference category with an odds of 1.000.

b Includes depression or anxiety attacks, fear, afraid for children, more cautious or aware, sleep problems, shock or disbelief, hurt or disappointment, and upset, confused, or frustrated.

c Includes ashamed or guilty, lowered self-esteem, problems relating to men, and increased self-reliance.

† Statistics Canada would not release the result to maintain respondent confidentiality. Statistical significance test was not released.

also indicated that Aboriginal victims were no more likely than non-Aboriginal victims to perceive that their children witnessed the violence.

The zero-order odds ratios for victims' help-seeking behaviours for both surveys are presented in Table 9.8. Among victims who were physically injured, the 1999 data indicated that there was no difference in Aboriginal and non-Aboriginal victims' odds of visiting a health care professional for treatment. The results in Table 9.8 showed that Aboriginal victims had a pattern across both surveys of higher odds of confiding in someone about the violence, including a friend or neighbour. The 1999 data also suggested that Aboriginal victims may have lower odds than non-Aboriginal victims of confiding in a health care professional or a religious adviser.

The results in Table 9.8 further indicated a pattern across both surveys of Aboriginal victims having had slightly higher odds of contacting a service. The 1999 data suggested that Aboriginal victims had higher odds of contacting a crisis centre/line, a counsellor, community/family centre, shelter/transition house, women's centre, and police or court-based victim service.

Table 9.8 Zero-order odds ratios for Aboriginal relative to non-Aboriginal victims' help-seeking behaviours in the 1999 and 2004 GSS

Dependent variable	Aboriginal/Non-Aboriginal status[a]			
	1999		2004	
	OR	n	OR	n
Visit doctor/nurse/hospital for treatment	1.033	73	†	
Confided in someone:	1.355	258	1.826	209
Family	2.032	258	0.945	208
Friend/neighbour	1.825	257	1.438	209
Co-worker	1.913	256	†	
Doctor/nurse	0.723	256	†	
Lawyer	1.931	257	†	
Minister/priest/clergy/ spiritual adviser	0.693	256	†	
Services contacted:	1.179	259	1.480	209
Crisis centre/line	1.576	259	†	
Another counsellor/psychologist	1.192	259	†	
Community/family centre	2.039	259	†	
Shelter/transition house	3.037*	259	†	
Women's centre	3.064*	259	†	
Police/court-based victim service	2.593	259	†	
Interested in mediation/ conciliation	1.506	252	0.856	196

Notes
*$p \leq 0.10$.
a Non-Aboriginal is the reference category with an odds of 1.000.
† Statistics Canada would not release the result to ensure respondent confidentiality. Statistical significance test was not released.

Table 9.9 contains the zero-order odds ratios for the police intervention variables for Aboriginal relative to non-Aboriginal victims in both surveys. The results in Table 9.9 showed a pattern across both surveys for Aboriginal victims to have reported higher odds of the police having found out about the violence. The 1999 data indicated that the police may have been more likely to find out about the violence from the respondent. Aboriginal victims who contacted the police had higher odds of reporting having done so to stop the violence/receive protection and to have their partner arrested or punished.

In terms of action taken by the police, the 1999 data suggested that Aboriginal victims had lower odds of the police visiting the scene and higher odds of the police taking no action. On the other hand, Aboriginal victims in the 1999 survey also reported higher odds of the police making a report/conducting an investigation, giving a warning to the partner, taking him away, and being put in touch with community services. Also, Aboriginal victims who had contact with the police had higher odds of reporting being satisfied with the police as well as reporting that the violence decreased or stopped following police intervention.

The results in Table 9.9 also showed that Aboriginal victims had higher odds of having not contacted the police because they dealt with it in another way, it was a personal matter that did not concern the police, the police could not do anything about it, fear of publicity or news coverage, and because they did not want anyone to find out about the violence. There was a pattern across both surveys of Aboriginal victims not contacting the police because they did not want to get involved with the police at similar or lower odds compared to non-Aboriginal victims. As well, Aboriginal victims had lower odds of not contacting the police out of concern that the police would not help.

Discussion

Aboriginal Women's Elevated Risk for Violent Victimization in the 1999 and 2004 Surveys

The review of the literature on prevalence rates of violence against Aboriginal women showed that these women tend to be at high risk for IPV. Moreover, the majority of studies that compared Aboriginal women's risk to that of non-Aboriginal women found that Aboriginal women have about three times the risk for partner violence compared to non-Aboriginal women. The data analysed in this chapter showed that, while the prevalence of violence against Aboriginal women in Canada declined, Aboriginal women's elevated risk for violence remained fairly stable across the 1999 and 2004 surveys. Across both surveys Aboriginal women had about four times the odds of violence compared to non-Aboriginal women. Although in the 2004 survey Aboriginal women no longer were significantly more likely to report having experienced

Table 9.9 Zero-order odds ratios for police intervention for Aboriginal relative to non-Aboriginal victims in the 1999 and 2004 GSS

Dependent variable	Aboriginal/Non-Aboriginal status[a]			
	1999		2004	
	OR	n	OR	n
Police found out	2.013	259	1.615	208
Police found out from respondent	1.564	68	†	
Reason police contacted:				
Stop violence/receive protection	1,245.668	53	†	
Arrest/punish spouse/partner	1.224	54	†	
Duty to notify police	0.915	53	†	
Recommendation of someone else	0.495	54	†	
Police action:				
Visited scene	0.422	65	†	
Made report/conducted investigation	7.261*	65	†	
Gave warning to spouse/partner	1.268	65	†	
Took spouse/partner away	1.620	65	†	
Put you in touch with community services	31.861***	65	†	
Made arrest/laid charges	NA		†	
None	2.242	65	†	
Respondent satisfied w/police	4.252	66	†	
Post-police violence decreased/stopped	2.711	41	†	
Reasons police not contacted:				
Dealt with in another way[b]	2.155	190	†	
Did not want to get involved with police	0.997	190	0.916	166

Fear of spouse/partner	0.611	190	†	
Personal matter that did not concern police	6.141	189	†	
Police couldn't do anything about it	1.746	190	†	
Police wouldn't help[c]	0.003	189	†	
Police wouldn't think it was important enough	1.625	190	0.254*	165
Fear of publicity/news coverage	4.752	190	†	
Did not want spouse/partner arrested or jailed	0.886	190	†	
Did not want anyone to find out about it (e.g., shame)	2.894*	190	†	
Other reason	0.003	189	†	

Notes

$*p \leq 0.10$; $***p < 0.01$.

a Non-Aboriginal is the reference category with an odds of 1.000.

b Includes left him, reported to another official, private matter that took care of myself, etc.

c Includes police wouldn't think it was important enough, wouldn't believe, wouldn't want to be bothered or get involved, police would be inefficient or ineffective, police would be biased, would harass/insult respondent, offender was police officer.

† Statistics Canada would not release the result to ensure respondent confidentiality. Statistical significance test was not released.

sexual assault in the 5 years prior to the study, a most welcome finding, they were still significantly more likely to report having experienced the remaining nine individual forms of violence over the preceding 5 years. In fact, the results suggested that Aboriginal women's relative risk of being slapped, choked and kicked, bit, or hit with a fist increased from the 1999 to the 2004 survey. It is important to note that particular caution must be exercised with respect to the results of these comparisons of individual forms of violence due to the small number of cases contributing to each estimate. Nevertheless, the overall pattern clearly suggested that the state of affairs had not improved with respect to Aboriginal women's relative risk for partner violence between the 1999 and 2004 surveys.

Key Findings on Risk Factors for Violence Against Aboriginal Women in the 1999 and 2004 Surveys

PATRIARCHAL DOMINANCE

Aboriginal women were consistently overrepresented on factors that have been associated with partner violence with one exception: patriarchal domination. In the 2004 survey Aboriginal women were no longer significantly more likely to report having a male partner who prevented them from having access to the family income even if they asked for such access. As shown in the logistic regressions in Table 9.5, patriarchal domination was one of the few risk markers whose impact was similar for both Aboriginal and non-Aboriginal women across both surveys. Hence, although patriarchal domination was linked to violence for both groups in both surveys, given that Aboriginal women's partners were no longer significantly more likely to behave in such a manner compared to non-Aboriginal women's partners in the 2004 survey, patriarchal domination was no longer a particularly important variable for understanding Aboriginal women's elevated odds of violence. Indeed, the results of the sequential logistic regressions in Table 9.6 showed that controlling for patriarchal domination accounted for only 16% of Aboriginal women's elevated odds of violence in the 2004 survey. There are a couple of possible explanations for this finding. The first, and most desirable possibility is that there was a real reduction in patriarchal domineering behaviour by partners of Aboriginal women. An alternative explanation is that this result, as well as others, could be due to random fluctuations in samples. Hamby (2000) noted that levels of factors associated with violence, including patriarchal domination, vary widely across Aboriginal groups. Given the small samples of Aboriginal women in the current study, it is possible that the 1999 data overestimated and/or that the 2004 survey underestimated Aboriginal women's partners' patriarchal domination relative to that of non-Aboriginal women's partners. It is also important to note that, while the vast majority of families in Canada are ethnically endogamous (Kalbach &

Richard, 1989), not all partners of Aboriginal women are themselves Aboriginal. For example, in two convenience samples of 431 and 312 Native American women in rural western Oklahoma, Malcoe and colleagues (2005, 2004) reported that 31.9% and 59% of the women, respectively, had non-Native partners. In the latter sample, Native American and African American partners had higher annual perpetration rates compared to White and Hispanic partners (Malcoe et al., 2004). By contrast, in a study of American Indians and crime, Greenfeld and Smith (1999) reported that 75% of intimate partner victimizations involved a non-American Indian offender. Unfortunately, it was not possible with the data analysed in this chapter to examine the ethnicity of women's partners. Future research needs to allow the identification of Aboriginal women's partners' ethnicity as well as include a larger sample of Aboriginal women to provide greater data reliability.

PARTNER'S EMPLOYMENT

Another noteworthy difference concerned the impact of male partner's unemployment on the odds of violence. Partner's unemployment did not have a significant impact on violence for either Aboriginal or non-Aboriginal women in the 1999 survey. In the 2004 survey, not only was this variable significant for both groups, but it also had a significantly larger impact on the odds of violence against Aboriginal women compared to non-Aboriginal women. It is difficult to speculate why the impact of partner's unemployment became significant and particularly strong for Aboriginal women in the 2004 survey. One possibility may stem from the fact that, as shown in Table 9.4, partners of Aboriginal women had half the rate of unemployment in 2004 than in 1999. If the employment prospects of these men improved, and this was the case for both Aboriginal and non-Aboriginal men (Statistics Canada, 2005a), it is possible that those who remained unemployed in the 2004 survey were the least employable and that they tended to share some characteristic(s) that increased their risk of perpetrating violence. For example, perhaps they experienced distress over being unable to find employment in such a favourable market. Whatever the specific mechanisms underlying this relationship, it is evident in the current study that partners' unemployment became a significant factor in predicting violence against women in the 2004 survey, especially for Aboriginal women.

RURAL/URBAN RESIDENCE

As identified in the chapter of this book on materials and methods (see Chapter 3), due to coding differences, rural/urban residence was the only variable in the study that was not directly comparable between the 1999 and 2004 surveys. Hence, when interpreting the difference between the results on the rural/urban variable in the 1999 and 2004 surveys the different coding must be taken into consideration and it is not possible to identify changes between time periods from such a comparison. For non-Aboriginal women, the proportion living in a rural area was 2.3% greater in the 1999 than the 2004 survey. This was likely because rural areas in the 2004 survey excluded areas adjacent to urban areas that had a high degree of social and economic integration with the urban cores. For Aboriginal women, the proportion living in a rural area was 15.9% greater in the 2004 than the 1999 survey. A possible explanation for this difference was that some reserves considered urban in the 1999 survey (those that had a minimum population concentration of 1,000 and a population density of at least 400 per square kilometre based on the previous census counts) were considered rural in the 2004 survey (those that had a population of 1,000 to 9,999 and a population density of 400 inhabitants per square kilometre according to the previous census). The results of the logistic regression in Table 9.5 showed that Aboriginal women in rural areas in the 1999 survey had 372% greater odds of violence compared to Aboriginal women in urban areas. In the 2004 survey, there was no significant difference between rural and urban Aboriginal women in their odds of violence. If this difference was due to different coding, then the results may suggest that smaller reserves (those with minimum population concentrations of less than 1,000 and population densities of less than 400 per square kilometre) have a higher prevalence of violence than larger reserves.[7] Future research with a larger sample of Aboriginal peoples is needed to disentangle whether differences exist in the prevalence and experience of violence in small compared to larger reserves.

HEAVY ALCOHOL CONSUMPTION

In both the 1999 and 2004 surveys Aboriginal women were significantly more likely to report that their partner abused alcohol compared to non-Aboriginal women. Although heavy drinking had a similarly strong positive impact on the odds of violence for both groups in the 1999 survey, this variable had a significantly stronger impact on the odds of violence against Aboriginal women in the 2004 survey. It is important to add, however, that controlling for alcohol abuse, along with other situational characteristics, accounted for Aboriginal women's elevated odds of violence in neither the 1999 nor the 2004 survey. Hence, while alcohol abuse is a particularly important risk marker of violence for Aboriginal women, it does not account for their elevated odds of violence. As Duran et al. (1998) have commented

> Academics and clinicians believe that alcohol may be the most significant contributing factor to domestic violence. This type of thinking is simplistic and fails to place the problem in the proper context. Alcohol may be closely related to the problems underlying domestic violence thus being more parallel than hierarchical in relationship.

(pp. 97–98)

Indeed, there appears to be a connection between colonization and alcohol abuse. Research has demonstrated that American Indians have frequent thoughts of historical losses (e.g., losing their culture) and they associate these losses with negative feelings (e.g., anger/avoidance and anxiety/depression; Whitbeck, Adams, Hoyt, & Chen, 2004). In a sample of 452 American Indian parents/caretakers of children aged 10 to 12, Whitbeck, Chen, Hoyt, and Adams (2004) found that these thoughts of historical loss were significantly positively associated with alcohol abuse. This research provided empirical support for a connection between perceptions of historical loss resulting from colonization and alcohol abuse. Thus alcohol excess can be seen as one manifestation of the psychopathology that has resulted from the social and cultural distress of Aboriginal peoples' past and continuing colonization (Kahn, 1982; Robin et al., 1998).

The Contribution of Risk Factors to Understanding Aboriginal Women's Elevated Risk of Experiencing Violence

Although there were interesting differences in the impacts of risk markers across the two surveys, in general, there were fewer differences between Aboriginal and non-Aboriginal women within the 2004 survey than within the 1999 survey. The *t*-tests in Table 9.5 showed that there were significant differences between Aboriginal and non-Aboriginal women on six of the variables in the 1999 survey and on three of the variables in the 2004 survey. This was also reflected in the proportion of the variance accounted for by each model as well as in the extent to which these risk markers accounted for Aboriginal women's elevated odds of violence. While the variables in the models accounted for a substantial proportion of the variance in violence for Aboriginal women (41% in 1999 and 31% in 2004), these variables, in general, accounted for less of the variance in 2004 than 1999 for both groups of women. The changes in the operation of several of the risk markers also had an impact on the extent to which these risk markers accounted for Aboriginal women's elevated odds of violence. That is, controlling for all of the risk markers in Table 9.6 showed that these variables accounted for less of the difference in odds in 2004 (85%) than in 1999 (194%). Although Aboriginal women may be becoming increasingly similar to non-Aboriginal women with respect to the impact of available risk markers on violence, as already discussed, their relative risk has remained essentially the same. Therefore, the 2004 results provide an even stronger suggestion than those of 1999 that these risk markers do not completely capture all elements of colonization that may be impacting violence against Aboriginal women. That is, the 2004 results provide even greater indirect support for colonization theory.

Consequences of Violence and Experiences with Services for Aboriginal
Relative to Non-Aboriginal Victims

The comparison of Aboriginal to non-Aboriginal victims in terms of consequences of violence yielded findings that were generally consistent with
Aboriginal women having higher odds of experiencing severe violence. Specifically, Aboriginal victims had greater odds of being physically injured, being
angry, having an altered psyche, taking time off from everyday activities, and
staying in bed for all or most of the day as a result of the violence. Encourag-
ingly, injured Aboriginal victims did not have lower odds of being treated by a
health care professional.

In a study of Aboriginal women in the Comox Valley of British Columbia,
it was reported that most Aboriginal women in the area relied on family and
friends for support, given their fear and distrust of the mainstream service
agencies (cited in Jiwani et al., 1998). The results of the analyses in this
chapter revealed that, while Aboriginal victims consistently had higher odds
of confiding in friends, they also consistently had higher odds of contacting a
service compared to non-Aboriginal victims. However, despite being more
likely to be injured, and being no less likely to seek medical treatment from a
health care professional, the 1999 data suggested that Aboriginal victims may
have lower odds of confiding in a physician or nurse. This was consistent with
past research, which suggested that Aboriginal women underreport their victimization to physicians (Lapham, Henley, & Kleyboecker, 1993). There are
indications, however, that American Indian victims of violence prefer to dis-
close to medical staff, as well as other service providers, if they are asked
directly about IPV (Lee, Thompson, & Mechanic, 2002). Hence, service
providers, and particularly health care professionals, should be made aware
that Aboriginal clients in particular may prefer to be asked directly about
issues of violence.

The victim data on police intervention were also consistent with a greater
average severity of violence against Aboriginal women, to the extent that the
police were more likely to be contacted about the violence. Among those who
contacted the police, Aboriginal victims had lower odds of reporting that the
police visited the scene and higher odds of reporting that they took no action.
Although the former finding may partially have reflected the fact that Aboriginal women were more likely to live in a rural area (the chapter on violence
against rural women showed that rural victims had 44% lower odds of reporting that the police visited the scene compared to urban victims), the latter
finding was perplexing. Conversely, Aboriginal victims had higher odds of
reporting that the police took a number of actions, of being satisfied with the
police, and of the violence stopping or decreasing following police intervention. Past research has also suggested that Aboriginal peoples have mixed
views of dealings with the police (Amnesty International, 2004). Overall, these

findings were encouraging in the sense that the police appeared to be a useful source of help for those victims that had contact with them.

In terms of victims who did not contact the police, Aboriginal victims had higher odds of reporting having not done so because they dealt with it in another way, it was a personal matter, the police could not help, fear of publicity, and not wanting anyone to find out. Not wanting to get involved with the police and viewing the police as being unwilling to help were not endorsed by Aboriginal victims more than by non-Aboriginal victims. Hence, it appeared that these victims were not aversive to the police per se, but preferred to deal with the violence in a different manner.

Limitations

In addition to the limitations already noted above, there were other limitations in the analyses contained in this chapter that need to be overcome in future research. First, the use of the telephone survey method automatically excluded persons without telephones. This represents about 4% of Canadian households (Johnson, 2006). However, research on Native Americans suggests that a larger proportion of those living on reservations, as many as 60%, do not have telephones (Bachman, 1992). Those living on reservations, then, were likely underrepresented in the current study. An examination of American Indians found that those without phones had lower SES and higher rates of binge and chronic drinking and marijuana use (Pearson, Cheadle, Wagner, Tonsberg, & Psaty, 1994). Hence, the prevalence of violence against Aboriginal women and the impact of these variables may have been underestimated in the current study.

A second limitation, which may also have led to the underrepresentation of Aboriginal women in the analyses contained in this chapter, concerned the language of the interviews. All of the surveys were conducted in either English or French. Those Aboriginal women who were not fluent in either of these languages could not participate. However, it is noteworthy that this is particularly problematic in the northern territories of Canada (Johnson, 2006), which were not included in the data analysed in this book.

Third, the study included only risk markers that were available in the GSS data. For example, the multigenerational experience of continuing colonization would suggest that a cycle of violence has existed in which Aboriginal children have been at elevated risk for exposure to violent models. Of course, this chapter and past research suggest that not all Aboriginal women experience partner violence and not all Aboriginal men are violent. Consistent with research on social learning theory, it is likely that not all of those who were exposed have modelled the violence (Kaufman & Zigler, 1987). Future research should examine this as well as all other potential factors that may place Aboriginal women at risk, and protect them from, partner violence.

A fourth limitation concerns the treatment of Aboriginal women as one group. As noted above, Hamby (2000) suggested that wide variation in risk factors exists across Aboriginal groups. Due to data limitations, it was not possible to compare Aboriginal groups in this chapter. Even if it were possible, the relatively small subsample of Aboriginal women would have limited the analysis. If, as the results of this chapter suggest, the elevated risk for violence against Aboriginal women is not due to any single risk marker but, rather, a constellation of factors linked to the larger experience of colonization, then a comparison across Aboriginal communities would also provide a fruitful direction for future research. That is, the extent to which a given Aboriginal community has maintained or reclaimed its culture should be inversely related to levels of violence against women within that community. A study of suicide among Aboriginal youth suggests that this is the case. Noting extensive variation in suicide rates across Aboriginal communities, Chandler, Lalonde, Sokol, and Hallett (2003) examined youth suicide rates across 196 Aboriginal communities in British Columbia. Using a measure of cultural continuity based on the extent to which each community had attempted to gain control from government supervision, these researchers found that youth suicide rates were inversely related to indicators of cultural continuity. Similarly, in the aforementioned study of alcohol abuse by Whitbeck, Chen et al. (2004), while thoughts of historical loss were a risk factor for alcohol abuse, enculturation was an equally powerful protective factor. Hence, future research should examine individual and community level continuity across cultural groups for a more complete understanding of the impact of Aboriginal peoples' experience of colonization on violence against women. A recent study of six Native American tribes also suggests that there may be nuances to understanding the relationship between cultural affiliation and violence against Aboriginal women. Yuan et al. (2006) found significant differences across tribes in rates of physical and sexual assault of women. Surprisingly, the authors found that some elements of cultural affiliation were positively associated with violence against women, though they noted that they were unable to determine whether victims increased their tribal affiliations subsequent to the violence as a coping mechanism. To be sure, future research on individual and community level continuity needs to be based on accurate measures and research designs that will maximize the ability to test the effect of these factors on violence against women.

Conclusion

Bearing these caveats in mind, the results of this chapter point to the conclusion that Aboriginal women in Canada continue to face an elevated risk of IPV. Aboriginal women also appear to be more likely to experience severe violence, and this is buttressed by several findings in the victim subsample. The results of this chapter also indirectly suggest support for the theory that much of this elevated risk may be linked to past and continuing colonization of Aboriginal peoples. The results further suggest that making the connection between the history of colonization and the impacts this experience has had on various aspects of Aboriginal peoples' lives, including violence, may be important for prevention. Future research is needed to test directly whether a link exists between colonization and Aboriginal women's elevated risk of violent victimization. Such studies should examine violence in the context of cultural continuity at the individual and community levels. Support for colonization theory would serve as a basis for change through buttressing efforts to reclaim essential cultural elements that have been diminished or lost through colonization. Of course, this does not absolve perpetrators from responsibility for violence and, in fact, in pre-colonial times perpetrators of violence were dealt with harshly (Bopp et al., 2003). It also does not mean a step back in time. As Kahn (1982) noted when writing of the need for Aboriginal peoples to reclaim cultural cohesion, pride, identity, and productive mastery over their world,

> it is, of course, totally naïve to think that the clock can be turned back several hundred years to pre-western contact, or that the past experiences can be wiped out. Their culture would have evolved and changed in any event.
>
> (p. 558)

If future research determines that cultural continuity is a protective factor for partner violence against Aboriginal women, then efforts to reclaim and enhance essential elements of Aboriginal culture would be important for reducing Aboriginal women's elevated risk of violent victimization. Kahn (1982) has suggested that

> whatever the approach, it needs to be an intervention that the aboriginal people want, and by means and by personnel that they select.... This probably cannot be achieved without the control and the finances of the services being in the hands of the indigenous people themselves.
>
> (p. 559)

Kahn's comments suggest that Aboriginal self-government, which would allow Aboriginal peoples some autonomy to have control over matters of special importance to them (Frideres, 2001), may help lay the groundwork for alleviating Aboriginal women's elevated risk for violence in Canada. To the extent that the findings of the current study are replicated in other nations in which Aboriginal peoples have experienced a similar history of colonization, self-government may also be a fruitful basis on which to reduce Aboriginal women's elevated risk for violence elsewhere. In the meantime, the results of the victim subsample were somewhat encouraging in the sense that it appeared that Aboriginal victims were accessing available services and often finding the contacts with the police helpful. The data also indicate that, consistent with past research, it may be helpful for health care professionals to ask directly Aboriginal women about their potential IPV victimization.

10
Violence Against Immigrant Women
A Reversal of Fortunes

The immigrant population of Canada is growing at a rate that is four times faster than the Canadian-born population. According to the 2006 Canadian Census, the proportion of immigrants in the population, representing one-fifth (19.8%) of the Canadian population, was at its highest in 75 years (Chui, Tran, & Maheux, 2007). Particularly in light of their increasing representation in Canada's population, an understanding of immigrant women's experiences of violence in Canada is a major gap in our knowledge of IPV. Raj and Silverman (2002) noted that a review of the literature across disciplines showed "a paucity of research on both the prevalence of IPV in immigrant communities and how immigrant status impacts women's risk of violence" (p. 368). These researchers added that "the few quantitative studies are not representative samples and include little data on immigrant status" (p. 368). Indeed, most Canadian research consists of qualitative studies of battered immigrant women (e.g., MacLeod & Shin, 1993) or social service workers engaged with this population (e.g., MacLeod & Shin, 1990). One might expect representative sample data to show that immigrant women are in a situation of double jeopardy with respect to violence. Women living in Canada, in general, face a number of problems such as overrepresentation in "pink-collar" jobs, wage discrimination, and expensive child care facilities. However, in addition to being disadvantaged by virtue of their sex, immigrant women face several circumstances that may exacerbate their likelihood of violence.

The purposes of this chapter are: (a) to examine the prevalence of violence against immigrant women in Canada; and (b) to explore what risk factors may account for differences in risk for violence between groups of immigrant women and Canadian-born women in two large-scale representative surveys.

Theoretical Framework

It is reasonable to argue that partner violence against immigrant women is a multifactorial problem. Thus, to understand fully the situation of immigrant women we must account for factors at various levels in immigrant women's environment. The best theoretical framework in which to accomplish this task is derived from ecological theory. To arrive at a thorough understanding

Table 10.1 Application of ecological framework to the problem of partner violence against immigrant women

System	Definition	Indicators
Macrosystem	Culture	Patriarchal domination Length of residence Age at arrival
Exosystem	Formal and informal Social networks	Female employment Religiosity Rural/urban residence
Microsystem	Family setting	Female education Male education Male employment Duration Children
Ontogenic	Individual development	Sexual jealousy Possessive behaviour

of the unique and complex problem of violence against immigrant women, what follows synthesizes various potential explanations for violence against immigrant women within an ecological framework. Table 10.1 provides an overview of the manner in which the ecological framework has been applied to violence against immigrant women in this chapter. This application of the ecological framework divides the environment into four levels: the macrosystem, the exosystem, the microsystem, and the ontogenic level.

Before surveying how risk factors at each level of the ecological framework may be related to violence against immigrant women, it is important to make a distinction between immigrant women from developing nations and those from developed nations. More than three-quarters of recent immigrants to Canada are from developing countries (Statistics Canada, 2001). Among immigrants that arrived in Canada between 2001 and 2006, nearly 60% were born in Asian countries (including the Middle East), with China being the single largest individual nation contributing immigrants to Canada (14%; Chui et al., 2007). The relationship of risk factors in immigrant women's ecology to violence may vary according to this broad distinction of place of origin. Hence, although the application of the ecological framework will speak of risk factors identified for immigrant women in general, in the analyses of risk factors a distinction will be drawn between immigrant women from developed and developing nations in recognition of the potential uniqueness of their situations with respect to IPV.

At the macrosystem level patriarchy may have an influence. Feminist theory suggests that violence is directly related to the extent to which members of a couple espouse a patriarchal ideology (Smith, 1990a). In many immigrants' cultures of origin, patriarchy is thought to be the norm and violence against women may be socially accepted as a way of life. One can therefore infer that, despite living in Canada, these women may have a different experience of violence from the average Canadian victim.

Other factors that may be linked to violence against immigrant women at the macrosystem level concern how long ago one immigrated and how old they were when they immigrated. One can reason that those who immigrated long ago have had more time to acculturate and that those who immigrated at a younger age are more amenable to acculturation. Since acculturated individuals should more closely resemble native-born Canadians, those who are more acculturated should have a similar likelihood of violence as those found in the mainstream Canadian culture while their less acculturated counterparts may have a higher likelihood of violence.

The exosystem refers to the formal and informal social networks in which the family is involved. Since contact with third parties can help to provide victims of violence with support, advice, and means of leaving an abusive relationship, it is possible that connectedness to others through both formal and informal social networks would help to insulate immigrant women from violence. More specifically, one might expect immigrant women who were socially connected to others through employment and religious participation would be more insulated from violence by their partner than those who do not participate in such networks. Another interesting comparison in this regard is rural/urban residence. Over the past 20 years many immigrants from several European countries have immigrated to the prairie region of Canada to run farms. The isolation of these immigrant women may be compounded by geographical segregation and the restricted movement associated with farm life. This suggests that immigrant women in rural areas may have a higher likelihood of violence than those in urban areas.

The microsystem consists of the family setting in which violence occurs. Immigrant women may stay in a violent relationship because they lack the skills necessary to survive on their own. For example, they may lack the skills to make financial transactions in this country, to drive a car, and so forth. This may be reflected in their level of education because one would expect more highly educated immigrant women to be more adaptable to acquiring the skills necessary to survive in their new country.

Among the factors operating at this level, the resources of an immigrant woman's partner may be of particular importance. Resource theory holds that the use of violence within a relationship depends on the resources a family member controls (Brownridge & Halli, 2000; Goode, 1971). Males who lack resources, such as education or employment status, may resort to violence against their spouse to feel in control. Immigrant men are more likely than Canadian-born men to lack these resources (Thompson, 2000). Hence, following resource theory, lower education and employment resources of immigrant women's partners may contribute to a greater likelihood of violent behaviour.

In addition, there are other components of the family setting that have been linked to partner violence and should therefore also be included at this level. For instance, relationships of short duration and those with children have been linked to partner violence (Brownridge & Halli, 2001). A possible explanation for these relationships is stress in the family. Establishing norms of interaction, which is particularly intense at the beginning of a relationship, may be stressful, as is raising children. One might expect the impact of these stressors to be exacerbated in the context of the stress associated with immigration, which in turn may also exacerbate their likelihood of violence.

Finally, the ontogenic level comprises the individual's development and, as a result, what they bring to the other levels based on their development. It can be argued that an individual's developmental history is strongly linked to their attitudes and behaviour. Men who hold attitudes that lead them to behave in a sexually proprietary way towards their partner have clearly learned at some point that this kind of behaviour is acceptable. They then bring this unique developmental history with them and it interacts within the context of the other three levels of the theoretical framework. Sexually proprietary behaviour has been linked to violence against women (cf. the discussion of sexual proprietariness in Chapter 2). Sexually proprietary behaviour may be related to patriarchy at the macrosystem level. That is, if the cultures of origin of immigrant women's partners are more likely to be patriarchal, then such socialization may also lead these men to engage in sexually proprietary behaviours.

Subsamples and Risk Factors

Subsamples

The data employed in this chapter were from the 1999 and 2004 surveys (see Chapter 3 for details of the surveys and methods). Since this chapter focuses on male partner violence against immigrant and Canadian-born women, the subsample from the 1999 survey consisted of 7,115 heterosexual women living married or common-law at the time of the survey (5,737 Canadian-born women, 844 immigrant women from developed countries, and 534 women who have immigrated from developing countries) and the subsample from the 2004 survey included 6,627 heterosexual women living married or common-law at the time of the survey (5,182 Canadian-born women, 710 women from developed nations, and 735 women from developing nations).

Risk Factors

As indicated in Table 10.1, three variables were included at the macrosystem level. These were patriarchal dominance, length of residence, and age at arrival. Risk factors at the exosystem level were woman's employment, religiosity, and rural/urban residence. Several measures were included at the microsystem level; woman's and partner's education, partner's employment, duration of relationship, and the presence of children. Finally, two indicators of sexual proprietariness were included at the ontogenic level. The first was sexual jealousy and the second was possessive behaviour.

Results

Figures 10.1 and 10.2 provide the prevalence rates of violence for immigrant women from developing nations, developed nations, and Canadian-born women in both surveys, respectively. The results in Figures 10.1 and 10.2 showed that the differences in prevalence between the groups were not statistically significant in the 1-year period prior to each survey. However, the 1-year prevalence rates followed the same pattern as did the 5-year prevalence rates, which were significantly different.

In the 1999 survey, the group with the highest prevalence of violence was immigrants from developing countries. A total of 5.5% of women in this group reported that their partner had been violent towards them in the 5 years preceding the survey. Surprisingly, the next highest prevalence of violence was not among immigrants from developed nations; rather, it was among Canadian-born women who had a rate of 3.7%. Indeed, the lowest prevalence of violence was found among immigrants from developed countries, 2.4% of whom reported violence having occurred in the 5 years prior to the survey. In the 2004 survey, Canadian-born women continued to fall between the two immigrant groups in terms of their prevalence of violence with a rate of 3.3%. However, the rates for the groups of immigrant women were reversed in the 2004 survey. That is, in the 2004 survey immigrant women from developed nations had the highest rate of violence (3.9%) and immigrant women from developing nations had the lowest rate of violence (1.4%). Given these findings, much of the remainder of this part of the chapter will systematically examine the differences in these rates across groups in the context of the ecological framework separately for each survey. Specifically, the questions to be answered are: do the groups differ in terms of risk factors in the ecological framework and, if so, do these differences in risk factors account for the observed differences in risk for violence across the groups?

Violence Against Immigrant Women in the 1999 GSS: Double Jeopardy and Double Advantage

The analysis of the prevalence of violence in the 1999 GSS suggested that two sets of comparisons were needed; one between immigrant women from developing and developed nations, and another between Canadian-born women and immigrant women from developed nations.

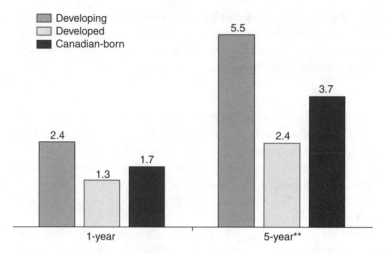

Figure 10.1 One-year and 5-year prevalence of violence against immigrant women from developing nations, developed nations, and Canadian-born women in the 1999 GSS (%).

Note
**$p < 0.05$ (p values refer to Chi-square tests of significance).

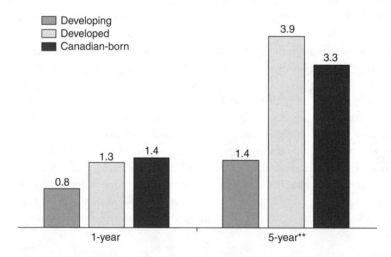

Figure 10.2 One-year and 5-year prevalence of violence against immigrant women from developing nations, developed nations, and Canadian-born women in the 2004 GSS (%).

Note
**$p < 0.05$ (p values refer to Chi-square tests of significance).

IMMIGRANT WOMEN IN DEVELOPING NATIONS IN DOUBLE
JEOPARDY: ONTOGENIC FACTORS ARE KEY

As noted at the outset of this chapter, conventional wisdom suggested that immigrant women in general would be in a situation of double jeopardy with respect to violence. The 1999 survey data suggested that only women from developing nations were in a situation of double jeopardy with respect to their risk for violence. Table 10.2 provides the results of the cross-tabulations of the risk factors by whether the respondent was from a developed or developing nation in the 1999 GSS. As one would expect, given Canadian immigration trends in recent years, the majority of immigrant women from developed countries arrived before 1975 while most of those from developing countries have arrived since 1975. The results in Table 10.2 also showed that immigrant women from developed countries tended to be younger than immigrant women from developing countries when they arrived in Canada. On the other hand, the results showed very little difference across the two immigrant groups in terms of the exhibition of patriarchal dominance. Although, generally speaking, the two groups of immigrant women tended to come from quite different backgrounds in terms of patriarchy, the results of the analyses in this chapter suggested that their partners were not exhibiting patriarchal dominance through preventing access to the family income at significantly different levels.

Immigrant women from developing countries were less likely to have worked in the year prior to the 1999 GSS. However, it did appear that this same group of immigrant women were more likely to be frequent church attendees. The results in Table 10.2 suggested the possibility that immigrant women from developed countries were more likely to be socially isolated by virtue of their greater likelihood of being geographically segregated in rural areas of Canada.

Women from developing countries were more likely to have a high education in the 1999 GSS, suggesting that these women were no less likely to possess the skills needed to survive without their partner. The results also showed that partners of women from developing countries were more likely to be highly educated than partners of women from developed nations. In both groups, the majority of couples had been together for 10 or more years. However, substantially more couples in the group of immigrants from developing nations had been together for less than 10 years. Women from developing countries were much more likely to have children less than age 15 living in the household.

Finally, the results of the cross-tabulations on individual risk markers of violence in the ontogenic level showed that male partners of women from developing nations were significantly more likely to commit both acts of sexual proprietariness (i.e., jealousy and possessive behaviour). Thus, it appeared that partners of women from developing countries were more likely to be sexually proprietary.

Table 10.2 Independent variables by whether the respondent was from a developed or developing nation in the 1999 GSS (%)

Independent variable	Place of origin	
	Developed nation	Developing nation
Macrosystem		
Period of immigration		
Before 1965	42.6	5.4
1965–1974	23.9	15.6
1975–1989	19.9	37.0
1990–1999	13.5	42.0***
Age at immigration		
Less than 20	41.7	21.6
20–29	34.8	45.4
30 and over	23.5	33.0***
Patriarchal dominance		
Yes	0.9	1.8
No	99.1	98.2
Exosystem		
Woman's employment		
Unemployed	27.8	33.4
Employed	72.2	66.6*
Religiosity		
Never	32.1	22.6
Once per year	4.8	6.0
A few times per year	16.5	11.8
One to three times per month	13.8	18.3
Once per week or more	32.8	41.3***
Urban/rural residence		
Rural	15.7	4.6
Urban	84.3	95.4***
Microsystem		
Woman's education		
Less than high school	23.0	15.2
High school	17.2	18.5
Some post secondary	12.7	6.9
Community college	24.4	25.2
University degree	22.7	34.1***
Partner's education		
Less than high school	23.3	11.6
High school	21.6	22.7
Some post secondary	8.1	6.7
Community college	18.8	18.8
University degree	28.3	40.2***
Partner's employment		
Unemployed	2.2	5.6
Employed	97.8	94.4***
Duration of relationship		
Less than 4 years	4.8	16.0
4–9 years	10.8	23.4
10 or more years	84.4	60.7***

Table 10.2 continued

Independent variable	Place of origin	
	Developed nation	Developing nation
Children <15		
Yes	27.2	51.4
No	72.8	48.6***
Ontogenic		
Know whereabouts		
Yes	3.7	9.3
No	96.3	90.7***
Jealousy		
Yes	3.2	8.5
No	96.8	91.5***

Note
$*p \leq 0.10$; $***p < 0.01$ (p values refer to Chi-square tests of significance).

To determine whether any of these differences accounted for the elevated odds of violence against immigrant women from developing nations in the 1999 GSS, sequential logistic regressions were performed at different levels of the ecological framework. Table 10.3 contains the results of these analyses. The first model in Table 10.3 contained the results for the place of origin variable without any controls. As one would expect, the odds of violence were higher for immigrant women from developing countries compared to women who had immigrated from developed nations. The difference in prevalence between the two groups translated to the former having 139% higher odds of violence than the latter. The second model in Table 10.3 controlled for the macrosystem variables. Although controlling for the macrosystem variables reduced the difference in odds, the difference remained significant. The third model in Table 10.3 controlled for the exosystem variables. Rather than reducing the difference, controlling for the exosystem variables actually increased the gap by 13%. The microsystem variables were controlled in the fourth model. With controls for the microsystem variables the difference in odds was reduced but remained significant. The fifth model in Table 10.3 contained the controls for the ontogenic level. While, in this model, women from developing countries still had 62% higher odds of violence, the significance of the difference disappeared. The final column in Table 10.3 contained the full model with all of the independent variables. In this model, the difference between the two groups of immigrant women was statistically insignificant, but the odds of violence for immigrant women from developing countries were not as low as when only the ontogenic variables were controlled. Thus, based on these sequential logistic regressions it appeared that it was the greater tendency of male partners of immigrant women from developing countries to be

Table 10.3 Results of sequential logistic regressions for immigrant women in developing relative to developed nations in the 1999 GSS

Covariates	Model 1 Place of origin n = 1,319 Odds ratio	Model 2 Macrosystem n = 1,300 Odds ratio	Model 3 Exosystem n = 1,257 Odds ratio	Model 4 Microsystem n = 1,203 Odds ratio	Model 5 Ontogenic n = 1,315 Odds ratio	Model 6 Full model n = 1,174 Odds ratio
Place of origin						
Developing	2.386***	1.837*	2.521***	1.914*	1.620	1.820
Developed	1.000	1.000	1.000	1.000	1.000	1.000
Macrosystem		Block				Block
Exosystem			Block			Block
Microsystem				Block		Block
Ontogenic					Block	Block
Constant	0.038***	0.018***	0.036***	0.045***	0.015***	0.012***
−2 Log likelihood	400	388	390	362	313	271
χ^2	9***	20***	15**	29***	95***	118***

Note
*$p \leq 0.10$; **$p < 0.05$; ***$p < 0.01$.

sexually proprietary that was responsible for the significantly higher prevalence of violence in these unions in the 1999 GSS.

IMMIGRANT WOMEN FROM DEVELOPED NATIONS WITH A DOUBLE
ADVANTAGE: MICROSYSTEM FACTORS ARE KEY

The results in Figure 10.1 indicated that immigrant women from developed nations were in a situation of double advantage in the 1999 GSS in the sense that they not only had an advantage over immigrant women from developing nations but also over Canadian-born women. Table 10.4 provides the results of the cross-tabulations of the risk factors by whether the respondent was from a developed nation or Canadian-born in the 1999 GSS. As shown in Table 10.4, there were no significant differences between immigrant women from developed nations and Canadian-born women in terms both of their partner's level of patriarchal domination and their own employment levels. There were, however, significant differences on the remaining exosystem variables and on all but one of the microsystem variables.

Immigrant women from developed nations were more likely to attend church frequently than were Canadian-born women. Canadian-born women were almost twice as likely (28% vs. 16%) to be living in a rural area. In terms of risk factors at the microsystem level, immigrant women from developed nations were more likely both to be of low education and of high education, though the gap between the two groups was greater for the respective proportions having a university degree (23% vs. 19%) than for the respective proportions having less than a high school education (23% vs. 21%). Partners of immigrant women from developed nations were significantly more likely to be highly educated, though there were no significant differences in these men's employment levels. There was a clear pattern of immigrant women from developed nations having had relationships of a longer duration and to be less likely to have young children living in the household.

There were no significant differences on variables at the ontogenic level. That is, partners of immigrant women from developed nations did not significantly differ from Canadian-born women's partners in terms of sexually possessive and jealous behaviours.

To identify which variables, if any, accounted for Canadian-born women's higher prevalence of violence, sequential logistic regressions were conducted to assess the difference in odds of violence for the two groups while controlling for the effects of the independent variables at the exosystem and microsystem levels.[1]

Table 10.5 contains the results of sequential logistic regressions for Canadian-born women relative to immigrant women from developed nations in the 1999 GSS. The first model in Table 10.5 contained the results for the place of origin variable without any controls. The results showed that the higher prevalence of violence for Canadian-born women translated to them

Table 10.4 Independent variables by whether the respondent was from a developed nation or Canadian-born in the 1999 GSS (%)

Independent variable	Place of origin	
	Developed nation	Canadian-born
Macrosystem		
Patriarchal dominance		
Yes	0.9	1.0
No	99.1	99.0
Exosystem		
Woman's employment		
Did not work in past year	27.7	29.5
Worked past year	72.3	70.5
Religiosity		
Never	32.0	34.8
Once per year	4.8	7.6
A few times per year	16.5	22.3
One to three times per month	13.9	11.5
Once per week or more	32.8	23.8***
Urban/rural residence		
Rural	15.7	27.9
Urban	84.3	72.1***
Microsystem		
Woman's education		
Less than high school	23.0	20.6
High school	17.2	16.9
Some post secondary	12.7	14.6
Community college	24.4	28.7
University degree	22.7	19.2**
Partner's education		
Less than high school	23.3	25.0
High school	21.6	25.3
Some post secondary	8.1	8.3
Community college	18.7	20.8
University degree	28.4	20.5***
Partner's employment		
Did not work in past year	2.2	2.9
Worked past year	97.8	97.1
Duration of relationship		
Less than 4 years	4.9	12.3
4–9 years	10.7	17.8
10 or more years	84.4	69.9***
Children <15		
Yes	27.2	37.2
No	72.8	62.8***
Ontogenic		
Know whereabouts		
Yes	3.7	3.5
No	96.3	96.5
Jealousy		
Yes	3.2	4.4
No	96.8	95.6

Note
**$p < 0.05$; ***$p < 0.01$ (p values refer to Chi-square tests of significance).

having 56% higher odds of violence than immigrant women from developed nations. The second model in Table 10.5 controlled for the exosystem variables. The results showed that controlling for the exosystem variables reduced Canadian-born women's higher odds of violence by only 8%. Moreover, with controls for the exosystem variables, Canadian-born women's odds of violence remained significantly higher than the odds of violence for immigrant women from developed nations. The third model in Table 10.5 controlled for the microsystem variables. The results showed that when the microsystem variables were controlled Canadian-born women had 16% higher odds of violence compared to immigrant women from developed nations. In other words, Canadian-born women's higher odds of violence were reduced by 40% when the microsystem variables were controlled such that Canadian-born women's odds of violence were no longer significantly higher than those of immigrant women from developed nations. The final column in Table 10.5 contained the full model with all of the independent variables. In this model, the difference between the two groups remained statistically insignificant, but the odds of violence for Canadian-born women were not any lower than they were when only the microsystem variables were controlled. Thus, based on these sequential logistic regressions it appeared that the microsystem variables were responsible for the significantly higher odds of violence experienced by Canadian-born women.

Violence Against Immigrant Women in the 2004 GSS: A Reversal of Fortunes

Recall from Figure 10.2 that in the 2004 survey there appeared to be a reversal of fortunes for immigrant women with respect to their prevalence of violence. In 2004, immigrant women from developed nations reported the highest rates of violence while those from developing nations reported the lowest rate of violence. This begged similar comparisons in the context of the ecological framework to those that were conducted for the groups in the 1999 GSS, but in this case the first comparison involved the odds of violence against immigrant women in developed nations relative to developing nations and the second involved comparing Canadian-born women's odds relative to immigrant women from developing nations.

IMMIGRANT WOMEN FROM DEVELOPED NATIONS MOST AT RISK IN 2004

Table 10.6 presents the results of the cross-tabulations of independent variables by whether the respondent was from a developed or developing nation in the 2004 GSS. With few exceptions, the differences between immigrant women from developed and developing nations in the 2004 GSS were very similar to those observed in the 1999 GSS (see Table 10.2). Unlike those from developed nations, the majority of immigrant women from developing nations had arrived since 1990. Immigrant women from developing nations

Table 10.5 Results of sequential logistic regressions on 5-year prevalence of violence for Canadian-born women relative to immigrant women from developed nations in the 1999 GSS

Covariates	Model 1 Place of origin n = 6,483	Model 2 Exosystem n = 6,328	Model 3 Microsystem n = 6,163	Model 4 Full model n = 6,105
	Odds ratio	Odds ratio	Odds ratio	Odds ratio
Place of origin				
Canadian-born	1.557*	1.482*	1.158	1.172
Developed	1.000	1.000	1.000	1.000
Exosystem		Block		Block
Microsystem			Block	Block
Constant	0.025***	0.030***	0.201***	0.228**
−2 Log likelihood	1,973	1,956	1,824	1,819
χ^2	4	11	91	93

Note
$*p \leq 0.10$; $**p < 0.05$; $***p < 0.01$.

Table 10.6 Independent variables by whether the respondent was from a developed or developing nation in the 2004 GSS (%)

Independent variable	Place of origin	
	Developed nation	Developing nation
Macrosystem		
Period of immigration		
Before 1965	36.5	2.6
1965–1974	24.9	13.0
1975–1989	20.4	33.6
1990–1999	18.2	50.8***
Age at immigration		
Less than 20	42.4	22.0
20–29	37.1	43.2
30 and over	20.5	34.8***
Patriarchal dominance		
Yes	0.9	1.6
No	99.1	98.4
Exosystem		
Woman's employment		
Unemployed	29.6	31.2
Employed	70.4	68.8
Religiosity		
Never	19.4	14.2
Once per year	7.7	4.9
A few times per year	21.0	18.6
One to three times per month	21.0	18.4
Once per week or more	30.9	43.9***
Urban/rural residence		
Rural	11.9	2.3
Urban	88.1	97.7***
Microsystem		
Woman's education		
Less than high school	20.7	9.5
High school	21.1	13.8
Some post secondary	7.9	10.6
Community college	25.9	30.3
University degree	24.4	35.8***
Partner's education		
Less than high school	22.2	9.0
High school	22.9	20.5
Some post secondary	7.1	10.6
Community college	22.4	19.0
University degree	25.4	40.8***
Partner's employment		
Unemployed	2.2	6.3
Employed	97.8	93.8***
Duration of relationship		
Less than 4 years	7.2	12.8
4–9 years	11.6	22.4
10 or more years	81.3	64.8***

continued

Table 10.6 continued

Independent variable	Place of origin	
	Developed nation	Developing nation
Children <15		
Yes	25.6	50.8
No	74.4	49.2***
Ontogenic		
Know whereabouts		
Yes	2.8	3.8
No	97.2	96.2
Jealousy		
Yes	2.8	3.8
No	97.2	96.2

Note
***$p < 0.01$ (p values refer to Chi-square tests of significance).

tended to be older when they immigrated. As in the 1999 survey, the two groups did not report significant differences in their partner's patriarchal domineering behaviour.

Although women from developing nations were slightly more likely to be unemployed in the 1999 GSS, there was no difference on this variable in the 2004 survey. Immigrant women from developing nations remained more likely to be frequent church attendees in the 2004 survey. Despite the different measure of rural/urban status in the 2004 survey, the results continued to show that most immigrant women living in rural areas of Canada are from developed nations.

Immigrant women from developing countries and their partners continue to be more likely to have a high education relative to immigrant women from developed nations and their partners. Despite their tendency to have higher education levels, partners of immigrant women from developing nations continued to have a higher rate of unemployment. Immigrant women from developing nations also continued to be more likely to have been in their union for less than 10 years and to have children less than age 15 living in the household.

In the 2004 survey there was no significant difference between immigrant women from developing and developed nations in terms of reports of possessive and sexually jealous behaviours by male partners. This was in stark contrast to the 1999 survey in which partners of immigrant women from developing nations were more than twice as likely as those of immigrant women from developed nations to have been reported to engage in sexually proprietary behaviours (see Table 10.2).

To explore whether any of the variables in the ecological framework account for the higher prevalence of violence against immigrant women from

Table 10.7 Results of sequential logistic regressions for immigrant women from developed relative to developing nations in the 2004 GSS

Covariates	Model 1 Place of origin n = 1,100 Odds ratio	Model 2 Macrosystem n = 1,100 Odds ratio	Model 3 Exosystem n = 919 Odds ratio	Model 4 Microsystem n = 1,049 Odds ratio	Model 5 Ontogenic n = 1,098 Odds ratio	Model 6 Full model n = 873 Odds ratio
Place of origin						
Developed	2.900**	4.564***	2.886**	3.800**	3.419**	5.128**
Developing	1.000	1.000	1.000	1.000	1.000	1.000
Macrosystem		Block				Block
Exosystem			Block			Block
Microsystem				Block		Block
Ontogenic					Block	Block
Constant	0.014***	0.003***	0.012***	0.033**	0.008***	0.000***
−2 Log likelihood	258	247	226	211	223	143
χ^2	7**	18**	8	20**	43***	14*

Note
$*p \le 0.10$; $**p < 0.05$; $***p < 0.01$.

developed nations in the 2004 survey, sequential logistic regressions were performed. Table 10.7 contains the results of those analyses. As shown in Model 1 of Table 10.7, the difference in prevalence between the two groups translated to immigrant women from developed nations having 190% greater odds of violence compared to immigrant women from developing nations in the 2004 survey ($p < 0.05$). A quick examination of the results in Table 10.7 showed that none of variables included in the ecological framework reduced immigrant women from developed nations' elevated odds of violence.

COMPARING CANADIAN-BORN WOMEN TO IMMIGRANT WOMEN FROM DEVELOPING NATIONS

As shown in Figure 10.2, Canadian-born women reported more than double the rate of violence compared to immigrant women from developing nations in the 5 years prior to the 2004 GSS. Although not discussed in the chapter, a separate cross-tabulation with only these two groups showed that this difference was statistically significant ($p < 0.05$). Hence, it was also important to explore variables in the ecological framework to determine whether any of these variables help to understand Canadian-born women's elevated risk of violence compared to immigrant women from developing nations in the 2004 GSS.

Table 10.8 contains the results of the cross-tabulations of the independent variables by whether the respondent was from a developing nation or Canadian-born in the 2004 GSS. The results in Table 10.8 showed that partners of Canadian-born women were less than half as likely to behave in a patriarchal domineering manner compared to partners of immigrant women from developing nations.

With respect to exosystem factors, Canadian-born women were less likely than immigrant women from developing nations to be unemployed and they also attended church services less frequently. Approximately one-quarter of Canadian-born women lived in a rural area compared to only 2% of immigrant women from developing nations.

Canadian-born women and their partners tended to be less highly educated than their counterparts from developing nations. Despite this, partners of Canadian-born women were less than half as likely to be unemployed. Canadian women were slightly more likely both to have relationships of a short duration (less than 4 years) and of a long duration (more than 10 years). Nevertheless, Canadian-born women were less likely to have young children with about one-third of these women having children under age 15 compared to just over one-half of immigrant women from developing nations.

Finally, in terms of the ontogenic factors, the results in Table 10.8 showed that partners of Canadian-born women were less likely than those of immigrant women from developing nations to behave in a possessive and sexually jealous manner.

Table 10.8 Independent variables by whether the respondent was from a developing nation or Canadian-born in the 2004 GSS (%)

Independent variable	Place of origin	
	Developed nation	Canadian-born
Macrosystem		
Patriarchal dominance		
Yes	1.7	0.7
No	98.3	99.3**
Exosystem		
Woman's employment		
Unemployed	31.2	25.7
Employed	68.8	74.3***
Religiosity		
Never	14.2	23.9
Once per year	4.9	9.7
A few times per year	18.6	26.0
One to three times per month	18.3	15.2
Once per week or more	43.9	25.2***
Urban/rural residence		
Rural	2.3	27.0
Urban	97.7	73.0***
Microsystem		
Woman's education		
Less than high school	9.5	16.8
High school	13.8	18.3
Some post secondary	10.6	14.0
Community college	30.3	29.5
University degree	35.9	21.5***
Partner's education		
Less than high school	9.0	23.7
High school	20.5	25.1
Some post secondary	10.7	8.7
Community college	19.1	21.0
University degree	40.8	21.5***
Partner's employment		
Unemployed	6.2	2.6
Employed	93.8	97.4***
Duration of relationship		
Less than 4 years	12.8	15.1
4–9 years	22.5	17.4
10 or more years	64.7	67.5***
Children <15		
Yes	50.7	36.3
No	49.3	63.7***
Ontogenic		
Know whereabouts		
Yes	3.7	2.4
No	96.3	97.6**
Jealousy		
Yes	3.9	2.7
No	96.1	97.3*

Note

$*p \leq 0.10; **p < 0.05; ***p < 0.01$ (*p* values refer to Chi-square tests of significance).

Table 10.9 contains the results of the sequential logistic regressions that were conducted to determine if any of the variables in the ecological framework accounted for the higher prevalence of violence against Canadian-born women relative to immigrant women from developing nations in the 2004 GSS. The first model in Table 10.9 showed that the difference in prevalence between the two groups translated to Canadian-born women having 145% greater odds of violence compared to immigrant women from developing nations. The results in Table 10.9 showed that controlling for macrosystem variables, microsystem variables, ontogenic variables, as well as all variables in the ecological framework simultaneously, did not account for Canadian-born women's elevated odds of violence in the 2004 survey. However, controlling for the exosystem variables did reduce Canadian-born women's elevated odds by 54%. Even after controlling for the exosystem variables, however, Canadian-born women still had 92% greater odds of violence ($p \leq 0.10$).

A Comparison of Immigrant and Canadian-Born Victims' Post-Violence Experiences

The analyses in this chapter involved a comparison of victims who were immigrants to Canadian-born victims in terms of their post-violence experiences in the 1999 and 2004 surveys. Although, based on the above analyses, it would have been enlightening to make the distinction between immigrant women from developing and developed nations in these analyses, the decision was made to retain immigrant victims as one group for two reasons: (a) separating immigrant victims would have exacerbated the problem of small samples; and (b) despite differences in their prevalence of violence, there is reason to believe that immigrant victims in general possess unique circumstances with respect to their post-violence experiences relative to Canadian-born women. Indeed, the matter of differences in prevalence rates for immigrant women may be independent of post-violence consequences for victims. For example, independent of prevalence rates in Asian or African cultures, the emphasis in these cultures on collectivism, family, hierarchy, and their gender-role expectations within marriage may be barriers to help-seeking among victims who are immigrants from these locales (Ting, 2007).

Table 10.10 contains the zero-order odds ratios for the consequences of violence in the 1999 and 2004 GSS. The results in Table 10.10 showed no clear pattern across the surveys in terms of the consequences of psychopathology, an altered psyche, or having to take time off from everyday activities as a result of the violence. There was, however, a pattern for immigrant victims to have slightly lower odds of physical injury. Immigrant and Canadian-born victims had similar odds of being angry as a result of the violence across both surveys. However, there was a pattern for immigrant victims to have higher odds of reporting that children witnessed the violence.

Table 10.9 Results of sequential logistic regressions for Canadian-born women relative to immigrant women from developing nations in the 2004 GSS

Covariates	Model 1 Place of origin n = 5,963	Model 2 Macrosystem n = 5,955	Model 3 Exosystem n = 4,988	Model 4 Microsystem n = 5,802	Model 5 Ontogenic n = 5,956	Model 6 Full model n = 4,849
	Odds ratio	Odds ratio	Odds ratio	Odds ratio	Odds ratio	Odds ratio
Place of origin						
Canadian-born	2.452**	2.786***	1.915*	2.912***	2.638***	3.079***
Developing	1.000	1.000	1.000	1.000	1.000	1.000
Macrosystem		Block				Block
Exosystem			Block			Block
Microsystem				Block		Block
Ontogenic					Block	Block
Constant	0.014	0.012***	0.015***	0.011***	0.010***	0.002***
−2 Log likelihood	1,630	1,583	1,244	1,525	1,500	1,057
χ^2	10***	56***	6	47***	139**	148***

Note
$*p \le 0.10$; $**p < 0.05$; $***p < 0.01$.

Table 10.10 Zero-order odds ratios for consequences of violence in the 1999 and 2004 GSS for immigrant relative to Canadian-born victims

Dependent variable	Immigrant/Canadian-born status[a]			
	1999		2004	
	OR	n	OR	n
Physical injury	0.805	261	0.715	210
Psychopathology[b]	1.217	254	0.986	202
Altered psyche[c]	0.374*	254	2.635**	202
Anger	0.974	254	1.002	202
Time off everyday activities	0.785	260	1.770	210
Stay in bed all/most of day	0.857	261	†	
Children witnessed violence	2.084**	210	1.691	148

Notes

*$p \le 0.10$; **$p < 0.05$.

a Canadian-born is the reference category with an odds of 1.000.

b Includes depression or anxiety attacks, fear, afraid for children, more cautious or aware, sleep problems, shock or disbelief, hurt or disappointment, and upset, confused, or frustrated.

c Includes ashamed or guilty, lowered self-esteem, problems relating to men, and increased self-reliance.

† Statistics Canada would not release the result to ensure respondent confidentiality. Statistical significance test was not released.

The zero-order odds ratios for victims' help-seeking behaviours across both surveys are presented in Table 10.11. The results in Table 10.11 showed that in the 1999 survey immigrant victims had much greater odds than Canadian-born women of visiting a health care professional for treatment. The 1999 survey data also suggested that, overall, immigrant victims did not have higher odds than Canadian-born victims of confiding in someone about the violence. However, there was a pattern across the 1999 and 2004 surveys for immigrant women to have higher odds of confiding in a family member, a doctor or nurse, and/or a minister, priest, clergyman, or spiritual adviser. The 1999 data also suggested that immigrant women had lower odds of contacting a lawyer relative to Canadian-born women. In terms of victims contacting services, the 1999 data suggested that immigrant women generally had higher odds of contacting a service. On the other hand, the 2004 survey suggested the opposite. The 1999 data clearly suggested that immigrant women had much higher odds than Canadian-born women of contacting a crisis centre or crisis line and of contacting a police or court-based victim service. In both surveys immigrant victims were certainly no less interested than Canadian-born women in trying mediation or conciliation.

Table 10.12 provides the zero-order odds ratios for the police intervention variables in the 1999 and 2004 surveys. There was a clear pattern across both surveys of immigrant victims having higher odds of police finding out about the violence. Among those for whom the police found out about the violence,

Table 10.11 Zero-order odds ratios for victims' help-seeking behaviours in the 1999 and 2004 GSS for immigrant and Canadian-born victims

Dependent variable	Immigrant/Canadian-born status[a]			
	1999		2004	
	OR	*n*	OR	*n*
Visit doctor/nurse/hospital for treatment	4.819**	73	†	
Confided in someone:	1.006	258	†	
Family	1.266	258	1.397	208
Friend/neighbour	0.722	257	1.733	209
Co-worker	0.554	256	†	
Doctor/nurse	1.735	256	1.868	209
Lawyer	0.266	257	†	
Minister/priest/clergy/ spiritual adviser	1.320	256	3.892***	208
Services contacted:	1.321	259	0.502	209
Crisis centre/line	2.315**	259	†	
Another counsellor/psychologist	0.967	259	0.684	209
Community/family centre	0.846	259	†	
Shelter/transition house	1.325	259	†	
Women's centre	1.150	259	†	
Police/court-based victim service	2.471	259	†	
Interested in mediation/ conciliation	1.867*	252	1.148	196

Notes

*$p \leq 0.10$; **$p < 0.05$; ***$p < 0.01$.

a Canadian-born is the reference category with an odds of 1.000.

† Statistics Canada would not release the result to ensure respondent confidentiality. Statistical significance test was not released.

the 1999 data suggested that immigrant victims may be more likely to report violence to the police, to do so on their own accord, and to do so to stop the violence and receive protection. Immigrant victims had lower odds, though, of contacting the police out of a desire to have their partner arrested or punished. Among those victims for whom the police had been contacted, the 1999 data suggested that immigrant women had higher odds of the police visiting the scene and giving a warning to the woman's partner. The 1999 data clearly showed that immigrant victims had lower odds both of being satisfied with the police and of reporting that the violence decreased or stopped following police intervention. Among victims for whom the police were not contacted, the 1999 data suggested that immigrant victims had lower odds of not contacting the police because they dealt with it in another way, because it was a personal matter, or because they believed the police could not do anything about it. On the other hand, the 1999 data suggested that immigrant victims had much higher odds of not contacting the police out of fear of their

Table 10.12 Zero-order odds ratios for police intervention in the 1999 and 2004 GSS for immigrant and Canadian-born victims

Dependent variable	Immigrant/Canadian-born status[a]			
	1999		2004	
	OR	n	OR	n
Police found out	2.043**	259	1.969*	208
Police found out from respondent	1.809	68	†	
Reason police contacted:				
Stop violence/receive protection	2.004	53	†	
Arrest/punish spouse/partner	0.301	54	†	
Duty to notify police	0.723	53	†	
Recommendation of someone else	0.347	54	†	
Police action:				
Visited scene	1.595	65	†	
Made report/conducted investigation	0.974	65	†	
Gave warning to spouse/partner	2.106	65	†	
Took spouse/partner away	1.028	65	†	
Put you in touch with community services	0.000	65	†	
Made arrest/laid charges	NA		†	
None	0.613	65	†	
Respondent satisfied w/police	0.187**	66	†	
Post-police violence decreased/stopped	0.106**	41	†	
Reasons police not contacted:				
Dealt with in another way[b]	0.480*	190	†	
Did not want to get involved with police	1.342	190	0.865	166
Fear of spouse/partner	3.181**	190	†	

Personal matter that did not concern police	0.539	189	†	166
Police couldn't do anything about it	0.276*	190	1.678	
Police wouldn't help[c]	0.419	189	†	
Police wouldn't think it was important enough	0.515	190	0.474*	165
Fear of publicity/news coverage	3.932**	190	4.439***	164
Did not want spouse/partner arrested or jailed	1.380	190	2.025	164
Did not want anyone to find out about it (e.g., shame)	0.823	190	3.653**	165
Other reason	4.005**	189	5.089***	165

Notes

$*p \leq 0.10$; $**p < 0.05$; $***p < 0.01$.

a Canadian-born is the reference category with an odds of 1.000.

b Includes left him, reported to another official, private matter that took care of myself, etc.

c Includes police wouldn't think it was important enough, wouldn't believe, wouldn't want to be bothered or get involved, police would be inefficient or ineffective, police would be biased, would harass/insult respondent, offender was police officer.

† Statistics Canada would not release the result to ensure respondent confidentiality. Statistical significance test was not released.

NA Not available in the data.

partner. The 1999 and 2004 data showed a pattern for immigrant victims to have lower odds of not contacting the police because they did not think it was important enough. On the other hand, there was a pattern of immigrant victims having higher odds of not contacting the police out of fear of publicity or news coverage, because they did not want their partner arrested or jailed, and for some other reason.

Discussion

The comparison of prevalence rates yielded some surprising findings. As expected, immigrant women did have an elevated risk for violence, but in the 1999 survey only immigrant women from developing nations had an elevated risk. Not only did the immigrant women from developed nations have a lower risk than immigrant women from developing nations, but they also had a lower risk than Canadian-born women in the 1999 survey.

Immigrant Women from Developing Nations' Double Jeopardy in the 1999 Survey

The analyses suggested that, although there were many differences in risk factors between the two groups of immigrant women, the double jeopardy faced by immigrant women from developing nations was due to the greater representation of partners of immigrant women from developing nations on variables measuring sexual proprietariness at the ontogenic level of the ecological framework. That is, partners of immigrant women from developing nations were far more likely to behave in a possessive and sexually jealous manner, and these differences accounted for the elevated risk of violence against immigrant women from developing nations in the 1999 survey. The rationale behind the inclusion of these variables in the application of the ecological framework in this chapter was that immigrant women may be more likely to come from cultures that are more patriarchal than that of Canada. Hence, one would expect that these women would be more likely to be partnered with men who were similarly socialized, and that socialization would also lead them to engage in sexually proprietary behaviours. However, the descriptive analyses showed that partners of both groups of immigrant women were not significantly different in their levels of patriarchal domineering behaviour. While it could be that the failure to find a difference in levels of patriarchal domineering behaviour was a result of an insufficient measure of patriarchal domination, it seems more likely that the importance of the ontogenic variables reflected the insecurity of sexual proprietariness. Brownridge and Halli (2002a) tested interaction effects using the 1999 GSS data and found that this insecurity worked in tandem with high education among women from developing nations (AOR = 2.006; $p < 0.05$) and low education among their male partners in the production of violence (AOR = 0.569; $p < 0.05$). This suggested the possibility that the elevated risk of violence for immigrant women from developing nations in the 1999 survey was particularly linked to sexual insecurity by less well-educated partners and partners of well-educated immigrant women from developing nations.

Immigrant Women from Developed Nations' Double Advantage in the 1999 Survey

The finding in the 1999 GSS data that immigrant women from developed nations had a lower prevalence of violence than both immigrant women from developing nations and Canadian-born women was, in the context of an expected higher prevalence rate, a welcome surprise. This finding contradicted the common perception that immigrant women in general have a higher prevalence of violence compared to Canadian-born women. The descriptive analyses identified a number of differences in risk factors at the exosystem and microsystem levels between immigrant women from developed nations and Canadian-born women that may have accounted for Canadian-born women's elevated risk. However, sequential logistic regressions demonstrated that controlling for microsystem variables removed the elevated odds of violence against Canadian-born women. The cross-tabulations showed that immigrant women from developed nations and their partners tended to have higher levels of education, to have relationships of longer duration, and to be less likely to have children under the age of 15, all of which have been related to a reduced risk of violence against women (Brownridge & Halli, 2003). Hence, a selection effect may have been operating such that the lower risk for immigrant women from developed nations was due to these individuals being in a later stage of their life course.

Immigrant Women's Reversal of Fortunes in the 2004 Survey

The 2004 GSS data indicated a surprising reversal of fortunes in terms of immigrant women's risk of violence in Canada. In the 2004 survey, immigrant women from developed nations had the highest prevalence and those from developing nations had the lowest prevalence of violence. A comparison of the two groups in terms of risk factors showed few changes between the two immigrant groups across the 1999 and 2004 surveys. The major difference concerned the sexual proprietariness variables. There were no significant differences in rates of possessive and sexually jealous behaviours of partners of immigrant women in the 2004 survey. This appeared to be largely the result of fewer reports of possessive and sexually jealous behaviours by partners of immigrant women from developing nations, which declined by 5.5% and 4.7%, respectively (derived by comparing rates on these variables for immigrant women from developing nations across Tables 10.2 and 10.6). Given the analyses of the 1999 data showing that these variables were responsible for the higher risk among immigrant women from developing nations, as well as the similarity on the other risk factors between the two surveys, the

decline in sexually proprietary behaviour in the 2004 survey could be speculated to account for the lower prevalence rate for immigrant women from
developing nations in the 2004 survey. Why partners of immigrant women
from developing nations might be less sexually proprietary than in the past is
an interesting question for future research. To address the question of why
immigrant women from developed nations had an elevated risk for violence
relative to immigrant women from developing nations in the 2004 survey,
sequential logistic regressions were performed. However, none of the variables included in the application of the ecological framework had anything to
offer with respect to understanding the elevated odds of violence against
immigrant women from developed nations in the 2004 survey, hence another
interesting question to be addressed in future research.

From Double Advantage to Double Jeopardy for Immigrant Women from Developed Nations in the 2004 Survey

The final comparison in terms of understanding an elevated risk of violence
in this chapter concerned the higher prevalence of violence against Canadian-
born women relative to immigrant women from developing nations in the
2004 survey. The descriptive analysis identified some differences between the
two groups that may have accounted for Canadian-born women's elevated
odds of violence. The sequential logistic regressions indicated that only the
exosystem variables contributed to some reduction in Canadian-born
women's elevated odds. Based on the theoretical rationale for the inclusion of
the variables at the exosystem level, the female employment variable should
not be responsible for the aforementioned reduction. The application of these
variables in the ecological framework in this chapter suggested that unemployed women would be more socially isolated and thus face a higher risk of
violence. The descriptive analysis, which showed that immigrant women were
more likely than Canadian-born women to be unemployed, suggested that, in
this regard, Canadian-born women had the advantage of having a social
network of co-workers that could serve a protective function. Hence, it
seemed unlikely that this variable accounted for the reduction in Canadian-
born women's elevated risk. On the other hand, based on the theoretical
rationale for inclusion of the variables at the exosystem level, it would appear
likely that the religiosity and/or the rural/urban variables were responsible for
the reduction in Canadian-born women's elevated odds of violence relative to
immigrant women from developing nations. Canadian-born women were
much less likely to attend church services frequently and they were far more
likely to live in a rural area. Based on the theoretical framework, it is possible
that both of these factors may have contributed to less social connectedness,
thereby increasing Canadian-born women's risk for violence. Nevertheless,
because the exosystem variables did not fully account for Canadian-born
women's elevated risk for violence, it remains to be known what was fully

responsible for their elevated odds of violence relative to immigrant women from developing nations in the 2004 GSS.

Immigrant Victims' Post-Violence Experiences Relative to Canadian-Born Victims

To shed light on the post-violence experiences of immigrant relative to Canadian-born victims a number of variables were explored. Most of the past research on victims had been based on women who sought help by either leaving the relationship or staying in a shelter, and those who seek help are believed to be different from those who do not leave an abusive relationship (Ting, 2007). One of the main advantages of the post-violence data in this book is that they were based on a representative sample, and so provided access to victims who did not leave the relationship and/or seek help in a shelter.

The results showed relatively few differences between immigrant and Canadian-born victims in terms of consequences. However, the results indicated that children of immigrant women may be more likely to have been exposed to inter-parental violence through witnessing their mother's victimization. The negative effects of exposure to IPV on children are widely known (Barnett et al., 2005) and exposure to IPV through witnessing the violence may be a particularly pernicious mode of intergenerational transmission (Brownridge, 2006a). These results imply that immigrants to Canada should be considered in the development of violence prevention programmes through, for example, educational campaigns showing parents the potentially dire consequences of their children witnessing violence.

In terms of help-seeking behaviours, overall it appeared that immigrant victims were no less likely than Canadian-born victims to seek help. Of course, seeking help and finding the assistance required are quite different, and, with the exception of the police response, the data in the current study could not speak to the latter. It was, however, noteworthy that immigrant victims in the 1999 survey had lower odds (OR = 0.266) of confiding in a lawyer about the violence. Although past researchers have suggested that immigrant women may not realize that violence by their husbands is illegal (Jang, Lee, & Morello-Frosch, 1990), more recent research suggests that immigrants are aware of the illegality of IPV, at least in the American context (Sorenson, 2006). Other research has suggested that a tendency for immigrant women to avoid confiding in a lawyer may be because immigrant women are less likely to know how to find lawyers that can help them and those that do tend to find them culturally insensitive (MacLeod & Shin, 1993). Hence, measures to enhance immigrant victims' ease of access to and experience with lawyers may be beneficial for their help-seeking.

With respect to police intervention, there was a clear pattern of immigrant victims having higher odds than Canadian-born women of having their violence come to the attention of the police and there were indications that immigrant victims themselves are seeking the assistance of the police to stop the violence. Given that, one may have been surprised to see that these women had lower odds of wanting their partner arrested or punished. However, several writers have pointed out that wanting violence to stop does not mean that all women want criminal charges to be laid against their abusive partners (Currie, 1998; Martin & Mosher, 1995; Snider, 1995). Past research has suggested that many immigrant victims are afraid that if their partner is arrested they will lose their means of financial support (Das Dasgupta, 1998; MacLeod & Shin, 1990; Pratt, 1995). As Martin and Mosher (1995) have observed,

> For women ... who have limited education (or whose foreign qualifications are not recognized), few marketable employment skills, limited fluency in English, and who face a discriminatory workplace which siphons them into job ghettoes characterized by low pay and lack of job security, the risk of economic insecurity is obviously great.
>
> (p. 25)

Indeed, immigrant victims in both surveys appeared to have higher odds than Canadian-born women of not contacting the police because they did not want their partner arrested or jailed. There were also indications in the data that immigrant victims had lower odds of being satisfied with the police response and that the police response was less effective in stopping or decreasing the violence, suggesting that work needs to be done to enhance the efficacy of police intervention. In terms of immigrant victims that did not contact the police, in addition to the aforementioned desire not to have their partner arrested, the element of fear appeared likely to have played an important role. Immigrant victims had much higher odds of not reporting the violence to the police out of fear of their partner and fear of publicity or news coverage. Past research has indeed revealed that many immigrant victims are reluctant to contact the police because they fear retaliation from their spouses (Bauer & Rodriguez, 2000; McDonald, 1999).

Limitations

A number of limitations may have affected the results contained in this chapter. The structure of the data and size of the samples did not allow comparisons of violence across individual nations. Hence, the findings had limited generalizability when referring to immigrants from specific countries that fell within either the developing or developed categories. Sample size was also an important concern for the post-violence comparisons, and these results must be interpreted with particular caution. However, patterns did emerge in the data that, based on representative data, lent support to past research that has identified some unique aspects to immigrant women's post-violence experiences. Nevertheless, the aforementioned limitations restricted the ability to make specific statements about strategies for policy development. The collection of more reliable data in future research would allow the placement of previous analyses in context as well as provide important information for the development of policies and programmes to address more effectively the problem of partner violence against immigrant women. In addition, more information about immigration itself, such as the reason for immigration, needs to be collected in future research.

Conclusion

Based on the analyses of the 1999 and 2004 GSS data, violence against immigrant women in Canada appears to be a complex and dynamic phenomenon. To be sure, the data indicate that immigrant women do face an elevated risk for violence and unique post-violence circumstances. But the changes in immigrant women's prevalence rates of violence between the 1999 and 2004 surveys and the inability of the data to account for all of these changes preclude firm conclusions about violence against immigrant women. It does, however, appear that the reality is quite different from the common perception that at any given time immigrant women in general face an elevated risk for violence and possess more difficulties post-violence. Future research needs to overcome the limitations identified above so that we might have a more concrete understanding of the situation of violence against immigrant women in Canada.

11
Violence Against Women with Disabilities
Perpetrator Characteristics are Key

Despite the fact that women with disabilities rank issues of violence as their most important research and health priorities, there has been a paucity of research on this issue. The dearth of research on violence against women with disabilities has contributed to the invisibility of this social problem (Curry, Hassouneh-Phillips, & Johnston-Silverberg, 2001). This has been the case especially regarding IPV against women with disabilities, which may have stemmed from societal myths that these women are single and asexual (Barnett et al., 2005). Research suggests, however, that intimate partners are the most common perpetrators of violence against women with disabilities (Martin et al., 2006; Milberger et al., 2003; Ridington, 1989; Young, Nosek, Howland, Chanpong, & Rintala, 1997), particularly current partners (Diaz-Olavarrieta, Campbell, Garcia De la Cadena, Paz, & Villa, 1999). Moreover, women with disabilities face an elevated risk for violence by their current marital/common-law partners compared to women without disabilities (Brownridge, 2006b).

While early research was important and helpful in raising awareness of violence against women with disabilities, it was plagued by methodological problems (Nosek, Howland, & Hughes, 2001). Recent years have seen a surge in research on violence against women with disabilities, some of which has overcome many of these methodological problems through the use of stronger samples and more sophisticated techniques of analysis (Renzetti, 2006). However, no study had previously examined the prevalence and risk markers of partner violence against women with disabilities over time to get a sense both of trends in partner violence against these women as well as the extent to which particular risk factors are important in understanding this phenomenon. Indeed, researchers have called for future studies to include a "focus on determining risk factors for abuse among women with disabilities using prospective, multiple time-point, research designs with comparison samples of women without disabilities" (Nosek, Hughes, Taylor, & Taylor, 2006, p. 848). While longitudinal data were not available, the availability of cross-sectional surveys, which included measures with the intention of monitoring changes across time (Federal-Provincial-Territorial Ministers Responsible for the Status of Women, 2002; Johnson, 2006), provided the ability to begin to address this gap in the literature.

The purpose of this chapter, then, is to compare reports of male partner violence against women with and without disabilities across three nationally representative surveys of Canada conducted between 1993 and 2004 to identify: (a) trends in the risk for violence against women with disabilities relative to women without disabilities; (b) patterns in risk markers of violence; and (c) the extent to which risk markers account for the higher rate of violence against women with disabilities relative to women without disabilities between 1993 and 2004.[1]

Explanatory Framework

Most theoretical applications in the literature on violence against women with disabilities organize risk markers for violence based on where they fit within an ecological context (Brownridge, 2006b; Curry et al., 2001; Petersilia, 2001; Sobsey, 1994; Sobsey & Calder, 1999). Based on these studies, this chapter organizes available risk markers into an ecological framework based on whether they related primarily to the context of the relationship, to the victim, or to the perpetrator.

Relationship Factors

A couple's education compatibility can serve as an indication of potential dependence on the relationship (Anderson, 1997). The more resources a woman with disabilities has relative to her partner, the more power she should have in the relationship. Women with disabilities who have fewer relative education resources may be more dependent, less powerful, and thus more prone to violent victimization.

Although both union duration and disability increase with age (Brownridge & Halli, 2001; Statistics Canada, 2002d), in the general population it is primarily women in short duration unions who are most at risk for violence (Brownridge & Halli, 2001; Johnson, 1996; Statistics Canada, 2002d). Brownridge (2006b) found that union duration was negatively related to disabled women's odds of violence, though this impact was not statistically significant.

Victim-Related Characteristics

Women with disabilities are more likely than their non-disabled counterparts to be of low SES. They tend to have lower educational attainment, which serves as a barrier to employment and increases the likelihood that they live in poverty (Curry et al., 2001; Nosek et al., 2001). Low SES is generally associated with violence (Barnett et al., 2005), thereby potentially increasing disabled women's risk.

In addition to socioeconomic characteristics, it is also important to include controls for age and Aboriginal status. Women with disabilities in Canada are more likely to be older (Statistics Canada, 2002d) and Aboriginal women are more likely than non-Aboriginal women to have a disability (Melcombe, 2003).

Perpetrator-Related Characteristics

Feminist disability theory directs attention to the fact that women with disabilities are in a position of double vulnerability, given that they live in a society that is both *disablist* and patriarchal (Curry et al., 2001; Thomson, 1994). This double vulnerability may be compounded by the fact that many crimes against persons with disabilities are motivated by an effort to gain control over the victim's behaviour. Given a connection between violence and both patriarchal domineering (Brownridge, 2002; Smith, 1990a) and controlling behaviour through possessiveness and sexual jealousy (Brownridge, 2004a), women with disabilities may be particularly vulnerable to violence.

Finally, dependency–stress models suggest that caregivers who cannot cope with stress associated with their caregiving are more likely to abuse their charges (Petersilia, 2001). Partners of women with disabilities who feel affected by their partner's disability, particularly if they are the primary caregiver, may experience stress (Melcombe, 2003). Heavy alcohol consumption is an indication of stress that has been linked to partner violence (Johnson, 2001). Hence, partners of women with disabilities who feel stressed may turn to alcohol, which may, in turn, increase their likelihood of violence.

Subsamples and Risk Factors

Subsamples

The data employed in this chapter were from all three surveys (see Chapter 3 for details of the surveys and methods). Before identifying the subsamples of women with and without disabilities in this study, it is important to discuss the definition of disability used in this chapter.

No single definition of *disability* is universally agreed upon (United Nations, 2001). The three main sources of definitions in the literature come from the World Health Organization (WHO), the United Nations (UN), and the Americans with Disabilities Act (ADA; Curry et al., 2001; Gilson, DePoy, & Cramer, 2001; Howe, 2000). Statistics Canada adopted the WHO definition in the early 1980s (Statistics Canada, 2002c). Known as the International Classification of Impairments, Disabilities and Handicaps (ICIDH), disability was defined by the WHO as "any restriction or lack (resulting from an impairment) of ability to perform an activity in the manner or within the range considered normal for a human being" (De Kleijn-De Vrankrijker, 2003, p. 563). To measure disability, Statistics Canada adapted Activities of Daily Living (ADL) questions that were developed by the Organization for Economic Cooperation and Development (OECD; Statistics Canada, 2002c).

To maximize the inclusion of persons with disabilities, in 1997 Statistics Canada revised its questions. Noting that these questions are not perfect, they can nevertheless be used as a "global disability indicator" (Statistics Canada, 2002c, p. 14). Meanwhile, the WHO revised its model of classification of disability, termed the International Classification of Functioning, Disability and Health (ICF; De Kleijn-De Vrankrijker, 2003). Statistics Canada uses the ICF as its framework, defining disability as "the relationship between body structures and functions, daily activities and social participation, while recognizing the role of environmental factors" (Duclos & Langlois, 2003, p. 18). Using this definition in its 2001 Participation and Activity Limitation Survey (PALS), persons having a disability were defined as "those who reported difficulties with daily living activities, or who indicated that a physical, mental condition or health problem reduced the kind or amount of activities they could do" (Duclos & Langlois, 2003, p. 18).

There were some differences in the specific questions that measured disability in the three surveys. The 1993 survey asked respondents "Are you limited in the amount or kind of activity you can do at home, at work or at school because of a long-term physical condition or health problem?" (Statistics Canada, 1994b, p. 26). In the 1999 survey, respondents were asked, "Does a long term physical or mental condition or health problem reduce the amount or the kind of activity that you can do at home, at school, at work or in other activities?" (Statistics Canada, 2000, p. 114). In the 2004 survey, respondents were asked, "Do you have any difficulty hearing, seeing, communicating, walking, climbing stairs, bending, learning or doing any similar activities?"[2] If respondents indicated "yes sometimes" or "yes, often," they were asked three additional questions as follows: "Does a physical condition or mental condition or health problem reduce the amount or the kind of activity you can do ... at home? ... at work or at school? ... in other activities, for example, transportation or leisure?" (Statistics Canada, 2005b, pp. 326–327). A variable was then derived from these questions. The resulting prevalence rates of disability were 15.1% in the 1993 survey, 15.7% in the 1999 survey, and 11.3% in the 2004 survey. Hence, the largest difference in operationalization and prevalence of disability across the three surveys was in the 2004 survey. This was unlikely to be due to an actual decrease in the population of women with disabilities, especially given an ageing population in general. It appeared likely that some women who did not have difficulty hearing, seeing, communicating, walking, climbing stairs, bending, learning, or doing any similar activities would nevertheless perceive themselves as having a reduced ability to engage in activities at home, work, or school because of a physical or mental health problem. Given that women with activity limitations have been shown to face an elevated risk for violence regardless of whether they experience activity limitations sometimes or often (Cohen, Forte, Mont, Hyman, & Romans, 2005), as well as research suggesting that level of disability severity does not impact the prevalence of violence (Powers et al., 2002), if anything, the impact of this operationalization should have been to make the relative risk in 2004 a conservative estimate. That is, some high-risk women who were coded as disabled in the 1993 and 1999 surveys may have been coded as non-disabled in the 2004 survey.

Since this chapter concerns violence against women in their current relationship, the subsamples of heterosexual women living married or common-law at the time of the survey consisted of 8,417 women (1,268 with disabilities and 7,149 without disabilities) from the 1993 survey, 7,027 women (1,092 with disabilities and 5,935 without disabilities) from the 1999 survey, and 6,769 women (748 with disabilities and 5,866 without disabilities) from the 2004 survey.[3]

Risk Factors

Relationship factors available in the data were education compatibility and duration of relationship. Victim-related characteristics included woman's education, woman's employment, woman's age, and Aboriginal status. Perpetrator-related characteristics included patriarchal dominance, possessive behaviour, sexual jealousy, and heavy alcohol consumption.

Results

Descriptive Analysis

VIOLENCE BY DISABILITY STATUS

The first two columns of Table 11.1 provide the lifetime prevalence of violence in the 1993 VAWS and the 1-year and 5-year prevalence of violence in all three surveys for women with and without disabilities. The results showed that women with disabilities had a significantly higher prevalence of violence in all time frames with the exception of the year prior to the 1999 GSS. The most inclusive rate in Table 11.1 is the lifetime prevalence recorded in the 1993 survey. A total of 21% of women with disabilities reported having ever experienced violence by their current partner compared to 14% of women without disabilities in the VAWS.

There also appeared to be an overall pattern of an increased risk for violence against women with disabilities relative to women without disabilities. To express the relative risk of violence for women with and without disabilities, as shown in the third column of Table 11.1, zero-order odds ratios were calculated for the disability status variable on each prevalence rate in Table 11.1. The final column reports whether the differences between the odds from 1993 to 1999 and from 1999 to 2004 were statistically significant. The odds of violence for women with disabilities relative to women without disabilities using a 5-year time frame increased from 1.2 times in 1993 to 1.4 times in 1999. Although this increase was not statistically significant, the increase from

Table 11.1 Prevalence rates (%) of violence for women with and without disabilities in the 1993 VAWS, 1999 GSS, and 2004 GSS, corresponding zero-order odds ratios, and significance of the change across surveys

	Disabled	Non-disabled	Odds ratio	Difference in odds
1993 VAWS				
1-year prevalence	4.6	2.8***	1.675***	
5-year prevalence	9.1	7.8*	1.187	
Lifetime prevalence	21.3	14.4***	1.615***	
1999 GSS				*1993 vs. 1999*
1-year prevalence	2.0	1.7	1.169	1.789**
5-year prevalence	4.9	3.5**	1.390**	–1.168
2004 GSS				*1999 vs. 2004*
1-year prevalence	2.7	1.1***	2.476***	–3.014***
5-year prevalence	5.3	2.9***	1.853***	–1.679**

Note

$*p \leq 0.10$; $**p < 0.05$; $***p < 0.01$ (p values for prevalence rates refer to Pearson Chi-square, for odds ratios the Wald Chi-square was used, and for the difference in odds the t-statistic was used).

1.4 times in 1999 to 1.9 times in 2004 was statistically significant. With respect to the 1-year time frame, the odds of violence decreased from 1.7 in 1993 to 1.2 in 1999, which represented a statistically significant decline in risk. However, the odds of violence against women with disabilities compared to women without disabilities increased significantly from 1999 to 2004, with women reporting a disability having 2.5 times the odds of violence in the year prior to the 2004 survey.

Figures 11.1, 11.2, and 11.3 contain the 5-year prevalence of each component of violence in the 1993, 1999, and 2004 surveys, respectively.[4] An examination of the results in these figures showed that there were significant differences on a similar number of items across all three surveys (seven out of ten in the 1993 and 2004 surveys, and six out of ten in the 1999 survey). Across all three surveys women with disabilities were consistently more likely to report having been threatened to be hit with a fist or anything else that could hurt, being slapped, and being beaten. On two of the three surveys, women with disabilities were more likely to report having been pushed, grabbed, or shoved in a way that could hurt; being choked; being kicked, bit, or hit with a fist; and being forced into any sexual activity by being threatened, held down, or hurt in some way. As well, the greatest disparities occurred on some of the more severe forms of violence. In the 1993 survey, women with disabilities were more than twice as likely to report being

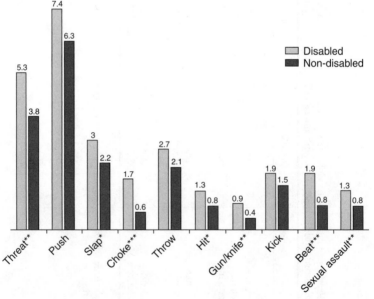

Figure 11.1 Five-year prevalence of each component of violence by disability status in the 1993 VAWS (%).

Note
$*p \leq 0.10$; $**p < 0.05$; $***p < 0.01$ (p values refer to Chi-square tests of significance).

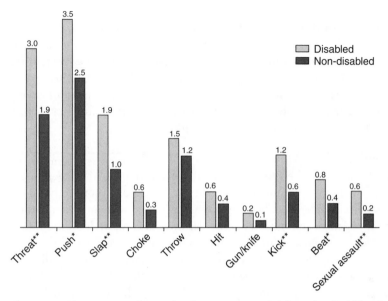

Figure 11.2 Five-year prevalence of each component of violence by disability status in the 1999 GSS (%).

Note
$*p \leq 0.10; **p < 0.05$ (p values refer to Chi-square tests of significance).

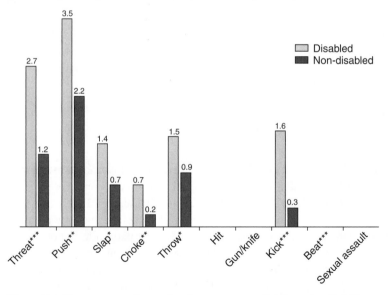

Figure 11.3 Five-year prevalence of each component of violence by disability status in the 2004 GSS (%).

Notes
$*p \leq 0.10; **p < 0.05; ***p < 0.01$ (p values refer to Chi-square tests of significance)
Blank categories indicate cross-tabulations that were not released by Statistics Canada to ensure respondent confidentiality. Statistical significance test is reported.

choked, threatened with or having a knife or gun used against them, and being beaten. In the 1999 survey women with disabilities were twice as likely to be kicked, bit, or hit with a fist and to be beaten. As well, they were three times more likely to report having been sexually assaulted. In the 2004 survey, women with disabilities were more than three times as likely to report having been choked and more than five times as likely to report having been kicked, bit, or hit with a fist compared to women without disabilities.

INDEPENDENT VARIABLES BY DISABILITY STATUS

Table 11.2 contains the results of the cross-tabulations of the independent variables by disability status for each survey. The results showed that there were significant differences between women with and without disabilities on all of the independent variables across all three surveys. Indeed, the differences between women with and without disabilities were very consistent across the three surveys. In terms of relationship factors, women with disabilities were more likely than women without disabilities to be in relationships that were educationally incompatible at both ends of the continuum. As well, women with disabilities were more likely to have longer duration unions. With respect to victim-related characteristics, women with disabilities were more likely to have less than high school education and less likely to have a university degree. They were also more likely to be unemployed, older, and Aboriginal. In terms of perpetrator-related characteristics, partners of women with disabilities were more likely to engage in patriarchal domination, possessiveness, and sexual jealousy. However, they were less likely to have consumed alcohol heavily and no more likely to have drunk heavily five or more times in the month prior to each survey.

Multivariate Analyses

LOGISTIC REGRESSIONS FOR WOMEN WITH AND WITHOUT DISABILITIES

To identify the impact of each variable on the odds of violence against women with and without disabilities, separate logistic regressions were run for each group. The results of these analyses are presented in Table 11.3.

In terms of relationship factors, as shown in Table 11.3, holding all other variables in the models constant, there was no clear pattern in the operation of the education compatibility variable across the three surveys. Union duration appeared to have slightly less impact on disabled and non-disabled women's odds of violence over time. This was especially true for women with disabilities whose odds of violence changed from a 4% reduction for each additional year the couple was together in the 1993 survey to having no impact on the odds of violence in the 2004 survey.

With respect to victim-related characteristics, education shifted from having no impact on the odds of violence for either group of women in 1993 and 1999 to having a positive impact on the odds of violence for both groups in 2004. Each unit of increase in a woman's education was accompanied by an 18% increase in the odds of violence for those with disabilities and a 10% increase for those without disabilities. Unemployment did not have a significant impact on the odds of violence in any of the surveys. Age tended to be negatively related to women's odds of violence in both groups, though the significance of the impact varied across the surveys. Aboriginal status had a strong positive impact on the odds of violence against women without disabilities in both 1999 and 2004. For women with disabilities this variable did not have a significant impact on the odds of violence in 1999 but it did in 2004. In the latter survey Aboriginal women with disabilities had 357% greater odds of violence compared to non-Aboriginal women with disabilities.

In terms of perpetrator-related characteristics, patriarchal dominance had a stronger impact on the odds of violence against women without disabilities than for women with disabilities across all three surveys. Indeed, the impact of this variable on the odds of violence for women with disabilities was significant only in the 1999 survey. Possessive and sexually jealous behaviour by partners of women both with and without disabilities was linked to significantly increased odds of violence across all three surveys. Finally, heavy alcohol consumption had a strong positive impact on the odds of violence against women without disabilities in all three surveys. This variable did not have a significant impact on the odds of violence against women with disabilities in either the 1993 or the 1999 survey. However, in the 2004 survey heavy drinking had an even larger impact on the odds of violence against women with disabilities than it did for women without disabilities. Each additional occasion in which a woman's partner consumed alcohol heavily in the month prior to the 2004 survey was linked to a 14% increase in the odds of violence against women with disabilities and a 9% increase in the odds of violence against women without disabilities.

LOGISTIC REGRESSIONS FOR WOMEN WITH AND WITHOUT
DISABILITIES COMBINED

Table 11.4 provides the results of the sequential logistic regressions on the 5-year prevalence of violence for women with and without disabilities in each survey. The first model in Table 11.4 contains the odds of violence for women with and without disabilities without any controls (also found in Table 11.1). In the second model, relationship factors were controlled; in the third, victim-related characteristics were controlled; in the fourth, perpetrator-related characteristics were controlled; and in the fifth, all variables were controlled simultaneously.

With respect to the 1993 data, although the odds of violence in the 5 years prior to the study were not significantly higher for women with disabilities,

Table 11.2 Independent variables by disability status in the 1993 VAWS, 1999 GSS, and 2004 GSS (%)

Independent variables	1993		1999		2004	
	n = 1,268 Disabled	*n = 7,149* Non-disabled	*n = 1,092* Disabled	*n = 5,935* Non-disabled	*n = 748* Disabled	*n = 5,866* Non-disabled
Relationship factors						
Education compatibility						
Woman has much less education	17.9	15.2	18.3	15.2	15.9	13.7
Woman has less education	10.6	14.1	10.5	14.2	11.3	13.2
Woman has same education	37.1	39.0	33.8	33.3	34.5	34.5
Woman has more education	11.4	13.1	14.9	18.4	15.0	18.9
Woman has much more education	23.1	18.7***	22.5	18.9***	23.2	19.7**
Duration of relationship						
Less than 4 years	9.0	15.0	8.4	12.3	9.1	14.6
4–9 years	11.3	18.2	11.4	18.4	9.8	18.3
10 or more years	79.6	66.8***	80.1	69.2***	81.1	67.1***
Victim-related characteristics						
Education						
Less than high school	38.8	22.2	35.0	17.7	27.7	14.7
High school	23.5	29.7	13.7	17.7	15.3	18.5
Some post secondary	12.6	14.2	13.6	13.8	14.2	12.8
Community college dip./cert.	15.1	16.6	24.1	28.6	29.3	29.2
University degree	10.0	17.3***	13.5	22.3***	13.5	24.8***
Employment						
Unemployed	55.4	32.5	42.5	27.8	38.3	25.7
Employed	44.6	67.5***	57.7	72.2***	61.7	74.3***

Age						
18/15–34	15.9	32.1	12.0	27.7	8.8	24.3
35–54	41.4	46.1	39.4	50.8	41.1	49.8
55+	42.7	21.8***	48.6	21.5***	50.1	25.8***
Aboriginal status						
Aboriginal	NA	NA	2.9	1.8	3.5	2.2
Non-Aboriginal	NA	NA	97.1	98.2**	96.5	97.8**
Perpetrator-related characteristics						
Patriarchal dominance						
Yes	11.4	6.0	2.1	0.8	2.3	0.7
No	88.6	94.0***	97.9	99.2***	97.7	99.3***
Possessiveness						
Yes	13.1	9.9	5.6	3.7	3.8	2.5
No	86.9	90.1***	94.4	96.3***	96.2	97.5**
Jealousy						
Yes	8.5	5.3	7.1	4.1	4.2	2.6
No	91.5	94.7***	92.9	95.9***	95.8	97.4**
Heavy drinking (past month)						
None	82.6	75.2	83.3	79.1	80.4	74.5
Once	5.8	10.8	6.6	9.4	8.4	10.9
2–4 times	7.9	10.6	6.9	8.5	8.9	11.1
5 or more times	3.6	3.4***	3.2	3.1**	2.3	3.5**

Notes

**$p \leq 0.05$; ***$p < 0.01$ (p values refer to Chi-square tests of significance).

NA Not available in the data.

Table 11.3 Results of logistic regressions on the 5-year prevalence of violence in the 1993 VAWS, 1999 GSS, and 2004 GSS for women with and without disabilities

Covariates	1993			1999			2004		
	Disabled n = 1,158	Non-disabled n = 6,699		Disabled n = 966	Non-disabled n = 5,338	n = 748	Disabled n = 5,432	Non-disabled	
	OR	OR	t	OR	OR	t	OR	OR	t
Relationship factors									
Education compatibility									
Woman much less edu.	1.411	1.122	0.879	0.670	0.834	-0.499	1.173	1.576	-0.550
Woman less edu.	0.375*	0.852	-2.016**	0.892	1.023	-0.313	4.531***	1.504	2.615***
Woman same edu.	1.000	1.000		1.000	1.000		1.000	1.000	
Woman more edu.	1.658	1.288*	0.928	0.454	1.303	-2.370***	0.566	1.269	-1.491*
Woman much more edu.	1.412	1.396**	0.048	1.360	0.867	1.327*	1.242	1.563*	-0.546
Duration of relationship	0.964**	0.972***	-0.680	0.981	0.975*	0.415	1.006	0.981	1.384*
Victim-related chars.									
Education	1.030	0.963	1.667**	1.033	1.002	0.487	1.175*	1.101*	0.848
Employment									
Unemployed	1.061	1.092	-0.145	1.433	0.925	1.431*	1.129	1.015	0.262
Employed	1.000	1.000		1.000	1.000		1.000	1.000	
Age	0.981	0.969***	1.204	0.957**	0.981	-1.482*	0.960	0.982	-1.119
Aboriginal status									
Aboriginal	NA	NA		1.136	2.795**	-1.491*	4.573**	2.250**	1.262
Non-Aboriginal	NA	NA		1.000	1.000		1.000	1.000	

Perpetrator-related chars.

Patriarchal dominance									
Yes	1.231	2.083***	−2.108**	3.689**	12.602***	−2.388***	1.059	12.358***	−3.278***
No	1.000	1.000		1.000	1.000		1.000	1.000	
Possessiveness									
Yes	2.434***	2.965***	−0.879	3.412**	4.521***	−0.702	2.936*	3.452***	−0.323
No	1.000	1.000		1.000	1.000		1.000	1.000	
Jealousy									
Yes	3.144***	2.739***	0.537	2.293*	4.975***	−2.013**	9.094***	4.313***	1.570*
No	1.000	1.000		1.000	1.000		1.000	1.000	
Heavy drinking	1.032	1.108***	−3.742***	1.044	1.106***	−2.440***	1.137***	1.088***	1.544*
Constant	0.200**	0.371**		0.237	0.067***		0.013**	0.012***	
−2 Log likelihood	593	3,043		305	1,310		230	1,219	
χ^2	118***	557***		79***	332***		67***	185***	

Notes
*$p \leq 0.10$; **$p < 0.05$; ***$p < 0.01$.
NA Not available in the data.

Table 11.4 Results of sequential logistic regressions on the 5-year prevalence of violence in the 1993 VAWS, 1999 GSS, and 2004 GSS

Covariates	Model 1 Disabled/ non-disabled Odds ratio	Model 2 Relationship factors Odds ratio	Model 3 Victim-related characteristics Odds ratio	Model 4 Perpetrator-related characteristics Odds ratio	Model 5 Full model Odds ratio
1993 VAWS	$n = 8,338$	$n = 8,135$	$n = 8,329$	$n = 8,039$	$n = 7,857$
Disability status					
Disabled	1.187	1.592***	1.675***	1.053	1.443***
Non-disabled	1.000	1.000	1.000	1.000	1.000
Relationship factors		Block			Block
Victim-related characteristics			Block		Block
Perpetrator-related characteristics				Block	Block
Constant	0.084***	0.177***	1.119	0.052***	0.294***
−2 Log likelihood	4,628	4,242	4,373	3,968	3,653
χ^2	3	276***	255***	437***	662***
1999 GSS	$n = 6,912$	$n = 6,610$	$n = 6,806$	$n = 6,544$	$n = 6,304$
Disability status					
Disabled	1.390**	1.867***	2.008***	1.025	1.409*
Non-disabled	1.000	1.000	1.000	1.000	1.000
Relationship factors		Block			Block
Victim-related characteristics			Block		Block
Perpetrator-related characteristics				Block	Block
Constant	0.037***	0.079***	0.331**	0.023***	0.085***
−2 Log likelihood	2,196	2,048	2,061	1,779	1,641
χ^2	4**	86***	110***	320***	390***
2004 GSS	$n = 6,532$	$n = 6,343$	$n = 6,475$	$n = 6,375$	$n = 6,180$
Disability status					
Disabled	1.853***	2.217***	2.442***	1.666**	2.000***
Non-disabled	1.000	1.000	1.000	1.000	1.000
Relationship factors		Block			Block
Victim-related characteristics			Block		Block
Perpetrator-related characteristics				Block	Block
Constant	0.030***	0.038***	0.054***	0.021***	0.009***
−2 Log likelihood	1,819	1,677	1,719	1,610	1,462
χ^2	10***	61***	69***	192***	240***

Note: $* p \leq 0.10$; $** p < 0.05$; $*** p < 0.01$.

sequential logistic regressions were performed to identify whether a pattern exists in the impact of controlling for the independent variables on the odds ratio. The results showed that only the perpetrator-related characteristics reduced the odds of violence against women with disabilities.

In the 1999 data, where women with disabilities had significantly higher odds of violence than women without disabilities, the same pattern was evident. That is, the only variables that reduced disabled women's relative odds of violence were the perpetrator-related characteristics. Indeed, controlling for these variables fully accounted for the elevated odds of violence against women with disabilities in the 1999 data.

In terms of the 2004 data, the same general pattern emerged. Once again, the only independent variables that reduced the odds of violence against women with disabilities were the perpetrator-related characteristics. Controlling for these variables reduced the odds of violence against women with disabilities by 19%. Nevertheless, even after controlling for these variables in the 2004 data women with disabilities had 67% greater odds of violence compared to women without disabilities, a difference that was statistically significant.

Post-Violence Experiences for Victims With Disabilities Relative to Victims Without Disabilities

Table 11.5 contains the zero-order odds ratios for the consequences of violence for victims with disabilities compared to victims without disabilities in all three surveys. Victims with disabilities reported much higher odds of being physically injured as a consequence of the violence compared to those without disabilities across all three surveys (1993 OR = 1.995, $p < 0.01$; 1999 OR = 2.020, $p < 0.05$; 2004 OR = 1.844, $p \leq 0.10$). Victims with disabilities also tended to report higher odds of having an altered psyche, taking time off from everyday activities, and staying in bed all or most of the day as a consequence of the violence. On the other hand, with the exception of the 1993 survey, victims with disabilities tended not to have higher odds of being angry as a result of the violence.

The zero-order odds ratios for disabled relative to non-disabled victims' help-seeking behaviours for all three surveys are presented in Table 11.6. Among victims who were physically injured, victims with disabilities were as likely, or more likely, to seek medical treatment for their injuries. Victims with disabilities consistently had higher odds of confiding in someone about the violence. Specifically, they had higher odds of confiding in a family member, a friend or neighbour, a physician or nurse, and/or a religious adviser about the violence.

Victims with disabilities consistently had higher odds of contacting a service. Those with disabilities had a pattern of higher odds of contacting a crisis centre or crisis line across all three surveys. The 1993 and 1999 data

Table 11.5 Zero-order odds ratios for consequences of violence for victims with disabilities relative to victims without disabilities in the 1993 VAWS, 1999 and 2004 GSS

Dependent variable	Disabled/non-disabled[a]					
	1993		1999		2004	
	OR	n	OR	n	OR	n
Physical injury	1.995***	619	2.020**	262	1.844*	210
Psychopathology[b]	1.232	594	1.720	255	0.574	202
Altered psyche[c]	1.695**	594	1.877*	255	1.145	202
Anger	1.254	594	0.799	255	0.753	202
Time off everyday activities	3.314***	617	2.218**	261	1.062	210
Stay in bed all/most of day	NA		1.632	262	3.268*	210
Children witnessed violence	1.217	521	1.205	211	0.992	148

Notes
$*p \leq 0.10$; $**p < 0.05$; $***p < 0.01$.
a Non-disabled is the reference category with an odds of 1.000.
b Includes depression or anxiety attacks, fear, afraid for children, more cautious or aware, sleep problems, shock or disbelief, hurt or disappointment, and upset, confused, or frustrated.
c Includes ashamed or guilty, lowered self-esteem, problems relating to men, and increased self-reliance.
NA Not available in the data.

were contradictory with respect to disabled victims' odds of contacting a shelter or transition house and/or a women's centre, with the 1993 data suggesting that disabled women had lower odds while the 1999 data suggested they had higher odds on these variables. Data from the 1999 survey suggested that they may have higher odds of being in contact with a police or court-based victim service. Victims with disabilities also expressed higher odds of being interested in mediation or conciliation in the 1999 and 2004 surveys.

Table 11.7 contains the zero-order odds ratios for police intervention variables for victims with disabilities relative to those without disabilities in all three surveys. Victims with disabilities tended to report higher odds of the police finding out about the violence across all three surveys. The 1999 data suggested that victims with disabilities had higher odds of reporting the violence to the police to have their partner arrested or punished than on the recommendation of someone else. In terms of action taken by the police for those who had police contact, the 1999 data suggested that violent partners of victims with disabilities had higher odds of receiving a warning from the police. Victims with disabilities consistently reported lower odds of the police taking their partner away, slightly higher odds of being put in touch with community services, and lower odds of the violence decreasing or stopping following police intervention. They also had lower odds of reporting being satisfied with the response of the police. Among victims that did not contact the police, the 1999 and 2004 data showed that those with disabilities had higher odds of having not done so because they dealt with the violence in

Table 11.6 Zero-order odds ratios for victims' help-seeking behaviours for women with disabilities relative to women without disabilities in the 1993 VAWS, 1999 and 2004 GSS

| Dependent variable | Disabled/non-disabled[a] | | | | | |
| | 1993 | | 1999 | | 2004 | |
	OR	n	OR	n	OR	n
Visit doctor/nurse/hospital for treatment	1.901*	141	0.976	73	†	209
Confided in someone:	1.527**	615	2.690**	259	3.222**	208
Family	1.455*	615	2.630***	259	2.376**	209
Friend/neighbour	1.522**	615	2.156**	258	1.262	209
Co-worker	NA		1.526	257	0.803	209
Doctor/nurse	3.089***	615	4.705***	257	1.533	
Lawyer	NA		0.995	258	†	
Minister/priest/clergy/spiritual adviser	2.495**	615	1.841	257	†	
Services contacted:	1.441*	618	3.984***	260	1.383	209
Crisis centre/line	1.746	618	3.953***	260	1.995	208
Another counsellor/psychologist	1.636**	618	2.862***	260	0.737	209
Community/family centre	0.755	618	1.111	260	†	
Shelter/transition house	0.773	618	2.963**	260	†	
Women's centre	0.702	618	2.788**	260	†	
Police/court-based victim service	NA		4.080**	260	†	
Interested in mediation/conciliation	NA		1.482	253	1.739	196

Notes
*p ≤ 0.10; **p < 0.05; ***p < 0.01.
a Non-disabled is the reference category with an odds of 1.000.
† Statistics Canada would not release the result to ensure respondent confidentiality. Statistical significance test was not released.
NA Not available in the data.

Table 11.7 Zero-order odds ratios for police intervention for victims with disabilities relative to victims without disabilities in the 1993 VAWS, 1999 and 2004 GSS

Dependent variable	Disabled/non-disabled[a]					
	1993		1999		2004	
	OR	n	OR	n	OR	n
Police found out	1.299	616	1.992**	260	1.985*	208
Police found out from respondent	NA		0.872	68	†	
Reason police contacted:						
Stop violence/receive protection	NA		0.349	53	†	
Arrest/punish spouse/partner	NA		1.319	54	†	
Duty to notify police	NA		0.689	53	†	
Recommendation of someone else	NA		1.302	54	†	
Police action:						
Visited scene	NA		0.798	65	†	
Made report/conducted investigation	NA		0.557	65	†	
Gave warning to spouse/partner	NA		2.055	65	†	
Took spouse/partner away	0.342*	64	0.568	65	†	
Put you in touch with community services	1.119	64	1.222	65	†	
Made arrest/laid charges	NA		NA		†	
None	NA		1.063	65	†	
Respondent satisfied w/police	0.448	63	0.136***	66	†	
Post-police violence decreased/stopped	0.833	63	0.389	41	†	

Reasons police not contacted:						
Dealt with in another way[b]	NA		1.703	191	1.186	167
Did not want to get involved with police	1.511	533	0.986	191	1.971	167
Fear of spouse/partner	0.687	533	0.354	191	1.785	167
Personal matter that did not concern police	NA		0.967	190	0.437*	167
Police couldn't do anything about it	0.670	533	2.482**	191	0.678	167
Police wouldn't help[c]	NA		1.904	190	†	
Police wouldn't think it was important enough	NA		0.686	191	0.628	166
Fear of publicity/news coverage	NA		3.252**	191	0.673	165
Did not want spouse/partner arrested or jailed	1.024	533	1.766	191	2.295*	165
Did not want anyone to find out about it (e.g., shame)	0.763	533	1.433	191	0.816	166
Other reason	2.242	533	0.717	190	†	

Notes
*$p \leq 0.10$; **$p < 0.005$; ***$p < 0.01$.
a Non-disabled is the reference category with an odds of 1.000.
b Includes left him, reported to another official, private matter that took care of myself, etc.
c Includes police wouldn't think it was important enough, wouldn't believe, wouldn't want to be bothered or get involved, police would be inefficient or ineffective, police would be biased, would harass/insult respondent, offender was police officer.
† Statistics Canada would not release the result to ensure respondent confidentiality. Statistical significance test was not released.
NA Not available in the data.

another way and lower odds of having not done so because they felt that the police would not think the violence was important enough.

Discussion

The Elevated Risk of Violence Against Women With Disabilities from 1993 to 2004

The prevalence of violence against women with disabilities is generally described in the literature as being "equal to or greater than their non-disabled peers" (Gilson, DePoy et al., 2001, p. 419). The current study revealed a pattern for women with disabilities to have a high risk for partner violence compared to women without disabilities in Canada. Women with disabilities had an elevated lifetime prevalence of violence, 5-year prevalence of violence, and, with only one exception, annual prevalence of violence.

The results in this chapter also suggested the possibility of a trend towards an increase in the gap in risk for women with disabilities between the 1993 and 2004 surveys. Using the example of the 5-year prevalence rates, which were available in all three surveys and which represented the most adequate account of all women across the three surveys who had experienced violence, the odds of violence against women with disabilities relative to women without disabilities changed from being insignificant in 1993 (19%), to being significantly higher in 1999 (39%), and even higher in 2004 (85%). An examination of the prevalence rates from the two most comparable surveys, both iterations of the GSS, suggested that the growing gap in the risk for violence against women with disabilities was due to an increase in the prevalence of violence against women with disabilities and a simultaneous decrease in the prevalence of violence against women without disabilities. The 5-year and 1-year prevalence of violence against women with disabilities in the 1999 and 2004 surveys increased by 0.4% and 0.7%, respectively, and each decreased by 0.6% for women without disabilities.

The results also revealed that women with disabilities were consistently more likely to report experiencing the majority of individual violence items. On all three surveys women with disabilities were more likely to report having been threatened to be hit with a fist or anything else that could hurt, being slapped, and being beaten. The results also suggested that women with disabilities had a particularly high risk of experiencing severe forms of violence. Women with disabilities were two to five times more likely than women without disabilities to report some of the more severe forms of violence, including being choked; kicked, bit, or hit with a fist; and being beaten by their partner.

It has been argued that "investigators rarely assume that disabled women have intimate partners, so IPV often goes undetected" (Barnett et al., 2005, pp. 353–354). With respect to the Canadian situation, the evidence suggests not only that disabled women's risk for violence by their intimate partners is greater than women without disabilities, and especially so on some of the more severe forms of violence, but also that there may have been a widening of the gap in their risk over time. Clearly, effective prevention of partner violence against women with disabilities requires all stakeholders to be aware of the reality of the problem. This also requires an understanding of why women with disabilities face such a high risk for IPV.

Examining the Elevated Risk of Violence Against Women With Disabilities using an Ecological Framework

To investigate the elevated risk of partner violence against women with disabilities an explanatory framework that organized risk markers in terms of relationship factors, victim-related characteristics, and perpetrator-related characteristics was examined.

RELATIONSHIP FACTORS

Although women with disabilities were more likely to be in relationships that were educationally incompatible across all three surveys, there was no clear pattern in the impact of this variable on disabled women's odds of violence across the three surveys. Women with disabilities were more likely to have longer duration unions across all three surveys. This variable appeared to have less of an impact on disabled women's odds of violence over time. Controlling for both of these relationship factors did not reduce the odds of violence against women with disabilities in any of the surveys. Hence, relationship factors were not important for understanding the elevated risk of violence against women with disabilities.

VICTIM-RELATED CHARACTERISTICS

Women with disabilities were consistently more likely to have had lower levels of education, to be unemployed, older, and Aboriginal. Across the three surveys unemployment did not have a significant impact on the odds of violence and age tended to be negatively related to violence for both groups of women. Although women with disabilities tended to have lower levels of education, this variable did not have an impact on the odds of violence in the 1993 and 1999 surveys. In 2004, however, education was positively associated with the odds of violence for both groups. The impact of Aboriginal status also shifted from the 1999 to 2004 surveys. In 1999, Aboriginal women with disabilities did not have higher odds of violence than non-Aboriginal women with disabilities. However, in 2004 Aboriginal women with disabilities had 357% greater odds of violence compared to their non-Aboriginal counterparts. Despite some variation in these risk markers across the surveys, the results showed that these victim-related characteristics did not reduce disabled women's elevated odds of violence in any of the surveys.

PERPETRATOR-RELATED CHARACTERISTICS

An examination of the data on perpetrator-related characteristics across all three surveys showed that male partners of women with disabilities were about two to three times more likely to behave in a patriarchal domineering manner, one to 1.5 times more likely to behave in a possessive manner, and 1.6 times more likely to behave in a sexually jealous manner towards their partners. While patriarchal dominance had a significant impact on the odds of violence against women with disabilities only in the 1999 survey, posses-siveness and jealousy had a significant impact on both disabled and non-disabled women's odds of violence in all three surveys. These results lent some support to the application of feminist disability theory. Contrary to the dependency–stress model, across all three surveys partners of women with disabilities were not more likely to abuse alcohol. In 1993 and 1999 alcohol abuse did not have a significant impact on disabled women's odds of violence. However, in 2004 this variable not only had a significant impact on disabled women's odds of violence, but also the impact was greater for women with disabilities compared to women without disabilities. Moreover, the perpetrator-related characteristics were the only variables that reduced the elevated odds of violence against women with disabilities. This pattern was evident in all three surveys. However, despite the new importance of the heavy alcohol consumption variable in the 2004 data, the results showed that as the extent of disabled women's elevated odds of violence increased, the perpetrator-related characteristics measured in this study were unable to account fully for this gap in risk.

Although the study was limited to available variables in the VAWS and GSSs, and therefore several relationship, victim-related, and perpetrator-related variables could not be examined, the apparent importance of the perpetrator-related characteristics suggested that unmeasured characteristics of the perpetrators were most likely responsible for the remaining elevated risk in the 2004 data. Hence, while future research should examine all poten-tial explanations for disabled women's elevated risk for violence, the results of this study clearly suggested that perpetrator-related characteristics were central. Several perpetrator-related characteristics that were not available for analysis in this chapter have been identified by researchers. These include the perpetrator's need for control, low self-esteem, authoritarianism, displaced aggression, poor impulse control, exposure to abusive models, anxiety, devaluing attitudes, and antisocial behaviour (Curry et al., 2001; Sobsey, 1994). Although these characteristics are not unique to perpetrators of viol-ence against women with disabilities, other factors have been identified that are unique to the situation of women with disabilities. For example, Martin et al. (2006) suggested that perpetrators may view women with disabilities as less able to resist and/or less likely to report the violence.

Copel's (2006) investigation into the lived experiences of partner abuse against women with physical disabilities has also provided insights into the perpetrators of partner violence against women with physical disabilities. Using a convenience sample of 25 women with physical disabilities, the analysis identified a process in which stressors would accumulate to the point where they exceeded the partner's ability to cope, which in turn led to abuse. This was followed by a period of separation where the partner would leave the scene. Eventually, the situation would return to normal but the stressors would accumulate again, continuing the cycle. Copel noted that the cycle of violence for these women with physical disabilities was different from that found in a general sample by Walker (1993) due to the absence of a loving contrition phase. Copel (2006) wrote that "for disabled women, there was the feeling that since their disability rendered them physically 'different from' or 'less than' other women, there was no compelling reason for the male partner to be remorseful" (p. 124). Indeed, Copel (2006) identified the source of physically disabled women's vulnerability to abuse in "the lack of value for the woman and the couple relationship, along with a punitive view of the woman's disability and difficulty functioning in her former roles" (p. 124). These women were dehumanized by their partner and his "distortion of power and misuse of male privilege replaced his sense of moral behaviour and responsibility and served as a justification for his violent actions" (p. 124). Similarly, it has elsewhere been argued that violence against women with disabilities must be understood in the context of societal hatred, fear, and loathing of persons with disabilities, where deformities of the body symbolize deformities of the soul; and so, persons with disabilities are perceived as being less human (Waxman, 1991).

While Copel's (2006) study was not generalizable and examined only women with physical disabilities, it suggested a connection between a disablist society, disabled women's partner's resentment over the disability, and their partner's controlling behaviour and violence. This may also help to account for the importance of the perpetrator-related characteristics in the current study. The results of the analyses contained in this chapter suggested overall that efforts to reduce men's patriarchal domineering, possessive, and sexually jealous behaviours in the general population may also help to reduce partner violence against women with disabilities, especially given that they are more likely than partners of women without disabilities to express these behaviours. However, as both Copel's study and feminist disability theory suggest, this needs to be accompanied by efforts to change our disablist society. A society that is not disablist is one that would provide to those with disabilities and their partners, among other things, the resources they need to cope with stress associated with the disability and whose collective conscience would inculcate an ideology of absolute respect for, patience with, and understanding of the situation of persons with disabilities.

Consequences of Violence and Experiences with Services for Victims With Disabilities Relative to Victims Without Disabilities

A number of the results in the post-violence comparison were consistent with the finding that victims with disabilities tended to be more likely to experience severe forms of violence and/or were more vulnerable to consequences associated with violence. This included that victims with disabilities had greater odds of physical injury, an altered psyche, taking time off from everyday activities, and staying in bed for all or most of the day as a result of the violence. Past research has, indeed, suggested that victims with disabilities may be more vulnerable to serious or lasting injury than their non-disabled counterparts (Andrews & Veronen, 1993). The observation that victims with disabilities tended to be more likely to experience severe violence was also buttressed by the finding that the police tended to be more likely to find out about their victimization and that the violence was less likely to decrease or stop following police intervention.

Despite a higher likelihood of violence in general, and severe violence in particular, victims with disabilities tended not to have higher odds of being angry as a result of the violence. One potential explanation for this apparent contradiction is that some of the women with disabilities may have been more accepting of or willing to tolerate a certain amount of violence. Research has shown that women with disabilities who have poor body and sexual esteem "explicitly stated that they had lowered their expectations and standards with regard to selection of intimate partners and were willing to tolerate a certain level of abuse rather than be alone" (Hassouneh-Phillips & McNeff, 2005). This desire to stay with an abusive partner may also have been reflected in the finding that victims with disabilities had higher odds of being interested in mediation or conciliation. That is, they may have been less eager to separate to end the violence because of their dependence on their partner and/or concerns about loneliness.

Nevertheless, victims with disabilities, having higher odds of both confiding in someone about the violence and contacting a service, were clearly actively reaching out for assistance. In addition to educating the general public about the issue of violence against women with disabilities, so that family, friends, and neighbours will be aware of how best to deal with this issue, the finding that victims with disabilities had higher odds of confiding in medical professionals and religious advisers suggested that special training in issues of violence in general, and violence against women with disabilities in particular, is warranted for these professions.

Disabled victims' higher odds of contacting a crisis centre or crisis line may have reflected issues of mobility for some victims or a lack of accessibility among other services. There were contradictory indications with respect to disabled victims' relative odds of contacting a shelter or transition house.

Although shelters need to be accessible to all victims with disabilities, past research has shown this largely not to be the case (Barile, 2002; Chang et al., 2003; Hassouneh-Phillips, 2005; Hassouneh-Phillips & McNeff, 2005; Swedlund & Nosek, 2000; Young et al., 1997). For instance, in a statewide survey of community domestic violence programmes, Chang et al. (2003) reported that there were two main challenges in providing services for clients with disabilities: (a) lack of funding resulted in inadequate staffing, training for staff, equipment, and an inability to make structural changes to meet the needs of clients with disabilities; and (b) limitations of their facilities resulted in problems providing services to women with physical disabilities, including a lack of space to store medical equipment or house personal care attendants, inability to accommodate assistant dogs, lack of bedrooms on the ground floor, lack of entrance ramps and wheelchair-accessible bathrooms, and lack of special equipment for the hearing or visually impaired. Indeed, Barile (2002) has identified how a lack of funding has resulted in many shelters being inaccessible to women with disabilities, which, in turn, leads to "institutional, system-based violence caused by inaction" (p. 6).

In terms of police intervention, the finding that victims with disabilities had higher odds of the police giving their partners a warning and being put in touch with community services, and lower odds of the police taking their partners away, was disturbing. It was possible that the police were more reluctant to remove partners when they were the caregivers or that officers were less able to make a determination that abuse had occurred for victims with disabilities. In addition to being consistent with disabled victims tending to have experienced more severe violence, the finding that the violence was less likely to decrease or stop following police intervention may have also reflected the lower odds of the violent partner being taken away by the police. The data clearly suggested that victims with disabilities were less satisfied with the police response than those without disabilities. Past research has indicated a mix of views on experiences with the police held by victims of violence with disabilities (Roeher Institute, 1995). In a study of 200 women with disabilities, victims identified calling the police as one of the least helpful strategies for help-seeking (Powers et al., 2002). Such findings have been interpreted to suggest that the police response is largely determined by individual officers' knowledge, sensitivity, and awareness of issues related to victims with disabilities (Powers et al., 2002; Roeher Institute, 1995). This implies that there is a need to improve officer training to ensure that all police officers are equally knowledgeable about, sensitive to, and aware of these issues.

Limitations

While the research in this chapter overcame many of the methodological problems of past research on violence against women with disabilities identified by Nosek et al. (2001), it nevertheless possessed limitations. Although the surveys used in the current study included measures with the intention of monitoring changes over time, they nevertheless need to be compared with caution (Federal-Provincial-Territorial Ministers Responsible for the Status of Women, 2002; Johnson, 2006). As already noted, not all of the measures were identical across the three surveys. This included the specific measures of disability. Although the slight differences in measurement of these variables along with a consideration of these differences in light of past research suggested that, if anything, the 2004 data would provide more conservative estimates of violence against women with disabilities, it is nevertheless the case that caution must be exercised in extrapolating from the results. Although, on the basis of these data, it was not possible to conclude that there is a trend towards increasing rates of violence against women with disabilities, these data have certainly provided food for thought and suggest that future research using standardized longitudinal measurement is warranted. It is also noteworthy that the two surveys that had very similar measures of disability, the 1993 VAWS and 1999 GSS, also suggested an increase in the risk for violence against women with disabilities relative to women without disabilities.

Although this study was the first to compare partner violence against women with disabilities across comparable large-scale nationally representative studies conducted over multiple time points, prospective data were not available. It was not possible with the data to determine whether the women's disability preceded or followed the onset of partner violence, though existing research suggests that disability is usually a precursor to intimate violence. For instance, in Copel's (2006) study, 21 of the 25 participants became disabled following their marriage and for these women the abuse was "associated with the onset of the disability and the changes in role functioning" (p. 121). Ideally, future research will also collect longitudinal data to examine in greater detail the lifespan trajectories of violence against women with disabilities.

Women with disabilities have also been found to experience forms of violence that were not measured with the modified version of the CTS used in the current study (Gilson, Cramer, & Depoy, 2001; Gilson, DePoy et al., 2001), which resulted in an underestimation of the prevalence of partner violence against women with disabilities. As well, women with disabilities that would have prevented them from answering the phone or from understanding the survey were excluded.

Conclusion

Despite the aforementioned limitations, this chapter has added to a growing body of research showing that stakeholders need to recognize and increase their efforts to prevent partner violence against women with disabilities. This is particularly the case in light of the evidence from the analyses contained in this chapter suggesting that the elevated risk of violence against women with disabilities is a social problem that may be growing. In addition to the efforts to change disablist and patriarchal societal views and accompanying behaviours, those who come into contact with women with disabilities, such as persons in the medical field, religious advisers, and the police, need to be trained with respect to issues around disability and violence. As well, services need to be appropriate and accessible for women with disabilities.

12

Conclusion
Assembling Pieces of an Intersectional Puzzle

This book has contributed new knowledge to help assemble pieces of the intersectional puzzle of violence against women. What follows will overview some of the key findings in terms of evidence against essentializing women, the need to apply unique explanatory frameworks to vulnerable populations, the variable interplay of feminist and evolutionary psychology approaches with these unique explanations, how the findings fit with an intersectionality approach, and implications for prevention and future research.

Evidence Against Essentializing Women

A comparison of women's risk for violence in vulnerable populations, as well as a comparison of trends in their relative risk over time, provides insights into the issue of essentializing women.

Differing Vulnerabilities Across Vulnerable Populations

Figure 12.1 contains the 1-year prevalence rates of violence against women in each vulnerable population reported in the 1999 and 2004 surveys. The 1-year rate was presented because it was the only time frame on which there was data for comparison across all vulnerable populations. Only data from the 1999 and 2004 surveys were included in this comparison because data were not available in the 1993 survey on several vulnerable populations (women in stepfamilies, women in rental housing, Aboriginal women, and immigrant women), and the purpose of the current analysis was to compare the 1-year prevalence rates across each vulnerable population. An examination of the prevalence rates in Figure 12.1 showed that separated women had the highest prevalence rate of violence in both the 1999 and 2004 surveys. Separated women's prevalence of violence was 1.7 times the prevalence of the next highest vulnerable population in both the 1999 and 2004 surveys. Clearly, separated women represent a particularly vulnerable population. The results in Figure 12.1 also showed that Aboriginal women consistently had the second highest 1-year prevalence of violence. In the 1999 survey Aboriginal women had a prevalence rate that was 1.5 times that of the vulnerable population with the next highest prevalence, and in the 2004 survey Aboriginal

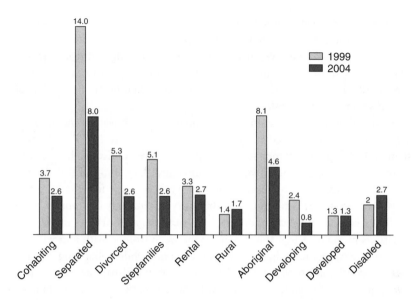

Figure 12.1 One-year prevalence rates of violence against women in each vulnerable population reported in the 1999 and 2004 surveys (%).

women's prevalence rate was 1.7 times that of the next highest ranked vulnerable population. The rank for the remaining vulnerable populations was variable across the 1999 and 2004 surveys. In the 1999 survey divorced women had the next highest prevalence, followed by women in stepfamilies, cohabiting women, women in rental housing, immigrant women from developing nations, women with disabilities, women living in rural settings, and immigrant women from developed nations. In the 2004 survey, women living in rental housing and those with disabilities tied for third highest prevalence. Divorced women, those in stepfamilies, and cohabiting women had the fourth highest prevalence rate. These women were followed by women living in rural settings, immigrant women from developed nations, and immigrant women from developing nations.

Trends in Risk for Violence Against Women in Vulnerable Populations

A comparison of trends in each vulnerable population's risk of violence relative to its comparison group provided further evidence that the vulnerable populations were unique with respect to violence.

For about half of the vulnerable populations, the relative risk of violence was consistent over time. Separated women had a consistent pattern of elevated risk over both divorced and married women. Their elevated risk was three to four times that of divorced women and six to nine times that of married women. Similarly, divorced women's risk was consistently higher compared to married women. Aboriginal women also had a consistent pattern of elevated risk, with rates of violence that were about four times that of non-Aboriginal women. Women living in rental housing had twice the rate of violence as those living in owner-occupied housing across the surveys. Rural-dwelling women's risk for violence was consistently similar to that of urban-dwelling women's risk.

For the other half of the vulnerable populations, there were some interesting nuances in their elevated risk of violence across the surveys. The elevated risk of violence against women in stepfamilies appeared to decline from about 2.3 times to 1.8 times that of women in biological families, and this decline appeared to be the result of a lower prevalence of less severe forms of violence against women in stepfamilies in the 2004 survey. Not only did women with disabilities consistently have elevated odds of violence, but also there were indications in the data that the gap in risk between women with and without disabilities may be increasing. On the other hand, while cohabiting women also consistently had higher odds of violence compared to married women, their relative risk for violence appeared to have declined over time. Finally, immigrant women's relative risk of violence completely reversed across the surveys, with those from developing nations having the highest risk and those from developed nations having the lowest risk in the 1999 survey, and vice versa in the 2004 survey.

Deducing from Differing Vulnerabilities and Trends in Risk

A comparison of results on the prevalence and trends of violence against women in each vulnerable population identified a number of important differences in risk of violence between these groups of women. The sampled women clearly did not have a universal risk of violence. Nor did their risk always appear to be stable. These results suggested that a complete understanding of violence against women requires that women not be essentialized and that the separate analysis of these vulnerable populations was warranted.

Vulnerable Populations Require Unique Applications of Explanatory Frameworks

The analysis of vulnerable populations also demonstrated that a one-size-fits-all theoretical approach did not reflect the complex reality of violence against women. That is to say, the study of each vulnerable population required a unique theoretical treatment. While the most appropriate theoretical framework for guiding the analyses of three of the vulnerable populations (women who had experienced a separation, who had disabilities, and who were immigrants) was an ecological framework (to capture risk factors at various levels of these women's environment), the applications of the framework to each of these vulnerable populations was unique. As noted in the chapter that situated research on vulnerable populations (Chapter 2), there is considerable room for interpretation and application within the ecological framework. This flexibility made it well suited for application to different vulnerable populations. So, for example, even the main levels of the environment analysed were not the same across all three applications of the framework. Based on the review of the literature, the ecological framework applied to violence against women with disabilities was organized around the ecology of the individuals in the couple and their relationship (victim-related, perpetrator-related, and relationship characteristics). That is, the application of the framework to women with disabilities was essentially focused on the microsystem and onto-genic levels. The other two vulnerable populations also included risk factors at the macrosystem level. Moreover, even within the ecological framework, the risk factors that were theoretically relevant to the study of each of these three vulnerable populations varied.

The explanatory frameworks relevant to the other five vulnerable populations were unique to each. For example, the notion that stepfamilies are incomplete institutions, and that a consequent lack of norms for guiding behaviour within them is connected to violence in these families, was certainly tailored to this vulnerable population. Similarly, the unique experience of past and continuing colonization of Aboriginal peoples is, by definition, not applicable to the other vulnerable populations as an overarching explanatory framework.

The Variable Interplay of Feminist and Evolutionary Psychology Approaches with Explanations Unique to Vulnerable Populations

Although patriarchal domination and sexual proprietariness tended to be important factors for understanding violence against women in a number of vulnerable populations, the contribution of these factors was variable and the reality of violence against women in vulnerable populations tended to be much more nuanced. What follows identifies the extent to which there was variable interplay of feminist and evolutionary psychology approaches with unique explanations for the vulnerable populations in this book.

Unique Factors Implicated in Post-Separation Violence

The analyses in the chapter on violence against women post-separation (Chapter 5) showed that separated and divorced women's partners were much more likely than married women's partners to have behaved in a patriarchal dominating and sexually proprietary manner. However, married women with patriarchal dominating, jealous, and possessive partners faced a particularly high risk of having experienced violence. This was because a larger proportion of ex-partners of separated and divorced women who did not behave in a patriarchal dominating or sexually proprietary manner were violent compared to the partners of married women. That finding lent further credence to the notion that there were unique dynamics and factors operating in post-separation violence, and supported the argument that these unique factors needed to be identified and understood for a more complete understanding of violence against women. Indeed, the results showed that youth was a particularly important factor for separated women, and, to a slightly lesser extent, divorced women. Female unemployment and the presence of children tended to be important predictors of violence for divorced women. It may be that the motive of retribution for the woman having left the relationship is a strong motive linked to the young age of many separated and divorced men who perpetrate post-separation violence. Resentment over having to support an ex-wife and issues involving children of the former union may be a particularly salient motive in violence against divorced women. Hence, although it is useful to combine current and former partners in epidemiological studies that attempt to gain an understanding of the prevalence and risk factors involved in violence against women in general, a complete understanding of violence against women requires that research attention also be paid to the unique factors implicated in post-separation violence.

Patriarchal Dominance not a Factor in Aboriginal Women's Elevated Risk of Violence

Results showed that Aboriginal women's partners were more likely to engage in patriarchal domination compared to non-Aboriginal women's partners in only one of the two surveys examined. Moreover, patriarchal domination had a similarly strong positive impact on Aboriginal and non-Aboriginal women's odds of violence and controlling for patriarchal domination did not account for Aboriginal women's elevated odds of violence in either of the surveys. Instead, the results were consistent with the theory that much of Aboriginal women's elevated risk of IPV was due to Aboriginal peoples' past and continuing colonization.

Patriarchal Dominance, Sexual Proprietariness, and Union Duration were Key Factors for Understanding the Elevated Odds of Violence Against Women in Rental Housing

Factors related to male domination and control, family life course, SES, and additional control variables were needed to account fully for the elevated odds of violence against women in rental relative to owner-occupied housing. However, the most important variables were derived from the male control and domination (i.e., feminist and evolutionary psychology) and family life course explanations. Partners of women living in rental housing were more likely than those of women in owner-occupied housing to have engaged in sexual proprietary and patriarchal dominating behaviour. Couples in rental housing were more likely than those in owner-occupied housing to have been together for a short period of time. These factors tended to be associated with increased odds of violence. Hence, variables derived from feminist and evolutionary psychology theories were of key importance, but they needed to be combined with insights from other explanations, particularly union duration, to account fully for the elevated risk of violence against women in rental housing.

Insights from Evolutionary Psychology as well as Unique Factors were
Required to Understand the Elevated Risk of Violence Against Women in
Stepfamilies

Variables derived from the application of evolutionary psychology theory were partially responsible for the elevated odds of violence against women in stepfamilies. In particular, partner's jealousy appeared to be an important variable associated with increased odds of violence against women in stepfamilies. However, insights from institutional incompleteness, union duration, and a selection factor explanation were also required to account fully for the elevated odds of violence against women in stepfamilies.

Jealousy and Possessiveness were Particularly Important for Understanding
the Elevated Risk of Violence Against Women with Disabilities

Although an ecological framework was best suited for organizing risk factors for violence against women with disabilities, results showed that the most powerful variables for understanding the elevated odds of violence against women with disabilities were the perpetrator-related characteristics. In particular, partners of women with disabilities were more likely to behave in a jealous and possessive manner and these variables were consistently positively associated with increased odds of violence for women. Perpetrator-related characteristics fully accounted for the elevated odds of violence against women with disabilities in the 1993 and 1999 surveys, and were responsible for the largest reduction in disabled women's elevated odds of violence in the 2004 survey.

Sexual Proprietariness Variables Needed to be Combined with Selection and
Other Relationship Factors to Understand the Elevated Risk of Violence
Against Cohabiting Women

Although over time it appeared that cohabiting men had become similar to married men in their patriarchal domineering behaviour, they were consistently more likely to engage in a sexually proprietary manner across the surveys. Jealousy and possessiveness were fairly consistently associated with increased odds of violence against cohabiting women (as well as married women). But there were other relationship factors that also appeared to be important, particularly the partner's alcohol abuse and the woman's depression. Moreover, both selection and relationship factors were required to account for the elevated risk of violence against cohabiting relative to married women. Hence, it appeared that sexual proprietariness variables made an important contribution, but they needed to be combined with other relationship factors as well as selection variables to account fully for the elevated odds of violence against cohabiting relative to married women.

Patriarchal Domination was an Important Variable for Rural and Urban Women Alike

Results showed that partners of rural- and urban-dwelling women were equally likely to engage in patriarchal dominating behaviour. Patriarchal domination had a strong positive impact on the odds of violence against both rural- and urban-dwelling women. Risk factors that appeared to make a unique contribution to understanding violence against women in rural areas were the male partner's alcohol abuse and Aboriginal status.

The Varying Importance of Insights from Feminist and Evolutionary Psychology Explanations for Understanding Violence Against Immigrant Women

The sexual proprietariness variables appeared to be important for understanding the double jeopardy faced by immigrant women from developing nations in the 1999 GSS. The reversal of fortunes in the 2004 survey, in which immigrant women from developed nations had the highest prevalence of violence, also appeared to have been impacted by the disappearance of any differences between the two immigrant groups in terms of the partner's sexually proprietary behaviours. However, these variables were not relevant for understanding the Canadian-born women's elevated risk of violence compared to immigrant women from developed nations in the 1999 survey and developing nations in the 2004 survey.

A Brief Statement on Intersectionality and Vulnerable Populations

As noted in Chapter 2, a main weakness of intersectionality is the difficulty in applying it to empirical analyses. This book has moved beyond intersectionality by focusing on populations of women based on their vulnerability with respect to violence, rather than oppression. In so doing it has opened the door to the application and empirical testing of various explanatory frameworks for understanding the unique vulnerabilities of each population, rather than merely contextualizing them in terms of economic or structural factors. Although the research in this book was too different from most articulations of intersectionality to be considered as such, the results certainly can contribute to intersectional understandings of violence against women. In addition to understanding how various factors may contribute to violence against a given vulnerable population of women, an examination of the results across vulnerable populations also can identify some interesting intersections. For instance, the chapter on violence against cohabiting women (Chapter 4) showed that these women had a high risk of violence relative to married women. However, in the chapter on stepfamilies (Chapter 6), it was evident that, controlling for other risk factors relevant to understanding the elevated risk of violence against women in stepfamilies, cohabiting women who lived in stepfamilies consistently had lower odds of violence than their married counterparts living in stepfamilies. This suggested the possibility that cohabiting women in stepfamilies may choose to live common-law out of cautiousness because of the failure of their past union, and that cautiousness may lead them to choose better partners who are less likely to be violent. Understanding this intersection of cohabiting in a stepfamily added an important nuance to our grasp of how both cohabitation and living in a stepfamily impact women's risk for violence.

Implications for Prevention

Research on vulnerable populations can yield important insights for violence prevention. If some groups in society tend to possess characteristics that give them an elevated risk of violence or possess unique circumstances surrounding their violence, we need to address these unique factors. The current study of violence against women in vulnerable populations has shown that *universal prevention* strategies, those that are offered to a broad group of eligible people for whom they may be beneficial, will help to reduce the risk of violence against women in general, including in vulnerable populations. In particular, efforts to change patriarchal and sexually proprietary attitudes and behaviours in society will lower women's risk for violence in general. In the language of epidemiological risk researchers, efforts to reduce patriarchal domination and sexual proprietariness will have an impact on reducing the overall risk for the population of women, or the population attributable risk (PAR; Arnold, Keane, & Baron, 2005). However, the above discussion of the variable interplay of feminist and evolutionary psychology approaches with explanations unique to vulnerable populations suggests that additional efforts will be necessary to reduce further the elevated risk of violence against women in vulnerable populations. These *selective prevention* efforts, which are designed for groups with an elevated risk of violence, need to include a focus on the factors that account for a given vulnerable population's elevated risk. While such efforts will reduce the risk for violence against vulnerable populations of women, it must also be noted that, from a statistical perspective, reducing these women's elevated risk will also contribute to an overall reduction in the prevalence of violence against women in society. Although it is beyond the scope of this book to engage in a detailed application of the findings to violence prevention, it is hoped that violence prevention experts will utilize the information herein, in combination with recommendations from past research, to develop or enhance violence prevention initiatives. What follows summarizes some of the key implications for violence prevention in each vulnerable population.

Providing Women with Resources and Knowledge to Make Informed
Decisions Regarding Separation

The research on post-separation violence has shown that it is an extremely complex phenomenon. Stakeholders need to be aware of the various issues surrounding post-separation violence, including that there appear to be some different dynamics operating in the violence experienced by separated and divorced women. Additional efforts to deal with separated men's anger and desire for retaliation, as well as efforts to deal with divorced men's resentment over having to support their ex-partner and children, would appear to be fruitful directions for reducing separated and divorced women's risk of violence. Service providers also need to ensure that women are aware of the complexities of violence post-separation, so that they can make informed decisions and choices for their, and their children's, futures.

Reclaiming Diminished or Lost Elements of Aboriginal Culture

Among the implications of the research on violence against Aboriginal women contained in this book, including that smaller rural reserves may be particularly important sites for violence prevention and that service providers should ask directly about experiences of violence, the main suggestion from the research concerns efforts to reclaim essential elements of Aboriginal culture. The indirect evidence in support of colonization theory suggests that efforts to reclaim diminished or lost elements of Aboriginal culture, including through Aboriginal self-government, may be crucial for reducing Aboriginal women's elevated risk of violence.

Directing Efforts Towards Those Living in Rental Housing, Particularly
Recently Coupled Individuals

In addition to universal programmes to promote the equality and rights of women, the results from the chapter on homeownership and violence (Chapter 7) suggest that there should be efforts directed towards the prevention of violence against women who are living in rental housing, particularly those who have recently moved in and so are more likely to be in newer unions. For example, information pamphlets on prevention and available services in the local area could be sent to landlords and renters by the governmental organization that oversees housing.

Enhancing the Efficacy of Services by Making Stakeholders Aware of the
Complexity of Violence Against Women in Stepfamilies

Practitioners working with women in stepfamilies should be aware that these women face an elevated risk of violence and that there is some truth to each of the explanations for this phenomenon. Issues stemming from the complexity of stepfamilies, particularly depression, the partner's jealousy, and the stresses in the early years of these families appear to be important foci for the prevention of violence against women in stepfamilies.

Raising Awareness and Enhancing Efforts to Prevent Violence Against Women with Disabilities

The results in the chapter on violence against women with disabilities (Chapter 11) show that stakeholders need to be aware of the reality of violence against women with disabilities. Among the various stakeholders, medical professionals, religious advisers, and the police may be good targets for specialized training for the prevention of violence against these women. Efforts to change disablist and patriarchal views in society will encourage the allocation of resources to enhance coping with stress around disability, ensure that services are appropriate and accessible, and combat negative perceptions of women with disabilities that may contribute to their violent victimization.

Prevention Efforts Directed Towards Cohabitors

The data suggest that cohabitation will have to become much more prevalent before the selection bias, which with its attendant effects on relationship factors appeared to be responsible for the elevated risk of violence against cohabiting women, is eliminated. In the meantime, stakeholders need to keep in mind the "cohabitation effect." For example, it appears that more work needs to be done by the police to get cohabiting victims to feel comfortable contacting them for help.

Improvements to Services for Rural Victims

There were a number of implications to enhance the efficacy of service provision for victimized women living in rural settings. The data suggest that there is a need for more appropriate and culturally sensitive services for Aboriginal women living on rural reserves. The research also suggests that improving the accessibility of alcohol abuse treatment programmes in rural areas would enhance violence prevention efforts. As well, religious advisers need to be made aware that rural victims are particularly likely to turn to them for assistance. Training of these professionals should include components on how best to assist these women. Public education campaigns that encourage women who are victims of violence to contact the police are needed, and these campaigns should include a rural focus to send the message to rural victims in particular that the police are a source of assistance for them. Also, police training should be enhanced to ensure that all police officers are sensitive to issues specific to rural victims, which would improve the consistency of the police response to rural victims.

Enhancing Prevention Efforts for Immigrant Women

Given immigrant victims' reports that their children may be more likely to be exposed to violence, prevention programmes that serve immigrants should ensure that their services deal with issues around children's exposure. Programmes that address the effects of exposure should consider the circumstances of immigrants. The lower likelihood of immigrant victims confiding in a lawyer suggests that efforts are needed to enhance immigrant victims' ease of access to, and experience with, lawyers. There are also a number of indications in the data suggesting that efforts to improve the police response for immigrant victims of violence are needed. At a minimum, this could include enhanced police training in sensitivity to issues specific to immigrant victims' experiences of violence.

Implications for the Future

This book has demonstrated the value of studying vulnerable populations, and so has articulated a promising new focal area in the field of family violence. Understanding violence against women in vulnerable populations is a necessary step in completing the complex intersectional puzzle posed by this vexing social problem. Targeting our efforts to those most at risk will, ultimately, reduce all women's risk of violence. The intersectionality of the puzzle suggests that reducing the risk of violence against women in vulnerable populations will not only reduce the overall prevalence of violence on a statistical level, but will also help to reduce all women's risk of violence. Hence, further analysis of vulnerable populations is warranted in future research.

Although this book is an important first step in developing the study of vulnerable populations as a focal area in the family violence field, the data on which it was based possessed several limitations that need to be overcome in future research that is designed specifically to examine vulnerable populations. There were some limitations that were applicable to most vulnerable populations. Future research needs to oversample vulnerable populations so that there will be large enough subsamples of vulnerable populations to allow more reliable estimates and analyses. As well, risk and protective factors that were not available in the data need to be included. Measures of risk factors specifically designed for the study of violence are also needed, instead of single item proxy measures. Furthermore, the same measures need to be employed across studies to enhance comparability (e.g., measures of disability and rural/urban residence). More information is also needed on women's partners, such as their ethnicity. Additionally, triangulation of data collection methods would help to overcome the limitations of telephone surveys, though the telephone survey method remains, on balance, the best method for eliciting these kinds of data in the Canadian and American contexts. Ideally, future research will include longitudinal data collection to provide definitive statements on cause and effect.

Other limitations more specific to individual vulnerable populations also need to be overcome in future research. For example, research on post-separation needs to overcome the inability to distinguish between violence that happened when the union was intact, during separation, and while divorced. Future research also needs to allow the determination of temporal ordering, such as knowing whether disability preceded or followed violence. Forms of violence unique to vulnerable populations should also be included for more accurate prevalence estimates (though these would need to be left out of analyses of relative risk to ensure comparability). It would be helpful if respondents had the option to complete interviews in languages other than English and French, particularly for Aboriginal and immigrant women. For the study of violence against these latter vulnerable populations of women, it would also be ideal to be able to distinguish between different communities. More information is also needed on the respondents' and their partners' history of cohabitation and immigration.

Future research also needs to include other missing pieces of the puzzle. There were a number of vulnerable populations for which there were insufficient data to be included in the analyses in this book, but which need to be submitted to such analyses as those found in this book. These include violence against pregnant women, violence in same-sex relationships, violence in dating relationships, and violence against women in the military. Fortunately, these populations are not understudied to the same extent as those that were included in this book. However, it would be fruitful for future research to examine these groups using the same approach to vulnerable populations found here.

Despite these limitations, this book has identified a promising and unique method for studying vulnerable populations with survey data, and so has demonstrated how empirical analyses can contribute to our understanding of the intersectionality of violence against women. This unique method includes: (a) a focus on understanding women's *elevated* risk in vulnerable populations; (b) comparisons across surveys to obtain a sense of trends in elevated risk for women in vulnerable populations, as well as the ability to make more concrete statements about the veracity of both risk factors and explanations for their elevated risk of violence; (c) a focus on relative rates, which helps to attenuate the effects of methodological differences across surveys; and (d) an examination of victims' post-violence experiences based on representative samples, which is a rarity in research on violence against women. Future researchers studying vulnerable populations with surveys should consider the use of these methods as appropriate.

Theories specific to understanding the unique circumstances of violence against women in vulnerable populations also need to be developed and tested. As shown in Chapter 2, researchers need to keep in mind the samples they are using when applying theoretical frameworks. For instance, future research examining perpetrators of violence against women in vulnerable populations in clinical samples should include measures of attachment and personality disorders to identify how these factors interact with those identified in this book.

In addition to encouraging the further study of violence against women in vulnerable populations, it would also be fruitful to engage in cross-cultural research on vulnerable populations in the future. Such research would allow a determination of the extent to which the same vulnerable populations are unique with respect to their experiences of violence and whether the same factors predict violence in vulnerable populations across different cultures.

Although it appears that there is a long road ahead, it is hoped that the new knowledge and approaches provided in this book will help move us towards the elimination of the elevated risk and unique circumstances of violence against women in vulnerable populations. Through assembling these pieces of the intersectional puzzle of violence against women, we will ultimately move one step closer to the eradication of this devastating social problem.

Notes

3 Materials and Methods

1 Although the research and analysis are based on data from Statistics Canada, the opinions expressed do not represent the views of Statistics Canada.

2 Women in same-sex relationships were excluded from the analyses in all three data sets.

3 For further information on the comparability of these data sets, readers should refer to Statistics Canada (2005b).

4 It must be noted that this is an individual-level indicator of patriarchal domination between a couple rather than a measure of patriarchal culture. For further elaboration of this conceptualization of patriarchal domination, readers may wish to refer to Brownridge (2002).

5 The chapters in this book that use this variable do not include the VAWS, and so the maximum age when this variable is used is 14 years.

6 Although there are exceptions within the developing category that are developed, particularly Australia and New Zealand, this did not have a significant influence on the results since very few individuals from these places migrate to Canada. For example, data from Statistics Canada (2001) showed that only 0.23% of recent immigrants report Australasia as their country of last residence. An examination of the original variable in the masterfile of the 2004 GSS showed that such countries from which there were relatively few immigrants were lumped into an "other" category. All of the nations that were identifiable were coded appropriately as developing or developed according to the United Nations (2007).

7 For a justification for the operational definition of culture see Brownridge (2002).

8 In both versions of the GSS, the question included "(prescription or over the counter)."

9 Using the 1993 VAWS and 1999 GSS public use microdata files, it was not possible to determine whether participants from Prince Edward Island (PEI) lived in a rural or urban area. It was decided to code all participants from PEI as rural. This decision was based on the fact that PEI is largely a rural province. For example, according to the 1996 census, the majority of the population of PEI was rural (Department of Provincial Treasury, 2000).

10 Information in parentheses refers to subtle differences in the GSS.

11 Ex-partners included men from either a marriage or a common-law relationship. Data restrictions did not allow disaggregation of ex-partners by whether they had been living in a marital or common-law relationship.

12 One difference between the VAWS and iterations of the GSS was that the VAWS asked all respondents with ex-partners about past experiences of violence that ever occurred from their ex-partner, while the GSS asked respondents who had been in contact with their ex-partner in the previous 5 years about experiences of violence from their ex-partner during that 5-year period. This did not pose a problem in the chapter on post-separation violence since a 1-year time frame was used.

13 The psychopathology and altered psyche variables were constructed based on the conceptualization of Ratner (1998).

14 An odds ratio is a ratio of the odds of a condition (in this case violence) in an exposed population (i.e., a given vulnerable population) to the odds of the same condition in a non-exposed population (i.e., the comparison group).

15 This is the same as the zero-order odds ratio.

16 A t-test is a test used for examining hypotheses about means of quantitative variables. Interested readers may wish to refer to an introductory text on research methods. In this book, the calculation of t involved taking the difference between the two regression coefficients and dividing that difference by the square root of the average of the square of the standard errors corresponding to each regression coefficient.

17 In an analysis of a subsample of a given survey, the weights provided with the data must be rescaled in a manner that preserves the variability of the original weights but that has an average value of one. This is accomplished first by calculating the average weight for those respondents in a given analysis and then dividing each respondent's weight by this average. The resulting weighting factor is used in the analysis. With the 2004 GSS, Statistics Canada added a bootstrapping program to refine further the variance estimates. Readers interested in bootstrapping may wish to refer to Efron and Tibshirani (1985). Since the purpose of the analysis was to compare estimates and their significance across the surveys, with the permission of the Manitoba RDC analyst, the bootstrapping program was not applied.

4 Violence Against Cohabiting Women: Present Perspective and Future Prospective

1 In Canada the terms cohabitation and common-law union are used interchangeably.
2 This chapter is an expansion of Brownridge (2008).
3 Although the duration variable was not included as a risk marker of violence per se, it has been noted in the literature that it is important to control for duration of relationship in multivariate analyses of partner violence (Brownridge & Halli, 1999).
4 This analysis was not comparable to an earlier analysis that used the 1993 VAWS (Brownridge & Halli, 2002b). Among the differences between the two analyses, the latter was conducted on the lifetime prevalence of violence and differentiated between married women with and without a prior history of cohabitation.

5 Differing Dynamics: Violence Against Women Post-Separation

1 Although this definition reflects the intent of much of the research in the area, as will be identified later in the chapter, much of the research is unable to make a specific determination regarding when post-separation violence occurred.
2 Crawford and Gartner (1992) were not able to determine if this was also true for estranged common-law partners and boyfriends, though they speculated that the results would be similar for these relationships.
3 It is also noteworthy that the majority of intimate homicide victims are female and women are much more likely to be killed by a separated partner than are men (Beattie, 2005; Johnson & Hotton, 2003).
4 For further elaboration, interested readers are referred to Chapter 9.
5 Ex-partners included men from either a marriage or a common-law relationship. Data restrictions did not allow disaggregation of ex-partners by whether they had been living in a marital or common-law relationship.
6 In the 2004 survey only the children of the ex-partner were included.
7 Married victims could not be included in the comparison because the dependent variables were not applicable to them.
8 Research on same-sex domestic violence has also identified differing motives and contexts for perpetrating violence such as retaliation and revenge rather than only as a means to restore power and control (Ristock, 2002).

6 Violence in "The Future Traditional Family": Stepfamilies and Violence Against Women

1 Although Daly et al. (1997) used the term uxoricide, their sample included victims in common-law unions.
2 In some cases statistically insignificant odds ratios were greater for women in stepfamilies than were statistically significant odds ratios for women in biological families. Had the subsample of women in stepfamilies been larger these odds ratios would likely be statistically significant. Hence, while they were not statistically significant, they were likely substantively significant.

9 Violence Against Aboriginal Women: The Role of Colonization

1 This chapter is an expansion, with kind permission from Springer Science+Business Media, of: *Journal of Family Violence*, Understanding the elevated risk of violence against Aboriginal women: A comparison of two nationally representative surveys of Canada, 23, 2008, pp. 353–367, Douglas A. Brownridge.

2 The 1-year rate was not specifically identified. It was noted that nearly one-third of men and women reported violence in this time frame and a figure of 31% appears in the abstract. This suggests that the actual rate for women was 31%. Oetzel and Duran (2004) have made this assumption.

3 Norton and Manson (1995) examined a convenience sample of 198 American Indian women who completed a mental health needs assessment survey and found that 46% reported having a history of spouse abuse. However, this rate appeared to confound victimization and perpetration and so should not be taken as the rate of partner violence against women in the sample.

4 It is also noteworthy that American Indian/Alaska Native women were significantly more likely to have been raped and/or physically assaulted in their lifetime and to report significantly more stalking victimization in their lifetime in a nationally representative sample of 16,005 American women and men 18 years of age and older (Tjaden & Thoennes, 1998a, 1998b). However, figures specific to partner violence were not provided. Aboriginal women in Canada have also been shown to have nearly double the rate of stalking compared to non-Aboriginal women (Johnson, 2006).

5 The risk marker of patriarchal domination is not repeated given its treatment in the previous part of the chapter.

6 In some cases statistically insignificant odds ratios are greater for Aboriginal women than are statistically significant odds ratios for non-Aboriginal women. Had the subsample of Aboriginal women been larger these odds ratios would likely be statistically significant. Hence, while they are not statistically significant, they are likely substantively significant.

7 The off-reserve Aboriginals in rural areas are reported by Statistics Canada mostly to be in isolated northern communities (Statistics Canada, 1998). Given that the data in this book did not include the Yukon, the Northwest Territories, and Nunavut, these Aboriginal women were excluded from the study.

10 Violence Against Immigrant Women: A Reversal of Fortunes

1 Since the main purpose of the analysis was to uncover differences that may account for Canadian-born women's elevated risk relative to immigrant women from developed nations, it was decided to eliminate from this analysis variables on which the two groups did not significantly differ.

11 Violence Against Women with Disabilities: Perpetrator Characteristics are Key

1 This chapter is an expansion of Brownridge et al. (2008).

2 According to the documentation for the 1999 GSS, this question was also asked of respondents in 1999 but it was not used as a screening question.

3 Given that the Participation and Activity Limitation Survey (PALS), the VAWS and the GSS were representative of the Canadian population and used the same definition of disability, the data from the PALS suggested that women with disabilities in this chapter included disabilities that spanned the continuum in terms of severity. Of the women reporting disabilities in the PALS, 32.2% reported mild disabilities, 25.3% moderate disabilities, 28.3% severe disabilities, and 14.1% very severe disabilities (Statistics Canada, 2002d).

4 Readers should extrapolate from these results with caution since many of the estimates are based on cell sizes of less than 15.

References

Adelman, M. (2000). No way out: Divorce-related domestic violence in Israel. *Violence Against Women, 6*(11), 1223–1254.

Amato, P. R., & Previti, D. (2003). People's reasons for divorcing: Gender, social class, the life course, and adjustment. *Journal of Family Issues, 24*(5), 602–626.

Ambert, A.-M. (2005). *Cohabitation and marriage: How are they related?* Ottawa, ON, Canada: The Vanier Institute of the Family.

Amnesty International. (2004). *Stolen sisters: A human rights response to discrimination and violence against Indigenous women in Canada.* Retrieved February 2, 2008, from www.amnesty.ca/campaigns/resources/amr2000304.pdf.

Anderson, D. K., & Saunders, D. G. (2003). Leaving an abusive partner: An empirical review of predictors, the process of leaving, and psychological well-being. *Trauma, Violence and Abuse, 4*(2), 163–191.

Anderson, K. L. (1997). Gender, status, and domestic violence: An integration of feminist and family violence approaches. *Journal of Marriage and the Family, 59*(3), 655–669.

Andrews, A. B., & Veronen, L. J. (1993). Sexual assault and people with disabilities. *Journal of Social Work and Human Sexuality, 8*(2), 137–159.

Arendell, T. (1995). *Fathers and divorce.* Thousand Oaks, CA: Sage.

Arnold, R., Keane, C., & Baron, S. (2005). Assessing risk of victimization through epidemiological concepts: An alternative analytic strategy applied to routine activities theory. *Canadian Review of Sociology and Anthropology, 42*(3), 345–364.

Babcock, J., Green, C. E., & Robie, C. (2004). Does batterers' treatment work? A meta-analytic review of domestic violence treatment. *Clinical Psychology Review, 23*(8), 1023–1053.

Bachman, R. (1992). *Death and violence on the reservation: Homicide, family violence, and suicide in American Indian populations.* New York: Auburn House.

Bachman, R., & Saltzman, L. E. (1995). *Violence against women: Estimates from the redesigned survey* (No. NCJ-154348). Rockville, MD: U.S. Department of Justice Bureau of Justice Statistics.

Barile, M. (2002). Individual-systemic violence: Disabled women's standpoint. *Journal of International Women's Studies, 4*(1), 1–14.

Barnett, O. W., Miller-Perrin, C. L., & Perrin, R. D. (1997). *Family violence across the lifespan: An introduction.* Thousand Oaks, CA: Sage.

Barnett, O. W., Miller-Perrin, C. L., & Perrin, R. D. (2005). *Family violence across the lifespan: An introduction* (2nd ed.). Thousand Oaks, CA: Sage.

Bauer, H. M., & Rodriguez, M. A. (2000). Barriers to health care for abused Latina and Asian immigrant women. *Journal of Health Care for the Poor and Underserved, 11*(1), 33–44.

Beattie, K. (2005). Spousal homicides. In K. AuCoin (Ed.), *Family violence in Canada: A statistical profile 2005* (pp. 48–51). Ottawa, ON, Canada: Minister of Industry.

Bechard, M. (2007). *Family structure by region* (No. 89–625-XIE). Ottawa, ON, Canada: Statistics Canada.

Belsky, J. (1980). Child maltreatment: An ecological integration. *American Psychologist, 35*(4), 320–335.

Belsky, J. (1993). Etiology of child maltreatment: A developmental-ecological analysis. *Psychological Bulletin, 114*(3), 413–434.

Berger, P., & Kellner, H. (1994). Marriage and the construction of reality: An exercise in the microsociology of knowledge. In G. Handel, & G. G. Whitchurch (Eds.), *The psychosocial interior of the family* (4th ed., pp. 3–17). New York: Aldine de Gruyter.

Berger, R. (1995). Three types of stepfamilies. In C. A. Everitt (Ed.), *Understanding stepfamilies: Their structure and dynamics* (pp. 35–49). Binghamton, NY: The Haworth Press.

Bersani, C., & Chen, H.-T. (1988). Sociological perspectives in family violence. In V. V. Hasselt, R. Morrison, & A. Bellack (Eds.), *Handbook of family violence* (pp. 57–86). New York: Plenum Press.

Biesenthal, L., Sproule, L. D., Nelder, M., Golton, S., Mann, D., Podovinnikoff, D., et al. (2000). *The Ontario Rural Woman Abuse Study (ORWAS) final report* (No. rr2000–15e). Belmont, ON, Canada: Community Abuse Program of Rural Ontario.

Blackstock, C., Trocmé, N., & Bennett, M. (2004). Child maltreatment investigations among Aboriginal and non-Aboriginal families in Canada. *Violence Against Women, 10*(8), 901–916.

Boba, R. L. (1996). *Violence between married and unmarried cohabiting partners: An analysis using couple-level data.* Unpublished Doctoral Dissertation, Arizona State University.

Bograd, M. (1999). Strengthening domestic violence theories: Intersections of race, class, sexual orientation, and gender. *Journal of Marital and Family Therapy, 25*(3), 275–289.

Bohn, D. K. (2002). Lifetime and current abuse, pregnancy risks, and outcomes among Native American women. *Journal of Health Care for the Poor and Underserved, 13*(2), 184–198.

Bohn, D. K. (2003). Lifetime physical and sexual abuse, substance abuse, depression, and suicide attempts among Native American women. *Issues in Mental Health Nursing, 24*(3), 333–352.

Bopp, M., Bopp, J., & Lane, P., Jr. (2003). *Aboriginal domestic violence in Canada.* Ottawa, ON, Canada: Aboriginal Healing Foundation.

Bowker, L. H. (1983). *Beating wife-beating.* Lexington, MA: D. C. Heath.

Brinkerhoff, M. B., & Lupri, E. (1988). Interspousal violence. *Canadian Journal of Sociology, 13*(4), 407–434.

Bronfenbrenner, U. (1977). Toward an experimental ecology of human development. *American Psychologist, 32*(7), 513–531.

Brownridge, D. A. (2002). Cultural variation in male partner violence against women: A comparison of Québec with the rest of Canada. *Violence Against Women, 8*(1), 87–115.

Brownridge, D. A. (2003). Male partner violence against Aboriginal women in Canada: An empirical analysis. *Journal of Interpersonal Violence, 18*(1), 65–83.

Brownridge, D. A. (2004a). Male partner violence against women in stepfamilies: An analysis of risk and explanations in the Canadian milieu. *Violence and Victims, 19*(1), 17–36.

Brownridge, D. A. (2004b). Understanding women's heightened risk of violence in common-law unions: Revisiting the selection and relationship hypotheses. *Violence Against Women, 10*(6), 626–651.

Brownridge, D. A. (2006a). Intergenerational transmission and dating violence victimization: Evidence from a sample of female university students in Manitoba. *Canadian Journal of Community Mental Health, 25*(1), 75–93.

Brownridge, D. A. (2006b). Partner violence against women with disabilities: Prevalence, risk and explanations. *Violence Against Women, 12*(9), 805–822.

Brownridge, D. A. (2006c). Violence against women post-separation. *Aggression and Violent Behavior, 11*(5), 514–530.

Brownridge, D. A. (2008). The elevated risk for violence against cohabiting women: A comparison of three nationally representative surveys of Canada. *Violence Against Women, 14*(7), 809–832.

Brownridge, D. A., & Halli, S. S. (1999). Measuring family violence: The conceptualization and utilization of prevalence and incidence rates. *Journal of Family Violence, 14*(4), 333–350.

Brownridge, D. A., & Halli, S. S. (2000). "Living in sin" and sinful living: Toward filling a gap in the explanation of violence against women. *Aggression and Violent Behavior, 5*(6), 565–583.

Brownridge, D. A., & Halli, S. S. (2001). *Explaining violence against women in Canada.* Lanham, MD: Lexington.

Brownridge, D. A., & Halli, S. S. (2002a). Double jeopardy? Violence against immigrant women in Canada. *Violence and Victims, 17*(4), 455–471.

Brownridge, D. A., & Halli, S. S. (2002b). Understanding male partner violence against cohabiting and married women: An empirical investigation with a synthesized model. *Journal of Family Violence, 17*(4), 341–361.

Brownridge, D. A., & Halli, S. S. (2003). Double advantage? Violence against Canadian migrant women from "developed" nations. *International Migration, 41*(1), 29–46.

Brownridge, D. A., Ristock, J., & Hiebert-Murphy, D. (2008). The high risk of IPV against Canadian women with disabilities. *Medical Science Monitor, 14*(5), PH27–32.

Brzozowski, J.-A. (Ed.). (2004). *Family violence in Canada: A statistical profile 2004.* Ottawa, ON, Canada: Minister of Industry.

Brzozowski, J.-A., Taylor-Butts, A., & Johnson, S. (2006). Victimization and offending among the Aboriginal population in Canada. *Juristat, 26*(3), 1–31.

Burch, T. K., & Madan, A. K. (1986). *Union formation and dissolution: Results from the 1984 family history survey* (No. 99–963). Ottawa, ON, Canada: Statistics Canada, Housing, Family and Social Statistical Division.

Campbell, J. C. (1992). "If I can't have you, no one can": Power and control in homicide of female partners. In J. Radford, & D. E. H. Russell (Eds.), *Femicide: The politics of woman killing* (pp. 99–113). New York: Twayne.

Carlson, B. E. (1984). Causes and maintenance of domestic violence: An ecological analysis. *Social Service Review, 58*(4), 569–587.

Centres of Excellence for Women's Health. (2002). Research as a spiritual contract: An Aboriginal women's health project. *Centres of Excellence for Women's Health Research Bulletin, 2*(3), 14–15.

Chandler, M. J., Lalonde, C. E., Sokol, B. W., & Hallett, D. (2003). *Personal persistence, identity development, and suicide: A study of Native and non-Native North American adolescents.* Retrieved July 8, 2006, from www.turtleisland.org/front/s4.pdf.

Chang, J. C., Martin, S. L., Moracco, K. E., Dulli, L., Scandlin, D., Loucks-Sorrel, M. B., et al. (2003). Helping women with disabilities and domestic violence: Strategies, limitations, and challenges of domestic violence programs and services. *Journal of Women's Health, 12*(7), 699–708.

Cherlin, A. (1978). Remarriage as an incomplete institution. *American Journal of Sociology, 84*(3), 634–650.

Chui, T., Tran, K., & Maheux, H. (2007). *Immigration in Canada: A portrait of the foreign-born population, 2006 Census.* Ottawa, ON, Canada: Statistics Canada.

Cohen, M. M., Forte, T., Mont, J. D., Hyman, I., & Romans, S. (2005). Intimate partner violence among Canadian women with activity limitations. *Journal of Epidemiology and Community Health, 59*(10), 834–839.

Copel, L. C. (2006). Partner abuse in physically disabled women: A proposed model for understanding intimate partner violence. *Perspectives in Psychiatric Care, 42*(2), 114–129.

Crawford, M., & Gartner, R. (1992). *Woman killing: Intimate femicide in Ontario 1974–1990.* Toronto, ON, Canada: Women We Honour Action Committee.

Crenshaw, K. (1989). Demarginalizing the intersection of race and sex: A Black feminist critique of antidiscrimination doctrine, feminist theory and antiracist politics. *University of Chicago Legal Forum,* 139–167.

Crenshaw, K. (1993). Race, gender, and violence against women: Convergences, divergences and other Black feminist conundrums. In M. Minow (Ed.), *Family matters: Readings on family lives and the law* (pp. 230–232). New York: The New Press.

Currie, D. H. (1998). The criminalization of violence against women: Feminist demands and patriarchal accommodation. In K. D. Bonnycastle, & G. S. Rigakos (Eds.), *Unsettling truths: Battered women, policy, politics, and contemporary research in Canada.* Vancouver, BC, Canada: Collective Press.

Curry, M. A., Hassouneh-Phillips, D., & Johnston-Silverberg, A. (2001). Abuse of women with disabilities: An ecological model and review. *Violence Against Women, 7*(1), 60–79.

Daly, M., Singh, L., & Wilson, M. (1993). Children fathered by previous partners: A risk factor for violence against women. *Canadian Journal of Public Health, 84*(3), 209–210.

Daly, M., Wiseman, K. A., & Wilson, M. I. (1997). Women with children sired by previous partners incur excess risk of homicide. *Homicide Studies, 1*(1), 61–71.

Daly, M. M., & Wilson, M. (1996). Evolutionary psychology and marital conflict: The relevance of stepchildren. In D. M. Buss, & N. M. Malamuth (Eds.), *Sex, power, conflict* (pp. 9–28). New York: Oxford University Press.

Das Dasgupta, S. (1998). Women's realities: Defining violence against women by immigration, race, and class. In R. K. Bergen (Ed.), *Issues in intimate violence* (pp. 209–219). Thousand Oaks, CA: Sage.

Dauvergne, M. (2005). Family homicides against children and youth. In K. AuCoin (Ed.), *Family violence in Canada: A statistical profile 2005* (pp. 51–59). Ottawa, ON, Canada: Minister of Industry.

Dauvergne, M., & Johnson, H. (2001). Children witnessing family violence. In C. Trainor, & K. Mihorean (Eds.), *Family violence in Canada: A statistical profile 2001* (pp. 19–25). Ottawa, ON, Canada: Minister of Industry.

De Kleijn-De Vrankrijker, M. W. (2003). The long way from the International Classification of Impairments, Disabilities and Handicaps (ICIDH) to the International Classification of Functioning, Disability, and Health (ICF). *Disability and Rehabilitation, 25*(11–12), 561–564.

DeKeseredy, W. S. (2000). Current controversies on defining nonlethal violence against women in intimate heterosexual relationships. *Violence Against Women, 6*(7), 728–746.

DeKeseredy, W. S., & Joseph, C. (2006). Separation and/or divorce sexual assault in rural Ohio: Preliminary results of an exploratory study. *Violence Against Women, 12*(3), 301–311.

DeKeseredy, W. S., Rogness, M., & Schwartz, M. D. (2004). Separation/divorce sexual assault: The current state of social scientific knowledge. *Aggression and Violent Behavior, 9*(6), 675–691.

DeKeseredy, W. S., & Schwartz, M. D. (2003a). Backlash and whiplash: A critique of Statistics Canada's 1999 General Social Survey on victimization. *Online Journal of Justice Studies, 1*(1), 1–14.

DeKeseredy, W. S., & Schwartz, M. D. (2003b). Theorizing public housing woman abuse as a function of economic exclusion and male peer support. *Women's Health and Urban Life, 1*(2), 26–45.

Department of Provincial Treasury. (2000). *Province of Prince Edward Island twenty-sixth annual statistical review 1999.* Charlottetown, PEI, Canada.

Diaz-Olavarrieta, C., Campbell, J., Garcia De la Cadena, C., Paz, F., & Villa, A. R. (1999). Domestic violence against patients with chronic neurologic disorders. *Archives of Neurology, 54*(6), 681–685.

Dobash, E. R., & Dobash, R. P. (1979). *Violence against wives: A case against the patriarchy.* New York: Free Press.

Duclos, É., & Langlois, R. (2003). *Disability supports in Canada, 2001* (No. 89–580-XIE). Ottawa, ON, Canada: Statistics Canada.

Duran, E., Duran, B., Woodis, W., & Woodis, P. (1998). A postcolonial perspective on domestic violence in Indian country. In R. Carrillo, & J. Tello (Eds.), *Family violence and men of color: Healing the wounded male spirit* (pp. 95–113). New York: Springer.

Durst, D. (1991). Conjugal violence: Changing attitudes in two northern native communities. *Community Mental Health Journal, 27*(5), 359–373.

Dutton, D. G. (1995). *The domestic assault of women: Psychological and criminal justice perspectives* (revised and expanded ed.). Vancouver, BC, Canada: UBC Press.

Dutton, D. G. (2006). *Rethinking domestic violence.* Vancouver, BC, Canada: UBC Press.

Dutton, D. G., & Painter, S. (1993). Emotional attachments in abusive relationships: A test of traumatic bonding theory. *Violence and Victims, 8*(2), 105–120.

Efron, B., & Tibshirani, R. (1985). The bootstrap method for assessing statistical accuracy. *Behaviormetrika, 12*(17), 1–35.

Ellis, D. (1987). Post-separation woman abuse: The contribution of lawyers as "barracudas," "advocates," and "counsellors." *International Journal of Law and Psychiatry, 10*(4), 403–411.

Ellis, D. (1992). Woman abuse among separated and divorced women: The relevance of social support. In E. C. Viano (Ed.), *Intimate violence: Interdisciplinary perspectives* (pp. 177–189). Bristol, PA: Taylor and Francis/Hemisphere.

Ellis, D., & DeKeseredy, W. S. (1989). Marital status and woman abuse: The DAD model. *International Journal of Sociology of the Family, 19*(Autumn), 67–87.

Ellis, D., & DeKeseredy, W. S. (1997). Rethinking estrangement, interventions, and intimate femicide. *Violence Against Women, 3*(6), 590–609.

Ellis, D., & Stuckless, N. (1992). Preseparation abuse, marital conflict mediation, and postseparation abuse. *Mediation Quarterly, 9*(3), 205–225.

Ellis, D., & Wight, L. (1997). Estrangement, interventions, and male violence toward female partners. *Violence and Victims, 12*(1), 51–67.

Fairchild, D. G., Fairchild, M. W., & Stoner, S. (1998). Prevalence of adult domestic violence among women seeking routine care in a Native American health care facility. *American Journal of Public Health, 88*(10), 1515–1517.

Federal-Provincial-Territorial Ministers Responsible for the Status of Women. (2002). *Assessing violence against women: A statistical profile* (No. SW21–101/2002E). Ottawa, ON, Canada: Status of women Canada.

Fine, M. (1985). Unearthing contradictions: An essay inspired by women and male violence. *Feminist Studies, 11*(2), 391–407.

Fishwick, N. (1998). Issues in providing care for rural battered women. In J. C. Campbell (Ed.), *Empowering survivors of abuse* (pp. 280–290). Thousand Oaks, CA: Sage.

Flake, D. F. (2005). Individual, family, and community risk markers for domestic violence in Peru. *Violence Against Women, 11*(3), 353–373.

Fleury, R. E., Sullivan, C. M., & Bybee, D. I. (2000). When ending the relationship does not end the violence: Women's experiences of violence by former partners. *Violence Against Women, 6*(12), 1363–1383.

Frideres, J. S. (1998). *Aboriginal peoples in Canada: Contemporary conflicts* (5th ed.). Scarborough, ON, Canada: Prentice Hall Allyn and Bacon Canada.

Frideres, J. S. (2001). *Aboriginal peoples in Canada: Contemporary conflicts* (6th ed.). Toronto, ON, Canada: Prentice Hall.

Gagné, M.-A. (1998). The role of dependency and colonialism in generating trauma in First Nations citizens: The James Bay Cree. In Y. Danieli (Ed.), *International handbook of multigenerational legacies of trauma* (pp. 355–372). New York: Plenum.

Ganong, L. H., & Coleman, M. (1994). *Remarried family relationships*. Thousand Oaks, CA: Sage.

Gaquin, D. A. (1977/1978). Spouse abuse: Data from the National Crime Survey. *Victimology, 2*(3/4), 632–643.

Gartner, R., Dawson, M., & Crawford, M. (1998/1999). Woman killing: Intimate femicide in Ontario, 1974–1994. *Resources for Feminist Research, 26*(3/4), 151–173.

Gelles, R. J. (1993). Through a sociological lens: Social structure and family violence. In R. J. Gelles, & D. R. Loseke (Eds.), *Current controversies on family violence* (pp. 31–46). Newbury Park, CA: Sage.

Giles-Sims, J. (1983). *Wife battering: A systems theory approach*. New York: The Guilford Press.

Giles-Sims, J., & Finkelhor, D. (1984). Child abuse in stepfamilies. *Family Relations, 33*(3), 407–413.

Gilson, S. F., Cramer, E. P., & Depoy, E. (2001). Redefining abuse of women with disabilities: A paradox of limitation and expansion. *Affilia, 16*(2), 220–235.

Gilson, S. F., DePoy, E., & Cramer, E. P. (2001). Linking the assessment of self-reported functional capacity with abuse experiences of women with disabilities. *Violence Against Women, 7*(4), 418–431.

Goode, W. J. (1971). Force and violence in the family. *Journal of Marriage and the Family, 33*(4), 624–636.

Grama, J. L. (2000). Women forgotten: Difficulties faced by rural victims of domestic violence. *American Journal of Family Law, 14*(3), 173–189.

Grandin, E., & Lupri, E. (1997). Intimate violence in Canada and the United States: A cross-national comparison. *Journal of Family Violence, 12*(4), 417–443.

Green, R. K. (2001). Homeowning, social outcomes, tenure choice, and U.S. housing policy. *Cityscape: A Journal of Policy Development and Research, 5*(2), 127–138.

Green, R. K., & White, M. J. (1997). Measuring the benefits of homeowning: Effects on children. *Journal of Urban Economics, 41*(3), 441–461.

Greenfeld, L. A., & Smith, S. K. (1999). *American Indians and crime* (No. NCJ 173386). Washington, DC: U.S. Department of Justice.

Hamberger, L. K., & Hastings, J. E. (1986). Personality correlates of men who abuse their partners: A cross-validation study. *Journal of Family Violence, 1*(4), 323–346.

Hamby, S. L. (2000). The importance of community in a feminist analysis of domestic violence among American Indians. *American Journal of Community Psychology, 28*(5), 649–669.

Hamby, S. L., & Skupien, M. B. (1998). Domestic violence on the San Carlos Apache reservation: Rates, associated psychological symptoms, and current beliefs. *Indian Health Service Primary Care Provider, 23*(3), 103–106.

Hannawa, A. F., Spitzberg, B. H., Wiering, L., & Teranishi, C. (2006). "If I can't have you, no one can": Development of a Relational Entitlement and Proprietariness Scale (REPS). *Violence and Victims, 21*(5), 539–560.

Hardesty, J. L. (2002). Separation assault in the context of postdivorce parenting. *Violence Against Women, 8*(5), 597–625.

Hart, B. J. (1990). Gentle jeopardy: The further endangerment of battered women and children in custody mediation. *Mediation Quarterly, 7*(4), 317–330.

Harwell, T. S., Moore, K. R., & Spence, M. R. (2003). Physical violence, intimate partner violence, and emotional abuse among adult American Indian men and women in Montana. *Preventive Medicine, 37*(4), 297–303.

Hassouneh-Phillips, D. (2005). Understanding abuse of women with physical disabilities: An overview of the abuse pathways model. *Advances in Nursing Science, 28*(1), 70–80.

Hassouneh-Phillips, D., & McNeff, E. (2005). "I thought I was less worthy": Low sexual and body esteem and increased vulnerability to intimate abuse in women with physical disabilities. *Sexuality and Disability, 23*(4), 227–240.

Heise, L. L. (1998). Violence against women: An integrated, ecological framework. *Violence Against Women, 4*(3), 262–290.

Hewitt, B., Baxter, J., & Western, M. (2005). Marriage breakdown in Australia: The social correlates of separation and divorce. *Journal of Sociology, 41*(2), 163–183.

Holtzworth-Munroe, A., & Stuart, G. L. (1994). Typologies of male batterers: Three subtypes and the differences among them. *Psychological Bulletin, 116*(3), 476–497.

Hornosty, J., & Doherty, D. (2001, July 22–25). Barriers women face in leaving abusive relationships in farm and rural communities: The importance of understanding the social and cultural context of abuse. Paper presented at the 7th International Family Violence Research Conference, Portsmouth, NH.

Horton, A. L., & Johnson, B. L. (1993). Profile and strategies of women who have ended abuse. *Families in Society, 74*(8), 481–492.

Hotton, T. (2001). Spousal violence after marital separation, *Juristat* (Vol. 21, pp. 1–19). Ottawa, ON, Canada: Statistics Canada.

Howe, K. (2000). *Violence against women with disabilities: An overview of the literature.* Retrieved April 28, 2003, from www.wwda.org.au/keran.htm.

Hubbard, M., & Davis, W. (2002). *Community advantage panel study: Social impacts of homeownership.* Chapel Hill, NC: Center for Community Capitalism.

Hukill, S. L. (2006). Violence in Native America: A historical perspective. *Journal of Transcultural Nursing, 17*(3), 246–250.

Hull, J. (2006). *Aboriginal women: A profile from the 2001 Census* (No. QS-3557–020-EE-A1). Winnipeg, MB, Canada: Women's Issues and Gender Equality Directorate.

Jackson, N. A. (1996). Observational experiences of intrapersonal conflict and teenage victimization: A comparative study among spouses and cohabitors. *Journal of Family Violence, 11*(3), 191–203.

Jacobson, N. S., & Gottman, J. M. (1998). *When men batter women: New insights into ending abusive relationships.* New York: Simon & Schuster.

Jakubec, L., & Engeland, J. (2004). Canada's metropolitan areas, *2001 Census Housing Series: Issue 4* (pp. 1–16). Ottawa, ON, Canada: Canada Mortgage and Housing Corporation.

Jang, D., Lee, D., & Morello-Frosch, R. (1990). Domestic violence in the immigrant and refugee community: Responding to the needs of immigrant women. *Response, 13*(4), 2–7.

Jiwani, Y., Moore, S., & Kachuk, P. (1998). *Rural women and violence: A study of two communities in British Columbia* (No. TR1998–16e). Ottawa, ON, Canada: Department of Justice Canada.

Johnson, H. (1990). Wife abuse. In C. McKie, & K. Thompson (Eds.), *Canadian social trends* (pp. 173–176). Toronto, ON, Canada: Thompson Educational Publishing.

Johnson, H. (1996). *Dangerous domains: Violence against women in Canada*. Scarborough, ON, Canada: Nelson Canada.

Johnson, H. (2001). Contrasting views of the role of alcohol in cases of wife assault. *Journal of Interpersonal Violence, 16*(1), 54–72.

Johnson, H. (2005). Assessing the prevalence of violence against women in Canada. *Statistical Journal of the United Nations, 22*(3–4), 225–238.

Johnson, H. (2006). *Measuring violence against women: Statistical trends 2006* (No. 85–570-XIE). Ottawa, ON, Canada: Statistics Canada.

Johnson, H., & Hotton, T. (2003). Losing control: Homicide risk in estranged and intact intimate relationships. *Homicide Studies, 7*(1), 58–84.

Johnson, H., & Sacco, V. F. (1995). Researching violence against women: Statistics Canada's national survey. *Canadian Journal of Criminology, 37*(3), 281–304.

Johnston, J. R., & Campbell, L. E. G. (1993). A clinical typology of interparental violence in disputed-custody divorces. *American Journal of Orthopsychiatry, 63*(2), 190–199.

Kahn, M. W. (1982). Cultural clash and psychopathology in three Aboriginal cultures. *Academic Psychology Bulletin, 4*, 553–561.

Kahn, M. W., & The Behavioral Health Technical Staff. (1980). Wife beating and cultural context: Prevalence in an Aboriginal and Islander community in Northern Australia. *American Journal of Community Psychology, 8*(6), 727–731.

Kalbach, W. E., & Richard, M. A. (1989). Ethnic intermarriage and the changing Canadian family. In J. Legare, T. R. Balakrishnan, & R. P. Beaujot (Eds.), *The family in crisis: A population crisis?* (pp. 213–226). Ottawa, ON, Canada: Lowe-Martin.

Kalmun, M., & Bernasco, W. (2001). Joint and separated lifestyles in couple relationships. *Journal of Marriage and Family, 63*(3), 639–654.

Kalmuss, D., & Seltzer, J. A. (1986). Continuity of marital behavior in remarriage: The case of spouse abuse. *Journal of Marriage and the Family, 48*(1), 113–120.

Kalmuss, D. S., & Straus, M. A. (1990). Wife's marital dependency and wife abuse. In M. Straus, & R. Gelles (Eds.), *Physical violence in American families: Risk factors and adaptations to violence in 8,145 families* (pp. 369–382). New Brunswick, NJ: Transaction.

Kanuha, V. (1996). Domestic violence, racism, and the battered women's movement in the United States. In J. L. Edleson, & Z. C. Eisikovits (Eds.), *Future interventions with battered women and their families*. Thousand Oaks, CA: Sage.

Kaufman, J., & Zigler, E. (1987). Do abused children become abusive parents? *American Journal of Orthopsychiatry, 57*(2), 186–192.

Kaukinen, C. (2004). Status compatibility, physical violence, and emotional abuse in intimate relationships. *Journal of Marriage and Family, 66*(2), 452–471.

Kennedy, L. W., & Dutton, D. G. (1989). The incidence of wife assault in Alberta. *Canadian Journal of Behavioural Science, 21*(1), 41–54.

Kenney, C. T., & McLanahan, S. S. (2006). Why are cohabiting relationships more violent than marriages? *Demography, 43*(1), 127–140.

Kershner, M., & Anderson, J. E. (2002). Barriers to disclosure of abuse among rural women. *Minnesota Medicine, 85*(3), 32–37.

Kershner, M., Long, D., & Anderson, J. E. (2001). Abuse against women in rural Minnesota. *Public Health Nursing, 15*(6), 422–431.

Kiernan, K. (2002). Cohabitation in Western Europe: Trends, issues, and implications. In A. Booth, & A. C. Crouter (Eds.), *Just living together: Implications of cohabitation on families, children, and social policy* (pp. 3–31). Mahwah, NJ: Lawrence Erlbaum Associates.

Kraus, R. F., & Buffler, P. A. (1979). Sociocultural stress and the American Native in Alaska: An analysis of changing patterns of psychiatric illness and alcohol abuse among Alaska Natives. *Culture, Medicine and Psychiatry, 3*(2), 111–151.

Krishnan, S. P., Hilbert, J. C., & VanLeeuwen, D. (2001). Domestic violence and help-seeking behaviors among rural women: Results from a shelter-based study. *Journal of Family and Community Health, 24*(1), 28–38.

Kung, W. W. (2000). The intertwined relationship between depression and marital distress: Elements of marital therapy conducive to effective treatment outcome. *Journal of Marital and Family Therapy, 26*(1), 51–63.

Kurz, D. (1989). Social science perspectives on wife abuse: Current debates and future directions. *Gender and Society, 3*(4), 489–505.

Kurz, D. (1995). *For richer, for poorer: Mothers confront divorce.* New York: Routledge.

Kurz, D. (1996). Separation, divorce and woman abuse. *Violence Against Women, 2*(1), 69–81.

Kurz, D. (1998). Old problems and new directions in the study of violence against women. In R. K. Bergen (Ed.), *Issues in intimate violence* (pp. 197–208). Thousand Oaks, CA: Sage.

Lane, K. E., & Gwartney-Gibbs, P. A. (1985). Violence in the context of dating and sex. *Journal of Family Issues, 6*(1), 45–59.

Lapham, S. C., Henley, E., & Kleyboecker, K. (1993). Prenatal behavioral risk screening by computer among Native Americans. *Family Medicine, 25*(3), 197–202.

LaRocque, E. D. (1994). Violence in Aboriginal communities (pp. 72–89). Ottawa, ON, Canada: Royal Commission on Aboriginal Peoples.

Le Bourdais, C., & Lapierre-Adamcyk, E. (2004). Changes in conjugal life in Canada: Is cohabitation progressively replacing marriage? *Journal of Marriage and Family, 66*(4), 929–942.

Lee, R. K., Thompson, V. L. S., & Mechanic, M. B. (2002). Intimate partner violence and women of color: A call for innovations. *American Journal of Public Health, 92*(4), 530–534.

Logan, T., Stevenson, E., Evans, L., & Leukefeld, C. (2004). Rural and urban women's perceptions of barriers to health, mental health, and criminal justice services: Implications for victim services. *Violence and Victims, 19*(1), 37–62.

Logan, T., Walker, R., Cole, J., Ratliff, S., & Leukefeld, C. (2003). Qualitative differences among rural and urban intimate violence victimization experiences and consequences: A pilot study. *Journal of Family Violence, 18*(2), 83–92.

Logan, T., Walker, R., & Leukefeld, C. G. (2001). Rural, urban influenced, and urban differences among domestic violence arrestees. *Journal of Interpersonal Violence, 16*(3), 266–283.

Ludvig, A. (2006). Differences between women? Intersecting voices in a female narrative. *European Journal of Women's Studies, 13*(3), 245–258.

Lupri, E. (1990). Male violence in the home. In C. McKie, & K. Thompson (Eds.), *Canadian social trends* (pp. 170–172). Toronto, ON, Canada: Thompson Educational Publishing.

Lupri, E., Grandin, E., & Brinkerhoff, M. B. (1994). Socioeconomic status and male violence in the Canadian home: A reexamination. *Canadian Journal of Sociology, 19*(1), 47–73.

McCall, L. (2005). The complexity of intersectionality. *Signs: Journal of Women in Culture and Society, 30*(3), 1771–1800.

McCloskey, L. (2001). The "Medea complex" among men: The instrumental abuse of children to injure wives. *Violence and Victims, 16*(1), 19–37.

McCracken, M., & Watson, G. (2004). *Women need safe, stable, affordable housing: A study of social housing, private rental housing and co-op housing in Winnipeg* (No. 74). Winnipeg, MB, Canada: The Prairie Women's Health Centre of Excellence.

McDonald, S. (1999). Not in the numbers: Domestic violence and immigrant women. *Canadian Woman Studies, 19*(3), 163–167.

MacDonald, W. L., & DeMaris, A. (1995). Remarriage, stepchildren, and marital conflict: Challenges to the incomplete institutionalization hypothesis. *Journal of Marriage and Family, 57*(2), 387–398.

McEachern, D., Winkle, M. V., & Steiner, S. (1998). Domestic violence among the Navajo: A legacy of colonization. *Journal of Poverty, 2*(4), 31–46.

MacLeod, L., & Shin, M. (1990). *Isolated, afraid and forgotten: The service delivery needs and realities of immigrant and refugee women who are battered.* Ottawa, ON, Canada: National Clearinghouse on Family Violence.

MacLeod, L., & Shin, M. Y. (1993). *Like a wingless bird: A tribute to the survival and courage of women who are abused and who speak neither English nor French.* Ottawa, ON, Canada: National Clearinghouse on Family Violence.

MacMillan, R., & Gartner, R. (1999). When she brings home the bacon: Labor-force participation and the risk of spousal violence against women. *Journal of Marriage and the Family, 61*(4), 947–958.

McMurray, A. M. (1997). Violence against ex-wives: Anger and advocacy. *Health Care for Women International, 18*(6), 543–556.

McMurray, A. M., Froyland, I. D., Bell, D. G., & Curnow, D. J. (2000). Post-separation violence: The male perspective. *Journal of Family Studies, 6*(1), 89–105.

Magdol, L., Moffitt, T. E., Caspi, A., & Silva, P. A. (1998). Hitting without a license: Testing explanations for differences in partner abuse between young adult daters and cohabitors. *Journal of Marriage and the Family, 60*(1), 41–55.

Mahoney, M. R. (1991/1992). Legal images of battered women: Redefining the issue of separation. *Michigan Law Review, 90*(1), 1–94.

Malcoe, L. H., Carson, E. A., & Myers, O. B. (2005). Intimate partner violence against rural Native American women: Prevalence and socioeconomic risk factors. *American Journal of Epidemiology, 161*(Supplemental), S139.

Malcoe, L. H., Duran, B. M., & Montgomery, J. M. (2004). Socioeconomic disparities in intimate partner violence against Native American women: A cross-sectional study. *BMC Medicine, 2*(20), 1–14.

Manson, S. M., Beals, J., Klein, S. A., Croy, C. D., & The AI-SUPERPFP Team. (2005). Social epidemiology of trauma among two American Indian reservation populations. *American Journal of Public Health, 95*(5), 851–859.

Martens, P., Bond, R., Jebamani, L., Burchill, C., Roos, N., Derksen, S., et al. (2002). *The health and health care use of registered First Nations people living in Manitoba: A population-based study.* Winnipeg, MB, Canada: Manitoba Centre for Health Policy.

Martin, D. L., & Mosher, J. E. (1995). Unkept promises: Experiences of immigrant women with neo-criminalization of wife abuse. *Canadian Journal of Women and the Law, 8*, 3–44.

Martin, S. L., Ray, N., Sotres-Alvarez, D., Kupper, L. L., Moracco, K. E., Dickens, P. A., et al. (2006). Physical and sexual assault of women with disabilities. *Violence Against Women, 12*(9), 823–837.

Martz, D. J. F., & Saraurer, D. B. (2002). Domestic violence and the experiences of rural women in east central Saskatchewan. In K. M. J. McKenna, & J. Larkin (Eds.), *Violence against women: New Canadian perspectives* (pp. 163–195). Toronto, ON, Canada: Ianna Publications and Education.

Mauricio, A. M., Tein, J.-Y., & Lopez, F. G. (2007). Borderline and antisocial personality scores as mediators between attachment and intimate partner violence. *Violence and Victims, 22*(2), 139–157.

Melcombe, L. (2003). Facing up to facts. *AWARE: The newsletter of the BC Institute Against Family Violence, 10*(1), 8–10.

Menard, A. (2001). Domestic violence and housing: Key policy and program challenges. *Violence Against Women, 7*(6), 707–720.

Milberger, S., Israel, N., LeRoy, B., Martin, A., Potter, L., & Patchak-Schuster, P. (2003). Violence against women with physical disabilities. *Violence and Victims, 18*(5), 581–591.

Murty, S. A., Peek-Asa, C., Zwerling, C., Stromquist, A. M., Burmeister, L. F., & Merchant, J. A. (2003). Physical and emotional partner abuse reported by men and women in a rural community. *American Journal of Public Health, 93*(7), 1073–1075.

Native Women's Association of Canada. (2003). *Our way of being: Gathering of Indigenous women on self-government.* Retrieved June 26, 2006, from www.nwac-hq.org/OurWayof Being.pdf.

Navin, S., Stockum, R., & Campbell-Ruggaard, J. (1993). Battered women in rural America. *Journal of Humanistic Education and Development, 32*(1), 9–16.

Norton, I. M., & Manson, S. M. (1995). A silent minority: Battered American Indian women. *Journal of Family Violence, 10*(3), 307–318.

Nosek, M. A., Howland, C. A., & Hughes, R. B. (2001). The investigation of abuse and women with disabilities: Going beyond assumptions. *Violence Against Women, 7*(4), 477–499.

Nosek, M. A., Hughes, R. B., Taylor, H. B., & Taylor, P. (2006). Disability, psychosocial, and demographic characteristics of abuse women with physical disabilities. *Violence Against Women, 12*(9), 838–850.

O'Brien, J. E. (1971). Violence in divorce prone families. *Journal of Marriage and the Family, 33*(4), 692–698.

O'Leary, K. D. (1993). Through a psychological lens: Personality traits, personality disorders, and levels of violence. In R. J. Gelles, & D. R. Loseke (Eds.), *Current controversies on family violence* (pp. 7–30). Newbury Park, CA: Sage.

O'Neil, J. M., & Harway, M. (1999). Revised multivariate model explaining men's risk factors for violence against women: Theoretical propositions, new hypotheses, and proactive recommendations. In M. Harway, & J. M. O'Neil (Eds.), *What causes men's violence against women?* (pp. 207–241). Thousand Oaks, CA: Sage.

O'Neil, J. M., & Nadeau, R. A. (1999). Men's gender-role conflict, defense mechanisms, and self-protective defensive strategies. In M. Harway, & J. M. O'Neil (Eds.), *What causes men's violence against women?* (pp. 89–116). Thousand Oaks, CA: Sage.

Oetzel, J., & Duran, B. (2004). Intimate partner violence in American Indian and/or Alaska Native communities: A social ecological framework of determinants and interventions. *American Indian and Alaska Native Mental Health Research, 11*(3), 49–68.

Pagelow, M. D. (1993). Justice for victims of spouse abuse in divorce and child custody cases. *Violence and Victims, 8*(1), 69–83.

Pearson, D., Cheadle, A., Wagner, E., Tonsberg, R., & Psaty, B. M. (1994). Differences in sociodemographic, health status, and lifestyle characteristics among American Indians by telephone coverage. *Preventive Medicine, 23*(4), 461–464.

Petersilia, J. R. (2001). Crime victims with developmental disabilities: A review essay. *Criminal Justice and Behavior, 28*(6), 655–694.

Peterson, R. (1980). Social class, social learning and wife abuse. *Social Service Review, 54*(3), 390–406.

Phoenix, A., & Pattynama, P. (2006). Intersectionality. *European Journal of Women's Studies, 13*(3), 187–192.

Poelzer, D. T., & Poelzer, I. A. (1986). *In our own words: Northern Saskatchewan Metis women speak out.* Saskatoon, SK, Canada: One Sky.

Powers, L. E., Curry, M. A., Oschwald, M., Maley, S., Saxton, M., & Eckels, K. (2002). Barriers and strategies in addressing abuse: A survey of disabled women's experiences. *Journal of Rehabilitation, 68*(1), 4–13.

Pratt, A. (1995). New immigrant and refugee battered women: The intersection of immigration and criminal justice policy. In M. Valverde, L. MacLeod, & K. Johnson (Eds.), *Wife assault and the Canadian criminal justice system: Issues and policies* (pp. 85–103). Toronto, ON, Canada: Centre of Criminology, University of Toronto.

Prins, B. (2006). Narrative accounts of origins: A blind spot in the intersectional approach? *European Journal of Women's Studies, 13*(3), 277–290.

Raj, A., & Silverman, J. (2002). Violence against immigrant women: The roles of culture, context, and legal immigrant status on intimate partner violence. *Violence Against Women, 8*(3), 367–398.

Raphael, J. (2001). Public housing and domestic violence. *Violence Against Women, 7*(6), 699–706.

Rasche, C. E. (1993). "Given" reasons for violence in intimate relationships. In A. V. Wilson (Ed.), *Homicide: The victim/offender connection* (pp. 75–100). Cincinnati, OH: Anderson.

Ratner, P. A. (1998). Modeling acts of aggression and dominance as wife abuse and exploring their adverse health effects. *Journal of Marriage and the Family, 60*(2), 453–465.

Razack, S. (1994). What is to be gained by looking white people in the eye? Culture, race, and gender in cases of sexual violence. *Signs, 19*(4), 894–923.

Rennison, C. (2001). *Violence victimization and race, 1993–98* (No. NCJ 176354). Washington, DC: U.S. Department of Justice.

Renzetti, C. M. (1998). Violence and abuse in lesbian relationships: Theoretical and empirical issues. In R. K. Bergen (Ed.), *Issues in intimate violence* (pp. 117–127). Thousand Oaks, CA: Sage.

Renzetti, C. M. (2006). Editor's introduction. *Violence Against Women, 12*(9), 803–804.

Riddell, J., & Doxtator, P. (1986). *Native women's needs assessment survey.* Ottawa, ON, Canada: Women's Education and Research Foundation.

Ridington, J. (1989). Beating the "odds": Violence and women with disabilities (position paper 2). Vancouver, BC, Canada: DisAbled Women's Network of Canada.

Ristock, J. L. (2002). *No more secrets: Violence in lesbian relationships.* New York: Routledge Press.

Robin, R. W., Chester, B., & Rasmussen, J. K. (1998). Intimate violence in a Southwestern American Indian tribal community. *Cultural Diversity and Mental Health, 4*(4), 335–344.

Roeher Institute. (1995). *Harm's way: The many faces of violence and abuse against persons with disabilities.* North York, ON: L'Institute Roeher Institute.

Rohe, W. M., Zandt, S. V., & McCarthy, G. (2001). *The social benefits and costs of homeownership: A critical assessment of the research* (No. LIHO-01.12). Joint Center for Housing Studies of Harvard University.

Russo, N. F. (1990). Forging research priorities for women's mental health. *American Psychologist, 45*(3), 368–373.

Salari, S. M., & Baldwin, B. M. (2002). Verbal, physical, and injurious aggression among intimate couples over time. *Journal of Family Issues, 23*(4), 523–550.

Saunders, D. G. (1992). A typology of men who batter: Three types derived from cluster analysis. *American Journal of Orthopsychiatry, 62*(2), 264–275.

Saylors, K., & Daliparthy, N. (2006). Violence against Native women in substance abuse treatment. *American Indian and Alaska Native Mental Health Research, 13*(1), 32–51.

Schulman, M. A. (1981). *A survey of spousal violence against women in Kentucky* (Vol. 96). New York: Garland Publishing.

Schwartz, M. D. (1988). Marital status and woman abuse theory. *Journal of Family Violence, 3*(3), 239–248.

Sev'er, A. (1997). Recent or imminent separation and intimate violence against women. *Violence Against Women, 3*(6), 566–589.

Sev'er, A. (2002). *Fleeing the house of horrors: Women who have left abusive partners.* Toronto, ON, Canada: University of Toronto Press.

Shackelford, T. K. (2001). Cohabitation, marriage, and murder: Woman killing by male romantic partners. *Aggressive Behavior, 27*(4), 284–291.

Shackelford, T. K., & Mouzos, J. (2005). Partner killing by men in cohabiting and marital relationships: A comparative, cross-national analysis of data from Australia and the United States. *Journal of Interpersonal Violence, 20*(10), 1310–1324.

Shalansky, C., Ericksen, J., & Henderson, A. (1999). Abused women and child custody: The ongoing exposure to abusive ex-partners. *Journal of Advanced Nursing, 29*(2), 416–426.

Shannon, L., Logan, T., Cole, J., & Medley, K. (2006). Help-seeking and coping strategies for intimate partner violence in rural and urban women. *Violence and Victims, 21*(2), 167–181.

Shepherd, J. (2001). Where do you go when it's 40 below? Domestic violence among rural Alaska native women. *Affilia, 16*(4), 488–510.

Silver, C., & Diepen, R. V. (2004). *Canadian social trends.* Retrieved March 9, 2004, from www.statcan.ca/english/ads/11–008-XIE/housinge.html.

Silverstein, L. B. (1999). The evolutionary origins of male violence against women. In M. Harway, & J. M. O'Neil (Eds.), *What causes men's violence against women?* (pp. 61–83). Thousand Oaks, CA: Sage.

Smith, M. D. (1986). *Effects of question format on the reporting of woman abuse: A telephone survey experiment.* Toronto, ON, Canada: Institute for Social Research, York University.

Smith, M. D. (1990a). Patriarchal ideology and wife beating: A test of a feminist hypothesis. *Violence and Victims, 5*(4), 257–273.

Smith, M. D. (1990b). Sociodemographic risk factors in wife abuse: Results from a survey of Toronto women. *Canadian Journal of Sociology, 15*(1), 39–58.

Smock, P. J., & Gupta, S. (2002). Cohabitation in contemporary North America. In A. Booth, & A. C. Crouter (Eds.), *Just living together: Implications of cohabitation on families, children, and social policy* (pp. 53–84). Mahwah, NJ: Lawrence Erlbaum Associates.

Snider, L. (1995). Feminism, punishment and the potential for empowerment. In M. Valverde, L. MacLeod, & K. Johnson (Eds.), *Wife assault and the Canadian criminal justice system.* Toronto, ON, Canada: Centre of Criminology, University of Toronto.

Sobsey, D. (1994). *Violence and abuse in the lives of people with disabilities.* Toronto, ON, Canada: Paul H. Brookes.

Sobsey, D., & Calder, P. (1999). *Violence against people with disabilities: A conceptual analysis.* Washington, DC: National Research Council.

Sokoloff, N. J., & Dupont, I. (2005). Domestic violence at the intersections of race, class and gender: Challenges and contributions to understanding violence against marginalized women in diverse communities. *Violence Against Women, 11*(1), 38–64.

Sommer, R. (1994). Male and female perpetrated partner abuse: Testing a diathesis-stress model. Unpublished Doctoral Dissertation, University of Manitoba, Winnipeg, Canada.

Sorenson, S. B. (2006). Judgments about intimate partner violence: A statewide survey about immigrants. *Public Health Reports, 121*(4), 445–452.

Spiwak, R., & Brownridge, D. A. (2005). Separated women's risk for violence: An analysis of the Canadian situation. *Journal of Divorce and Remarriage, 43*(3/4), 105–118.

Statistics Canada. (1994a). *Violence Against Women Survey microdata file.* Ottawa, ON, Canada: Canadian Centre for Justice Statistics.

Statistics Canada. (1994b). *Violence Against Women Survey: Public use microdata file documentation and user's guide.* Ottawa, ON, Canada: Canadian Centre for Justice Statistics.

Statistics Canada. (1998). 1996 Census: Aboriginal data. *The Daily* (January 13), 1–8.

Statistics Canada. (1999). *1996 census dictionary: Final edition reference* (No. 92–351-UIE). Ottawa, ON, Canada: Minister of Industry.

Statistics Canada. (2000). *1999 General Social Survey, Cycle 13 victimization: Public use microdata file documentation and user's guide.* Ottawa, ON, Canada: Minister of Industry.

Statistics Canada. (2001). *Recent immigrants by country of last residence.* Retrieved May 23, 2001, from www.statcan.ca/english/Pgdb/People/Population/demo08.htm.

Statistics Canada. (2002a). 2001 Census: Marital status, common-law status, families, dwellings and households. *The Daily* (October 22), 1–3.

Statistics Canada. (2002b). *Changing conjugal life in Canada* (No. 98–576-XIE). Ottawa, ON, Canada: Minister of Industry.

Statistics Canada. (2002c). *A new approach to disability data: Changes between the 1991 Health and Activity Limitation Survey (HALS) and the 2001 Participation and Activity Limitation Survey (PALS)* (No. 89–578-XIE). Ottawa, ON, Canada: Minister of Industry.

Statistics Canada. (2002d). Participation and Activity Limitation Survey: A profile of disability in Canada. *The Daily* (December 3), 1–8.

Statistics Canada. (2002e). *Profile of Canadian families and households: Diversification continues* (No. 96F0030XIE2001003). Ottawa, ON, Canada: Minister of Industry.

Statistics Canada. (2003). *Aboriginal peoples of Canada: A demographic profile* (No. 96F0030XIE2001007). Ottawa, ON, Canada: Minister of Industry.

Statistics Canada. (2004). Divorces. *The Daily* (May 4), 1–5.

Statistics Canada. (2005a). *Aboriginal peoples living off-reserve in Western Canada: Estimates from the labour force survey.* Ottawa, ON, Canada: Minister of Industry.

Statistics Canada. (2005b). *General Social Survey Cycle 18: Victimization (2004): User's guide to the public use microdata file.* Ottawa, ON, Canada: Minister of Industry.

Statistics Canada. (2006). *Guide to the labour force survey* (No. 71–543-GIE). Ottawa, ON, Canada: Minister responsible for Statistics Canada.

Statistics Canada. (2008). *Aboriginal peoples in Canada in 2006: Inuit, Métis and First Nations, 2006 Census* (No. 97–558-XIE). Ottawa, ON, Canada: Minister of Industry.

Stets, J. E. (1991). Cohabiting and marital aggression: The role of social isolation. *Journal of Marriage and the Family, 53*(3), 669–680.

Stets, J. E., & Straus, M. A. (1989). The marriage license as a hitting license: A comparison of assaults in dating, cohabiting, and married couples. *Journal of Family Violence, 4*(2), 161–180.

Straus, M. A. (1979). Measuring intrafamily conflict and violence: The Conflict Tactics (CT) scales. *Journal of Marriage and The Family, 41*(1), 75–88.

Straus, M. A. (1990). Injury and frequency of assault and the "representative sample fallacy" in measuring wife beating and child abuse. In M. A. Straus, & R. J. Gelles (Eds.), *Physical violence in American families: Risk factors and adaptations to violence in 8,145 families* (pp. 75–91). New Brunswick, NJ: Transaction.

Straus, M. A. (1993). Physical assaults by wives: A major social problem. In R. J. Gelles, & D. R. Loseke (Eds.), *Current controversies on family violence* (pp. 67–87). Newbury Park, CA: Sage.

Straus, M. A., & Gelles, R. J. (1990). *Physical violence in American families: Risk factors and adaptations to violence in 8,145 families.* New Brunswick, NJ: Transaction.

Straus, M. A., Gelles, R. J., & Steinmetz, S. K. (1980). *Behind closed doors: Violence in the American family.* Garden City, NY: Anchor Press/Doubleday.

Swan, S. C., & Snow, D. L. (2006). The development of a theory of women's use of violence in intimate relationships. *Violence Against Women, 12*(11), 1026–1045.

Swedlund, N. P., & Nosek, M. A. (2000). An exploratory study on the work of independent living centers to address abuse of women with disabilities. *Journal of Rehabilitation, 66*(4), 57–64.

Tabachnick, B. G., & Fidell, L. S. (2001). *Using multivariate statistics* (4th ed.). Toronto, ON, Canada: Allyn and Bacon.

Taylor-Butts, A. (2007). *Canada's shelters for abused women, 2005/2006* (No. 85–002-XIE). Ottawa, ON, Canada: Statistics Canada.

Thompson, E. N. (2000, March 20–25). Immigrant occupational skill outcomes and the role of region specific human capital. Paper presented at the Fourth National Metropolis Conference, Toronto, ON, Canada.

Thomson, R. G. (1994). Redrawing the boundaries of feminist disability studies. *Feminist Studies, 20*(3), 582–598.

Timmons Fritz, P. A., & O'Leary, K. D. (2004). Physical and psychological partner aggression across a decade: A growth curve analysis. *Violence and Victims, 19*(1), 3–16.

Ting, L. (2007). Intimate partner violence in immigrants: Exploring acculturation and barriers to help seeking among victims. In K. A. Kendall-Tackett, & S. M. Giacomoni (Eds.), *Intimate partner violence* (pp. 9.1–9.18). Kingston, NJ: Civic Research Institute.

Tjaden, P., & Thoennes, N. (1998a). *Prevalence, incidence, and consequences of violence against women: Findings from the National Violence Against Women Survey* (No. NCJ 172837). Washington, DC: U.S. Department of Justice.

Tjaden, P., & Thoennes, N. (1998b). *Stalking in America: Findings from the National Violence Against Women Survey* (No. NCJ 169592). Washington, DC: Department of Justice, National Institute of Justice.

Toews, M. L., McKenry, P. C., & Catlett, B. S. (2003). Male-initiated partner abuse during marital separation prior to divorce. *Violence and Victims, 18*(4), 387–402.

Trainor, C., Lambert, M., & Dauvergne, M. (2002). Spousal violence. In C. Trainor (Ed.), *Family violence in Canada: A statistical profile 2002* (pp. 6–25). Ottawa, ON, Canada: Minister of Industry.

Trainor, C., & Mihorean, K. (2001). *Family violence in Canada: A statistical profile 2001.* Ottawa, ON, Canada: Minister of Industry.

Ulbrich, P. M., & Stockdale, J. (2002). Making family planning clinics an empowerment zone for rural battered women. *Women and Health, 35*(2/3), 83–100.

Umberson, D., Anderson, K. L., Williams, K., & Chen, M. D. (2003). Relationship dynamics, emotion state, and domestic violence: A stress and masculinities perspective. *Journal of Marriage and Family, 65*(1), 233–247.

United Nations. (2001). *Guidelines and principles for the development of disability statistics* (No. ST/ESA/STAT/SER.Y/10). New York: United Nations.

United Nations. (2007, August 28). Standard country or area codes for statistical use. *Series M, 49*(4) Retrieved November 22, 2007, from http://unstats.un.org/unsd/methods/m49/m49regin.htm#developed.

Ursel, J. (1986). The state and the maintenance of patriarchy: A case study of family, labour and welfare legislation in Canada. In J. Dickinson, & B. Russel (Eds.), *Family, economy and state* (pp. 150–191). Toronto, ON, Canada: Garamond.

Van Hightower, N. R., & Gorton, J. (2002). A case study of community-based responses to rural woman battering. *Violence Against Women, 8*(7), 845–872.

Van Hightower, N. R., Gorton, J., & DeMoss, C. L. (2000). Predictive models of domestic violence and fear of intimate partners among migrant and seasonal farm worker women. *Journal of Family Violence, 15*(2), 137–153.

Waldram, J. B. (1997). The Aboriginal peoples of Canada: Colonialism and mental health. In I. Al-Issa, & M. Tousignant (Eds.), *Ethnicity, immigration, and psychopathology* (pp. 169–187). New York: Plenum.

Walker, L. E. A. (1993). The Battered Woman Syndrome is a psychological consequence of abuse.

In R. J. Gelles, & D. R. Loseke (Eds.), *Current controversies on family violence* (pp. 133–153). Newbury Park, CA: Sage.

Walker, R., Logan, T., Jordan, C. E., & Campbell, J. C. (2004). An integrative review of separation in the context of victimization: Consequences and implications for women. *Trauma, Violence and Abuse, 5*(2), 143–193.

Waxman, B. F. (1991). Hatred: The unacknowledged dimension in violence against disabled people. *Sexuality and Disability, 9*(3), 185–199.

Websdale, N. (1995). Rural woman abuse: The voices of Kentucky women. *Violence Against Women, 1*(4), 309–338.

Websdale, N. (1998). *Rural woman battering and the justice system: An ethnography.* Thousand Oaks, CA: Sage.

Weekes-Shackelford, V. A., & Shackelford, T. K. (2004). Methods of filicide: Stepparents and genetic parents kill differently. *Violence and Victims, 19*(1), 75–81.

Whitbeck, L. B., Adams, G. W., Hoyt, D. R., & Chen, X. (2004). Conceptualizing and measuring historical trauma among American Indian people. *American Journal of Community Psychology, 33*(3/4), 119–130.

Whitbeck, L. B., Chen, X., Hoyt, D. R., & Adams, G. W. (2004). Discrimination, historical loss and enculturation: Culturally specific risk and resiliency factors for alcohol abuse among American Indians. *Journal of Studies on Alcohol, 65*(4), 409–418.

Wilson, M., & Daly, M. (1992). Till death us do part. In J. Radford, & D. E. H. Russell (Eds.), *Femicide: The politics of woman killing* (pp. 83–98). New York: Twayne.

Wilson, M., & Daly, M. (1993). Spousal homicide risk and estrangement. *Violence and Victims, 8*(1), 3–16.

Wilson, M., & Daly, M. (1998). Lethal and nonlethal violence against wives and the evolutionary psychology of male sexual proprietariness. In R. E. Dobash, & R. P. Dobash (Eds.), *Rethinking violence against women* (pp. 224–230). Thousand Oaks, CA: Sage.

Wuest, J., & Merritt-Gray, M. (1999). Not going back: Sustaining the separation in the process of leaving abusive relationships. *Violence Against Women, 5*(2), 110–133.

Yllö, K., & Straus, M. A. (1981). Interpersonal violence among married and cohabiting couples. *Family Relations, 30*(3), 339–347.

Young, M. E., Nosek, M. A., Howland, C. A., Chanpong, G., & Rintala, D. H. (1997). Prevalence of abuse of women with physical disabilities. *Archives of Physical Medicine and Rehabilitation, 78*(12), S34–S38.

Yuan, N. P., Koss, M. P., Polacca, M., & Goldman, D. (2006). Risk factors for physical assault and rape among six Native American tribes. *Journal of Interpersonal Violence, 21*(12), 1566–1590.

Yuval-Davis, N. (2006). Intersectionality and feminist politics. *European Journal of Women's Studies, 13*(3), 193–209.

Zack, N. (2005). *Inclusive feminism: A third wave theory of women's commonality.* Lanham, MD: Rowman and Littlefield.

Index